A NEW HISTORY OF SCOTLAND

WILLIAM CROFT DICKINSON, C.B.E., D.LIT., LL.D.
*Late Fraser Professor of Scottish History and Palaeography
in the University of Edinburgh*

GEORGE S. PRYDE, M.A., PH.D.
*Professor of Scottish History and Literature
in the University of Glasgow*

A New History of Scotland

1   SCOTLAND FROM THE EARLIEST TIMES TO 1603
     William Croft Dickinson, C.B.E., D.LIT., LL.D.

2   SCOTLAND FROM 1603 TO THE PRESENT DAY
     George S. Pryde, M.A., PH.D.

A NEW HISTORY OF SCOTLAND VOL. I

Scotland

from the earliest times to 1603

WILLIAM CROFT DICKINSON

NELSON

THOMAS NELSON AND SONS LTD
36 Park Street London W1
Parkside Works Edinburgh 9
10 Warehouse Road Apapa Lagos
P.O. Box 25012 Nairobi

THOMAS NELSON (AUSTRALIA) LTD
597 Little Collins Street Melbourne

THOMAS NELSON AND SONS (AFRICA) (Pty) LTD
P.O. Box 9881 Johannesburg

THOMAS NELSON AND SONS (CANADA) LTD
81 Curlew Drive Don Mills Ontario

THOMAS NELSON AND SONS
Copewood and Davis Streets Camden 3, N.J.

———

First published October 1961
Reprinted 1962
Second edition (revised) 1965

Printed in Great Britain by
THOMAS NELSON (PRINTERS) LTD, LONDON AND EDINBURGH

Contents

CONTENTS

Tables

Foreword

SOME fifty years have now elapsed since Hume Brown published his three-volume *History of Scotland*, which, upon its appearance, was at once accepted as the ' standard ' account. Since ' Hume Brown ' there have been many books on Scottish history, and, after half a century, a real need has arisen for a new ' History of Scotland ', written from a somewhat different approach and taking full account of our advancing knowledge. A new ' History of Scotland ', consecutive and comprehensive, but still manageable, seemed to be desirable alike for the general reader, for the university student, and for the advanced school pupil.

On several occasions I discussed this need with Professor George S. Pryde, of the University of Glasgow, and the two of us finally decided to compile a new two-volume History of Scotland ourselves, of which I should write the first volume, ' From the Earliest Times to 1603 ', while he would write the second, ' From 1603 to the Present Day '. So our joint effort began. In the course of our collaboration we have kept in constant touch with one another, exchanging our chapters, as they were written, not only for comment but also in the hope of securing a reasonable approach to uniformity in scope and treatment.

Because our History is intended for general use, footnotes have been kept to a minimum and there are few references to sources and authorities. For a like reason the Select Bibliography at the end of each volume is intended mainly to furnish details of the works which are referred to in the text or have been used in its preparation, and also to act as a guide to further reading; it does not pretend to be other than a select list of the more essential original authorities and the more important secondary works.

When writing chapters II, III and V of my own volume I benefited from advice and help freely given to me by Professor Stuart Piggott, Dr Kenneth Steer and Mrs M. O. Anderson; and, when the volume was in draft, my colleagues, Dr Gordon Donaldson, Mr A. A. M. Duncan and Dr W. Ferguson, generously read through the whole of the typescript and made a number of valuable suggestions for its improvement. I am also indebted to Dr I. B. Cowan for compiling the Index.

At every stage in the work I have been conscious of the dangers inherent in compression and simplification: in all my generalisations I have been aware of my temerity; in deciding what to include and what to omit I have realised that I might ' content few and displease many '.

Yet if, together, our two volumes stimulate interest and help to further the study of Scottish history we shall be satisfied.

W. CROFT DICKINSON

The University,
Edinburgh.
August 1959.

This second edition embodies a number of modifications in emphasis and interpretation.   Most of these have been made to meet the scholarly criticisms of friends and reviewers of whom, in particular, I must mention Dr Ian Cowan, Professor A. A. M. Duncan and Dr Ranald Nicholson; a few are my own ' second thoughts '.   The map has been improved by minor corrections and by the addition of the Roman walls.

W. C. D.

The University,
Edinburgh.
April 1963.

CHAPTER I

Introductory - Historical and Geographical

THE HISTORY of the Scottish people has been influenced in many ways by geography – not only by the physical structure of Scotland itself, but also by Scotland's position in relation to neighbouring countries.

In the first place, Scotland is the northern part of one island, with England forming the southern part. In prehistoric times there were immigrant movements of the same or similar peoples to both ' Scotland ' and ' England ', and some settlers moved from ' England ' to ' Scotland '. Then, in the second century A.D., a division between the northern and the southern parts of the island was made by the Roman walls; but towards the end of the fourth century Hadrian's Wall was overrun for the last time and never restored, and for many centuries thereafter the boundary between the northern and the southern parts was fluid and contested. At one time the Angles held the land up to the Forth; at another time ' Scotland ' had pressed far into the northern parts of ' England ' on both the east and the west, and the exclusion of the four northern counties of England from William the Conqueror's Domesday Survey may indicate a wide extent of ' no-man's land ' – territory disputed by the two countries. A boundary line between Scotland and England was formally recognised only with the treaty of York in 1237.

In the twelfth and thirteenth centuries many Anglo-Norman families came to Scotland from England, and many of them held lands in both countries. Norman law and administration were then introduced; a number of Scottish monasteries were founded and ' colonised ' from England; and there was much intermarriage, including intermarriage between the royal houses. In 1215 Scotsmen helped to wring Magna Carta from an unwilling John, and in the years between 1263 and 1282 Balliol College, Oxford, was endowed and given its first statutes by a Scottish lord and his lady. Closer fusion, and perhaps even union, between the two countries seemed possible and might have been secured at the end of the thirteenth century with the marriage of the ' Maid of Norway ' to Edward I's son. But when the death of the ' Maid ' ruined a plan that was in many ways statesmanlike, Edward I's claim to be sovereign lord of Scotland and his attempt to secure union by force led only to the War of Independence, and to a period of over 250 years during which Scotland was subject to intermittent invasion and raid by her more powerful southern neighbour.

Edward I is said to have vowed that he would ' bring in ' Scotland, as already he had ' brought in ' Wales; and, from Edward I's initial attempt to subdue Scotland in 1296, until the middle of the sixteenth century Scotland and England were ' at war ' with one another. The last of a long series of battles between Scottish and English armies was fought at Pinkie in 1547[1]; the last Border incident took place in 1596 when ' Kinmont Willie ' was rescued by ' the bold Buccleuch ' from the clutches of Lord Scrope and the castle of Carlisle.

This long period of hostilities between Scotland and England affected every aspect of Scotland's history until the union of the crowns in 1603. A country with little security on its border has small chance to prosper and to develop the arts of peace. The resources of Scotland, the efforts of her kings and councils, and the lives of many of her hardy men were too often given and lost in war. Moreover, the most fertile parts of Scotland, a number of wealthy abbeys, and many of her important towns, including her capital, Edinburgh, lie in the south and along the easily invaded eastern coastal plain. Thus, to Scotland, an invasion by England meant the ravaging of some of her best land and the burning of important monasteries and towns. Following one fortnight's invasion of Lothian in September 1545 the English commander, the Earl of Hertford, could boast that he had destroyed seven monasteries (including Dryburgh, Kelso and Melrose), sixteen castles, peels and towers, five market towns, and two hundred and forty-three villages; while in the previous year, 1544, he had burned and destroyed Edinburgh (so that neither within the walls nor in the suburbs was any house left unburned), the Abbey and Palace of Holyrood, Leith, Haddington, Dunbar (where men, women and children were suffocated and burned alive) and the Abbey of Newbattle. An English invasion of southern Scotland could always inflict greater harm than the harm which could be inflicted by a Scottish invasion of northern England.

[1] Though after Pinkie the English established themselves in Haddington, which they did not abandon until 1550.

The campaigns and battles of the mid-seventeenth century were part of a civil war which, in Scotland, was also a war of religion. The risings of the 'Fifteen and the 'Forty-five were supported by only a small section of the Scottish people, mainly Highlanders, and battles like those of Prestonpans and Culloden were not fought ' between Scottish and English armies '.

Continual warfare also hinders the maintenance of law and order and the government of the realm. In the warfare with England David II was captured and held prisoner from 1346 to 1357 – being then released only upon Scotland's agreement to pay an enormous ransom which, although never paid in full, crippled the finances of Scotland for more than a century; James II was killed at the early age of twenty-nine, at the recapture of Roxburgh castle from the English (1460); James IV, a king of high endeavour, was killed at Flodden (1513) at the age of forty. Because of the warfare with England, James, the son of Robert III, was captured at sea when on his way to France and was a captive king, James I, from 1406 to 1424.

But when kings were held prisoner, or were killed in battle at an early age and so left minors to succeed them (James III was in his ninth year when his father, James II, was killed at Roxburgh; and James V was only in his second year when his father, James IV, was killed at Flodden), the government of the country fell into the hands of regents, members of the royal family or great nobles who, from time to time, were more concerned with their own interests than with the interests of the realm. Then there were periods of lawlessness which further weakened the country and handicapped its development: periods when ' all men drew to factions ' and when the local lord ruled his neighbourhood as he willed.

When the king was a child, or when the king was weak (as Robert II and Robert III were weak), too many of the big nobility became overmighty and impatient of royal control. Thereby, the task of the Scottish kings in ' governing ' the realm was rendered more difficult, for the geography of the land necessitated loyal servants and loyal nobility in the distant parts; it was rendered more difficult still in face of the ever-present English threat to break through the southern gate; and even still more difficult when, upon occasion, England could rely upon the support of discontented or disloyal parties within Scotland itself. More than once, for example, MacDonald of the Isles, who was for long virtually an independent ruler in his Western Isles, made treaty with the English king to be his allies against the Scottish crown, though fortunately none of these treaties was effective.

Scotland's position as the northern part of one island, and her long enmity with her southern neighbour, retarded Scotland's economic and social development, preoccupied her government and, for over 250 years, helped to make her history largely one of warfare and strife. At the same time the long struggle with England gave to the people of

Scotland an intense love of freedom which Barbour, in his epic poem, *The Bruce*, proclaimed in immortal lines

> A! fredome is a noble thing!
> Fredome mays man to haiff liking;   [*makes*
> Fredome all solace to man giffis:
> He levys at es that frely levys.   [*ease*

It made the people of Scotland hardy; it inured them to a life of difficulty and danger; it gave them a new feeling for their own country and kindled in them a fervent national spirit. ' Scotland ', it has been aptly said, ' was born fighting.'

In the brief warfare of the Reformation-rebellion, however, English forces entered Scotland as allies and not as foes. With a common acceptance of Protestantism, conflict between Scotland and England came to an end. And in 1603 James VI, a Protestant king and a direct descendant of Henry VII, succeeded Elizabeth on the English throne. The two kingdoms were now ruled by one king; and a hundred years later, in 1707, by the Treaty of Union, the ' two kingdoms of Scotland and England ' were united into ' one kingdom by the name of Great Britain ' to be henceforth governed under one parliament. Since then, Scotland and England have formed friendly parts of a united Great Britain – though there have been, and still are, occasional discontents; and today, with increasing governmental control in every aspect of affairs, there is the danger that Scottish affairs may not be given sufficient ' parliamentary time ', that officials in Scotland may be too remote from the centre where decisions are made, and that officials in London may be unaware of Scottish sentiment, Scottish conditions and Scottish needs. There is the danger, too, that something distinctive in Scottish culture and in the Scottish way of life may be blurred and eventually lost.

Again, Scotland is close to northern Ireland, the intervening channel being only fifteen to twenty miles across. From Ireland, in prehistoric times, came the first visitors – fishers and beachcombers – to a ' Scotland ' which was still uninhabited after the retreat of the ice sheet; and in the Bronze Age there was a close connection between northern Ireland and western Scotland From Ireland came the Scots,[1] who

---

[1] Until the tenth century *Scotia* meant Ireland. In the tenth century *Scotia* was being used for the mainland of modern Scotland to the north of the Forth and Clyde, and the Forth was sometimes called ' The Scots Water '. From about the middle of the eleventh century *Scotia* gradually came to mean the whole of modern Scotland, though even at the beginning of the fourteenth century we still find modern Scotland

established a kingdom in Dalriada (modern Argyll), and to Dalriada, from Ireland, came the missionary Columba, and Scotland's early culture. Many Scots later fought against the English in Ireland in the fourteenth, fifteenth and sixteenth centuries. In the sixteenth century particularly, there was much mutual co-operation between Scottish and Irish rebels – the Irish helped the Islesmen and Highlanders against the Scottish government; the Islesmen and Highlanders helped the Irish against the English government. In modern times the close proximity of Ireland has led to a vast immigration of Irish labour, particularly into the industrial area around Glasgow.

To the north-east of Scotland lie the island groups of Orkney and Shetland – the first landfall in any western voyage from Scandinavia, as Scotland learned to her cost in the ninth century when the Vikings seized these island groups and held them as a base for further voyaging to Iceland or to Ireland. Then the Vikings, sailing round the north coast of Scotland and down the west coast to Ireland, took and held Caithness, Sutherland, parts of Ross, and the Western Isles and Man. These Vikings established themselves not only in northern Scotland and the Isles but also in Ireland and in northern and central England; and they had command of the sea. As a result Scotland was isolated and driven in upon herself. For more than a century and a half she was virtually cut off from Ireland, England and Europe; but that period of isolation also helped her to achieve unity in the face of a common foe.

Turning now to the geography of Scotland as revealed by an orographical map showing the gradations of high land and low land, we see at once that a great part of the country is high land. The low and fertile land is mainly confined to the 'Midland Valley' (including Lothian) with its continuation up the eastern coastal plain into the 'Laigh o' Moray'.

The Midland Valley, with its fertile soil, has always been Scotland's wealth. In early agrarian times, Picts, Scots, Britons and Angles all strove for it. In the twelfth and thirteenth centuries many Anglo-Normans were given lands there and colonised it. There (and in the fertile Tweed valley and in the south-west) were founded the principal monasteries. Today, in an industrial age, it is still the wealth of Scotland, not only because of its continuing agricultural fertility, but also because of its valuable mineral deposits, notably coal.

divided into the districts of ' Galloway ', ' Lothian ' and ' Scotland ' – this last district embracing the land to the north of the Forth and Clyde.

Here, in the heart of the Midland Valley, stands Stirling which, with its castle and its bridge over the Forth, guards all routes, north and south, east and west. Stirling is the strategic centre of Scotland. In a map drawn by Matthew Paris (died 1259) the estuaries of the Clyde and Forth are shown as practically meeting one another, the country to the north of them is called ' Scotland beyond the Sea ', and Stirling is there depicted as a bridge across the ' Sea ' and is called *Estrivelin pons*. ' At the Bridge of Stirling ', ran the old saying, ' the Forth bridles the wild Highlandman.' Again, any advance northwards from Stirling must go *via* Strathallan, Strathearn and Strathmore: and that route, in turn, is guarded by Perth which, with its castle and its bridge over the Tay, also guards any southward movement down the east coast plain or down the Perthshire Glengarry and through Dunkeld. To the south, on the Border, Berwick, with its castle and its bridge over the Tweed, is the gateway into Scotland, while Edinburgh, again with its castle on the natural fortress of a rock, guards the gap, nine miles wide, between the Pentlands and the sea, and so acts as a second ' gate ' to bar the easiest route of any English advance.

Here we should never forget that rivers and high hills are always difficult barriers to cross. Berwick, Edinburgh, Stirling and Perth all guarded important routes, and three of them also guarded important river-crossings. Those routes are still the main routes today, and, together with the passes followed in early times through the mountains and hills of the Highlands, are still the routes and passes followed by our modern system of roads and railways. Nevertheless, while rivers are difficult barriers to cross, rivers and river-valleys form easy routes of penetration into the interior of the country. The earliest peoples coming to Scotland moved inland up the river-valleys. At one period in the War of Independence the English were able to hold Stirling and Perth only because they could be reached and supplied by English ships.

In mediaeval times this fertile Midland Valley, and its continuation up the eastern coastal plain, embraced the cultural, economic and political life of Scotland. Here Scone (near Perth), with its Moot Hill, was for long regarded as the *caput*, or legal centre of the realm; but the building of Holyrood Palace by James IV, and the centralisation of the courts of justice in Edinburgh, eventually made Edinburgh the ' capital ', the seat of the king and the govenment. In 1472 and 1492, respectively, St Andrews and Glasgow were erected into archbishoprics. Universities were founded at St Andrews (1412), Glasgow (1451) and Aberdeen (1495). Here, too, were many monasteries – at Arbroath,

Coupar Angus, Scone, Lindores, Balmerino, St Andrews, Dunfermline, Culross and Cambuskenneth.

In this part of Scotland were nearly all Scotland's early trading centres, the burghs, with many of them on the east coast. For, in mediaeval times, Scotland looked east. Her trade was with the Baltic, the Low Countries and France, and it was a trade mainly in wool, woolfells (that is, sheepskins still bearing their wool), hides and skins from the good land of the Midland Valley, Lothian and the Tweed valley, and in barrelled fish (salmon, trout and eels) and cured fish (haddock and herring) from the rivers and the sea – for no part of Scotland is more than fifty miles from sea-water, and the river estuaries and the long sea-lochs encouraged fishing. In return, Scotland imported useful commodities (like iron and salt) or luxuries (like wines and rich cloths).

That ' string ' of burghs along the coast of Fife – Kinghorn; Dysart, Wemyss, Largo, Pittenweem, Anstruther, Crail and St Andrews (which Andrew Fairservice likened to a ' string o' ingans ' but which James VI called a ' golden fringe ') – tells part of the tale of Scotland's early trade, largely to the Baltic and the cloth towns of the Low Countries. But today those thriving burghs of the past, which proudly sent their commissioners to the Scottish Parliament, are little more than fishing villages, for political and economic changes in the seventeenth and eighteenth centuries turned Scotland's outlook from the east to the west.

Looking again at an orographical map of Scotland we see how much of the land is poor land. Of the total land area of Scotland, three-fifths are mountain, hill and wind-swept moor; and one-fifth is woodland, rough grazing and grass. Thus only one-fifth of the land area is good fertile land, concentrated, as we have seen, in the south-west, the Midland Valley, and the eastern coastal plain. We should remember too, that in early times when there was less skilled attention to the land (less draining, less ditching, less dyking) and, earlier still, when there were far wider stretches of forest and scrub and, in the valleys, far more bog and marsh,[1] the proportion of good land was even smaller than it is today.

The poor land lies mainly in the Highlands – a vast region of natural poverty where the hard schist and granite rocks bear only a thin covering of soil which a heavy rainfall, attracted by the mountains,

---

[1] The very many place-names with an element meaning ' bog ' or ' marsh ' are eloquent of the many stretches of ill-drained land.

sweeps away or keeps permanently wet.[1] The very nature of the country – small glens amid high hills and the penetrations of sea-lochs – meant isolated communities, each striving to eke out an existence on a limited patch of good land in strath or glen. The communities were small because the supply of food was small; they were isolated because of the great difficulties of communication. They tended to become self-reliant, self-supporting, self-interested.

Here there was nothing to attract the new settler or the colonist. So the people of the Highlands differed from the people of the Lowlands. The Highlander remained the Gael; his social organisation continued to be the old grouping by family and by kin. The Lowlander might be any admixture of Gael, Saxon, Angle, Norman, Fleming and Briton; his social organisation was based upon the working of a fertile land under a manorial or a feudal system. And a different language became a further barrier to fusion.

So, for long, Scotland was divided into two: into a Highland zone and a Lowland zone.[2] The distinctions between the two zones were both cultural and geographical. Moreover, the Highlander was apt to think of the Lowlands as land held by ' foreigners ', and land where there was ' gear to grip ' whenever he was in need, or whenever the occasion offered. The distinction between the Highlander and the Lowlander grew wider with Lowland fear and distrust; and the Lowlander's idea of the Highlander as a wild man dwelling in the woods and mountains, and a born thief, for long ran through Scottish history. Pitscottie, writing in Fife in the middle of the sixteenth century, relates how a MacGregor stole the crown of England at Bosworth Field and, when detected, boldly affirmed that, had he got the crown away to Blair Atholl, the English lords would never have seen it again. Towards the end of the sixteenth century one of the poems attributed to Montgomerie, a court poet,[3] describes how God made a Highlander out of a lump of horse manure, and then

> Quoth God to the Helandman † Quhair wilt thou now ?   [where
> I will doun to the Lowland, Lord, and thair steill a kow.

[1] We have already noted the (exceptional) fertile soils of the ' Laigh o' Moray ' – derived from Old Red Sandstone. Also the lime of the ' machair ' – flats of shell sand in certain of the Western Isles – was beneficial for agriculture.

[2] It is best to think of the Highland-Lowland line as one dividing the west from the east. The ' Lowlands ' extended beyond the Black Isle and into Sutherland and Caithness.

[3] Montgomerie (c. 1545-1610) is best known for his The Cherrie and the Slae, and The Banks of Helicon.

The Highlander, moreover, was long unwilling to be under the control of the Scottish king. In the twelfth and thirteenth centuries the best that the king could do was to establish his castles at Dumbarton and Inverness at either end of the Highland Line. Dumbarton guarded the route to or from the Highlands via Loch Lomond and Loch Long; Inverness guarded all routes, east and west, south and north. But outside those strongpoints the Scottish kings had little control. Alexander II is said to have made Dumbarton a royal burgh partly because of its services in defending the king's peaceful subjects in Lennox from the oppression of 'men dwelling in the neighbouring mountainous parts'; as late as 1592 James VI speaks of Inverness as 'surrounded on all sides by most aggressive and rebellious tribes, *the clans*'.

Here, in the Highlands, the mountain ranges and 'broken parts' which halted the invader (and no invasion, from the time of the Romans onwards, ever penetrated the Highland west) also arrested the reach of the king's law. In 1527, for example, when James V wished to issue letters against MacLeod of Dunvegan, we read in the records that, 'the said Alexander MacLeod dwells in the Highlands, where none of the king's officers dare pass for fear of their lives'. Moreover, no army could be supplied and maintained in a land of mountains and inland seas; and no roads existed. So, in the later Middle Ages, what law there was, was the unwritten law of the clan. Loyalty to the clan was the only loyalty that was known. Rights and pretensions were maintained by the arbitrament of arms: men fought and died at their chief's command, and in their chief and the unity of the clan found their protection. For long, the Highland chieftains ruled their own lands as a land apart; and we have already seen MacDonald of the Isles concluding treaties with English kings.

Here, too, the nature of the land, walled in by mountains and high hills, with deep indentations of the coast, with far-penetrating sea lochs, and with many off-shore islands, made communications by water easier than communications by land. The boat was the natural conveyance. A community was often united by the waters of a loch just as, in the southern Lowlands, a community might be united by a stretch of road. In these north-western Highlands and Islands the Vikings, relying upon sea communications, and finding a land similar to that which they had left, established themselves, and record of their settlements may be read in many place-names and heard in the terms that are used for much of the tackle of a boat. The strongholds at the openings of sea lochs and the positions of the brochs all speak of sea communications. Service to a lord might take the form of providing a galley with so many ' oars '; the sole entrance to Dunvegan Castle was its ' Sea-gate '; and Argyll bore on his arms the galley of Lorne.

Not until the seventeenth century did the Scottish kings begin to have *some* control in these difficult parts, and not until the measures taken after the Risings in 1715 and 1745 did the government secure effective control. Then, in addition to Disarming Acts, and Acts prohibiting the wearing of Highland dress and abolishing the heritable jurisdictions, roads and bridges were constructed to make land communications easier, garrisons were maintained at strategic points including Fort William,[1] Fort Augustus and Fort George, and, more important still, the officials appointed to administer the estates of those who had been forfeited for their support of the Stewart cause busied themselves with the encouragement of schools, agriculture, fishing, and industry.

Giving one last look at the map we see, close by the Borders, what are known as the Southern Uplands. There, again, the nature of the land and the difficulties of communication made royal control virtually impossible. There the Border ' clans ' were as difficult to control as the Highland clans. Moreover, the Borderers, constantly in the forefront of the battle with England,[2] and always the first to be raided and harried, were apt to rely more on the strength of their own right hands than on the slow processes of the courts of law, or the decisions of a distant government. There, in the words of the English historian Camden, ' men knew no measure of law other than the length of their own swords '. There we find the simple plan.

> That they should take, who have the power,
> And they should keep who can.

There the raid and the foray became part of the daily lives of the people. There

> Broken keep and burning farm
> Taught his fathers strength of arm;
> Feud and fight from gate to gate
> Showed them how to nurse their hate.

[1] Though the fort at Inverlochy was first built by General Monck during the Cromwellian régime, it was replaced by a stronger building, and named Fort William, by General Mackay in 1690. There was also a Cromwellian fort at Inverness.

[2] Not without reason the Scotts of Thirlestane carried on their coat of arms ' a sheaf of spears ' with the motto, ' Ready, aye ready '.

There men who slept with their swords ready to hand to resist English raids were not averse to using their swords to resist the officers of the Scottish king.

The Union of the Crowns in 1603, however, made the Border counties of both England and Scotland the ' Middle Shires '. And then the appointment of a body of Border Horse to maintain law and order was sufficient, under the spirited leadership of Sir William Cranstoun, to pacify and control a once difficult part – though only after a goodly number of executions and banishings of old Border thieves had been carried out. Old feuds and animosities occasionally flared up anew, but in 1609 the Borders were declared (though with some exaggeration) to be ' as lawful, as peaceable, and as quiet as any part in any civil kingdom in Christianity '.

CHAPTER II

Prehistoric Peoples

DURING THE ice age Scotland was covered with glaciers and was un-inhabitable. As the ice slowly retreated northwards and the climate became more genial, this uninhabited Scotland was first invaded by plants. Gradually vegetation covered large areas of the land, creeping up from England or coming as wind-borne seed. Then, when this food was available for them, came animals, moving northwards or migrating across the plain which still joined Britain to the continent. Lastly, and much later, came man, who was still dependent upon hunting and fishing for his food.

Meantime the melting waters of the ice had slowly formed a shallow new ' North Sea ' and, by flooding the land-ridge between south-east England and the mainland of Europe, had formed the ' Straits of Dover '. Britain had become an island.

During the following thousands of years various peoples came. We know little about them, though from their primitive tools, weapons, pottery and ornaments that have been found, and from the evidence of their forts, dwellings and graves it is possible to reconstruct something of their lives and history.

We speak of different ages – the stone age, the bronze age, the iron age – making these rough classifications according to the material used by each age for its weapons and tools. We can distinguish different cultures – some of these early peoples, for example, followed the custom of burying their dead collectively in tombs over which they erected large cairns of stones; some followed the custom of burying their dead individually in small stone-lined graves; others burned their dead. And these differing customs, we say, reveal different peoples, peoples of different cultures.[1] In a like way even finer distinctions can be made by a close examination of surviving pottery, ornaments, tools and weapons. When we find pottery of a better clay or of a neater or more ornate design, or when we find the use of a more efficient

---

[1] It is important to remember that both ' cultures ' and ' ages ' could flourish in different places at widely different times; and that, because of its remoteness and its difficult geography, Scotland was late in receiving new cultures and new developments. Even within the limited area of ' Scotland ' we find, for example, that in Orkney men were still using stone when, in Lothian, men were using bronze.

method of fastening an axe-head to a wooden haft, we deduce that these are the work of later cultures, of peoples who lived nearer to our own time – for we assume that over the long centuries men gradually improved their handiwork. Finally, by knowing that some particular culture (the same type of grave, for example, or the same type of pottery or axe) found, shall we say, in the south-west of Scotland or in Fife, has also been found in, say, the south of France or the Baltic region, archaeologists have been able to suggest how and whence some of these early peoples came.

Beyond that we know little. We know nothing, for example, of individual men and their actions, of their hopes and aspirations, or of leaders and the events with which they were concerned. All we can say is that for long these peoples must have been few in number, and their lives must have been hard, dangerous and short. Even when they possessed only crude weapons of stone they had to face bears, wolves and the wild boar.[1] Until they had learned how to till the land and to raise crops they clung to the sea-beaches, living on fish and shell-fish with possibly a little local hunting. Moreover, to venture forth into new territory, even to venture forth in the search for food, was to venture into the unknown. Fear was a constant companion: fear of hunger, fear of nature, fear of strangers; yet peril and want also sharpened man's wits and gave him reliance.

The land, too, was vastly different from the land we know today. The valleys were largely bog and marsh, and much of the higher ground was covered with scrub and forest. Even the levels of sea and land were not the same as they are now. On the floor of a cave near Oban, for example, some of the first visitors to Scotland left a few bone pins and a few serrated bone harpoons, or fish-spears, in amongst the thousands of empty shells of the winkles, limpets, cockles, mussels and whelks which they had eaten. When those visitors used that cave it was on the sea-shore; when their middens were discovered it was inland and well above the sea-level. Possibly the land, once it was released from the weight of the ice which had been pressing upon it for countless years, expanded and rose in an upheaval which took place gradually over many centuries – though we are not sure of the full reasons for the change. This movement of the land, moreover, was

---

[1] In the caves at Allt-nan-Uamh, near Inchnadamph in Sutherland, were found fragments of a large number of antlers of reindeer, the bones of wolves and the bones of bears comparable in size with the grizzly bears of North America. ' Caledonian bears ', we are told, appeared in the arena at Rome.

neither regular nor uniform; and the land of the east and south-east, composed of newer and softer rocks than the land of the west and north-west, even appears to have sunk under new tidal pressures. It would seem, indeed, that the whole island of Britain had tilted. In the south-east of England the earlier coastal areas are now beneath the sea, but all round Scotland there are raised sea-beaches, of varying heights above the beaches of today, showing how the land has risen above the earlier level of the sea.[1]

Probably the first people who came to Scotland after the retreat of the ice were visitors from Ireland – fishers and beachcombers, whose flints and barbed harpoons, or fish-spears, made from bone, have been found here and there in the west. Probably they were even regular visitors – if we are to judge by the enormous number of empty sea-shells found on their sites – very small groups coming again and again; but they were hardly settlers. Their tools and weapons show that they were people of the mesolithic age – people of the middle stone age, falling sometime between the palaeolithic (or old stone) and the neolithic (or new stone) ages. But hard on their heels came other visitors who made long visits amounting almost to settlement – more fishers and beachcombers came to the west coast; 'whalers' and 'forest folk' (who had axes) came from northern Europe and the Baltic to the river estuaries on the east. One of these 'whalers' left his axe, which was made from a stag's antler, in the skull of the whale he had killed; it was found there, in the whale's skeleton, in 1877, five miles up the Forth to the west of Stirling, so providing us with a record of that whaler's visit several thousands years earlier, and also showing that at the time of his visit the carses of the Forth and the Tay were still under water and that the land had not yet risen to its present level above the sea.

True settlement, however, came with immigrants in the neolithic age – men who brought cereals with them, and who also brought cattle and sheep which they had learned to raise for food; men who were farmers as well as hunters, even though farming and stock-raising only in 'a small way'.[2] The changes they brought were enormous and

---

[1] The conspicuous raised sea-beach at Ardaniaskin can be clearly seen from the opposite shore of Loch Carron.

[2] By an examination of the bones found in 'middens' it is possible to tell whether in early settlement depended mainly for its food upon hunting or upon stock-raising. If the bones which predominate are, shall we say, the bones of deer and other wild animals, then we know that that settlement was mainly dependent upon hunting; if, on the other hand, the bones which predominate are those of cattle and sheep, then we know that that settlement depended for its food mainly upon stock-raising.

far-reaching. Grain could be stored against the dangers of winter famine; flocks and herds could provide food in milk and flesh. The hungry hand-to-mouth existence of the hunter and fisher gave way to a more secure and stable existence. Tillage meant settlements; the land was cleared for pasture and arable, and men began to make the first of many changes in the face of the earth.

And now we have ample evidence of immigration by two distinct cultures – one coming to the west coast; the other, slightly later, coming to the east. To the west, came a long-headed people from the Mediterranean who voyaged round the Iberian peninsula, along the west coast of France, touched Brittany, Cornwall and the ' horns ' of Wales, passed up the Irish Sea and along the Atlantic coasts of the Hebrides, and made settlements on the west coast of Scotland (in Galloway, Kintyre, Arran and Bute), in the north-east of Ireland (whence some of them appear to have migrated to Scotland), in the Hebrides, Caithness and Sutherland, and in Orkney and Shetland. Their settlements, dating possibly from before 2000 B.C., are revealed by their remarkable burial cairns, for these people buried their dead collectively, in what might be called family vaults, or multiple graves,[1] with chambers of various kinds - for various groups of these people used various methods of building their tombs – and the chambers were then covered over with enormous long cairns of stones. The cairn was often vastly bigger than the tomb it covered: one at Yarrows, Caithness, for example, is over two hundred feet long, but the passage and the burial chamber together extend to only eighteen feet.

Because of the huge stones which they used for their burial chambers these people have been called megalithic (or big stone) folk; and in Orkney, at Maeshowe, one of their finest graves has a remarkable stone chamber with huge corner pillars – though there the chamber is covered with a mound of earth. Although we know that they were farmers as well as herdsmen, they probably relied for food as much on their herds as on their crops. Because they were still dependent upon stone for their tools moreover, their agriculture was bound to be poor with the few stone implements which they had at their command though large clearances could be made by burning as well as cutting – and some modern experiments in slash and burn clearances have shown that land so cleared was not only improved,[2] but also could be

---

[1] Though, exceptionally, some of these burial cairns have been found to contain the remains of only one or two burials.

[2] We now know that wood-ash is rich in potash, and the ' souring ' of the felled

farmed for a considerable length of time. Slowly, very slowly, more and more small patches of land were cleared and cultivated. And that these people had come with the intention of staying is clear from their choice of sites for their settlements – straths and glens where there was fertile land, and the forest-free lands of Caithness; they brought their families, their cattle and sheep, and their stocks of grain; and their multiple graves suggest successive burials over a long period of time.

To the east, on the other hand, during the later period of this colonisation of the west and north (and beginning probably from about 1800 B.C.), came a different people, a round-headed people who buried their dead individually and who came to the Tweed valley, the estuaries of the Forth and Tay, the eastern coastal areas, and the district round the Moray Firth. Their graves were like boxes, lined and covered with stone slabs, but so short that the body had to be placed in the grave in a doubled-up position with the knees drawn up to the chin; and occasionally over the grave they erected a small round cairn of earth and stones which is called a ' barrow '. Because of their shape these graves are usually known as ' short cists '. Moreover, in the grave, beside the body, these people placed a distinctively shaped pot called a ' beaker ', which probably contained the food or drink which was thought to be necessary for the journey of the dead to another world.

From their distinctively shaped grave-vessels these people are known as the beaker folk. Again there were various groups of them, shown by the various methods of decorating their beakers; but all of them came by the North Sea route, either direct from the mainland of Europe (probably from the Rhineland and Holland), or by moving further north from settlements they had already made on the coastal areas of eastern England. Like the megalithic folk they were farmers and herdsmen, but unlike the megalithic folk they were also using a little copper – copper knife-daggers and copper ornaments – and the earliest metal objects found in Scotland come from their graves. So the megalithic folk are said to belong to the new stone age (the neolithic age), but the beaker folk are said to belong to the early bronze age. Possibly some of the copper artifacts used by the early beaker folk

wood released ammonia; all that neolithic man knew was that land so cleared yielded better grass and crops. The modern experiments in ' slash and burn ' clearances have also shown that alder, hazel and birch thrive on the cleared land, and from analyses of pollen in the peat bogs we know that oaks, lime, elm and ash were succeeded by alder, birch and hazel.

were obtained by trade with Ireland, or possibly they were made by a few itinerant smiths who carried about with them their copper, their bellows and their moulds; but, in either case, it is clear that men already knew, and were using, trade routes. Now, too, the megalithic folk were beginning to use metal – copper, bronze and gold – for their ornaments and for a few of their tools, and the demand for new land and new hunting grounds meant that both the megalithic folk and the beaker folk were steadily moving inland, up the passes and the river valleys.

Possibly these beaker people, in their later, full metal-using period, or the people who immediately followed them, raised the stone circles which stand so impressively in many parts of Scotland, and notably in the north-east. More important, however, prehistoric men in Britain were now using more and more metal and less and less stone. In Ireland there was enough copper to meet all demands; tin was plentiful in Cornwall; smelted together, copper and tin made a hard bronze. Man had progressed from the neolithic age to the bronze age. The increasing use of bronze, moreover, led to an increasing use of the land. With bronze tools and implements the land could be cleared more easily, the soil could be worked more easily, and more crops could be sown and reaped.

Now, too, with the bronze age (and probably from about 1600 B.C.), we find another distinctively shaped pot used for ' grave goods ': a pot fatter and taller than the beaker and of a different shape. This pot has been called the ' food vessel '. Occasionally, moreover, the food vessels, and even beakers, have been found associated with burials in which the dead have been cremated.

It must be confessed that we know very little about either the food vessel folk or the ' incinerators '. Although the urn-fields (or cemeteries) of the incinerators are heavily concentrated in Lothian, in the north-eastern corner of Fife, and in Aberdeenshire, we cannot be sure that either the food vessel or the incinerary urn represents a new penetration of people of a new culture coming by the North Sea route from earlier settlements in England or from the European mainland. The incinerators may represent merely a group or groups of food-vessel or beaker folk who showed a preference for cremation and urn burial; and even the food vessel may represent merely a change in fashion adopted by later beaker folk, or perhaps some change brought about through the influence of earlier native pot-shapes. Moreover it is now more and more difficult to trace the movements of different peoples, or even to distinguish different peoples, because the cultures become related to each other and borrow from each other, while those coming to the east and to the west of Scotland meet each other as men use the overland routes through the passes of the mountains and by river-valley and loch.

Last of all came iron-using peoples, from both England and France, and by both the North Sea route and the Atlantic route. At first, bronze, which is a hard metal, was preferable to iron, which is a soft metal. One of the Roman historians, for example, tells us that the legionaries won a battle against the Insubres in Gaul, in 224 B.C., because each of the Insubres after one stroke with his iron sword could not deliver a second stroke until he had straightened out the bent blade under his foot. But once men had discovered how to temper iron, and so make it as hard as bronze, iron quickly replaced bronze. Moreover, whilst in Europe copper and tin are rare (although, as we have seen, the British Isles were fortunate in their deposits of both), iron is abundant everywhere; and abundance meant cheapness. Only the rich and powerful could afford bronze; almost everyone could afford iron.

With the coming – or perhaps we should say with the invasion – of the iron users (and, while their first invasions may have begun soon after the middle of the first millennium B.C., the pace may have increased in the first century B.C. with a series of refugee immigrations from troubled ' England ') the population of prehistoric ' Scotland ' must have entered upon a rapid expansion.[1]

Now too, these new invaders can be traced by their dwellings, many of which have survived. We do not know much about the dwellings of the peoples who preceded them, for while their graves were built of stone or covered with earthen mounds, the great majority of their houses were constructed wholly of wood, and, not being placed within any enduring form of enclosure, like a wall or bank, are now difficult to locate. Exceptionally, however, a remarkable group of connected stone houses, of the late neolithic age, has been discovered at Skara Brae in Orkney, and gives us some indication of how the people lived.[2] Wood is practically unknown in these northern isles, and these surviving stone houses at Skara Brae with their stone beds, stone cupboards and stone dressers, may be something like wooden

---

[1] The following revised paragraphs on the iron age owe much to the helpful criticisms of Mr R. W. Feachem.

[2] Recently, too, excavations in Shetland have revealed the remains of very solid, egg-shaped stone houses which can be assigned to the earlier part of the second millennium B.C.

counterparts which were in use in the timber houses on the mainland. But we cannot be sure. Prehistoric survivals in Orkney and Shetland are often so different from parallel survivals on the mainland that we cannot draw too close an inference from Skara Brae.

The Skara Brae pastoralists, who lived by breeding sheep and cattle, had built their stone settlement amid the sand-dunes and *beneath* sand and refuse, as a protection from the high winds: and it was exposed when a storm in 1866 cleared the covering sand. In a similar way at Jarlshof (near Sumburgh Head in Shetland) successive drifts of sand over the centuries engulfed successive settlements of the late stone age, the late bronze age and the iron age, and these have now been excavated to reveal a site that is unique in its evidence of changing ' house styles '.

But, while hardly any iron-age graves have as yet been recognised, the dwellings and settlements built by the iron-age people have survived in large numbers both on the mainland and on the western and northern islands; and it is noticeable that from the start of the iron age they were always defensible against attack. In the greater part of the country the iron age houses, invariably circular in plan, were made entirely of timber. But, unlike those of earlier periods, they were enclosed, at first within one or more palisades and later within a wall or a system of ramparts. Possibly the ' lords of the iron age ', after invasion and conquest, compelled the local people to work for them, perhaps even to build their strongholds. For, while the use of iron made agriculture and all the useful arts more easy, a multiplication of iron weapons may also have made war easier than work. Certainly there is now every indication that attack and defence were part and parcel of the iron-lord's life. Possibly there was now a temptation to try to take a neighbour's lands or cattle by force rather than to open up new land or raise larger herds by work. Moreover, if the iron-lords had subjugated the local people and made them slaves, there was always the risk that the local people might rise in revolt.

The farmsteads, settlements and ' places of strength ' of the iron age occur in great variety. They include single-house homesteads of timber or of stone, farmsteads, small and large settlements and hill-top towns measuring up to as much as 40 acres in extent. The circular timber houses vary from as little as 20 feet in diameter to more than 60 feet, an example of the largest, found at Scotstarvit in Fife, having a floor space of 3,000 square feet. Timber houses were built throughout the whole period of the pre-Roman iron age, but there is no evidence that the fashion carried on into post-Roman times when houses, though

19

at first still circular, had walls at least founded upon stone, if not indeed wholly constructed of drystone masonry.

The palisades enclosing the earliest iron age houses were, in their simplest form, merely single fences forming a farmyard boundary; but many much larger and more elaborate forms were developed. These include twin palisades bounding settlements more than one acre in extent, often accompanied by an outlying concentric single or double fence which formed an enclosure for cattle. When more robust defences were demanded, the circular timber houses were enclosed within walls or ramparts. Two of the largest of such defended settlements, the 'hill-forts' or 'towns' on Traprain Law in East Lothian, and on the north-west summit of the Eildon Hills in Roxburghshire, contained hundreds of dwellings and other buildings. At the latter settlement, the final form of the defences was a set of three concentric heavy ramparts which were not, however, maintained after the Roman conquest in the first century A.D. At Traprain Law, an important centre of the Votadini 'tribe' who may have been in treaty with the Romans, the defences were kept in repair until at least the fourth century A.D.

Some of the stone-walled settlements, or hill-forts, had walls of great thickness strengthened internally with timber beams. It has been shown that, in some cases, the houses or other internal buildings were timber-built lean-to erections attached to the inner face of the wall; and it may be assumed that this was a common arrangement. If such buildings were set on fire, by accident or during an attack, the conflagration would set alight the beams inside the wall. When this happened, many of the blocks of stone in the wall fused together in vitrified masses and even fused on to the underlying rock. Such 'vitrified forts' are to be found in every part of Scotland except the far north. Timber-laced walls, however, are found in southern Britain and in north-west Europe, and their great variety indicates that the technique developed over a long period and among different peoples. The only example known in Britain of the true *murus Gallicus*, in which iron bolts secured the timbers, is at Burghead in Moray, though the inner wall of the hill-fort in Angus known as the White Caterthun, which is about 40 feet thick, might be another.

In the west and north, where timber was not available for building, the homesteads were constructed of stone. Communal settlements of the hill-fort kind are not found in these parts, and only individual homesteads occur. Here the two principal varieties are the brochs and the structures now known as dùns. The latter are enclosures with very thick walls which often contain galleries and chambers, staircases and cells, and have entrences checked for a door and provided with bar-holes. There are dùns of circular, oval, and subrectangular plan; they often measure internally about 3,000 square feet; and it is assumed that within them light-weight lean-to buildings or tent-like shelters were used. The dùns occur mainly in the far west, in contradistinction to the brochs which occur mainly in the far north.

The broch was a dry-stone tower with a wall about fifteen feet thick surrounding a circular space usually about thirty feet in diameter. After some six feet or more of solid wall at the base (in which there were often cells), the wall became double with a space of from four feet to two feet or less between an inner and an outer wall, which were tied together by horizontal stone slabs which assisted stability and also served as scaffolding during the work of building. A broch may have risen to more than forty feet in height, as seen in the best preserved surviving example on the island of Mousa off the east coast of Shetland; and in several other cases the wall still stands to a height of more than twenty feet. It may be that a height of at least thirty feet was common. The few excavations that have been carried out in brochs suggest that the circular interior was covered by a roof, probably thatched and supported on posts set in or on the floor, with its edge resting on a scarcement formed on the inner face of the wall. Only one opening, the entrance, pierced the broch wall.

Almost all the brochs, which number about 600, lie in the territories of the Picts, the people dwelling north of the Forth-Clyde isthmus. The very few which have been found south of this region may be assigned to rare Pictish settlers among the Britons. No precise date can as yet be given to these remarkable structures, but an origin in the first century B.C. is probable, comparable to that also suggested for the dùns. Like the dùns, the brochs are usually found near good land – up the fertile river valleys and along the coastal strip. Like the dùns, they were strongholds, and the word broch means a fortified dwelling.

Other stone-built homesteads which can be assigned to the iron age are the aisled round-houses and the wheel-houses, distributed in remote peripheral western and northern areas. A round-house immediately succeeded the broch at Jarlshof, while the broch, in turn, was succeeded by a wheel-house. At this site, at least the sequence is clear; and it, is possible that both the aisled round-house and the wheel-house originated very early in the first millenium A.D., if not before.

To this period also can be assigned the crannogs – dwellings like circular farm-houses, but built on artificial islands in the lochs – and the strange subterranean chambers or galleries, variously called weems or Picts' Houses and technically known as *souterrains*.

Finally, as we have seen, the cheapness and abundance of iron meant a steady increase in the amount of land under cultivation and that meant a steady increase in population. Admittedly the archaeological evidence reveals that the economy of the iron age was still mainly pastoral, but only large local groups, or communities, could have built the brochs or, for example, the massive stone ramparts of the fort on Finavon Hill in Angus, with its walls 25 feet thick enclosing an area of some 100 by 300 feet. It has been calculated that when the Romans moved north the population of 'Scotland' was between 300,000 and 400,000; certainly the population was sufficiently large to be a worry to the Romans and to compel them eventually to build a fortified frontier for the protection of southern Britain. Writing of the year A.D. 297 a Roman author, Eumenius, speaks of attacks made on that fortified frontier by 'Picts and Irish [Scots] '. This is the first mention of 'Picts'. Possibly, to the Romans, the Picts were the painted (or tattooed) people attacking from the land-mass of Scotland, as opposed to attackers on the west (Scots) from Ireland. If so, the Picts would be the descendants of both the late bronze-age people and the later iron-age invaders.

CHAPTER III

The Roman Walls

AFTER THE successful invasion of England by the Emperor Claudius in
A.D. 43 the whole of its southern parts were quickly conquered and
colonised by the triumphant Roman arms. But the north and west
still remained unconquered. To maintain the conquest of Wales, the
Romans built legionary fortresses at Isca Silurum (Caerleon-on-Usk)
and Dēva (Chester); to hold down the turbulent Brigantes of the north,
they built a legionary fortress at Eborācum (York). But what of the
tribes who dwelt further north still – those who dwelt in the country
which is now Scotland ?

Although the story of the Romans in Scotland usually begins with
Agricola, and is based upon the life of Agricola written by his son-in-
law, the historian Tacitus, recent excavations at Milton, in Annandale,
suggest that there may have been a Roman ' push ' into south-west
Scotland before Agricola. It may be that Tacitus was ignorant of this,
or, possibly as a dutiful son-in-law he may have wished to give
Agricola the credit for the first Roman penetration into the farther
north.[1] Moreover, as yet, archaeologists who study the Roman period
can tell us little about these earlier penetrations and we must await the
results of further excavations of the various sites which have been
revealed by air photography. But it now seems possible that Lugu-
vallium (Carlisle) was reached by Petilius Cerealis (Governor of the
Province of Britain, 71-4) in the course of his campaigns against the
Brigantes, and that from there he sent forward strong reconnaissance
forces into south-west Scotland and established a number of outposts
there.

Nevertheless, even if there was a pre-Agricolan Roman push into
these northern parts, it is probable that it was little more than a reconnaissance in strength. The first real attempt at conquest came with
Agricola (Governor of the Province of Britain, 78-85) who, in 80, had
pushed into Scotland (advancing in two columns up Lauderdale and
Annandale, and converging upon Inveresk) and had reached the narrow
neck of land between the Forth (Bodotria) and the Clyde (Clota),

---

[1] And the account written by Tacitus must always be read with due allowance for
filial piety.

with, possibly, a lightning raid on the east as far as the River Tay, before withdrawing again. In the following year, 81, however, 'securing the ground which he had overrun', Agricola once more advanced to the Forth-Clyde isthmus and there built a chain of small stockaded posts, building also strategic roads and forts (like Dalswinton and Newstead) to the south of this new line.[1] Thus, says Tacitus, 'the enemy was pushed back into what was virtually another island'; and it must have seemed so to the Romans, for, as we have seen, the estuary of the Forth was then much wider than it is today, and the river ran through vast stretches of bog and marsh on either side. And, Tacitus observes, ' were such a thing compatible with the courage of our armies and the glory of the name of Rome, there would have been found, within the limits of Britain, an ultimate frontier line '.[2] That was undoubtedly what Rome was seeking; but it is doubtful if Agricola was satisfied with the Forth-Clyde line and still unconquered country lying to the north. A frontier line had as yet been neither found nor formed.

In the following year, 82, Agricola carried out a series of campaigns in the south-west, in modern Dumfriesshire, Galloway and southern Ayrshire, either in preparation for an invasion of Ireland, or to meet the possibility of an invasion from Ireland, but in either event certainly securing the left flank of his new line of forts. Recent air photographs and archaeological excavations have shown that the peoples of the south-west must have put up a strong resistance, for their country had subsequently to be strongly held. At this time, too, Agricola sent a fleet to explore the west coast and the western isles – possibly to see whether the Highlands could be outflanked by a landing on the west, But the answer he received must have been unfavourable, for, in 83, when Agricola moved his army northwards again, he took the route dictated by the geography of the land, the route up Strathallan, Strath-earn and Strathmore – a route signposted by the permanent forts built at Ardoch (near Greenloaning), Strageath (near Innerpeffray), Bertha (near Perth) and Cardean (near Meigle); and in Strathmore he built a legionary fortress at Inchtuthill, about seven miles south-east of Dun-keld, to form a permanent Scottish base. Marching still further north, and keeping in touch with a Roman fleet (for the very nature of the

---

[1] The difficulties of the land-routes, and the necessity of providing the Roman soldiers with their rations of corn, oil and wine, also meant the establishment of bases like Inveresk on the Forth and, later, Carpow on the Tay. Recent excavations moreover, have revealed that Carpow, near Abernethy, acted as a legionary base during the Campaign of Severus (*infra* p. 28).

[2] The word used by Tacitus is *terminus*.

country necessitated supplies by sea), he defeated a strong native force at the battle of Mons Graupius[1] – possibly Knock Hill, near Keith, Banffshire, though the site of the battle has not yet been identified with certainty. But the season was already late; the marching camp at Auchinhove (two miles north-east of Keith) is the northernmost camp which has been found[2]; and Mons Graupius possibly represents the limit of Agricola's advance before he turned southwards again. The fleet, however, sailed further north still, as far as the Orkney islands where it received the submission of the people.

Mons Graupius was probably fought in 84; in 85 Agricola was recalled by Domitian (through jealousy of his achievements, according to Tacitus – though under Domitian Rome was trying to reduce her commitments in far-afield campaigns which drained her resources and man-power); and in 86 the Second Legion Adiutrix was withdrawn from the Province of Britain.[3] The withdrawal of the Second Legion Aduitrix left only three legions in Britain – one each for Isca, Dēva, and Eborācum. No legion was available for Inchtuthil. That strong and ideally situated fortress commanding the route north and south through Strathmore, and guarding the descent from the hills down Glengarry, was abandoned. And the abandonment of Inchtuthil meant Rome's abandonment of Scotland. There was a slow, contested, but definite Roman retreat. For a time Newstead and Dalswinton appear to have become the main northern Roman bases; then there was further retreat to the line of the Tyne and Solway; and finally, after some unrecorded disaster to the Ninth Legion (probably inflicted upon it by the Brigantes of the modern Lancashire and Yorkshire), the retreat was stayed with the building of Hadrian's Wall.

Hadrian's Wall, begun about 122 under Aulus Platorius Nepos (whom the Emperor Hadrian, after his visit to Britain in 121 or 122, had left behind as Governor of the province) and completed about 128, was a definite attempt to protect Roman Britain from invasion and attack by the unconquered peoples of the north. It was a Roman frontier, a fortified boundary with a protected road providing a trans-

---

[1] Tacitus, following the fashion of historical writing in his time, ascribes an eloquent address to Calgācus, the leader of the barbarian army, which is notable for its indictment of Rome and Roman slavery, and which includes many phrases still frequently quoted, such as ' ubi solitudinem faciunt pacem appellant ' (' where they make desolation, they call it peace ').

[2] Unless, indeed, the as yet unexcavated site near Fochabers should prove to be Roman.

[3] The withdrawal of this legion, together with its auxiliaries, meant the withdrawal of some 10,000 men.

verse means of communication; it served the double purpose of holding back attacks and of enabling the garrison to move freely in either direction; and it was akin to the Roman frontiers on the Danube and the Rhine.   As finally built, the Wall was of ashlar, rubble-filled,[1] and ran from Wallsend on the Tyne to Bowness on the Solway.   Its height, to the top of the parapet walk, was about twenty feet; its thickness averaged about eight feet; and in front of it, to the north, ran a ditch some fifteen feet deep, while the upcast from the ditch, thrown out to the north, made the drop even deeper still.   It was, and still is, a work of stupendous magnificence, eloquent of the ability and might of Rome.   At first, along its course, there were only the small forts, or *milecastles*, built at every Roman mile, with signal-towers, or *turrets*, in between; but, almost immediately after its construction (or perhaps even during its construction), larger forts, sixteen in number and spaced at intervals of five or six miles, were added, emphasising the defensive nature of the new frontier line, while probably at the same time, the *vallum*, or ditch, some ten to twelve feet deep, was dug along its southern side. Clearly there was heavy pressure from the north; but the *vallum*, to the south, is in places so badly sited for defence against any supporting attacks by the still restless tribes to the immediate south, notably the Brigantes, that it may have been constructed only to prevent easy access to the Wall.   At this same time outposts were built at Bewcastle, Netherby and Birrens, and the western flank was protected (probably from attacks by the Scots of Ireland) by some form of continuation, including small forts, along the Cumbrian coast.

But Hadrian's Wall was apparently too far from the real trouble-makers of the north.   Less than twenty years later, Lollius Urbicus (Governor of Britain under the Emperor Antoninus Pius), probably influenced by continuing pressure from the north, pushed the Roman arms once more up to the narrow line of the Forth-Clyde isthmus, built a wall where Agricola had earlier built his forts, and apparently conscripted many of the young men of fighting age from the intervening territory (mainly, it would appear, men of the Selgovae in the central southern uplands) transported them to the continent, and enrolled them as auxiliaries in the Roman army on the Rhine.

[1] On the west the final stretch was at first built of turf and then gradually replaced by stone. The wall was built by the legionaries, for there were no pioneer troops and each legionary had to be able to dig and to build as well as to fight.   While certain of the inscribed stones along the wall bear the names of Hadrian and of Aulus Platorius Nepos, others name the contingents which built some of the forts and different sections of the wall.

This new push took place between 139 and 142, and the new wall – the Antonine Wall – completed by Lollius Urbicus about 144, ran, roughly, from Bo'ness to Old Kilpatrick. Like Hadrian's Wall, it was built from east to west. In contrast with Hadrian's Wall, however, it was a turf wall (a *murus caespiticius*) erected on a stone pitching. It was about ten feet high, fifteen feet thick at its base, and six feet thick at its top, while to the north of it ran a ditch some thirty-six feet wide and twelve feet deep. Along its course were nineteen forts or garrison strong-points, smaller than those of Hadrian's Wall (that at Duntocher being only half an acre in size, and that at Rough Castle only one acre) and closer to one another for mutual support.[1]

In many respects the Antonine Wall was thus far less strong than Hadrian's Wall. Nevertheless it was intended to be a new permanent line. The new wall was intended to be the new frontier. The route northwards was again partially opened up; Ardoch was once more occupied; and some twenty or more forts and fortlets were strung along a network of roads to the south. There is also evidence that the mile-castles (and presumably the turrets) on Hadrian's Wall were abandoned for a time, and that the Hadrianic forts were held by smaller garrisons. All this suggests that the tribes of the southern uplands were thought to be no longer dangerous. But, even though the garrisons of the Hadrianic forts had been reduced, and even though the forts of the Antonine Wall could have held only small contingents, it is clear that the demands of the two walls, together with the demands of the forts to the rear of the Antonine Wall (like Newstead, guarding the important route through Lauderdale) were stretching to its utmost the Roman strength in north Britain.[2]

The new wall, admittedly, was only thirty-seven miles long compared with the seventy miles' length of Hadrian's Wall; but, quite apart from its weaker constructional strength, the Antonine Wall could easily be turned by sea-borne landings (despite the protecting forts on both its flanks), its lines of support (and retreat) through the difficult country of the southern uplands were never good (despite the new Roman roads and forts), and, above all, the new frontier and a large proportion of the Roman forces in Britain were too far north with long and difficult lines of communication. Twice in the next forty years

---

[1] The fort at Cramond appears to have been built at this time to act as a supply base.

[2] Some 16,000 to 20,000 men would be required for the two walls and the network of intervening forts; and, though it was contrary to Roman practice to use legionaries in front-line garrisons, there is evidence that some legionaries were being used.

the Antonine Wall was overrun, and twice reoccupied and repaired. There is evidence that the line was probably still being held as late as 186; but shortly thereafter it was abandoned or lost, though we do not know when or how. Certainly it cannot have been held later than 196 or 197 when Clodius Albinus took most of the garrison of Britain over to Gaul in an attempt to set himself up as Emperor, and when Hadrian's Wall was promptly overrun and shattered. If the Antonines Wall was then still being held, it too must have been broken.

That is, by the end of the second century the land that is now Scotland had freed itself from the Roman arms. More than that, the Maeatae (of Strathmore and the Mearns) and the Caledonii (of the central Highlands), having overrun both walls, had joined the Brigantes, and, pushing south, had taken part in the sack of York. The rising, however, was eventually crushed; the 'barbarians' were driven back; work was begun on the broken Hadrianic Wall and forts; and in 208 the Emperor Sevērus himself supervised the restoration of the Hadrianic line and, during the next two years, campaigned in Scotland, marching up the eastern coastal plain, turning the naval base at Carpow into a legionary base (for the Sixth Legion) and apparently striving to hold the vale of Strathmore.[1]

Sevērus enjoyed no resounding victory like that of Agricola at Mons Graupius; but both the Maeatae and the Caledonii were subdued. With the death of Sevērus at York, in 211, however, Hadrian's Wall was apparently accepted by Rome as her frontier line and the garrisons were withdrawn from Scotland, though long-range patrols still maintained a certain hold over the country to the immediate north. Yet the success of the Sevēran campaign was to be seen in the large number of village settlements which flourished in south-eastern Scotland in the third century and which were witness to a period of peace.

For almost a hundred years the Hadrianic frontier apparently stayed secure. In 296-7, however, when Allectus took away the garrisons of the Wall in his attempt to set himself up as Emperor, the Hadrianic line was again broken; and this time we are told by a Roman writer of attacks by 'Picts and Irish (Scots)'. But Allectus had not taken the legionaries out of Britain; he was defeated in southern Britain by Constantius; and Constantius was able to restore the position. The Wall was repaired and rebuilt (about 305), and Constantius conducted a punitive expedition into the north much as Sevērus had done.

[1] It is possible that during this period some of the forts on the Antonine Wall were re-occupied – but only briefly, say 209-11.

In 367, however, we are told of Picts sweeping over the Wall, of Scots attacking the west coast, and of Saxons landing in the south-east. Rome's conflict with the barbarians was becoming more difficult. Once more the position was restored – this time by Theodosius who brought over fresh contingents to reinforce the army in Britain in 369. But now it was no longer possible to man the Wall as of old. Instead 'the new garrisons with their women and children, lived exclusively within the forts' which 'became little fortified townships. . . . A centurion of the old order would have blenched at the sight.'[1]

In these closing years the Romans appear to have tried to set up native buffer states, in front of Hadrian's Wall, to take the first shock of attacks from the north. Also they formed a mobile fleet of light vessels (called *Pictae*), based on harbours in Wales and the west, to spot or even to engage the invading Scots from Ireland. But the attackers were too many and the defenders too few; and the Saxon raids grew more and more serious. The Roman forces, moreover, were again sadly depleted when, in 383, Magnus Maximus took many men from Britain to Gaul in an attempt to set himself up as Emperor. Once more the Wall was overrun, and this time the frontier was never restored. A Roman poet, Claudian, writing in 399 and 400, speaks of a Britain freed from the attacks of Picts, Scots and Saxons in the first consulate of Stilicho; but, although Stilicho apparently took measures for the defence of Britain, it is doubtful how far Britain was defended north of the vale of York.

Thus, all in all, the Roman occupation of Britain hardly touched the land of modern Scotland. There were brief campaigns, such as those of Agricola and Severus; the land to the south of the Forth and Clyde was held for about fifty years; but, when the Antonine Wall ceased to be the Roman frontier (sometime before 200), Scotland (apart from lower Annandale) fell completely outside the Roman province.

As we have already indicated, the impossibility of manning the legionary fortress of Inchtuthil meant the impossibility of securing a Roman Scotland. The Roman road northwards, through Strathallan, Strathearn and Strathmore, can be traced no further than Kirriemuir; and the northernmost permanent Roman fort, so far discovered, as distinct from temporary marching camps, is that at Stracathro, near Edzell. Writing of Agricola's recall, Tacitus made the comment, 'Perdomita Britannia et statim omissa' (' Britain completely subdued

[1] I. A. Richmond, *Roman Britain* (1955), p. 63.

and at once relinquished '). But had the northern part of the island of Britain been ' completely subdued ' ? To try to hold back attacks from the difficult country of the central Highlands, Agricola had built small forts at Bochastle (near Callander), at Dalginross (near Comrie) and at Fendoch (in the Sma' Glen); but those forts merely sealed off an unknown and unconquered west. And, when the legionaries built their marching camp at Auchinhove and, looking northwards, saw, beyond the arm of the sea which is now called the Moray Firth, the tops of yet further mountains and hills in a still unreached land, did they themselves think that Britain had been wholly won ?

Thus this period in Scottish history is largely the history of Scotland's separation from Rome by two frontier walls. Scotland lay beyond the frontier of a ' far-flung empire '; and Rome's relations with Scotland were much like the relations, in recent time, of the British Empire with the tribes who lived beyond the north-west frontier of India. Scotland can have felt little of the cultural influence of Rome. It has been said, and with truth, that, even in that part of the Province of Britain which is now England, the Romans civilised the south but only occupied the north. In the south of England their occupation was marked by towns and villas and a civil government; in the north of England it was marked by forts, camps, signal stations, and a military government.[1] And the northern frontier of that military occupation was the fortified boundary of the Roman Wall. The Roman villa (a large house with an agricultural area based upon it) is rare even in north Yorkshire; no Roman villa at all has been found north of Hadrian's Wall.

The advent of the Roman legions possibly taught the peoples of Scotland something of new methods in the waging of war: though the very character of the Roman forts, and not merely the strength of Hadrian's Wall, indicates that those peoples had bravery and tenacity of purpose in the defence of their land and in their hatred of the newcomer. The Roman fort at Ardoch, in Strathallan (first built by Agricola, and the best preserved Roman fort in Scotland), eventually had an amazing series of banks and ditches (in some places seven deep) to guard its rampart; the rampart of the fort at Rough Castle, on the line of the Antonine Wall, was protected by a honeycomb of crisscrossed pits in which pointed stakes were concealed. Again, while the expeditions of Agricola and Severus may have brought about the first

[1] This is admirably illustrated by Plates 20 and 21 in Haverfield's *Roman Occupation of Britain* (ed. Macdonald), and by the Ordnance Survey Map of *Roman Britain*.

beginnings of a new unity fashioned in alliance against a common foe – Tacitus states that, at Mons Graupius, Calgācus was leading a ' confederacy of tribes ' – any such alliance was probably merely temporary. What is certain is that continuous warfare was bound to have its effect in continuous unsettlement.

A little of Rome's culture may have been acquired through trading contacts at the Wall and at posts held for a while, here and there, in advance of it. Archaeologists have shown that Housesteads, for example, in the very centre of Hadrian's Wall, developed a definite market, outside its fort, where Roman pottery, glass and metal-work were exchanged for native cattle, skins and hides. But, although Roman wares found their way far north of Hadrian's Wall, the volume of trade must have been small; and there is no indication that the native people learned any of the Roman arts and crafts. Above all, however, it may be that the Christian work of Ninian (and possibly of others whose names have not come down to us[1]) was facilitated by Roman stability in the Solway region; certainly the friendly contacts established between Rome and the Votadini (of Northumberland, the Merse and Lothian) secured stability in the east.[2]

Scotland, unlike England, was never completely opened up by a system of Roman roads[3]; unlike southern England, Scotland was never ' colonised '. Rome never touched the Highlands; and the Lowlands knew little of Rome apart from the strength of her defensive works and the might of the Roman arms. And yet, in a negative way, Rome may have left a different legacy unawares. Hadrian's Wall, holding until the close of the fourth century, protecting the ' Roman peace ' of the south, and barring the onslaughts of the tribes from the north, was the first division between the peoples of one island.

Unfortunately the Roman historians and geographers tell us little of the people to the north of that division. Tacitus, throughout, calls them either *Britanni* or the people inhabiting *Caledonia*; but this does not necessarily mean that the people who, to Tacitus (or Agricola), were the *Britanni* of the north were the same people as the *Britanni* of

---

[1] *Infra*, pp. 43-4.

[2] Samian pottery and Roman coins dating from the end of the first to the end of the fourth century have been found in the hill-top forts of Traprain Law (of the Votadini) in East Lothian. It should be remembered, too, that not until nearly two centuries after the demilitarisation of the Wall did the Angles conquer and occupy northern England.

[3] Though air photography and excavation are revealing a network of military roads in the Lowlands, constructed to connect the forts which were built to hold down that difficult part.

the south. Ptolemy (about 150) gives the names of a number of tribes, and of their strongholds, and places the *Caledonii* in the whole of the central Highland area.[1] An account of the campaign of the Emperor Sevērus places the *Maeatae* close to Hadrian's Wall with the *Caledonii* beyond them. In the fourth century, however, we read of 'the Caledonians, the Picts and others', or of 'the Caledonians and other Picts'. But the name Caledonians disappears, and then the peoples of the north are called Picts.

[1] See the map in *Roman and Native in North Britain*, p. 49.

CHAPTER IV

The Formation of the Kingdom of Scotland

THE Venerable Bede, who died in 735, and who had spent his whole life at Wearmouth and Jarrow in ' the land of the Angles ', closed his *Historia Ecclesiastica* with the year 731 and with this summary: ' The Picts are at this time at peace with the Angles; the Scots who inhabit Britain, satisfied with their own territories, meditate no hostilities against the Angles; the Britons, although in part they are their own masters, are elsewhere under subjection to the Angles'.

Here Bede refers to four different peoples – Picts, Scots, Britons and Angles: and, although there were then no definite boundaries, we know that at this time these peoples occupied four separate regions – the Picts in the land from the Forth to the Pentland Firth[1] (and probably also in Orkney, Shetland and the Hebrides); the Scots in Dalriada or, roughly, modern Argyll; the Britons in Strathclyde, Cumbria and Wales; and the Angles in Bernicia, the northern part of an Anglian kingdom stretching from the Humber to the Firth of Forth. Elsewhere, Bede refers to these four peoples as four ' tongues '. This problem of language is full of difficulties. In the very broadest terms we may say that the Britons, the Scots, and the Picts spoke a Celtic language, whereas the Angles, a Germanic people, spoke a Teutonic language. The Britons spoke a Celtic which has become modern Welsh; the Scots spoke a Celtic which has become modern Gaelic; and these two dialects (called P-Celtic and Q-Celtic, respectively) may represent two separate Celtic immigrations from Europe.

These four regions and their peoples were gradually united to form the kingdom of Scotland – though it should be noted that the regions of the Britons and the Angles stretched far down into modern England and that several centuries were to pass before a final boundary, short of the original southern limits of these two regions, was at last fixed and accepted to define the land of Scotland from the land of England.

As we have seen, the name Picts does not occur until the end of the third century when a Roman writer speaks of ' Picts and Irish (Scots) ' attacking the Roman (Hadrians') Wall. If, as we have sug-

---

[1] That is, the ' Pettaland ', or ' Pictland Firth '.

gested, the word meant to the Romans simply 'the painted people ',[1] it would be an indication that the peoples of the north were still following the custom of painting their bodies at a time when that custom had died out in the south. Probably, too, the Romans used the word as a general term for all the peoples living in the land-mass of Scotland to the north of the Forth: and another Roman writer's phrase *'Caledŏnes and other Picti '* seems to show that the term was a collective one. The name ' Picts ', however, passed into current use for the peoples of a Pictish kingdom which stretched northwards from the Forth. At first we hear of ' northern Picts ' and ' southern Picts ', probably the inhabitants of two separate kingdoms each under its own king[2]; but, by the seventh century, these two separate groups had united to form one Pictish kingdom with a shift southwards of political power. It was a united Pictland that defeated the Angles at Dunnichen in 685; and the peoples of that Pictland were the descendants of differing iron-age invaders and of the late bronze-age peoples whom they had overruled.

The strength and unity of the Pictish kingdom may have been impaired by a peculiar system of succession (sometimes called ' the Pictish Law of Succession '), which was still in force in Bede's time and which, it is thought, may have been taken from some system practised by the late bronze-age peoples. Probably the system was matrilinear (that is, descent was reckoned through the mother); and, while the general principle appears to have been that a man became king because his mother was the daughter of an earlier king, and that he was succeeded not by his son but by his mother's son (his brother) or by his mother's daughter's son (his nephew), the succession was also subject to choice.[3] Yet although this choice was made within a family group containing

---

[1] We have already noted that the Roman patrol-vessels operating off the west coast of England in the fourth century were called *Pictae*, presumably because they were camouflaged by being painted sea-green.

[2] And possibly developing from two separate iron-age invasions. We know from archaeological evidence that the iron-age invaders who settled between the Firth of Forth and the Moray Firth were of a different, but related, ' culture ' from the iron-age invaders who settled north of the Moray Firth and in Orkney and Shetland. Timber-laced (vitrified) forts are found mainly in the area between the Firth of Forth and the Moray Firth, and around the Moray Firth while the brochs, on the other hand, are found mainly north of the Moray Firth and in Orkney and Shetland. In historic times, however, the division appears to have been at the Mounth (a word akin to the Welsh *mynydd*, ' mountain '), the name given to the mass of high mountains on both sides of the valley of the upper Dee.

[3] Possibly, too, when the son of a daughter and the son of a son were equally eligible for succession, the son of a daughter would be preferred.

brothers, cousins and nephews, all descendants of a common great-grandmother, the system lacked the stability that comes from the direct succession of son to father – always providing such direct succession did not lead to minorities.

No Pictish literature has survived, but the Pictish sculptured stones – usually dressed slabs bearing designs in relief or rough pillars with designs incised[1] – are remarkable works of art. Certain of the designs like the ' V-rod and crescent ', the ' pair of spectacles ', the ' mirror and comb ' and other symbols, are stereotyped; but other designs showing, in relief, warriors, huntsmen and churchmen are bold in execution and give us some idea of Pictish costume and armour. Some of the designs are also associated with a cross – either the simple Latin cross or the more elaborate Celtic cross – and have borders and divisions of intricate interlacing mesh and spital patterns.

The Scots, as we have seen, came from Ireland. *Scotia* was originally Ireland, and the inhabitants of *Scotia* were *Scotti*.[2] Possibly some of them, after helping the Picts against the Romans, decided to settle in the west, in Argyll; possibly, on the other hand, in a period of general unrest, the Britons of Strathclyde invited the Scots to seize Argyll from the Picts and to colonise it, so that the flank of the British kingdom would be protected from attack by the Picts. We do not know. Or again, Scots of Dalriada in northern Ireland may have made a settlement in Argyll sometime in the fifth century. About 500 Domingart, son of Fergus [Mor] son of Erc, was apparently king of the Scots of Dalriada in Ireland and Argyll, while in an annal of much later date a like position is accorded to his father.

This Scottish kingdom in Argyll came to be known as Dalriada; and at first it was closely associated with the Scots of Dalriada in Ireland. Fergus Mor, we are told, ' with the people of Dalriada [in Ireland], held part of Britain '. In strife with the Picts, it was firmly established by Columba[3] and by Aidan, who was made king of Dalriada by Columba in 574. The Scots had already made some penetrations eastwards into the fertile midland valley – Strathearn probably means ' Strath of Eire ' rather than ' Strath of the river Earn '; and also north-eastwards – possibly even moving up the Great Glen into the area of the Moray

---

[1] The Pictish ' symbols ' are also to be found on the walls of caves, and on small objects of stone, bone and metal.

[2] *Supra*, p. 4, n. 1. The first mention of Scoti (Scotti) seems to be by Ammianus in the fourth century.

[3] According to Bede, Columba came to preach to the northern Picts and received the island of Iona from their king, Brude, son of Maelchon.

Firth – though these early penetrations cannot have been permanent. Pushing southwards, however, they came into conflict with the Angles who, in turn, had been steadily pushing westwards into the land of the Britons.

The old name for Britain was Albion[1]; but, under the Romans, the name was changed to *Britannia* (Britain), the land of the *Britanni* or *Brittŏnes* – the Britons. Then *Alba*, as opposed to *Britannia*, seems to have been used for the non-Romanised part of Britain north of the Roman Wall.[2] Later still, as we shall see, *Alba* was used for the united kingdom of the Picts and Scots north of the Forth-Clyde line.

After the departure of the Romans, the Britons, apparently divided into various kingdoms, were gradually pushed westwards by invading Angles and Saxons until they held only the western part of Britain from the Clyde to Cornwall. Between 613 and 616, moreover, Ethelfrith, Anglian king of Northumbria, by a victory at the battle of Chester, drove the first wedge between the Britons of the north and the Britons of Wales.[3] A further advance of the Angles up the valley of the Tyne and down the valley of the Irthing divided the Britons of the north, separating those of Strathclyde from those of Cumbria.

The main strong-point of the Britons of Strathclyde was Dumbarton which, in its British form, was Alclut (the rock of the Clyde), though the Irish form, which has survived, was Dūn Breattan (the fortress of the Britons). This kingdom of the Britons of Strathclyde was strong enough to retain its separate identity until the beginning of the eleventh century.[4]

The Angles, using the Humber as a river-base, moved northwards by sea, establishing themselves in such places as Bamburgh, St Abb's Head and Dunbar. Then, pushing inland, they built up a kingdom of north-Humber (Northumbria) from the Humber to the Forth. Spreading westwards, the Angles were met by Aidan, king of the Scots, at the battle of Degsa-stan[5] (603), where they gained a complete though costly victory. As a result, they were able, during the following decades, to push into the land of the Britons (though not, apparently, into the

[1] A name which possibly goes back as far as the voyage of Himilco the Carthaginian (c. 500 B.C.), is used by Ptolemy (about 150), and referred to by Bede.
[2] So Drum Alban is the ridge or spine of Alba, the high mountains running north and south from Ben Hope in Sutherland to Ben Lomond. Breadalbane is the upland of Alba.
[3] Even in the twelfth century the Britons of the north were still called the ' Welsh ' – a word given to the Britons by the invading Anglo-Saxons and apparently meaning ' strangers '.
[4] *Infra*, p. 39.   [5] The exact site of the battle is unknown.

land of the Scots), and even to expand northwards, over the Forth. Eventually, however, they were heavily defeated in 685 by Brude, son of Bile, king of the Picts, at Nechtansmere, the modern Dunnichen, near Forfar, when not only was their northward penetration halted but also, owing to the heavy Anglian losses, their pressure upon the Scots and the Britons was reduced and, although still powerful, their kingdom, in the words of Bede, thereafter had ' narrower bounds '.

The gradual union of these separate kingdoms with their fluctuating boundaries, and the formation of modern Scotland, began in the year 843 when Kenneth MacAlpin, king of the Scots, became also king of the Picts and, by crushing Pictish resistance during the period 843-50, firmly united Pict-land to Scot-land to form a new united kingdom of Alba.

How Kenneth MacAlpin gained the Pictish throne is difficult to understand. It was the last of many interpenetrations; more important, it was lastingly successful. Undoubtedly, however, the union of the Picts and Scots was facilitated by the attacks of the Scandinavians. The Picts may have been weakened through a heavy defeat which they suffered at the hands of the Danes in 839; the Scots may have received assistance from Ireland – and there are references to a continuing relationship and to a reinforcement (in 836) of ' Dalriada in Scotland '. Certainly the union became permanent in the face of a new danger. For, from being raiders, the Vikings became settlers. We are told of their raids on the Western Isles, beginning at the very end of the eighth century, but, by the middle of the ninth century (or even earlier), they had become settlers. Over-population on the west coast of Norway was undoubtedly the first cause of these new settlements overseas; but the settlements grew in number after the battle of Hafrsfjördr (872) when King Harald Fairhair assumed sovereignty over all Norway. Then many of the hitherto independent jarls, ' having no mind to beg for that which they had once possessed in their own right ', sailed with their families and followers to seize new lands and dwell there.[1] They

---

[1] It should be noted, however, that Scandinavian scholars would now put the battle of Hafrsfjördr some twenty to thirty years later, would discount the effects of Harald Fairhair's conflict with the jarls, and would stress over-population as the main reason for emigration and settlement which had probably begun as early as 800.

While ' longships ' may have been used for the earlier raids, it is almost certain that larger craft (the *hafskip* or the *knörr*) were used in the later settlements. Only thus could the settlers have brought with them their wives and families, their friends, their household gear and other cargo. The *hafskip*, as opposed to the *langskip*, was of deeper draught, broader, and with a higher freeboard; but both were clinker-built, prow-shaped at each end, and driven by one large square-sail which, with a good wind, made them fast sailing.

took and held the Shetland and Orkney Islands, Caithness, Sutherland,[1] part of Ross,[2] the Western Isles and the Isle of Man; they also settled in Iceland and Ireland, and they established themselves in the north and the midlands of England. And they had command of the sea. Thus Scotland was surrounded and isolated. The old link of Dalriada with Ireland was broken; and Scotland was cut off from southern England and the continent. The new kingdom of Alba was thrown in upon itself; it was welded together against the common foe.

With the Norsemen and Danes attacking both Scotland and England, however, and with both countries endeavouring to oust them, alliances and agreements began to be made. One of the most important of these was apparently made in 945 when Edmund of England, according to the *Anglo-Saxon Chronicle*, ' allowed ' all Cumbria to Malcolm I of Alba[3] on condition that Malcolm would be ' his helper on sea and land '. What ' Cumbria ' meant is doubtful (possibly it was Strathclyde – which Edmund had wasted – and included land south of the Solway), but the arrangement suggests that Edmund, wishing to delimit his difficulties in the north, hoped that if the king of Alba had control of Cumbria he would have a direct interest in preventing the Danes in Ireland from allying with Strathclyde and with the Danes in Northumbria. This appears to have been a new policy for a new relationship with Alba. As recently as 937, Edmund's predecessor, Athelstan, had fought and won a mighty battle at Brunanburgh against Constantine II, king of Alba (Malcolm I's predecessor), Owen, king of Strathclyde, and Olaf Godfrey's son, leader of the Danes in Dublin, who, fearing Athelstan's power in the north, had combined against him. But now, apparently, there was to be some English withdrawal from the north accompanied by an agreement with Alba.

This new policy may also have been continued in a similar arrangement for Lothian. If we are to trust an account contained in the *De Regibus Saxonicis* (written early in the twelfth century), Edgar, king of England, gave Lothian to Kenneth II, king of Scots,[4] ' and with great honour sent him back to his own '; and a glance at the map shows that if, after 945, the Scots had control of ' Cumbria ' or Strathclyde, Lothian was heavily outflanked and virtually untenable by England. Finally,

[1] Sutherland was so named because it was the land to the south of their first settlements in Caithness.

[2] Apparently as far south as the Beauly Firth. Dingwall is an interesting place-name, derived from *Thing-vollr*, the field or meeting-place of the *thing* (the assembly of the people). [3] Great-grandson of Kenneth MacAlpin.

[4] The ' gift ' was therefore made between 971 and 975.

38

the battle of Carham (in 1018), when Malcolm II defeated a North-umbrian army, confirmed the Scottish hold on the land between the Forth and the Tweed.[1]

About the same time as the battle of Carham, moreover, Owen, king of Strathclyde, died, and Malcolm II's grandson, Duncan, succeeded to Strathclyde (possibly through a dynastic connection) and became 'king of the Cumbrians'. Thus, when Duncan succeeded Malcolm II in 1034, and reigned as Duncan I, his kingdom included Pict-land, Scotland, Lothian, Cumbria and Strathclyde – roughly the land of modern Scotland, though large tracts in the north, as well as Orkney, Shetland and the Western Isles, were still held by the Scandinavians, and the boundary between Scotland and England had still to be defined.[2]

Above all, these old kingdoms and peoples had yet to be fused together to form one kingdom and one people, under one law and one king. In the twelfth century the Scottish kings were addressing their charters to their faithful subjects, French, English, Scots, Welsh and Galwegians – and even the order of address is important: for these different groups represent the new Anglo-Norman incomers, the Angles of Lothian, the [Picts and] Scots of Scotia (the old Alba), the British (Welsh) of Strathclyde, and the Galwegians[3] of the south-west. In 1305, for an English administration, the kingdom was divided into four regions[4]; and while, a little later, we find the simple administrative division 'north of the Forth' and 'south of the Forth', in the south-west Galloway was for long a 'difficult' part.[5] But steadily a strong central government, and more especially the feudal administration of the twelfth and thirteenth centuries, began to weld the different parts together. The organisation and work of the church also helped towards unification. Finally, the English attempts to conquer Scotland brought together the people of all ranks and aroused a strong patriotic spirit.

It only remains to be noted how the northern parts of the mainland, the Western Isles, and Orkney and Shetland, were brought in to become parts of the new kingdom of Scotland.

By an expedition in 1098 Magnus Barefoot, king of Norway, had strengthened the hold of the Norwegian king over Shetland, Orkney, the Western Isles, Anglesey and Man. Entering into treaty with Edgar, king of Scots (1097-1107), Magnus secured formal acknowledgement of

---

[1] In Symeon of Durham's account of Carham the Northumbrian army is said to have been composed of the people from the Tees to the Tweed, which suggests that Lothian was already held by the Scottish king.   [2] See *infra*, chap. viii.
[1] Possibly the *gall ghàidhil*, that is, a mixed people of Norse (or Danish) and Gael.
[4] *Infra*, p. 161, n. 2.   [5] Cf. *infra*, p. 109.

the Norse possession of the Isles,[1] but apparently made no claim to Norse possession of Ross and Caithness (including Sutherland), though those parts still remained in Norse hands. Moreover the difficulties of communication, and the ease with which the Norsemen could retire to Orkney and then return again, for long precluded any effective Scottish control in the far north. By campaigns of 1179, 1196-97 and 1202, William 'the Lion' strove to secure his authority there and built royal castles to maintain it, including Dunskaith and Redcastle to dominate the Cromarty and Beauly Firths. But not until the reign of James IV were these northern parts brought into something approaching control by the Scottish king.

Yet if the Scottish king had difficulty in maintaining his authority over the northern mainland, equally the king of Norway had difficulty in maintaining his authority over the distant Western Isles, and the 'kings' there, although paying, when necessary, allegiance to the king of Norway, were virtually independent rulers. Then, in 1156, Somerled,[2] a *regulus* in Argyll, defeated Godfrey, the Norwegian king of the Western Isles and Man, in a bitterly contested sea-fight and thereby gained the whole of the Islands south of Ardnamurchan. Shortly afterwards he invaded the Isle of Man and routed Godfrey who fled to Norway. Somerled was now all-powerful in the West. Feeling himself strong enough to challenge the Scottish king (though we do not know the background), he led an army of men from Argyll, Kintyre, the Isles and Ireland against Malcolm IV in 1164, but was defeated and slain near Renfrew.

The West, nevertheless, was still outside the control and sovereignty of the Scottish king. By a campaign in 1221 or 1222, Alexander II

---

[1] According to the story in the saga, Magnus Barefoot claimed Kintyre as an 'island' by being drawn in a skiff, with the rudder in its place, across the isthmus at Tarbert, and, interestingly, it became a tradition that whoever would hold the Western Isles must 'sail' across the isthmus of Kintyre. So Barbour tells us that Bruce and his ships were drawn and blown across and, when those 'in the Ilis' heard of this

Thai war abasit all utrely.	[utterly
For thai wist throu ald prophesy	[knew
That he that suld ger schippis swa	[make ships so
Betuix the seis with salis ga,	[sails go
Suld wyn the Ilis swa till hand,	
That nane with strynth suld him withstand.	

So all came into the king's 'bidding'.

[2] The name Somerled appears to be a form of *sumarlidi*, 'summer rover', a name given to the Vikings who came over the North Sea in the early summer when the prevailing wind is usually from the east and who returned when the prevailing wind had changed and blew from the south-west.

subjugated Argyll and enforced the allegiance of the mainland chiefs, but, in 1249, when he had assembled a fleet for an attempt to subdue the Isles, and had arrived at Kerrera, he was taken ill and died there. His successor, Alexander III, sent an embassy to Hakon, king of Norway to negotiate for the cession of the Isles, but the mission was unsuccessful. In view of these and other developments, and to secure his hold over the Isles, Hakon determined on a show of strength. In 1263 he assembled a large fleet[1] and sailed round the north of Scotland and down the west coast, to meet the challenge of the Scots. Anchoring off Arran (for he had a claim to Arran and Bute) he was drawn into negotiations by Alexander III – who was probably 'driving time' until he could assemble the Scottish host. Because of bad weather, Hakon had now to draw up his fleet between the Cumbraes and Cunningham, and prepared to land at Largs. Then came the great storm of 1 and 2 October. Most of the Norwegian ships were soon out of control; the men of those driven ashore were attacked by the Scottish army, whilst those still under control were unable to land their men to help their fellows in the fight. Wind and weather helped the Scots to win the battle of Largs. The battered and heavily depleted expedition withdrew as best it could; and its leader, King Hakon, died in Orkney on the return voyage to Norway. Magnus, king of Man, now submitted to Alexander; hostages were taken from a number of the Isles; and Hakon's son and successor, Magnus IV of Norway, was able to persuade the Norwegian assembly that the Western Isles were of little value to Norway, that they were difficult to hold because of their remoteness, and that, if held, they were likely to be a constant cause of war. In the result, by the Treaty of Perth of 1266, the Western Isles and the Isle of Man[2] were ceded to Scotland in return for a payment of 4,000 merks[3] and an annual rent of 100 merks.[4] But, although the Western Isles had now become part of the kingdom of Scotland,[5] the

---

[1] The Norwegian account, which is probably exaggerated, states that he had some 160 ships and 20,000 men, and that the king's own ship held 300 men – 240 warriors and 60 oarsmen.

[2] In the treaty the Western Isles and the Isle of Man are called the *Sudreys* (that is, the *Southern* islands). The *Nordreys*, Orkney and Shetland, were still reserved to Norway. The old name, *Sudreys*, still survives in the title of the Bishop of Sodor and Man.

[3] A merk was not a coin but a reckoning of value. It was two-thirds of a pound, that is, 13s. 4d.   [4] Which was often in arrears.

[5] During the War of Independence the Isle of Man changed hands several times. In the period of Edward Balliol's attempt to wrest the crown from David II it fell once more into English hands, and thereafter the Scottish kings were apparently content to allow it to remain an English possession.

chiefs of the Clan Dougall or MacDougall, in direct descent from
Somerled, were powerful there until finally suppressed by Bruce;
while later the chiefs of Clan Donald, the Lords of the Isles, also in
direct descent from Somerled, long enjoyed there a virtually independent
authority. The Lordship of the Isles was brought to an end in the
reign of James IV, but it was not until the Statutes and Band of Iona
of the early years of the seventeenth century that the government began
to have any effective control in those remote and almost inaccessible
parts.

Finally, Orkney and Shetland, of which Norway retained her
sovereignty by the Treaty of Perth, became part of Scotland in an
unusual way. By a treaty of 1468, which arranged for the marriage of
James III to Margaret, daughter of Christian I, king of Denmark,
Sweden and Norway, not only was the annual from the Western Isles
finally extinguished but also Christian pledged and mortgaged the
royal lands and rights in Orkney for payment of the greater part of
Margaret's dowry; and in 1469 he apparently further pledged Shetland
for the greater part of the remainder.[1] The balance of the dowry was
never paid, and the pledges were never redeemed. Then, in 1470, the
Earl of Orkney (William St Clair) resigned the earl's lands and rights
to James III in exchange for lands in Fife, and in 1472 the Scottish
parliament annexed and united the earldom of Orkney and the lordship
of Shetland to the Scottish crown. It is possible that Christian, like
Magnus IV in 1266, realised the difficulties of holding Orkney and
Shetland in view of a steady Scottish infiltration; and he may have had
no intention of redeeming the pledge. Later, however, Denmark made
several attempts to raise the question of redemption and the return of
the islands – even as late as the middle of the eighteenth century – but
always unsuccessfully. Today, the long Scottish occupancy and
administration of Orkney and Shetland are held in international law
to have created a Scottish sovereignty *de jure* as well as *de facto*.

[1] Margaret's dowry was to be 60,000 gold florins, and at first Christian agreed to
pay 10,000 florins and pledged his lands and rights in Orkney for the remaining
50,000. Then, finding it impossible to pay the promised 10,000 florins, he agreed to
pay 2,000 florins and apparently pledged Shetland for the remaining 8,000.

CHAPTER V

Early Saints and the Early Church

IN THE 1860s a visiting antiquary noticed that two stones serving as gateposts at the graveyard of Kirkmadrine, Wigtownshire, bore at their heads, and within a circle, an equal-armed cross of which, in each case, one of the arms was also used to form the Greek letter ρ.[1] Further examination revealed inscriptions – on the one stone, HIC JACENT SANCTI ET PRAECIPUI SACERDOTES ID EST VIVENTIUS ET MAVORIUS; on the other, and unfortunately broken, . . . S ET FLORENTIUS. At the very top of one stone were also cut the Greek letters α ET [ω]; while a third stone discovered in the same neighbourhood in 1916 also bore the *chi-rho* monogram and the words INITIUM ET FINIS.[2]

The *chi-rho* monogram, in various forms, was widely used by the early Christians, and the design of the monogram cut on these Wigtownshire stones is found in use from the end of the fourth century to the middle of the sixth century. Thus, sometime within that period Christian priests were at work in Galloway.

The names of three of these priests, Viventius, Mavorius and Florentius, have survived only on their grave-stones; but Bede writes cautiously of another, Ninian, of the race of the Britons, 'a most reverend bishop . . . who had been regularly trained at Rome' and who ' is said ' to have converted the southern Picts and, at a place called *Candida Casa*, to have built a church of stone, which was unusual among the Britons. Yet although, in addition to Bede's short statement, we possess an eighth-century poem on the Miracles of Ninian, written at Whithorn, and also a twelfth-century *Life* (based on the poem, or on a source of the poem, but written primarily to commend the reorganisation of the Scottish church, which was then taking place under David I, as being a return to the good old ways of Ninian), Ninian still remains a shadowy figure. He may have done more than we know;

[1] The equal-armed cross represented the cross of Christ and also the Greek letter χ; when one of the arms was also used to form the Greek letter ρ, the initial letters of the word χριστς (i.e. Christ) were thus shown. This combination of the cross and the Greek letters *chi* and *rho* (the *chi-rho* monogram) is known as the *Chrisma*.

[2] The three stones had previously been noted, about 1820, by a local antiquary who also spoke of a fourth stone (of which the whereabouts is not now known) bearing the name VENTIDIUS.

he may have done less than some historians would have us believe. Nevertheless, excavations conducted at Whithorn in 1949 brought to light a small and very early primitive religious cell, built of the local dark-coloured stone but covered over on the outside with a light-coloured lime mortar – a cell that *may* have been the *Candida Casa* (the ' white cell ') referred to by Bede.

All in all, it would appear that in late Roman or early post-Roman times Christianity had reached south-west Scotland, and had become established there, and that Christian missionaries had carried the faith into southern Pictland. Among these early Christian priests Ninian was apparently one of the more outstanding: so much so that reports of his life and work survived in an oral tradition which, in the eighth century, was recorded by Bede. On the other hand, Bede's cautious statement was made just after Nechtan, king of the Picts, had accepted the Roman calculation for Easter and had rejected the calculation used by the Columban (Irish) church.[1] We should not overlook the possibility that Nechtan, in order to support his adherence to Rome and his rejection of the Celtic Church, furthered the tradition of an early saint who had been ' regularly ' (*regulariter*: according to the rule) trained at Rome and who had then converted the Picts.

After Ninian we have traditions of other early Christian missionaries of whom we know little more than their names and possibly the areas of their work. Even Kentigern (or St Mungo) and St Serf of Culross[2] are also shadowy figures, though both, like Ninian, were ' of the race of the Britons '. Kentigern (died *c*. 612) appears to have been the founder of the church at Glasgow and a missionary in Cumbria; but the accounts of his work in carrying the faith into the north of Scotland are probably little more than twelfth-century inventions.[3] Interestingly, in a late twelfth-century *Life* of Kentigern (probably written to exalt the church of Glasgow and to claim for it an early direct relationship with the Pope in Rome – and thereby defeat the claim to obedience made by the church of York[4]), we are told of a meeting between Kentigern and Columba. The passage was probably intended to show the high

---

[1] *Infra*, p. 48.

[2] According to a twelfth-century account, Kentigern (there said to mean *chief lord*) was baptised with that name by St Serf who also affectionately called him Munghu, *dearest friend*.

[3] The dedications of churches are far from trustworthy. They may represent a tradition of a ' missionary tour ' by the saint; on the other hand they are more likely to represent a ' fashion ' of the time and the revival of a ' cult '.

[4] See *infra*, p. 137 and n. 2.

standing of Kentigern, and undoubtedly his work was of great importance; but with Columba, who came from the church in Ireland,[1] the real history of the Scottish church begins.

Columba, who crossed from Ireland about 563, and probably established his monastery in Iona in 565, is no shadowy figure. In his case we are fortunate in possessing a *Life* written by Adamnan, himself an abbot of Iona, who appears to have used an earlier *Life*, and who died in 704. Admittedly Adamnan's ' Life of Columba ' is full of legends and miracles, but that is true of all such works, for they were written for the edification of the people and not as histories; and the ' Life of Columba ', written within three generations of the saint, is far more trustworthy than the ' Lives ' of Ninian and Kentigern. There is inevitably the danger that, because we know more of Columba through Adamnan's *Life*, he has been given a larger place than others in the history of the early church; yet undoubtedly his work was great, and his labours gave to Christianity in Scotland a firm and lasting foundation.

Leaving Ireland partly because of a quarrel with King Diarmait,[2] and partly to further the work of the church in Britain, Columba, with twelve companions, eventually settled in Iona and there built his monastery – for the Irish church at this time was largely monastic in character. But, whereas the Benedictine monks of the Roman church were cloistered, and lived within their monasteries, the monks of this Irish church moved freely among the people. The larger monastic communities were independent of one another, each having its own organisation, with an abbot as its head – an office which, in each monastery of importance, was often filled from within a particular noble family.[3] Usually the bishop was under the abbot, though often (but never at Iona) the abbot was also the bishop. While the bishop had sacramental functions – he had authority to ordain – he exercised no administrative office.

This Irish church thus differed from the Roman church in many

[1] The Irish church had been established by St Patrick before the middle of the fifth century, but the retreat of the legions from Britain and Gaul left it isolated from Rome and it had developed its own organisation which was closely allied to the tribal and kinship organisation of Irish society.

[2] A quarrel that led to the battle of Cuil-dremne which, with its heavy slaughter (for which Columba was later blamed), seems to have influenced Columba in his decision to leave Ireland.

[3] Columba himself was said to be of noble descent, with a right to the kingship of Ireland which he renounced for the work of God. The political influence of these early churchmen was thus two-fold – by birth and by priestly office.

ways. There was no central organisation: indeed, there were many individual 'saints' who went out to preach and to convert. There was no idea of any organisation by parishes, dioceses and provinces, as in the Roman church; and therewith there was no hierarchy, no organisation similar to that which developed in the Roman church under bishop, archbishop, provincial council, pope and general council. Moreover, the Irish church observed its own reckoning for the date of Easter, and it had its own form of tonsure. Yet both were within the Catholic (Universal) Church, and the differences were less than the bonds.

About the year 559 the Irish annals record a flight of the Scots before Brude, Maelchon's son, the king of the Picts, and, according to Bede, Columba received the island of Iona from Brude. Sometime after establishing his monastery in Iona, however, Columba journeyed to Brude, by whom, after certain 'miracles' in the name of God, he was honoured and revered. And it is noteworthy that after that visit there is little evidence of hostility between the Picts and the Scots until the early part of the eighth century. Again, in 574, when Conall, king of the Scots, died, Columba, claiming divine guidance, ordained Aidan as king rather than Eoganan, Aidan's brother; and Aidan, as we have seen, apparently halted the advance of the Angles into the land of the Scots. Finally, about 575, Columba and Aidan crossed to Ireland where, in a council or assembly at Drumceta, they met Aed, king in the northern part of Ireland, doubtless in an endeavour to secure his protection for the men of Irish Dalriada. All the accounts of the meeting are late and obscure, but it would appear that friendly agreement was reached – an agreement which must have strengthened the relations between Irish and Scottish Dalriada; and those close relations (as has already been noted) were probably of great importance at a later time when the Norse and Danish attacks began.

In addition to all these important political achievements, Columba's missionary zeal, and the work of those who went out from Iona, saw Scotland gradually studded here and there with small monastic communities and with the isolated cells of individual holy men. All preached the one God. Christianity was beginning to bind men together.

Columba died in 597, the year in which Augustine landed in the Isle of Thanet; and, in due course, the Celtic church found itself face to face with the church of Rome.

In brief, under Oswald, king of Northumbria (633-41), who, during the reign of Edwin, had taken refuge in Iona[1] and had there caught the

[1] Edwin had defeated and slain Ethelfrith, king of Northumbria, in 616. Ethel-

46

fervour of the monks, Northumbria was regained for Christianity and the monk Aidan, sent from Iona at Oswald's request, established his monastery at Lindisfarne. After the death of Oswald, Oswiu, his brother (who had also lived in exile at Iona), likewise furthered the work of the church. Indeed, missionaries sent out from Lindisfarne by Aidan and his successor, Finan (who also came from Iona), spread the truth through all the provinces of the Angles and from the Thames to the Forth, for the movement was both northwards and southwards. A monastery (a 'double monastery' with separate communities of men and women) was founded at Coldingham about 640 and placed under the superintendence of King Oswald's sister, Ebba; and from a monastery at Old Melrose (so called to distinguish it from the later Cistercian Abbey built nearby), founded before 650, Cuthbert went on his missionary tours through the modern Lothian and the Border country.

But Oswiu's queen came from Kent where she had been brought up in the church of Rome: and one of the major differences between the Celtic church and the church of Rome lay, as has been said, in the calculation of the date of Easter.[1] Already some of the Northumbrian clergy who were not in the traditions of Lindisfarne and Iona were beginning to accept the Roman computation, and the more zealous among them regarded the Celtic church as deliberately maintaining errors which had been corrected by Rome. Gradually the Roman party grew in strength, and, according to Bede, Easter began to be kept twice in the one year, according to the two different forms of reckoning. Thus, when it happened that in the king's court the queen was still fasting and observing Palm Sunday while the king had ended his fasting and was observing Easter Sunday and the glory of the risen Lord, when, too, the king's son, Alfrid, insisted upon observing the reckoning of Rome, Oswiu determined to seek the advice of a local council of the clergy.[2]

frith's sons, including Oswald and Oswiu, had fled into exile, and Edwin had ruled as king of Northumbria until 632 when he was killed in battle against Cadwallon and Penda. In 633, however, Oswald had slain Cadwallon and had become king of the whole of Northumbria, both Deira and Bernicia. In 641 Oswald was defeated and slain by Penda; but in 654 Penda was in turn defeated and slain by Oswiu, Oswald's brother, and Oswiu ruled over an again united Northumbria.

[1] Apparently the Celtic church still used an old method of calculation which had been abandoned by Rome, and there were other differences in the two methods of determining the date.

[2] It should be remembered, too, that the date of Easter determined the Church's Calendar for the greater part of the year including the dates of Lent, Pentecost and Ascension.

This council, the ' Synod of Whitby ',[1] met in 663. Colman, who had succeeded Finan in Lindisfarne, spoke for the Celtic church; Wilfrid of Ripon spoke for Rome. And when Wilfrid, after speaking of the observance of all the churches in Christendom (save only in ' these two remote islands, and only in part even of them '), finally claimed the unique authority of St Peter to whom the Lord had said, ' Thou art Peter, and upon this rock I will build my church . . . and to thee I will give the keys of the kingdom of heaven ',[2] Oswiu turned to Colman and asked if it were true that those words were spoken to Peter by our Lord. Colman agreed that it was true. Then said the king, ' I will obey the decrees of Peter in all things, lest, when I come to the gates of the kingdom of heaven, there should be none to open them, he being my adversary who is proved to have the keys.'[3]

With the decision at Whitby, the Northumbrian church became united in its acceptance of the usages of the church of Rome. The great southern expansion of the Celtic church was over. More than that, the Celtic church now began to retreat before the advance of Rome. Colman retired to Iona, and Cuthbert, in his closing years, advocated Catholic unity. About 710 Nechtan, king of the Picts, sent to Ceolfrid of Jarrow for ' exhortatory letters ' by which he could confute those ' who presumed to observe Easter not at its proper time ', and, upon Ceolfrid's reply, ordered the Roman Easter and the Roman tonsure to be observed in his kingdom.[4] In 717 he is said to have expelled ' the community of Iona ' from his kingdom, driving them across Drum-Alban – possibly because of the refusal of some of the monks to accept the Roman Easter and Roman usages. In 716 Iona itself, and other churches in 'Scotland,' are said to have conformed. Unity and uniformity were being achieved.

It is, perhaps, important to stress that Rome had regarded the

---

[1] A misnomer: for it was, in reality, simply a meeting of local representatives of two rival traditions and was neither a synod nor a diocesan council. At the same time it was a meeting of two churches – the church of Rome and a church which had been in full vigour long before Augustine set foot on Thanet.

[2] Matthew, 16: 18-19.

[3] Eddi, Wilfrid's biographer, says that Oswiu gave this decision ' with a smile ' – which may well mean that he had previously made up his mind and was glad to seize the opportunity so fortunately presented by Wilfrid's appeal to Peter and Colman's reply. Moreover, Oswiu undoubtedly saw the danger that, if Bernicia remained closely associated with the Celtic church, while Deira favoured the Roman church, Bernicia and Deira might again fall apart. (They had been temporarily united under Oswald, and were united again under Oswiu after the defeat of Penda in 654.)

[4] Nechtan also asked for architects to be sent to him to make among his people *a church of stone after the manner of the Romans.*

Celtic church as being in error, and not in schism. No question of doctrine had arisen, and Colman had admitted the authority of Rome. Yet, although the church in Scotland now accepted the Roman Easter and the Roman tonsure, and although a diocesan episcopate began to emerge, a certain monasticism still remained. But the new uniformity with Rome was of vital importance. The church in Scotland was brought into closer contact with western Christendom; and, later, it was able the more easily to change from a lingering monasticism to the full and more efficient organisation of the Roman church, with its system of territorial bishoprics and parishes which, although only slowly built up in Scotland, and notably in the twelfth and thirteenth centuries, could be dovetailed into the territorial government of the feudal state.

At the same time we should not forget Bede's words, written in appreciation of Lindisfarne and the Celtic monks – 'The whole care of those teachers was to serve God, not the world; to feed the soul, and not the belly. . . . If any priest happened to come into a village, the inhabitants flocked together to hear from him the word of life; for the priests and clergy went to the villages only to preach, to baptise, and to visit the sick: in brief, to care for souls.'

Finally, no account of the Celtic church could be complete without paying tribute to the beauty of many of the manuscript books written by its monks. In these books – mainly copies of the four Gospels, in Latin – individual scribes of the Celtic church devoted themselves to the joy of multiplying in loveliness the Word of God. One of the most beautiful of all those which have survived is the 'Book of Kells', which was begun, if not completed, in the Columban monastery at Iona. In the twelfth century Giraldus Cambrensis thought it so beautiful that it seemed to be 'rather the result of angelic than of human skill', and in the nineteenth century an archaeologist wrote that he had examined its ornamentation for hours together under a magnifying glass 'without ever detecting a false line or an irregular interlacement'.

The 'Book of Deer', a much later work (and consisting only of parts of the Gospels of St Matthew, St Mark and St Luke, the whole of the Gospel of St John, a fragment of an Office for the Visitation of the Sick, and the Apostles' Creed), cannot compare with the 'Book of Kells' in its ornamentation and workmanship; but the 'Book of Deer' is important in another way. In its margins and blank spaces, and written in Gaelic sometime late in the eleventh century or early in the twelfth century, is the story of Columba's foundation of the monastery at Deer, followed by a number of entries noting various grants of lands and rights that were subsequently made to the monastery. These *notitiae*, or entries made *pro memoria*, are exceedingly valuable because of their references to early Celtic officers, like the *mormaer* and the *toisech*, and to the Celtic organisation of society by ' townships '.

We know that the beautiful manuscript books of the church were frequently kept in gold and silver shrines, rich in filigree work and often set with precious stones. Unfortunately no such shrine has survived in Scotland.[1] Other shrines, equally beautiful, were used to house sacred relics, and, of these, one or two have fortunately been preserved. The most famous is the jewelled and enamelled Monymusk Reliquary[2] which, enshrining a relic of St Columba, was known as the *Brecbennoch*. When borne by its keeper into battle, it was held to bring victory provided the cause was just, and it appears to have been so borne on the field of Bannockburn.[3]

For a time it had seemed possible that all the churches in Scotland and in the north and midlands of England would look to Iona as their *matrix ecclesia*; but the decision at the Synod of Whitby determined the supremacy of Rome. Nevertheless, although all Scotland gradually came within the obedience of Rome, the church in Scotland remained separate from the church of England. Whithorn, exceptionally, became the seat of an Anglian bishop who owed obedience to York. Moreover, as Scottish bishoprics were slowly established (often at early monastic sites), their bishops claimed that they were subject to neither Canterbury nor York – a claim which, as we shall see, was recognised only after a long struggle.

Early in the tenth century Columba was apparently regarded as the ' apostle ' of the Scots, and his name was invoked in battle. Some verses which seem to belong to the time of Alexander I (1107-24) ask him to be *ensis Scottorum et munimen eorum*.[4] But, by the twelfth century, and with the growth in importance of St Andrews – with its priory and cathedral, and with its legend that St Regulus (St Rule) had brought thither certain relics of St Andrew – and possibly also because

---

[1] A shrine containing a copy of the Gospels at one time lay on the high altar at St Andrews. A number of Irish shrines are to be seen in the National Museum in Dublin.

[2] Now in the National Museum of Antiquities of Scotland.

[3] Likewise beautiful, in their silver and gold, set with precious stones, were the casings made for the heads of pastoral staffs – that of St Fillan, also in the National Museum of Antiquities of Scotland, being a lovely example.

[4] Sword and defence of the Scots.

of the stronger influence of the church of Rome, the patron saint of the church at St Andrews had become the patron saint of Scotland.[1] Then, too, a white cross placed diagonally on a blue field (for St Andrew was said to have been crucified on a *crux decussata*, **X**, known heraldically as a *saltire*) became the national flag.

[1] Though it should be noted that the cult of St Andrew had been introduced into Scotland in the eighth century, and that St Andrews had become the chief episcopal seat by the tenth century – an indication of the acceptance of Roman usages and the Roman organisation.

CHAPTER VI

The Early Scottish Kingship

WE KNOW very little about the early kings of Scotland. The ' Lists of the Kings ' show that, for some time after Kenneth MacAlpin, the reigning king of Alba was succeeded by his brother, his nephew, or his cousin – a system of succession that was probably derived from Ireland. Thus the early table of royal successions runs[1]:

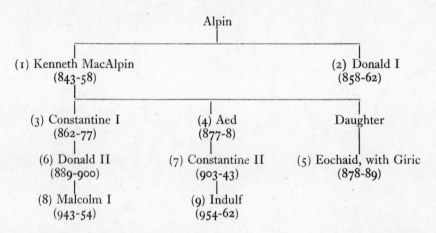

Such a system was not without its advantages: notably it generally ensured that the king would be of age, and thus minorities and the rule of regents were avoided.[2] On the other hand, it is clear from the fuller table of kings (on the opposite page) that kingship came to alternate between two main collateral branches of the royal house. Such an order of succession was apparently known and agreed; under such an order of succession the senior collateral of the alternate branch could expect to succeed as of right. There is no evidence of any formal election, and the ' Seven Earls ',[3] if they played any part, would partici-

---

[1] The dates of these early kings' reigns cannot be given with absolute exactness; the are to be taken as being approximately correct.

[2] Though Eochaid was probably a minor and Giric, possibly his foster-father and guardian, ruled with him; or, alternatively, Giric may have been a usurper. Certainly it is Giric's name, rather than Eochaid's, which appears in the lists of the kings.

[1] For the ' Seven Earls ' see *infra*, p. 61.

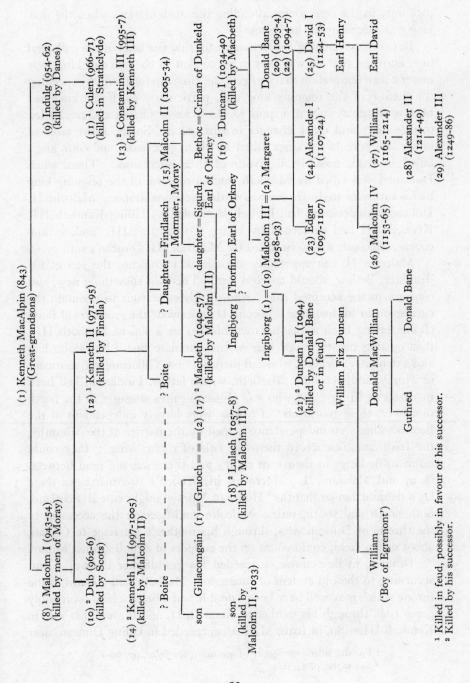

(1) Kenneth MacAlpin (843)
(Great-grandsons)

(8) 1 Malcolm I (943-54) (killed by men of Moray)

(9) Indulg (954-62) (killed by Danes)

(10) 2 Dub (962-6) (killed by Scots)

(11) 1 Culen (966-71) (killed in Strathclyde)

(12) 1 Kenneth II (971-95) (killed by Finella)

(13) 2 Constantine III (995-7) (killed by Kenneth III)

(14) 2 Kenneth III (997-1005) (killed by Malcolm II)

? Boite

? Boite

son Gillacomgain (1)=Gruoch=(2) (17) 2 Macbeth (1040-57) (killed by Malcolm III)

son (killed by Malcolm II, 1033)

(18) 2 Lulach (1057-8) (killed by Malcolm III)

? Daughter=Findlaech Mormaer, Moray

(15) Malcolm II (1005-34)

daughter=Sigurd, Earl of Orkney

Bethoc=Crinan of Dunkeld

(16) 2 Duncan I (1034-40) (killed by Macbeth)

Ingibjorg | Thorfinn, Earl of Orkney ?

Ingibjorg (1)=(19) Malcolm III=(2) Margaret (1058-93)

Donald Bane (20) (1093-4) (22) (1094-7)

(21) 2 Duncan II (1094) (killed by Donald Bane or in feud)

(23) Edgar (1097-1107)

(24) Alexander I (1107-24)

(25) David I (1124-53)

Earl Henry

William Fitz Duncan

(26) Malcolm IV (1153-65)

(27) William (1165-1214)

Earl David

Donald MacWilliam

Donald Bane

William ('Boy of Egremont')

Guthred

(28) Alexander II (1214-49)

(29) Alexander III (1249-86)

1 Killed in feud, possibly in favour of his successor.
2 Killed by his successor.

pate only in the ceremonies attending the inauguration, when the new king was placed upon the ' Stone '.

But such a system of succession meant that the head of the collateral line, knowing that he was next in succession to the office of king, was under a sore temptation to try to gain the kingship forthwith by speeding the demise of the reigning king and, particularly so, if the king had been unfortunate in war or policy. So dynastic faction and rivalry led to insecurity and quick changes in succession. So the fuller table of kings also reveals six kings killed by their successors and four kings killed in feud, possibly in favour of their successors. Thus, when Duncan I was killed by Macbeth, such a removal of the reigning king by his successor to the throne was neither new nor strange. Malcolm II, Duncan's predecessor, had himself succeeded by killing Kenneth III; Kenneth III had succeeded by killing Constantine III; and, in due course, Macbeth was to be killed by Malcolm III, Duncan's son.

Malcolm II was apparently anxious that Duncan, the son of his daughter, Bethoc, should succeed him. This was something new, and contrary to the accepted rule. And, in his endeavour to maintain the succession in his own line, Malcolm II ' removed ' the grandson of Boite (Boite having been either his own brother or a son of Kenneth III), thus cutting out the male heir of the alternate line. But Boite had also a daughter, Gruoch, who had married, first, Gillacomgain, mormaer of Moray, and, secondly, Macbeth, whose father, Findlaech, had been mormaer of Moray, and who was Gillacomgain's cousin. In the north moreover, these mormaers[1] of Moray were largely independent of the Scottish king – an independence helped by the barrier of the Mounth[2]; the Irish annalists accord them the title of *ri*, or ' king '; they could claim to be kings in their own right; and there was old feud between them and Malcolm II. Moreover, in Gruoch's two marriages there lay a definite danger that the ' House of Moray ' might rule all Scotland, both north and south, unless Malcolm could secure the accession to the throne of Duncan who, through his mother's marriage to Crinan, abbot of Dunkeld, could count on the support of Atholl against Moray.

Duncan, in due course, succeeded his grandfather in 1034. But, according to the old system of succession, Macbeth had a claim to the throne which may well have been a double and a better claim – probably going back through his mother to Kenneth II, and through his wife to Kenneth III. So, in 1040, Macbeth succeeded in killing Duncan, near

---

[1] For the office and dignity of mormaer, see *infra*, pp. 60-1.
[2] See *supra*, p. 34, n. 2.

Elgin, in the Moray country (where doubtless Duncan was having trouble), and thereby succeeded to the throne. All *more Scottico*, but made to appear wild and strange by the genius of Shakespeare.

Macbeth appears to have ruled well. A reign of seventeen years is also indicative of a strong king; and he and his queen (Gruoch) were generous to the church. But in 1057 he was slain by Malcolm, son of Duncan I, near Lumphanan, in Mar (again in or near the Moray country to which he may have retreated in the hope of finding support); and in 1058 Malcolm also slew Lulach, the son of Gillacomgain and Gruoch – again in the same northern region, in Strathbogie. So Malcolm, son of Duncan I, became king as Malcolm III.

Malcolm III was twice married – first, to Ingibjorg, a daughter or the widow of Thorfinn, earl of Orkney,[1] and secondly (about 1068-70) to the Saxon princess, Margaret, who, after the Norman Conquest of England, had fled north to Scotland with her sister, Christina, and her brother, Edgar the Atheling. By his first marriage Malcolm III had a son, Duncan; and by his second marriage six sons, whose names illustrate the influence which Queen Margaret had over him – Edward, possibly named after Margaret's father; Edmund, possibly named after Margaret's grandfather; Ethelred, possibly named after Margaret's great-grandfather; Edgar, possibly named after Margaret's great great grandfather; Alexander, possibly named in honour of Pope Alexander II; and David, possibly named after David, the youngest son of Jesse.

Malcolm III had a long and, as we shall see, an eventful reign. But, when he was killed, near Alnwick, in his last invasion of England in 1093, the *Anglo-Saxon Chronicle* records that ' the Scots chose as king Donald, Malcolm's brother, and drove out all the English who were with King Malcolm before '. This was a clear preference for the old system of succession – the king's brother was chosen to be king; also it revealed a Celtic opposition to the English members of, and English influences in, the court of Malcolm and Margaret – and those influences may have included the concept of primogeniture. But although the Celtic opposition had chosen Donald (Bane) to be king, Duncan, the son of Malcolm III by his first wife, Ingibjorg, marched north in 1094 with Anglo-Norman aid (he had been an honourable

[1] More probably a daughter. This marriage may have been contracted in an attempt to secure the friendship of the Norsemen in the northern parts of the mainland, possibly even to recover some of the ' nine earldoms ' which the Scottish crown is said to have lost to Thorfinn during the reign of Duncan I. Thorfinn and Duncan I, it should be noted, were both grandsons of Malcolm II.

hostage at the court of William and had remained at the court of Rufus[1]), claiming the throne as his by inheritance, that is, as Malcolm III's eldest son.[2] For a few months he was able to oust Donald and to reign as Duncan II, though the *Anglo-Saxon Chronicle* states that the Scots slew most of his followers and that he reigned 'on the condition that he should never again introduce English or French into the land'; and when there was again a Celtic reaction, Duncan was slain and Donald Bane once more became king. In 1097, however, Edgar, the second son of Malcolm and Margaret,[3] again with Anglo-Norman aid, marched north and, overthrowing Donald Bane,[4] ruled as king from 1097 to 1107, though William, son of Duncan II, undoubtedly had the better claim to the throne under the system of primogeniture.[5]

Edgar died, unmarried, in 1107, and was succeeded by his brother, Alexander I.[6] Alexander I died, without lawful issue, in 1124, and was succeeded by his brother, David I. Both these successions satisfied both systems; both were successions of brothers; but in both cases the king had died without heirs of his body and thus, even under the system of primogeniture, the eldest surviving brother would succeed.

So we come to David I, who had a son, Henry; and in certain charters, of about the year 1145, Henry is styled *rex designatus*. That style suggests that not only is the king's eldest son heir apparent (according to primogeniture), but also, during the king's lifetime, he has been recognised as such. Henry, however, died in 1152, pre-

[1] See *infra*, p. 72.
[2] When William the Conqueror accepted him as a hostage at Abernethy he accepted him as Malcolm III's 'eldest son'; and in a charter granted by him to the monks of St Cuthbert at Durham, when on his way north, he calls himself 'Dunecanus filius regis Malcolumb, constans hereditarie rex Scotie', that is, 'Duncan,' son of King Malcolm, agreed to be the king of Scotland by inheritance'.
[3] The eldest son, Edward, who was with his father at Alnwick, was wounded there, and died of his wounds; the third son, Edmund, appears to have ruled part of Scotland, south of the Forth and Clyde, jointly with his uncle, Donald Bane, 1094-7, an action of which he apparently repented for he 'entered religion' and died a monk; the fourth son, Ethelred, became abbot of Dunkeld, an office his great-grandfather had held.
[4] Who, however, was not killed. He was blinded and kept in captivity.
[5] He was, however, a minor and was possibly regarded as the descendant of an illegal marriage. The near-contemporary William of Malmesbury, probably expressing the current Anglo-Norman opinion, calls Duncan II 'base-born', i.e. illegitimate. Malcolm III and Ingibjorg were within the forbidden degrees of marriage, and probably no dispensation had been obtained.
[6] Again William, son of Duncan II, had the better claim; but by now the sons of Malcolm and Margaret had full Anglo-Norman support, and it was left to William's son, Donald MacWilliam, to try to assert his right.

deceasing his father. And at once, according to the chroniclers, David took steps to ensure that Henry's eldest son – who was the heir apparent according to the law of primogeniture – should be named as his successor. We read that, immediately on the death of Henry, David ' took forthwith his son's first-born, Malcolm, and giving to him as guardian Duncan, earl [of Fife], with a numerous army, commanded that this boy should be conducted round the provinces of Scotland, and proclaimed to be the heir to the kingdom '. And upon the death of his grandfather, in the following year (1153), this boy, Malcolm, succeeded to the throne as Malcolm IV, though only eleven years old at his accession.

Malcolm IV died, without issue, in 1165, and was succeeded by his brother, William – a succession which again satisfied both systems. But when William died in 1214 he was succeeded by his son, Alexander II; and when Alexander II died in 1249 he was succeeded by his son Alexander III (although he was not yet eight years old). And now the system of primogeniture had become so well established that in February 1284, when the king's only surviving son had died,[1] the magnates of the kingdom at once acknowledged an infant girl, Margaret, the child of a daughter of Alexander III, to be heir to the throne if the king had no further issue.[2] Alexander III had no further issue and, upon his death in 1286, his granddaughter, Margaret, the ' Maid of Norway ' (who was only about three years old), became Queen of Scots.

Primogeniture had become established as the rule of the throne[3]; but not without opposition. Partly that opposition was dynastic, in favour of the ' House of Moray ' and the descendants of Ingibjorg, and directed against the sons of Malcolm and Margaret; and partly it was a Celtic opposition to the Anglo-Norman families, laws and customs which the sons of Malcolm and Margaret were steadily introducing into Scotland, with ' a new nobility and a new social order ', and with ' the charter instead of the pedigree, the feudal superior in place of the head of the kin ' – all of which will be examined later.

There were risings against the house of Malcolm and Margaret in 1124, 1130, 1134, 1151, 1153 and 1156. Galloway rose against the king and against ' the English and French ' in 1160 and 1174. And from 1181 to 1187 Donald MacWilliam, grandson of Duncan II, was a thorn

---

[1] Alexander, who died in January 1284, aged twenty.

[2] This acknowledgement of a female infant as heir to a kingdom was something most unusual, if not unique, for the time.

[3] See also infra, pp. 150-2, 154-5.

in the side of William. According to Fordun, Donald MacWilliam 'aimed at the whole kingdom '; and, indeed, he could claim to have a better title to the throne as being descended from Malcolm III's first marriage, whereas William was descended only from the second marriage, with Margaret.[1] At last William, seeing ' that he must either lose the kingdom of Scotland or slay MacWilliam, or else drive him from the bounds of his kingdom ', made a supreme effort, and, although there were apparently supporters of Donald MacWilliam among the Scottish magnates themselves, Donald MacWilliam was eventually overthrown and slain near Inverness in 1187. Again, in 1211-12, there was trouble in the north, this time stirred up by Guthred, son of Donald MacWilliam, and apparently once more with support from some of the magnates; but Guthred was captured and ' hanged by the feet, after his head had been cut off ', and, following royal practice, King William built further castles in the north in his attempt to hold it secure.

On the death of William, and the accession of Alexander II, there was further trouble in the north, this time led by Donald Bane, another son of Donald MacWilliam, ' with a numerous band of malignants ', but, according to the *Chronicle of Melrose*, ' Machentagar [Ferchar Maccintsacairt] attacked them, and mightily overthrew the king's enemies; and he cut off their heads, and presented them as new gifts to the new king. And because of this, the lord king appointed him a new knight.'[2] This is doubly interesting. It shows a Celtic leader in the north now on the side of the royal house descended from Malcolm and Margaret; and, because of his services, the Celtic leader is made a feudal knight.[3]

Thereafter there were no more serious challenges to the established royal line, though the problem of the succession was to be raised again upon the death of the ' Maid of Norway ' in 1290.

[1] But see *supra*, p. 56, nn. 5 and 6; while it is also possible that Donald was an illegitimate son. William, the ' Boy of Egremont ', had died while still a minor.

[2] He was later created Earl of Ross, and greatly assisted Alexander II in suppressing a rising in Galloway.

[3] See also *infra*, pp. 90-1.

CHAPTER VII

Early Society

AGAIN IT must be confessed that owing to the poverty of our records
we know very little about the structure of society and the life of the
people, or about government and the maintenance of law and order,
prior to the reign of David I and the introduction of Anglo-Norman
feudalism. The only extant ' laws ' that possibly pertain to this period
are those contained in a code known as the laws in use among the
' Bretts and Scots '[1] – that is, the laws of the Britons and the Scots:
Celtic laws, not applicable to the Angles of Lothian – but that code is
little more than a society valuation-roll. There the ranks of society
are given as, king; son of the king; earl; son of an earl; thane; son of a
thane; grandson of a thane; freeman; carl. There we are told how
much was the *cro* (or blood money) to be paid in compensation for
killing a person in any one of those ranks – the cro of the king, for
example, is given as 1,000 kye, while the cro of a grandson of a thane
is ' 44 kye and 21 pennies and 2 parts of a penny ' – and it is noticeable
that the son in each rank of society is assigned a cro equivalent to that
of the father in the next lower rank. But of machinery for the adjudg-
ment and enforcement of these payments we are told nothing.

Admittedly, each of the higher ranks of society appears to have
enjoyed a ' peace ' – we read of the peace of the king's son; the peace
of an earl; the peace of an earl's son, of a thane, of a thane's son, and
even of a thane's grandson – and a peace almost certainly meant
protection and a right to punish those who broke the peace. But again
we do not know how that was done.

Probably, too, the law varied from district to district, with many
local laws.[2] It was not a written law; it was known to its hereditary
holder and preserver, the brehon, by memory and tradition. The
brehon held the law ' in his breast ',[3] and he handed down to his ' pupil '

---

[1] In Edward I's ordinance of 1305 (*infra*, p. 161), where these laws are proscribed,
they are called ' lusage de Scotis et de Bretis '.

[2] Local laws persisted certainly until the end of the fourteenth century (cf. *infra*
p. 109). At the beginning of the fifteenth century James I enacted that all the king's
lieges were to be governed only by the king's own laws and statutes – an enactment
repeated by James IV.

[3] Because of this the Celtic laws of the Isle of Man were known as ' Breast Laws '.

his knowledge of what the law was.[1] When a dispute was decided by a legal assembly (and not, as was probably often the case, by force of arms) the brehon ' declared ' the law.

There is some evidence of a grouping by family and kindred, with loyalty to a chief. We have references to the privileges that pertained to the men of this or that kin, to the kindred, to the chief of a kindred, and so forth. But it is difficult to know how these groupings worked.

In those parts of the country which were difficult of access, and thus able to resist the new feudal organisation developed and encouraged by David I and his immediate successors,[2] such old groupings apparently long continued, and, because of that, the later records of these remoter regions may give some guidance as to conditions in Celtic Scotland at a much earlier time; but we must be careful not to lay too much stress on this evidence. Even in Ayrshire, in 1451, a royal charter confirmed to Gilbert Kennedy of Dunure the right of being head of his kin (*caput progeniei*), together with the right of leading his kin in war and judging in all matters touching his kin. In the northern parts, in 1476, Duncan Macintosh is described in a charter as ' capitaneus de Clanquhattane '; and in 1531 we find Torquil MacNeil designated as ' chief and principal of the clan and surname of MacNeil '. Other charters speak of the headship of a kindred under its old name of *kenkynnol*. On the other hand, it is amply evident that, at the time of these later records, admission to a clan and the acceptance of a chief were not limited to those who were of kin and blood-relationship.[3] As the Scottish parliament later put it, either ' pretense of blude or place of thare duelling ' might bind clansmen to their chief.

In the ' Book of Deer ',[4] where the *notitiae* provide us with tantalisingly brief references to the structure of Celtic society in Alba, we read of the *toisech* of the kindred of Cano, and the *toisech* of the kindred of Morgann. We read too of the *mormaer* of Buchan, and the *mormaer* of Mar. But again we know little of either *toisech* or *mormaer*. According to an early legend, the Kingdom of Alba was divided into seven provinces – Angus, Atholl, Strathearn, Fife, Mar, Moray and Caithness[5]

---

[1] The ' wise man', like the lawyer or the poet, had his ' pupils ' to whom he imparted his knowledge. Later there was a tendency for intellectual offices to become hereditary, and then the wise man handed down his knowledge to his son.

[2] *Infra*, chaps. ix and xi.

[3] The chief, however, was regarded as the ' father ' of the clan, and its members were his ' children '. Thus the concept of ' kindred ' could be maintained.

[4] See *supra*, pp. 49-50.

[5] Another enumeration omits Caithness and includes Argyll, possibly because Caithness was held by the Norsemen, and the Picts had pressed into Argyll.

– each under its own king, each of whom would be responsible to a high king (*ard ri*) of the whole kingdom. But there is no good evidence to prove that the legendary seven kings became seven mormaers who, in due course, became seven Celtic earls. Nor is there any good evidence to show that these were the ' Seven Earls ' who were said to take part in the inauguration of the king.[1] The evidence does suggest, however, that the mormaer was the head of a province. The word may mean a ' sea steward ', and the office may have arisen from arrangements made to meet the Norse attacks. In the east, we find mormaers of Moray, Buchan, Mar and Angus; the Mearns means ' the Stewardship '; in the west we find a mormaer of Lennox; and Morvern is said to mean ' mormaer's land '. The office apparently became hereditary; and it is possible that, in some cases at least, there was a transference from mormaer and province to Celtic earl and Celtic earldom.[2] The toisech (a word meaning ' leader ') was possibly the head of a ' family ' group, though later he is identified with the thane.[3] So the ' capitaneus ' of Clan Chattan and ' the chief and principal of the clan and surname of MacNeil ' may have been equivalent to the early toisechs. But all this is largely surmise, for we are dependent upon a few stray references and nothing more.

In the ' Book of Deer ' we also read of ' townships ' which, we know, had separate ' houses ' or ' households ': separate, because taxation could apparently be levied upon the house as well as upon the township. Also, owing to the nature of the land in the west and north, with its limited small patches of fertile ground, the houses of a ' township ' would often be scattered and not clustered together in one compact group; and, as we shall see, it is possible that a ' township ' was regarded as consisting of twenty ' houses '.

Each of these early townships appears to have had for its support a small amount of arable land and a much larger extent of grazing for both sheep and cattle. The stress was upon grazing; and the arable was cultivated by common, or community, working of a very primitive plough, or perhaps, in places, even by the men of the township working in a team with spades.[4] But we have no evidence of any measurement

---

[1] Cf. *supra*, pp. 52-4.

[2] It is to be noted that the Celtic word for an earl is *mormaer*.

[3] See *infra*, p. 67.

[4] Similarly in coastal areas there was common working of a boat. It must be remembered, too, that the foot-plough (cas-chrom) could be used on land unsuitable for the ox-drawn plough, and that although a ' primitive ' implement it was also very efficient for relatively small areas of arable.

of land otherwise than by the number of animals the land would support – a simple reckoning which took account of the widely differing nature and fertility of the soil.

The holder of a ' house ' was probably a ' freeman ', and since, in ' The Laws of the Bretts and Scots ', freemen and carls were the only ranks of society below a thane, those ranks must have comprised by far the greater part of the people. Moreover (if Celtic Scotland was in any way like Celtic Ireland), there would be varying ranks of freemen, the ranks being possibly determined by ' cattle grazings '. Thus, while a freeman of the lowest rank might hold a grazing for, say, six cattle, freemen of higher ranks might hold grazings for, say, twelve cattle, or twenty-four cattle, or more. Such ranks would also determine the number of oxen (and possibly also the nature of the gear) which the freeman had to contribute to the common plough.

By these freemen, tribute, services and supply would be paid to the toisech and the mormaer (as is clearly implied in certain passages in the ' Book of Deer '), and by them, in turn, to the king. Tribute and supply were also paid to the church. Payment was in kind because land paid tribute and services according to the number of animals it could support or the grain it could produce. There are references to a unit known as the *davoch*, upon which renders of service were based,[1] and which often occurs as a ' half-davoch ' or a ' quarter '; but we know little about this *davoch*.[2] Possibly it was the extent of land which would support the grazing of a known number of cattle and which, together with a small accompanying extent of arable, was regarded as the land that should pertain to one ' township ' and that rendered known services and tax. In the west, indeed, the *davoch* is sometimes equated with one *ounceland* (or twenty *pennylands*) – an extent of land formerly burdened with a Norse tax (or *scat*) of one ounce of silver; and the render of a silver penny ' from each fire-house ' suggests, but only suggests, that a ' township ' may have consisted of twenty ' houses '.

In the payment of tribute and the render of services and supply, we find references to *cain*, *conveth*, and *feacht* and *sluaged*. *Cain* was a tax, or tribute, paid to the king, to the local ' chief ', or to the abbot of the church, for his maintenance, and the maintenance of his ' dignity ',

---

[1] In feudal charters this usually appears as ' Scottish service ' to be rendered from each *davoch*. Cf. *infra*, p. 87, n. 2.

[2] Professor Barrow has adduced good evidence (*Scottish Studies*, vi, 131-6) to show that by the thirteenth century the arable of the *davoch*, or of the *half-davoch*, was probably similar in extent to the arable of the ploughgate (*infra*, p. 64).

that is, his household and retinue. It was rendered in cattle, grain, cheese and so forth.[1] *Conveth* was the provision of supply, either in the sending of food, or in the actual furnishing of hospitality (board and lodging) for the chief, or the king, or a churchman, and his following, when he was passing through the land. *Feacht* and *sluaged* entailed military service.

In the more fertile land between the Forth and the Tweed, however, the land possibly acquired by King Edgar's gift and firmly held after Carham,[2] there was naturally more stress upon arable and less upon grazing. Moreover, in Lothian, arable land was measured by the ' acre '; and gradually, from Lothian, this new superficial measurement of land spread over those parts of Scotland where the land was fertile and where arable farming, as opposed to the raising of cattle and sheep, could be developed. The ' tilling of the land ' is said to have been urged and encouraged by the kings of the twelfth and thirteenth centuries; and, in the fertile parts, arable gradually became more and more important.

This new measurement by the acre, moreover, was at first used solely for arable. The acre, indeed, was an extent of land related to ploughing and the ploughteam, and, originally, it may have been equivalent to ' one day's ploughing '.[3] In due course, however, its basis became the furlong, the pole and the rood. The furlong (or ' furrow-long ') was 220 yards – the optimum length for ploughing a furrow before giving the cattle a pause for rest; the pole was $5\frac{1}{2}$ yards – said to be the amount of turning-room required by the ploughteam, though that is largely surmise. One furlong (or 40 poles) by one pole constituted one rood; four roods lying side by side formed one acre – a piece of land comprising 40 poles by 4 poles, or roughly 220 yards long and 22 yards wide, and which could be ploughed to and fro in parallel furrows. At some period not earlier than the twelfth century, however, the Scottish acre became larger than the English acre because the Scottish acre came to be determined by the ' ell ' (slightly more than 37 inches, and thus longer than the English yard) and by the ' fall ' (which contained 6 ells and was thus longer than the English pole of $5\frac{1}{2}$ yards). A Scottish acre of 40 falls by 4 falls was thus nearly twenty-

---

[1] Later, we often find small rents in ' cain fowls '.

[2] See *supra*, pp. 38-9.

[3] It is important to bear in mind that there was no exactness in early measurements. So-called acres were often smaller, and sometimes larger that the exact acre of modern surveying. 'A man's foot was still a foot, even though it might be only ten inches.'

five per cent larger than an English acre of 40 poles by 4 poles. Other land-measurements based upon the acre, moreover, were all related to the plough and the ploughteam, and they indicate a system of agriculture, with related land-measurements, that was Anglo-Danish in origin and was common in northern and eastern England. That system eventually prevailed throughout Lowland Scotland until the middle of the eighteenth century.

So, in those parts of Scotland where arable prevailed, we find references to the *ploughgate* (or *carrucate*, from the Latin form *carrucata*) – generally, though not necessarily, 104 acres[1] – an area of arable land which one ploughteam was supposed to be able to cope with each year. Probably, however, with the primitive ploughs then in use, a plough-team would be able to work only about half that extent of land in any one year; and even in the middle of the eighteenth century, with better drained land and better tillage, but prior to the invention of Small's 'swing-plough', one plough could cope with only about 50 acres in one year. Thus, from the first, there may have been something like a 'two-field' system, each 'field', or half the ploughgate, being worked in alternate years; or there may have been an 'infield' and 'outfield' (or waste), with periodic intakes from the outfield as the infield became exhausted; but the evidence is insufficient to enable us to reach any definite conclusion, and there must have been many variations. Also the 'baulks' (or sometimes the ditches) and the 'head-dykes' (which, respectively, separated individual holdings and protected the ploughed land from invasion by the cattle) would considerably lessen the area actually ploughed and sown with crops.

The ploughgate, in turn, was divided into *oxgangs* (or *oxgates*, or *bovates* from the Latin form *bovata*) and, in the south-east, into *husbandlands*. Eight oxgangs, of approximately thirteen acres each,[2] formed one ploughgate; and two oxgangs formed one husbandland. Thus, if each oxgang provided an ox for the common plough, a ploughteam of eight oxen[3] could be formed to work the

---

[1] We find ploughgates as small as 64 acres and as large as 160 acres. But a plough-gate of 104 acres is defined in one of David I's charters; that was its 'official' extent; and that extent was finally laid down by the Scottish exchequer in 1585.

[2] Again the size of the oxgang varied. In the rental of the priory of Coldingham (1298) we find oxgangs of differing sizes between eight acres and fourteen acres.

[3] Oxen were preferred to horses for the drawing of the plough (as, later, they were preferred for drawing the early guns) because of their steady plodding gait. But it should be noted that some ploughteams consisted of more than eight oxen, and that eight was merely a notional figure. The five 'ploughs' of Reveden, belonging to the abbey of Kelso, had among them sixty oxen.

ploughgate.[1] Moreover, if a team of oxen was required to draw the plough, so also a team of men might be required to work it – one man to hold the plough, one man to drive the oxen (usually walking backward in front of them), at least one man to walk beside the plough to help to guide it and to adjust the plough-beam, and probably even one man to ride upon the plough to help to keep it steady in the soil; though in easily worked soil we might find only two men – the ' halder ' of the plough and the ' gadman ', or goader of the oxen.

While it should be constantly borne in mind that ploughgates, husbandlands and oxgangs were not definite measurements like those of our modern exact surveying, this stress upon arable, and the provision of ploughteams according to land-holding, meant that the men who provided the oxen for the common plough tended to live in compact groups of houses which Bede calls ' villages '. The village, with the arable surrounding it, was the heart of the settlement. The arable was divided into strips, which were separated from each other by ' baulks ' (or sometimes by ditches): to use a purely Scottish term, the arable was divided into ' rigs '. Apparently, at first, these rigs were allocated among the different families or households of the village in such a way that no one household held two or more contiguous rigs. It may be that the rigs were allocated to the members of the ploughteams as the work proceeded from rood to rood; certainly, whatever the method of allocation, the good land and the poor land appear to have been roughly apportioned among all the families in what were later called in Scotland ' runrig ' holdings; but we have not sufficient evidence to enable us to draw definite conclusions, and there is no evidence that an annual re-allotment of the rigs was customary. Later, however, many rigs became permanently assigned to particular tenements. Thus an oxgang or husbandland might consist of many scattered rigs, or, where a name was given to it, it might be one compact unit of adjacent rigs.

But although the stress was upon arable, the other land was not forgotten. So we find holdings like ' one ploughgate together with common pasture for twenty-four cattle (probably oxen) and one hundred sheep '; or again, ' two bovates with sufficient pasture for four hundred sheep, sixteen cattle, two draught-horses and twelve swine '. In the phraseology of the later charters, the arable was held with its

---

[1] In Kent there was a similar unit known as the *sulung* (from O.E. *sulh*, ' plough ') or ' ploughland '. A quarter of a sulung was called a ' yoke ' (clearly derived from the yoke of a pair of oxen), and the four ' yokes ' provided between them eight oxen for the common plough.

'pertinents' – that is, with wood and plain, pastures and hayfields, moor and marsh, fishings and peat-bogs[1] – all necessary for the community: providing grazing and pasture for their sheep, horses, milk-cows and plough-cattle, hay for winter feed, peat and dead wood for burning, thatch and green wood for building, pannage for their pigs, and so forth. The plough-oxen, indeed, consumed great quantities of fodder, so that one of the chief problems facing every community was that of trying to raise sufficient hay to feed the plough-cattle throughout the winter.

This emqhasis upon arable, as opposed to the emphasis upon grazing, distinguished the village from the township; and, as arable farming, based upon the ploughgate, spread to the south-west, into the midland valley and up the eastern coastal plain, the villages of Bede became the later Scottish 'ferm touns' – farm townships; and for long in Scotland a group of farm-steadings was called a 'toun'. With the introduction of Norman feudalism, the barony – a new unit of society – might have many such 'ferm touns' for its many farms or ploughgates,[2] including a 'Milton' (where the mill was), a 'Kirkton' (where the church was), and the 'Mains' (the 'ferm toun' of the lord's demesne or domain).

In the Highlands, where grazing still predominated, such 'ferm touns' were less common, and the houses of a township were usually more scattered; but again, with the introduction of Norman feudalism, we find that the new feudal services may be based upon the old Celtic units, or may run side by side with old renders from houses and townships. So we find a davoch of land to be held for the service of one-tenth part of a knight; we find a render of 'the service which pertains to ten township'; and there are continuing renders of 'two cheeses from each house in which cheese is made', and the payment of a silver penny 'from each house from which smoke comes', or 'from each fire-house'.[3]

In the Lowlands as in the Highlands, however, grazing was still for long reckoned according to the number of sheep or cattle it could support; usually only arable was measured and defined. Thus we frequently find such definitions as 'una carrucata terrae mensurata et

[1] Cf. infra, p. 86.
[2] In the Strathmore rentals of the mid-eighteenth century the separate farms were still called 'ploughgates', and individually they were from eighty to eighty-five acres in extent.
[3] That is from each *inhabited* house. Later there are similar renders of 'reek [smoke] hens' 'from ilk fyir hous ane reick hen'.

arabilis, cum communi pastura'. When, in the reign of William, Elena de Moreville gave to the abbey of Melrose part of the lands of the 'villa' (or 'toun') of Killebeccokestun, she gave it with sufficient of the common pasture, pertaining to the same villa, for 700 sheep with their lambs up to two years old, 40 cows with their calves up to two years old and one bull, 40 oxen, 8 horses, and 4 pigs with their young up to three years old. In the charter recording this gift we also see that, when boundaries were given, they were defined by natural features and that, when there were no suitable natural features, ditches were dug (*fossae factae ad divisas*) or boundary stones ('meith stones' or 'march stones'), often incised with a simple cross to stress their sanctity, were erected.

And now, in the twelfth and thirteenth centuries, with the steady growth of record, we learn more about the various ranks of society and the working of the land – and also of changes that take place. There is not sufficient evidence to prove that the thanes of the twelfth century were the old Celtic toisechs with their rights and duties more clearly defined, though such a theory has much to commend it, and identifications of thanes and toisechs can be cited in its support. Nor does such a theory necessarily contradict the identification of the toisech with the later 'capitaneus' or chief. By the early thirteenth century, however, the thane has become a royal official administering a parcel of the king's demesne land known as a thanage. These thanages are to be found predominantly between the Forth and the Spey; and from them the king draws rents, in victuals and money. Then, also in the thirteenth century, and as a further change, the thane begins to *hold* his thanage, instead of administering it on behalf of the king. He tends to be equated with the feudal baron, and in the reign of David II the king converted many thanages into baronies. Now, too, the freemen and carls appear under various designations, such as *husbandi*, *bondi*, *cottarii*, *rustici* and *nativi*. Of these, probably only the *nativi* (the neyfs or serfs) were unfree. Born unfree, they were *native* to the land where they were born. They were not necessarily slaves, as we understand that term today; some of them undoubtedly had 'substance' of their own, and might even have some right to their land; but they were tied to the land where they were born; they 'went with it' and could be sold with it, or given away with it. If a *nativus* fled he could be seized and brought back again to the land to which he belonged. So, in the records, we read of 'fugitive serfs',[1] and of lands being granted

---

[1] The last legal action on record for the return of a fugitive serf occurred in 1364.

with 'meadows, *men* and pastures'. The *husbandi*, although freemen, and although paying a money-rent for their land, were still under the burden of rendering certain services to their lord, and held by no title save that of possession and their lord's good will. Even the bondmen (*bondi*) appear to have been free; the word itself being probably derived from an earlier word meaning 'a small farmer', and having no connection with the 'bondsman' of later times. The cottagers were simply smaller holders still.

Much of this, moreover, can now be read in the earliest Scottish rental that has survived – a rental of the abbey of Kelso, describing the holding and working of the abbey's lands about the year 1290. There we find *husbandi* (each holding a 'husbandland') who pay a yearly rental of six shillings and eightpence, but who also render certain services to the abbey, such as five days' reaping in harvest-time, one day's carting of peats, the service of a man and a horse to and from Berwick once a year, and other tasks at the sheep-shearing and so forth. Sometimes, with his land, the husbandman received from the abbey the cattle and seed necessary for its cultivation. Certain husbandmen, for example, at one time received from Kelso with their land two oxen, a horse, three chalders[1] of oats, six bolls[2] of barley and three bolls of wheat, and these, or their equivalent, would have to be returned to the abbey when the husbandman ceased to work that land; and such a system, including the provision of implements, can be traced at work as late as the second half of the eighteenth century, when it is known as 'steelbow tenure'. Even at the time of this rental, however, some of these husbandmen were becoming sufficiently prosperous to pay a higher rent of eighteen shillings, and thereby escape the burden of their services at harvest-time and so forth, so that they could the better tend their own land. At least one 'tenant', moreover, no longer held at the will of his lord: he held half a ploughgate (two husbandlands) heritably and in perpetuity, paying an annual rent of eight shillings but also still rendering services in plough-time and harvest. The *cottarii*, we find, held varying extents of land from one to nine acres, paying a varying money rent of from one to six shillings a year, and rendering services which might amount to nine days' labour in the year.

[1] The chalder contained sixteen bolls (see the next note).

[2] The boll, which contained four firlots, was a measure of capacity at one time equal to twelve gallons. In the reign of James I its capacity was fixed at eight and a half gallons; but local variations soon crept in – in 1649, for example, the boll in Dumfriesshire and Annandale was two and a half times the size of the Linlithgow boll.

Although in this rental we have a reference to wheat, we know from the records in general that the chief crops were oats, barley, peas and beans. Ale was the common drink of the people, and the bishop or lord was already importing wine from France. Cheese was a staple food; meat and fish were plentiful; and there are many references to hens. But the dearth of hay and the absence of root crops (which did not appear until the agricultural improvements of the eighteenth century) meant that, if the plough-cattle were to be fed throughout the winter, most of the milk-cows would have to starve. Thus, with the approach of winter, cows would be killed and their carcases salted for winter food; since this was usually done about Martinmas (11 November) such salted carcases were known as ' marts '[1]. There was an abundance of wood and peat for fuel, and in the second half of the twelfth century the monks of Newbattle were already working the coal-seams near Dalkeith. Building was mainly of wood and, for humbler dwellings, of earth and turves. In one of the earliest Exchequer accounts there is a reference in 1287 to stone-masons at work ' building ' the castle of Stirling, and, in another account, their work is spoken of as ' the new stone work '. But this was exceptional. When, for example, a ' new hall ' was built for Alexander III at Kettenes it was built of ' boards ' and, for the same king, a *domus Scoticana*, built in the castle of Inverness, was likewise built of wood.

With the multiplication of charters and other records we are no longer dependent upon stray references from which to draw tenuous conclusions. It is not simply the case that for the Celtic period record has perished while for the feudal period it has survived. Record, in the form of charters confirming the holding of lands, or in the form of rolls for financial and judicial proceedings, was itself a definite part of the feudal system. And with the reign of David I, when the history of feudal Scotland begins, we come to know much more, not only about the organisation of society and the lives of the people, but also about the working of local and central government.[2]

[1] *Mart* and *Martinmas* are etymologically unconnected, but the coincidence appears to have led to a kind of folk-etynology.

[2] *Infra*, chaps. ix and xi.

CHAPTER VIII

The Border Line

FOR LONG the boundary between Scotland and England was undefined and indefinite. From time to time natural features, such as the Lammermuirs, the Tweed or the Solway, did serve as dividing lines; but the boundary was fluid and subject to change. Moreover, there were ' English ' settlements in ' Scottish ' lands, and vice-versa[1]; and changing allegiances might well result in changing spheres of influence. A definite border line was not drawn until 1237 – although by then it had probably been already long recognised. And yet, a hundred years later, England was holding most of Scotland south of the Forth; and today the town of Berwick, although on the north bank of the Tweed, is still part of England, and Berwickshire has been deprived of its ancient and natural ' head burgh '.

Clearly, if the new ' Kingdom of Scotland ', which had been formed, under Duncan I, from the union of Pictland, Scotland, Lothian and Strathclyde, was to expand, expansion could only be southwards; but although Malcolm III (1058-93, son of Duncan I), who succeeded to the throne after killing Macbeth and Lulach, made five invasions of northern England he failed to extend the lands of his kingdom. Indeed, at his death, England had succeeded in encroaching upon lands which were formerly regarded as in the possession of the king of Scots.

Malcolm's first wife, Ingibjorg, was probably a daughter of Thorfinn, earl of Orkney, and a granddaughter of Earl Sigurd the Stout who had married a daughter of Malcolm II; his second wife, whom he married about 1070, was the Saxon Margaret, sister of Edgar the Atheling – an alliance with the legitimate royal house of England.[2] Both marriages were important. Malcolm may well have hoped that through his first marriage, and through his royal descent, his invasions of northern England would not be accompanied in his absence by trouble in any part of what was still a loosely-knit ' Scotland '. In

---

[1] The population of Cumbria in the eleventh century included Britons, Angles, Danes and Scots; in Lothian there were Britons and Scots as well as Angles.

[2] After all, William of Normandy was a ' conqueror '. It is true that the Atheling had been passed by – possibly because he was felt to be too weak, or too young – but upon the death of Harold at Senlac, the Londoners at once chose the Atheling to be king; and the Atheling was the direct descendant (grandson) of Edmund Ironside.

the north he was assured of the friendship of the Norse earls by his marriage to Ingibjorg; in the heart of Scotland, in Atholl, his grand-father, Crinan, had been abbot of Dunkeld; in the south-west, his father, Duncan, had been 'king of the Cumbrians' before he became king of Scots, and Malcolm himself was known as 'the son of the king of the Cumbrians'. Through his second marriage into the English royal house, he doubtless counted upon some support in northern England from those who still opposed the Norman conqueror. More-over, if Scotland was still a loose-knit kingdom, so was England. While William was still busy consolidating his hold on the south, could not Malcolm seize part of the north ?

Even before the landing of William, however, and before Malcolm's marriage to Margaret, the Scottish king had invaded Northumbria in 1061: the Northumbria which had sheltered him during the reign of Macbeth, and whose earl, Siward (died 1055), had invaded Scotland on his behalf in 1054, and had fought for him against Macbeth, in a battle near Scone.[1] This invasion of 1061 might well seem to be an act of ingratitude; but, although the evidence is scanty, it may be that Malcolm was attempting to maintain the Scottish hold on Cumbria south of the Solway, for, during Macbeth's reign, Siward of Northumbria had apparently pushed westwards and had gained some control over part of southern Cumbria.[2] Certainly, in 1061, when Tostig, Siward's successor in the earldom, and Malcolm's sworn brother, was absent on a pilgrimage to Rome, Malcolm seized his opportunity and invaded Northumbria, harrying far and wide; but there is no record that he succeeded in making any territorial gains.

Again, in 1070, Malcolm invaded northern England, this time through his own lands in Cumbria, where recently he had been trying to consolidate his authority; but again there is no record of any terri-torial success, though an English chronicler writes mournfully that Malcolm drove away so many captives 'that even to this day there cannot be found a hamlet or even a hut [in Scotland] without slaves and handmaids of the English race'.

And now, probably in this same year, Malcolm married the Saxon Margaret, the sister of the Atheling, and his court became a refuge for

---

[1] After this battle, moreover, Malcolm apparently ruled southern Scotland in independence of Macbeth. Possibly in this battle, or in an earlier battle, of 1045 or 1046, fought near Dunkeld in an attempt to unseat Macbeth, lay the origin of the story of Birnam Wood and Dunsinane.

[2] It is probably impossible to say how far south this 'Scottish Cumbria' really ran. It may have run as far south as Stainmore.

all those who were at enmity with William. Moreover, in 1068 and 1069, William had had to face a series of risings in northern England (with at least one of which the Atheling was associated), and had finally harried and wasted the land so terribly that further revolt by the people there was wellnigh impossible. But the Atheling was still at Malcolm's court, and Malcolm was still a danger to stability in the north. Hence, in 1072, with a land army supported by a fleet, William invaded Scotland itself. According to the *Anglo-Saxon Chronicle*, Malcolm retreated before him until at last the two kings met at Abernethy, where they ' came to peace ', and Malcolm became William's ' man ', handing over his son, Duncan, as a hostage[1] – a clear indication that Duncan was accepted as Malcolm's legitimate first-born son.[2]

The peace thus secured at Abernethy lasted until 1079. Then, when William was absent in Normandy, fighting against his own son, Robert Curthose, Malcolm, ' unmindful of the treaty made between him and King William ', broke their relationship and again invaded Northumbria, harrying the land as far as the Tyne. Moreover, in the spring of the following year, a sudden revolt of the Northumbrians, against the Norman administration of the earldom, led to the massacre, at Gateshead, of the Bishop of Durham, his clerks, and all the knights and men who were with him – a massacre which William avenged, in the usual fashion, by the harrying and burning of the lands of those who had been involved.[3] Thus large tracts of northern England now lay waste and open to further invasion, and perhaps occupation, by the Scottish king. To prevent such a move, and also as an answer to Malcolm's raid, William, in the autumn of the same year (1080), sent an army under his son Robert Curthose (with whom he was now reconciled) against Scotland. But, in the words of the chronicler, Symeon of Durham, when Robert ' had come to Falkirk he returned without accomplishing anything, and founded a New Castle upon the river Tyne '.

The New Castle may have been designed simply to strengthen the English defences in the north. On the other hand, the land between

[1] Probably, too, under the terms there agreed, the Atheling had to leave Malcolm's court, for later he appears on record in Flanders.

[2] See *supra*, p. 56, n. 5. Although Duncan was released, as a hostage, upon the death of William in 1087, he still remained at the English court until 1094 when he marched north to claim the Scottish throne following the death of his father in November 1093. (See *supra*, pp. 55-6.)

[3] Here it is worthy of note that, had Malcolm III in 1079 wooed and not wasted Northumbria, an alliance between Malcolm and the north of England might have been too much for the resources of the Conqueror.

the Tweed and the Tyne was possibly still 'debatable land' or 'no-man's land', and the New Castle may well have been much in the nature of a border fortress.[1] If that were so, then, some forty years later, that no-man's land had clearly been overrun and consolidated from the south, and the border had been pushed northwards to the line of the Tweed. In 1121 Ranulf Flambard, the energetic bishop of Durham, built a castle at Norham, on the south bank of the Tweed, 'for there, as upon the boundary of the kingdoms of the English and the Scots, raiders had formerly [had] frequent opportunity for incursion, no fortress having been there to repel such attacks'. The border-line on the east was becoming fixed at the Tweed – but only for a time.

On the west the important date is 1092. In 1091 Malcolm III had again invaded Northumbria, at a time when William II (Rufus) was absent in Normandy, and had spoiled and harried as before. When Rufus heard of this, he returned to England and marched north into Lothian where Malcolm was glad to make peace with him, becoming his 'man' as earlier he had become the 'man' of the Conqueror, while Rufus, in term, promised that Malcolm should hold all the land he had held before. Yet that peace 'lasted only a little while', for, in 1092, Rufus, in the words of the *Anglo-Saxon Chronicle*, 'went north with a great army to Carlisle, and restored the town and built the castle. . . . And he garrisoned the castle with his vassals', and thereafter sent many people there, with women and cattle, to dwell there and to till the land. In effect, Rufus seized Carlisle and, with it, all Cumbria south of the Solway; and his intention to hold what he had seized was proved by his castle-building and his peopling of the land. Naturally Malcolm saw this as an invasion and settlement of his own land. Was he not himself 'son of the king of the Cumbrians?' And had not Rufus, only a year ago, sworn to maintain him in his lands? That Malcolm did not at once invade Cumbria and attack the new castle and its garrison may well have been due to a respect for the strength of the English king of which he had had experience in the preceding year; but, in the following year 1093, when Rufus fell ill and 'in his sickness vowed many vows to God', Malcolm sent to him, peaceably, and asked for the fulfilment of their late agreement. Rufus summoned him to Gloucester, but, when Malcolm reached Gloucester, Rufus had recovered from his illness and had recalled his vows. The English king

---

[1] It is to be noted, however, that the New Castle was built on the northern bank of the Tyne.

would neither hold speech with Malcolm nor grant a fulfilment of their agreement. 'Therefore they parted in great enmity, and King Malcolm went home to Scotland', where 'he gathered his army and advanced into England', harrying with great wantonness, but only to be trapped, treacherously, by the river Alne and there killed with his eldest son.[1] And when, three days later, the news was brought to Margaret, Malcolm's queen, she 'was distressed even to death . . . and gave up her spirit'. So, on the west, the boundary was fixed at the Solway – again for a time. And in 1133 Henry I erected Carlisle into a bishop's seat, with a diocese extending over Cumberland and Westmorland and possibly including lands and churches which had once been associated with the church of Glasgow.

For over a generation, after the death of Malcolm III, the Border question 'slept'. Both Duncan II and Edgar marched north from England to wrest the Scottish crown from Donald Bane, Malcolm's brother, and their successes were largely due to English aid.[2] Duncan II (1094), temporarily successful, reigned for only six months before being killed by Donald, who once more assumed the throne only to be finally ousted, three years later, by Edgar (1097-1107). Edgar, like Duncan II, had lived at the English court and his sister Matilda (Maud) married Henry I of England in 1100.

It has been suggested that Rufus gave support to Duncan II and to Edgar in an attempt to make royal amends to Malcolm III's sons for the killing of their father by Morel – 'a deed so base and cruel that the king [Rufus] and his nobles were greatly aggrieved and utterly ashamed that it had been done by Normans'. But Edgar, in anticipation and in hope of English aid, had accepted Rufus as his feudal superior for the kingdom of Scotland; and it seems to be clear that, whatever had been the relationship between Malcolm III and the English kings William I and William II, both Duncan II and Edgar were vassal kings.[3]

Alexander I (1107-24), Edgar's brother and successor, had likewise frequented the English court and had married Sybilla, a natural daughter of Henry I. His feudal relationship to Henry I is less clear, but it may be that as a feudal vassal he led a Scottish army to serve with

---

[1] He was apparently killed by Morel of Bamburgh (a nephew of Robert de Mowbray, who was also present), an act which horrified contemporaries for Morel was Malcolm's 'gossip' or 'sworn brother'.

[2] See *supra*, pp. 55-6.

[3] See A. A. M. Duncan, 'The Earliest Scottish Charters', in *Scottish Historical Review*, VOL. XXXVII (1958), pp. 103-35.

Henry I in the Welsh campaign of 1114. Certainly Anglo-Norman influences, inter-marriages between Anglo-Norman houses,[1] and a feudal relationship between the kings of the two kingdoms were drawing Scotland and England closer together. It seemed possible that a ' Border line ' might soon be forgotten.

David I (1124-53), Alexander I's brother and successor, had also spent much of his youth in England, but probably, in his reign, the feudal subjection of the Scottish kings lapsed. Then, for a time, the initiative passed to Scotland; for, with the death of Henry I in 1135, when Stephen was crowned as king of England, David seized the opportunity of conflict between Stephen and the Empress Matilda to reassert old Scottish territorial claims. David had sworn to Henry I that he would support the Empress as the rightful successor to the English throne; but, if the Empress Matilda, claimant to the English throne, was David's niece, so also was the other Matilda, Stephen's queen:

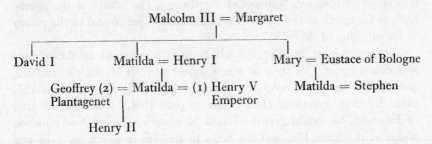

Malcolm III = Margaret

David I   Matilda = Henry I   Mary = Eustace of Bologne

Geoffrey (2) = Matilda = (1) Henry V   Matilda = Stephen
Plantagenet   Emperor

Henry II

Yet in 1136, and before civil war broke out in England, David invaded the north and seized Carlisle and Newcastle – the two strategic strongholds on the west and the east. It is clear that in this move David was in no wise concerned with the position of either of his two nieces; his sole concern was with the old claim to Cumbria (as grandson of Duncan, ' king of the Cumbrians '), and with his own new claim to Northumbria, through the right of his queen (another Matilda) who was the daughter and eldest co-heiress of Waltheof, earl of Northumbria.[2] Thus, when Stephen marched north against him, and the two kings met at Durham, their discussions appear to have been solely territorial. By their treaty at Durham (1136), David was to retain Carlisle, and his

---

[1] See the Table in *Source Book of Scottish History*, VOL. I (2nd edn.), p. 80.

[2] Matilda, David I's queen, also brought with her the earldom of Northampton and the honour of Huntingdon. (See *infra*, p. 77, n. 1.)

claim to Northumbria (made on behalf of his son, Henry) was to be taken into consideration. The retention of Carlisle, however, opened up the whole of southern Cumbria, and from certain of David's charters it would appear that the Scottish king soon extended his authority in the west as far south as the river Ribble in Lancashire.

Open civil war between Stephen and the Empress Matilda broke out in 1138, and David I promptly invaded England through Northumbria, pressing southwards into Yorkshire. But there, on Cowton Moor (near Northallerton), in a battle known as the ' Battle of the Standard ',[1] he was decisively beaten by an army gathered together by Thurstan, archbishop of York. Nevertheless, in the following year, 1139, by a second treaty at Durham, David was able to secure terms of peace from Stephen which could hardly have been more favourable had he been victorious in the battle. By this new treaty Stephen granted to Henry, David's son, the whole of Northumbria (except Newcastle and Bamburgh); and now, according to the near-contemporary chronicler, William of Newburgh, the whole of the north-east, as far south as the river Tees, remained in peace and in the power of David, king of Scots.

Ten years later, in 1149, the whole question of these northern lands was raised again, this time in a new agreement, in favour of Scotland, entered into between David and Henry of Anjou, the Empress Matilda's son. By that agreement Henry took an oath that, ' if he became king of England, he would give to David Newcastle, and all Northumbria and would permit him and his heirs to possess in peace for ever and without counter-claim the whole land which lies between the rivers Tweed and Tyne '. On the west, by a further agreement, Ranulf, earl of Chester, was to hold the honour of Lancaster (into which David had penetrated) while Carlisle and Cumbria were to be retained by the king of Scots. In return for Scottish help, Henry of Anjou gave to the Scottish king rights over the modern counties of Northumberland, Cumberland and Westmorland. And those northern lands of modern England were in future to be held by the kings of Scotland; though apparently they were to be held of the king of England.

David I died in 1153; his son Henry had predeceased him in 1152; and he was succeeded by his grandson, Malcolm IV, a boy only eleven years old. In the following year, 1154, Henry of Anjou, aged twenty-one, became king of England as Henry II; and he was to prove one of

[1] The English army had in its midst a ship's mast upon which were hung a silver pyx and the banners of St Peter of York, St John of Beverley and St Wilfrid of Ripon.

the most efficient of English kings. Nor was Henry II slow to perceive that the power of Scotland under her boy-king Malcolm IV was vastly different from her power under David I. In 1157, by a treaty at Chester, Malcolm IV was induced (or perhaps *compelled* would be the better word) to resign the northern counties to Henry solely in return for the confirmation of his rights in the lands of Huntingdon.[1] This treaty of 1157 was a clear breach of Henry's oath taken in 1149, and even the almost contemporary English chronicler, William of Newburgh, when recording the treaty, distinguishes between Malcolm's 'right' and Henry's 'might' –

To the king of Scots also, who possessed as his proper right the northern districts of England, namely Northumbria, Cumberland, Westmorland . . . [King Henry] took care to announce that the king of England ought not to be defrauded of so great a part of his kingdom, nor could he patiently be deprived of it. And [Malcolm] prudently considering that in this matter the king of England was superior to the merits of the case by the authority of might, although he could have adduced the oath which [Henry] was said to have given to David, his grandfather . . . restored to him the aforenamed territories in their entirety, and received from him in return the earldom of Huntingdon, which belonged to him by ancient right.

In 1173, however, when Henry II's sons (urged on by Louis VII of France) rose in rebellion against their father, King William, Malcolm IV's brother and successor, entered into alliance with them (receiving in return from the young Henry, son of Henry II, a new grant of Northumbria as far as the Tyne), and thereafter invaded the north as of old.[2] While most of his army was plundering and harrying widely, both east and west, William, with part of his force, laid siege to Alnwick. There he was unluckily taken prisoner by an English force which, moving northwards in a thick mist, found the Scottish king in the open with only a few attendant knights (July 1174). Brought to Henry II

[1] Matilda, David's queen, had held Huntingdon in her own right as the eldest of the co-heiresses of Waltheof, earl of Northumbria, and his wife, Judith. With David's intervention in England, however, Stephen appears to have forfeited Huntingdon, and it was apparently regarded as being still in the hands of the king of England, by forfeiture. Thus in 1157 Henry II could restore it to Malcolm, who conferred it upon his youngest brother, David.

It should be noted that the Scottish kings, or their sons, had to do homage to the king of England for their lands in England: a dangerous situation with regard to 'rights'.

[2] The Chronicle of Melrose says that William was 'hoping to make old losses good by a new conflict'. The Treaty of 1157 had deprived him of the earldom of Northumbria. If Henry II had restored to him his rights in Northumbria the story might have been different.

at Northampton, ' with his feet shackled beneath the belly of his horse ',
William was taken to Normandy where he was finally imprisoned at
Falaise; and, at Falaise, William concluded a treaty with Henry
(December 1174) by which he secured his release only in return for an
acknowledgment of Henry's feudal superiority over himself and his
kingdom.

The terms of the treaty of Falaise were clear and unambiguous.
William became the liege man of Henry II ' for Scotland and for all his
other lands '. More than that, the castles of Edinburgh, Stirling,
Roxburgh, Jedburgh and Berwick were to be handed over to England,
to be held by England with English garrisons at Scottish expense, ' for
the sure observance ' of the treaty.

That complete feudal subjection lasted for fifteen years. Henry II
died in July 1189; his son, Richard I, was crowned in September
1189; and Richard left England to join the third crusade in December
1189. For his crusade, however, Richard needed money. Accordingly,
at Canterbury, a week before his departure, and in return for a payment
of 10,000 merks of silver, Richard freed William from ' all compacts '
which Henry had ' extorted by new charters and by his capture ', and
restored to him his castles of Berwick and Roxburgh.[1] This release,
which is in the form of a feudal charter of quit-claim (that is, a charter
whereby an overlord renounces some right previously held by him),
definitely cancelled the humiliation of the treaty of Falaise. Scotland
was once more a free and independent country.

One clause in the charter of quit-claim granted at Canterbury ran,
' And whatever our father [Henry II] has granted to King William
aforesaid, we [Richard I] wish to support and confirm it.' Possibly
relying upon this clause, William constantly strove to secure the return
of the northern counties of England – demanding them from both
Richard I and John. But his demands were as constantly refused.

Richard's charter of 1189 was a statesmanlike move. He secured
a friendly north during his long absence from England; indeed, friendly
relations between Scotland and England continued throughout the
whole of Richard's reign. William contributed 2,000 merks towards
Richard's ransom, and he carried a sword of state before Richard at his
second coronation in 1194.

On the death of Richard in 1199 William might have supported the
claim to the English throne of his great-nephew, Arthur of Britanny –

---

[1] These are the only two castles mentioned in the release. Edinburgh had been
restored earlier, upon William's marriage to Ermengarde de Bellomonte.

78

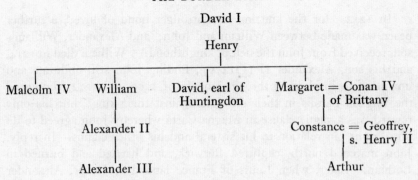

David I
|
Henry
|

| Malcolm IV | William | David, earl of Huntingdon | Margaret = Conan IV of Brittany |

Alexander II   Constance = Geoffrey, s. Henry II

Alexander III   Arthur

– instead, he promised to serve John with all his strength if John would restore to him his 'patrimony' in Northumbria and Cumbria. And, to that, John gave the vague reply that he would do what was 'just'.

Arthur was the strict heir of line –

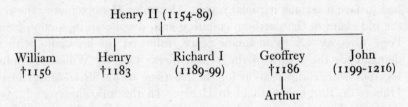

Henry II (1154-89)
|

| William †1156 | Henry †1183 | Richard I (1189-99) | Geoffrey †1186 | John (1199-1216) |

Arthur

– but there was as yet no clear-cut rule of succession to the English throne.[1] John had been recognised as king by England, Normandy and Aquitaine, and the boy Arthur was murdered, probably by John himself, in 1203. Yet John consistently refused William's claim to the northern counties; and in 1209, in a characteristic burst of energy, John advanced with a strong force to Norham and demanded satisfaction for the destruction of his castle at Tweedmouth which the Scots, regarding it as a threat to Berwick, had twice thrown down. At Norham, the ageing William (who was now sixty-six), 'wishing to have peace rather than war', agreed to pay to John 15,000 merks and to hand over two of his daughters, Margaret and Isabella, to be married to John's two sons, Henry (later Henry III) and Richard,[2] and the erection of a castle at Tweedmouth was to be abandoned.[3]

[1] See *infra*, pp. 154-5.
[2] The 15,000 merks could thus be regarded as *maritagium*: a gift, usually of lands, made by a father to a daughter at the time of her marriage in order to help to support her in her new married estate.
[3] We do not know the exact terms of the agreement reached at Norham between William and John, but they are said to have been greatly displeasing to the Scots.

In 1212, 'for the knitting of a stronger bond of love', a further peace was made between William and John; and Alexander, William's son, received from John the belt of knighthood.[1] William died in 1214, and his son, Alexander II (1214-49), finding John still obdurate and unwilling to implement the agreements of 1209 and 1212, supported the English barons in their struggle against their king; but his only reward was a vague clause in Magna Carta whereby John agreed to do him 'right' in relation to his sisters[2] and his other claims. In reply, John marched north, captured Berwick, and harried and burned in Lothian. Later, when Louis of France landed at Dover, Alexander marched south to join him, taking and holding Carlisle on his way; but, in the general settlement of 1217, he surrendered this, his only gain.

In 1221 Alexander II married Joanna (Joan), the eldest daughter of John and sister of Henry III, and friendly relations between Scotland and England seemed to be assured. But when, in 1232-4, Henry III had to face a serious baronial revolt, Alexander II once more renewed the old claim to the northern counties, and, despite an injunction from Pope Gregory IX to maintain peace, followed up his claim with a demand for the return of the 15,000 merks paid by William to John together with compensation for the marriage of his sister Margaret to Hubert de Burgh instead of to Henry. In the following year (1235) Alexander's third sister, Marjorie, was married to Gilbert, earl of Pembroke, the Earl Marshal of England, and a leader of the baronial opposition to Henry; and at one time it appeared as though Henry would have to face an alliance between Alexander, Llewelyn of Wales and a strong group of rebellious lords. War, however, was avoided. Alexander and Henry met at York in September 1236, with apparently friendly results, and in 1237, again at York (and with the good offices of a papal legate, Otto, sent by Gregory IX to reconcile the differences of the two kings), a final peace was concluded between Scotland and England. By the treaty of York of 1237 Alexander II abandoned his claim to the counties of Northumberland, Cumberland and Westmorland (and also his claim for the return of the 15,000 merks of silver paid by William to John, together with compensation for John's failure to marry Alexander's sisters into the English royal house), and, in return, accepted from Henry two hundred librates of land in Northumberland

---

[1] Possibly accepting John as his liege lord for Northumbria.

[2] Neither of Alexander's sisters, however, returned to Scotland, and neither was married into the English royal house. Margaret was married in 1221 to Hubert de Burgh, the justiciar, and Isabella was married to Roger Bigod, earl of Norfolk.

and Cumberland[1] to be held of the English king. Also, by the treaty, the two kingdoms returned to the relationship existing between them before the agreement of 1209 – again suggesting some promise of Northumbria, by John, at that time.

The treaty of York recognised the Tweed-Solway line as the line of the Border.[2] Inland, perambulations by mixed juries, under officials of the two countries, were held from time to time to determine the exact line of the boundary (though even in the sixteenth century there were still parts that were ' debatable '); and the administration of the Border was henceforth conducted by Wardens of the two countries[3] under ' Border law and custom ' and with special meetings (' Days of Trew ' or ' Days of Truce ') to hear and determine, by mixed juries, complaints of raiding, cattle-thieving and so forth made by the borderers of either side. In contrast with the Welsh March, the Border was never defined by a series of systematic fortifications.

After the treaty of York peace and friendly relations between Scotland and England continued until the eve of the War of Independence, though crises and periods of strain were not unknown. In 1244 Alexander II and Henry III faced one another, in arms, at Newcastle; but the settlement of 1237 was renewed in formal terms (of which a copy was sent to the Pope) and, in addition, Henry agreed to give his daughter, Margaret, in marriage to Alexander's son, later Alexander III.

The marriage of Alexander III (1249-86) to Margaret took place in 1251 when Alexander was ten years old and Margaret eleven. Then Henry III, although doubtless solicitous for the welfare of his daughter, took advantage of his position and of the youthfulness of the King and Queen of Scotland to try to assume a supervision over the royal court and the affairs of the realm. Inevitably this led to the formation of parties (pro-English and anti-English), in which rivalries and jealousies were also at work. For a time Henry was unable to interfere to any great extent in Scottish affairs; but, in 1255, on the argument that the queen was being treated dishonourably, he led an army to the Borders where, at Roxburgh, he was met by the lords of the ' English party ' who had seized and brought with them the king and queen. A council of regency, drawn from the ' English party ', was appointed by Henry

---

[1] That is, lands valued at £200 a year. The apportioning of the lands was made by a mixed commission of Scots and English, and ultimately the lands were defined as the honour of Tyndale and the manor of Penrith.

[2] But see *infra*, p. 178.

[3] Eventually there were three ' marches ' (East, Middle and West), each under its own warden.

himself; Alexander was placed under Henry's ' protection '; and it was announced that any who opposed these arrangements would be regarded by Henry as rebels against his authority. Two years later, however, the Comyns and other lords who had been removed from office in 1255, and who, in the words of an English chronicler, formed a ' native and natural ' party, fearing ' the dishonour of the king and of the kingdom ', themselves seized the king, assembled their forces in arms to oppose Henry and his supporters in Scotland, and, in 1258, concluded an alliance with the Welsh (then in revolt against Henry) for mutual support and defence. For a time the situation looked ugly; but open conflict was avoided, a compromise was reached, and a new council of regency was appointed which contained representatives of both parties.

In 1262 Alexander III came of age to govern his realm in his own name. The incidents of 1255-8, however, revealing that there were Scottish lords who could form an ' English party ', willing to work in agreement with the English king, boded ill for the ' native and natural ' men of Scotland in the years that were to follow Alexander's death, and not only then, but even after Scotland had secured her independence under Robert Bruce.

CHAPTER IX

Feudal Scotland - I

DAVID I, the youngest son of Malcolm III and Margaret, succeeded to the Scottish throne in 1124 when he was about forty-four years old. Much of his youth had been spent at the English court, and in 1113 he had married Matilda, the widow of Simon de Senlis, through whom he held the earldom of Northampton and the honour of Huntingdon.[1] Thus he had seen much of the central government of England under Henry I, and he had had experience of local government on his wife's vast estates. This new king at once strove to ' improve ' his kingdom by establishing and developing the Anglo-Norman institutions and the Anglo-Norman system of central and local government which he had learned in England and had come to admire.

Before long, Anglo-Normans whom he had brought with him to Scotland (many of them from his Northamptonshire estates), or whom he subsequently invited to come north, were holding most of the important offices in church and state. To them, and to other Anglo-Normans, the king gave large extents of Scottish lands, and, in Anglo-Norman society (and therewith, also, in its system of government), rights and duties, jurisdiction and administration, military service and agricultural organisation all rested upon a relationship which was both territorial and personal, a relationship between the ' lord ' of the land and the ' tenant ' who ' held of him '.

The new unit of administration was now a unit of land. With a grant of land there went authority over every aspect of the lives of those living on the land. So, gradually, many men in the south, in the midland valley and in the eastern coastal plain found themselves bound to serve new lords to whom their relationship was solely that of the tenure of land. Indeed, under David I and his immediate successors, something very like a peaceful ' Norman conquest ' of Scotland took place.[2] A French-speaking aristocracy was established which administered a new, precise and orderly rule, and the greater part of Scotland was gradually

---

[1] See *supra*, p. 77, n. 1.

[2] Under David I we find feudal tenures mainly in the south; but in the reigns of Malcolm IV and William there appears to have been an intensive feudalisation of ' Scotland ', north of the Forth and Clyde.

knit together by a well-organised system of government similar to that of England under Henry I and Henry II.

The essentials of this Anglo-Norman system of government and administration, or Anglo-Norman feudalism, were the 'fief' and 'vassalage' – the 'fief', a holding of land by a 'tenant' of a 'lord'; and 'vassalage', the rendering of certain services by the tenant to the lord in return for the enjoyment of his holding and also in return for his lord's protection. Moreover, because the tenant held his land 'of' his lord, he was subject to his lord's jurisdiction: his lord's court would hear actions touching the tenant or his holding.

The tenant, or vassal, however, might himself dispose of part of his holding to a sub-tenant who would then acknowledge him as his lord. He might 'subinfeudate' part of his fief.[1] And again, that new tenant, in turn, might subinfeudate part of his holding. So a large fief might contain within it a number of smaller fiefs, some or all of which might contain smaller fiefs still. And at the same time a concept emerged that the king was lord of all the land and fountain of all justice. So, in the fief of Molle, we find Helen de Lindsay holding of her father, Simon de Lindsay, who held of Robert de Pollock, who held of Simon de Mauleverer, who held of the abbot and convent of Melrose, who held of the king. The lord who holds of the king is the king's tenant-in-chief, he holds 'direct'; the lord who holds of a tenant-in-chief is called a mesne (or intermediate) lord.

Going a stage further, we may say that the king, in granting a fief to a great lord and making him one of his tenants-in-chief, has delegated, with the fief, part of his royal authority; the tenant-in-chief, in turn, in subinfeudating part of his fief, has likewise delegated part of his authority to a mesne lord. Behind such delegations lay the concept, 'I grant to you this part of *my* land to hold *of* me. You will keep it secure, and maintain law and order there, *for* me. In all this I will support you; and you can develop and improve the land and enjoy its fruits. But, as the holder of this part of *my* land, you must help *me* in battle, in my court, and with aid and counsel, whenever I call upon you to do so.' Moreover, in this relationship between 'lord' and 'man', so much depended upon the keeping of faith that often the tenant, in a solemn act on bended knees, with his hands placed between the hands of his lord, bound himself to be his lord's 'man' and to bear faith with him against all others – though, if his lord was not the king, with the

---

[1] But he could not sell, give away, or otherwise alienate so much of his fief as to endanger the rendering of the services due from the whole fief to his lord.

84

saving clause, ' except the faith that I owe to the king .' This ceremony was known as homage. Less solemn was the oath of fealty (*fidelitas*). It might be taken at the time of homage, or taken alone. Here the tenant stood, with his hand on the gospels or on some sacred relic, and swore to bear faith to his lord, again with a saving clause if his lord was not the king. Fealty was considered to be less binding than homage; in the oath of fealty the tenant did not bind himself to be his lord's ' man '.

Such a system of government and administration by delegation to local lords was an admirable one for holding down outlying (and possibly unruly) parts of the king's land and for maintaining law and order there. And particularly so when there were no roads and when communications were slow and difficult. Moreover, for holding down the land, the Normans had not only developed this new method of government by delegation, they had also evolved new methods of warfare[1] and a new art of castle-building – not the stone castle, which was still exceptional, but the *motte-and-bailey* castle: a wooden castle built on a raised mound and protected by a palisade and ditch – so that the lord with his castle could dominate his land.[2]

Thus, at the very beginning of his reign, David I granted Annandale to Robert Bruce to be held with its castle (the motte of Annan) and with those customs (feudal customs) which Randulfus Meschin had in Carlisle and his lands of Cumberland. So, gradually, motte-and-bailey castles were built here and there over the land. Some were the king's castles, into which he put his own officers; some were the castles of his Norman followers and friends to whom he had granted lands in those parts; but every castle was a strong-point for holding and governing an area of land.

A grant of lands, moreover, was confirmed by a charter – a written document, on vellum or parchment, stating that the lands had been granted, to be held for certain services therefrom, listing those who were witnesses to the charter confirming the grant, and authenticated with the grantor's seal. David I's charters are simpler than, for example,

[1] They had developed the use of cavalry, of the sword and the lance, and of armour. Protected by a shirt of mail, wearing a conical iron helmet, and carrying a kite-shaped shield and a sword (a far more efficient weapon than the cumbrous two-handed battle-axe of the foot soldier), the Norman 'knight' (or armoured horseman) was vastly superior to his contemporary English or Scottish adversary. At Senlac, the English fyrd fought mainly on foot and without any protective body-armour; at the battle of the Standard, the Galwegians charged ' naked '.

[2] For these motte-and-bailey castles, and for the subsequent development of the castle in mediaeval Scotland, see chap. x.

85

those of William[1]; but the charter soon takes a definite form, which with variations and extensions, runs roughly, ' Know that I have given and granted, and by this charter confirmed, the land of X to A, to be held by him and his heirs, of me and my heirs, in return for the service of Y. These are the witnesses.' And the royal charters clearly indicate that the king now regards all the land as his.

As an example we may take the charter by King William confirming the grant of the lands of Lundin to Walter, son of Philip the Chamberlain:

W[illelmus] Rex Scottorum episcopis abbatibus comitibus baronibus justiciariis vicecomitibus et omnibus probis hominibus totius terrae suae salutem: Sciant presentes et posteri me dedisse et concessisse, et hac carta mea confirmasse, Waltero, filio Philippi camerarii, Lundin in Fif cum omnibus justis pertinenciis suis per rectas divisas suas; Tenendum sibi et heredibus suis de me et heredibus meis in feudo et hereditate, libere et quiete, plenarie et honorifice, cum omnibus libertatibus et rectitudinibus ad idem feudum pertinentibus, in bosco et plano, in pratis et pascuis, in terris et aquis, in campis et moris et in omnibus aliis rectis pertinenciis suis per servicium unius militis. Quare volo et firmiter praecipio ut praedictus Walterus et heredes sui praedictum feudum teneant de me et heredibus meis, ita libere et quiete sicut alii milites mei liberius et quietius feuda sua de me tenent in regno Scocie, sicut carta regis M[alcolmi] fratris mei testatur et confirmat. Testibus: Engelramo episcopo de Glasgu, Nicholao cancellario, comite Waldevo, comite Dunecano, Ricardo de Morvill constabulario, Waltero filio Alani dapifero, Roberto Avenel, Willelmo de Mortemer, Radulfo de Clere, Waltero de Barkelai, Ricardo clerico: Apud castellum puellarum.

A straightforward translation would be:

William, king of Scots, to the bishops, abbots, earls, barons, justiciars, sheriffs and all upright men of his whole land, greeting. Let all men present and to come know that I have given and granted, and by this my charter have confirmed, to Walter, son of Philip the Chamberlain, Lundin in Fife, with all its just pertinents and according to its right boundaries; to be held by him and his heirs of me and my heirs, as a heritable fief, freely, quietly, fully and honourably, with all liberties and rights pertaining to it, in wood and plain, in hayfields and pastures, in lands and waters, in open fields and moors, and in all other its right pertinents, for the service of one knight. Wherefore I will, and firmly command, that the aforesaid Walter and his heirs shall hold the aforesaid fief of me and my heirs as freely and quietly as my other knights most freely and quietly hold their fiefs of me in the kingdom

---

[1] William's charter to Robert Bruce is not only fuller than David I's charter to Robert Bruce (the father) but also shows the development that had taken place in Scottish feudal administration. (See *Source Book of Scottish History*, i, 2nd edn., pp. 90-3).

of Scotland, as the charter of King Malcolm my brother witnesses and confirms. Witnesses: Engelram, bishop of Glasgow; Nicholas, the Chancellor; Earl Waldeve [of Dunbar]; Earl Duncan [of Fife]; Richard de Moreville, the Constable; Walter son of Alan, the Steward; Robert Avenel; William de Mortimer; Ralph de Clere; Walter de Berkeley; Richard the clerk. At the castle of Edinburgh.

In this charter the service to be rendered for the lands is the provision of one knight – an armoured horseman. For smaller holdings, the service might be the provision of half a knight or even one-twentieth part of a knight[1]; and sometimes we find the provision of a ' sergeant ' on a horse, or an archer with a horse, or simply one archer. On the western coast-line we find feudal grants involving the service of a galley with rowers. Such service is called military service.[2] A rule arises that the service shall be rendered for only forty days in any one year: though in Scotland there are also frequent references to twenty days' service. In addition, land held on military service must pay feudal ' casualties ' or ' incidents ' – money payments which *may* arise. When the holder of the land dies, the land returns ' into the hands of the lord of whom the land is held ', and the heir, if of age, must pay a ' relief ' (usually a sum equal to one year's issues of the land) when he ' takes up the land again ' (*re-levat*) out of the hands of his lord. If the heir is a minor, he becomes a ' ward ' of the lord; the lord holds the land in ' wardship ', providing a reasonable sustentation for the minor who, when he comes of age, takes up his land again. The lord has also a right of ' marriage ' – a male heir who is still a minor, or a female heiress of any age, can be disposed of by the lord in marriage to someone of his own choice, and he may make a profit thereby. If there is no heir at all, the lands ' escheat ' into the hands of the lord, who again holds that which he had formerly given away.[3] Again, the fief held upon military service may be called upon to pay an ' aid ' (*auxilium*) – a money payment to help the lord in his necessity; and towards the end of William's reign it is possible that, upon occasion, aids might be

[1] Which suggests a proportional money-payment towards the cost of one knight.

[2] In addition to this *feudal* service we should note that an older service, inherent in all land, was usually exacted. This older service (which in the north and west was based upon the davoch) was called ' forinsec service ', and appears to have embraced fighting service, works and the payments of ' aids ' (probably gelds).

[3] This applies even today, when estates for which no heir is known or can be found escheat to the crown. The national newspapers, like *The Scotsman*, frequently carry advertisements running in the name of the Queen's and Lord Treasurer's Remembrancer and announcing that an estate left by a named deceased will escheat to the crown unless heirs come forward to claim it.

restricted to three in number – ransoming the lord from captivity, meeting the expenses of the ceremony of the knighting of his eldest son, and meeting the expenses of the marriage of his eldest daughter. Finally, military service may include the provision of men to garrison the lord's castles, a service known as ' castle guard '.

Service for lands, however, could take other forms. It might be a service of prayers – the usual service for lands that were granted to endow a church or a religious house. Sometimes the saying of certain masses was stipulated in the grant, but usually the lands were simply stated to be given to the church in free alms (in *frankalmoign*, or *in liberam elemosinam*), that is, for the return of no secular service at all. It is to be noted, too, that lands once given to the church were given for ever. The church does not die (no relief is ever payable, and there is no possibility of escheat through lack of heirs); the church is never a minor (the lord can never enjoy the rights of wardship or marriage); the church does not break faith, or commit treason, whereby the lands can return to the lord through forfeiture. Because of all this, later kings, pressed for finance, regretted the pious generosity of their predecessors. The church held vast extents of land which rendered no tangible return and which could never be recovered. While, in the spirit of mediaeval times, the intangible returns were greatly valued, James I is said to have called David I a ' sair sanct for the croun '.

Again, lands might be held for service in some office: for acting, for example, as the King's High Constable, or his cup-bearer; or, on a lord's estate, for acting as his bailie, or his smith. Or lands might be held for a render of food – soon commuted into a money-payment – or for a direct monetary return. Later, as we shall see, such monetary payments become common; the land is said to be held in feu-ferme (it pays a *firma*, or rent, for the feu, or fief), which is a perpetual heritable holding,[1] as opposed to the tack, or lease, which is for a number of years only.

Lastly, and particularly after the later years of the reign of William, lands might be held of the king or of a lord for a token service only – such as ' rendering a rose in the season of roses ', or ' paying one penny if it is asked for '. This is known as ' blenche-ferme ' (*alba firma*) tenure. The token render, however small, still acknowledged the lord's superiority. Usually lands were granted by the king in blenche-ferme as a reward for some singular service rendered to him; though later,

---

[1] See *infra*, pp. 295-6. So today practically all land in Scotland is held in feu, on a perpetual heritable tenure, in return for the payment of a feu-duty to the superior.

in the fourteenth and fifteenth centuries, some of the very strange services to be rendered under blenche-ferme tenures suggest grants made in jovial mood. The barony of Carnwath, for example, was held in return for providing a pair of breeches of English ' bluecloth ' to be given every midsummer to the winner of a race from the eastern end of the town of Carnwath to the cross called ' Cawlo-Cross '; and the barony of Penicuik was held in return for blowing three blasts on a horn on that part of the burgh muir of Edinburgh which was once the forest of Drumsheugh, upon the occasion of the king's chief hunting there.[1]

Lands held by military service, moreover, also owed service to the lord's court.[2] This was known as ' suit of court '. It entailed personal presence, or the provision of a fully-qualified and accepted ' suitor ', at the sittings of the court.[3] The Latin word used for such suit clearly indicates the relationship of the lands to the court – suit is *secta*, from the verb *sequor*: the lands *follow* the court of the lord of whom they are held. Not only must actions relating to the lands, or to their holder, be heard in the lord's court, but also the holder of the lands must attend the lord's court, there to give his lord ' aid and counsel ' both in judicial causes and in general matters of administration – for all feudal courts were both judicial and administrative. In the court itself, it was the tenants of the lord, the suitors of his court, who made judgment or gave decision. The judgment, or decision, was said to be that of the ' body of the court '; so judgment by the tenants in any action relating to a tenant is the judgment of his peers (*judicium parium*), the judgment of his equals in rank.

The change-over from the Celtic organisation to the new Norman feudalism must have been slow and gradual, and subject, as we have seen, to some compromise. The new feudalism, based upon the holding of land, did not completely oust the older grouping by family and kindred and by acceptance of a chief and admission to a clan.

[1] The stables at Penicuik House still bear on their dome the words ' Held for a Blast '.

These odd tenures are very similar to some of the English ' serjeanties '; but there is no Scottish render to parallel that in England of holding the king's head whenever he crossed the Channel.

[2] Sometimes this burden was also imposed upon lands held in frankalmoign, and, very occasionally, upon blenche-ferme tenures – though both those tenures were held to be exempt. In such cases, however, the service was specifically defined and while, in military tenures, the service might also be defined, it was always understood.

[3] In due course, not at all sittings of the court, but only either when summoned to render suit, or at the three principal sittings of the court (the ' head courts '). Cf. *infra*, p. 91, n. 2.

Moreover the Celtic risings in the north and west in the twelfth and early thirteenth centuries[1] were, as we have seen, not solely dynastic; partly they were directed against the ' foreigners ' who were displacing the Gael, and partly they were an endeavour to uphold the old order against the new. But as, one after another, the risings were defeated, motte-and-bailey castles were built,[2] and another part of the difficult country was brought in. In the south, Anglo-Normans were settled peacefully, but in the north and west they penetrated only with difficulty or against active resistance. Admittedly in the reign of William we find Celtic earls, the sons of Celtic earls, and native landholders in the north-east parts of ' Scotia ' receiving from the king charters of infeftment of lands to be held for feudal services; but in the western highlands the new feudalism remained alien and largely unknown.

The importance of the Anglo-Normans whom David I introduced as administrators, officials, military leaders and local governors is to be read in the royal charters themselves. In the lists of witnesses, French names, and often the same names, either appear alone or heavily predominate: that is to say, Anglo-Normans predominate among those who are around the king. Regularly we find as witnesses Gervasius Ridel, Hugo de Morevilla, Robertus Corbet, Hugo Bret, Berengarius Engaine – all from David's Northamptonshire estates. The Bruces, with vast estates in Yorkshire, were given Annandale; FitzAlans became High Stewards and eventually established a royal line; and, somewhat later, the Balliols, with many manors in Durham, settled by intermarriage in Galloway and the Comyns acquired Buchan.

Walter of Coventry, writing at the end of the thirteenth century and describing the overthrow in 1212 of Guthred, son of Donald MacWilliam, ' of the ancient line of Scottish kings ',[3] tells us that ' the more recent kings of Scots profess themselves to be rather Frenchmen, both in race and in manners, language and culture; and, after reducing the Scots to utter servitude, they admit only Frenchmen to their friendship and service '.[4] Here, ' utter servitude ' may be an exaggeration, though, with the many grants made to Anglo-Normans by David I, Malcolm

[1] See *supra*, pp. 57-8.
[2] We have already noted how King William, after the defeat of Guthred, son of Donald MacWilliam, built castles in the north (*firmari fecit castella sua in Ros*) to hold it secure (*supra*, p. 58).
[3] *Supra*, p. 58.
[4] Walter of Coventry was writing of Malcolm IV and William, and it is to be noted that Jordan of Fantosme also wrote of William that he held only foreigners dear, and would never love his own people.

IV and William, there must have been many dispossessions, of both lands and rights, about which the records are silent[1]; and, although Scots, like Duncan, earl of Fife, and Malise, earl of Strathearn, may have been ' admitted to friendship and service ', the men who were around the king and gave him their ' aid and counsel ' were mainly Anglo-Normans, until, over the generations, the Scottish earls and lords themselves became as Normanised as the newcomers. Towards the end of William's reign we find Fergus, Celtic earl of Buchan, granting three davochs of land, by charter, for the render of one archer and suit to the earl's head courts[2] at Ellon, ' as any earl may freely infeft a vassal in Scotia '.

But some compromise is still there. The Celtic earls for long remained the only ' earls '.[3] Even the greatest and most important of the new Anglo-Normans were not given that dignity[4]; and at first they acquired it only by inter-marriage – as when the Comyns gained the earldom of Buchan, and the Bruces the earldom of Carrick.

Again turning to the evidence of the charters, we find in the reign of Robert I (1306-29), when feudal tenures become more strictly defined, that a fief can be held of the king *in liberam baroniam*, or ' in free barony '. This is a new term implying that certain rights and privileges are enjoyed by the lord: rights and privileges which may or may not have been previously enjoyed or exercised,[5] and which, in some cases, may have been covered by the old phrase ' cum sac et soc, et infangandthef et utfangandthef '.[6] The lord whose fief has been ' erected ' by the king into a ' free barony ' (and only the king could

---

[1] Also and apart from the ' bringing in ' of ' waste ', there must have been dispossessions owing to improvements in agriculture introduced by Anglo-Norman lords and by the new monastic houses. It must be remembered that the records and chronicles were largely written by Anglo-Norman churchmen: hence their silence.

[2] There were three ' head courts ' a year – at Yule, Easter and Michaelmas – at which *all* tenants had to compear. In addition smaller intermediate courts were held. This arrangement applied to the courts of the sheriffs and the burghs as well as to franchise courts.

[3] The earls of Dunbar may be cited as an exception, but they were descended from Gospatric, earl of Northumbria, and they did not use the title ' Earl of Dunbar ' until the end of the twelfth century.

[4] This may possibly support the argument that the Celtic earls were originally branches of the paramount royal house ruling over provinces that had been assigned to them.

[5] And probably, in distant parts, some feudal lords *exercised* rights and privileges which they did not *enjoy* by virtue of the grants they had received from the king.

[6] Meaning, in effect, a right to hold a court for his lands and, in his court, to try thieves caught with stolen goods in their possession which had been taken either inside or outside the lord's lands.

create a barony) now definitely enjoyed *haute justice*, with ' pit and
gallows ' (*fossa et furca*). His court could hear not merely the disputes
which might arise between the lord and his tenants, or between the
tenants themselves, relating to their holdings, to their services, and to
their labouring of the lands; in its general maintenance of law and
order, it could decide more than simple actions of assault with bloodshed
(*bloodwite*) and of ' strife and trublance '. The court of a barony enjoyed
a jurisdiction of ' life and limb '. The thief, the man-slayer, and often
simply the ' unwanted general nuisance ' could, by its sentence, be
hanged or drowned; and no question would be asked, for it was the
court of a barony.[1] Indeed, the king sometimes says in his charter
that he has erected the lands into a barony ' for the maintenance of
peace and to put down robbers '. Now, too, the barony tended to
become an autonomous unit, a little feudal state, or, in the words of the
lawyers, an *unum quid*. In it, the social and economic aspects of a
feudal holding became more clearly defined. The lord had his mill,
his brewery, his smithy – to all of which his tenants were ' thirled '.
Just as they had to attend the lord's court, so they had to grind their corn
at his mill (and pay ' multures ' for the miller's work), so had they to
take their iron-work to his smithy (and pay for the services of the
smith). The lord might build a church, endow it with a holding of
land, and appoint a priest; to it his tenants would pay their tithes and
oblations; and barony and parish would tend to become identical.
Later, when our records become fuller, we even find some lords
exercising through their courts a paternal authority over their people:
this young man (who has got into monetary difficulties) is ordered to
cease playing at the cards and dice; because of certain disorderly
scenes, ale must not be sold to women unless they are in the company
of their husbands.

More important, however, the greater lords soon obtained further
rights and privileges from the king. Again in the reign of Robert I,
we have references to ' regalities '; and the regality, a holding *in liberam
regalitatem*, or *in liberam regaliam*, was simply a barony with more
extensive rights – regal rights, as its name implies. The lord of regality
was virtually king in his own lands. The king's writ did not run in
the regality; the king's officers had no right to enter its lands. The

[1] Admittedly, as we shall see later, the king's sheriff was supposed to ensure that
baronial jurisdiction was not abused; but, although a right of ' appeal ' in civil causes
from baron court to sheriff court long continued, in criminal causes the sheriff's
supervision over the baron courts within his sheriffdom was apparently little exercised
and soon ceased altogether (see *infra*, pp. 101-2).

court of the regality had a jurisdiction virtually equal to that of the king himself: usually it could hear ' the pleas of the crown '[1]; and only treason (a crime against the king and his rule) was excluded from its cognisance.

The complete independence and power of a lord of regality are aptly illustrated in 1320 when an official return recorded that ' de Vesci held Sprouston [Roxburghshire] *regaliter*, by the same liberties and customs with which King Alexander III had held the lands of his kingdom; that de Vesci had the right to his own justiciary, his own chamberlain, his chancellor, his coroner, his sergeands, and also his standard measures in the manner of the said King Alexander '. Such extensive rights, often held over extensive lands, descended heritably, with the lands, from father to son; but the son did not necessarily inherit his father's loyalty and due service to the king. So we can begin to see how, in later years, there arose a long struggle between the crown and the ' overmighty barons ', when often a powerful lord in a distant part would put his king to defiance. All that, however, still lay in the future.

[1] At first the ' pleas of the crown ' were many and various; but soon they were reduced to four—murder, arson, rape and robbery. See also *infra*, p. 104.

CHAPTER X

The Lord and His Castle

WE ARE told that when William the Conqueror's army disembarked at Pevensey, on Thursday 28 September 1066, carpenters and smiths waded ashore with the soldiers and before evening had made a *castellum* at Hastings. It was undoubtedly a castle similar to that depicted in the Bayeux Tapestry – a ditch, an earthen mound raised from the upcast of the ditch (much as a child digs a sand-castle today),[1] and a wooden structure, with a surrounding wooden palisade, built on the top of the mound – in other words, a ' motte-and-bailey ' castle.

The general plan of the motte-and-bailey castle was always the same: though the *motte*, or mound, might vary in height from twenty to fifty feet, and a suitable existing mound or an outcrop of rock might be used to save the labour of raising an artificial one. The motte was surrounded by a wide, deep ditch (not always filled with water); its crest was protected by a close, strong palisade of timbers; and within that palisade the lord built his wooden tower or ' house '. To reach the house, a long ladder-like bridge led upwards from the outer edge of the ditch to the top of the mound. This bridge could be easily defended by a gate in the palisade round the top of the mound, and the foot of the bridge might also be defended by a gate of its own. All these features are again shown in the Bayeux Tapestry when it depicts the castle of Dinan. The *bailey* was a separate area round the base of the motte and was also defended by its own timber palisade and sometimes also with its own ditch. The lord lived in his wooden house on the motte; inside the bailey were wooden buildings for the lord's men, for stables, for brewhouses, for stores, and so forth. The whole area of an early motte-and-bailey castle varied between one and three acres.[2]

Wood, however, can easily be set on fire. Besiegers could use arrows carrying burning pitch.[3] Thus, in due course, the lord's wooden house, and the wooden buildings within the bailey, might be given an additional roof of turf, or they might have their walls faced

---

[1] In the Bayeux Tapestry we note that the *castellum* was ordered ' to be *thrown up* ', not *built* (*jussit ut foderetur castellum at Hestenga ceastra*), and the picture shows men digging with spades and throwing up the earthen mound.

[2] Impressive surviving mottes can be seen at Urr, Invernochty, and Inverurie.

[3] In the Bayeux Tapestry the Normans set fire to Dinan Castle, but by torches.

with puddled clay which set hard and firm to give them something like a concrete covering.

The 'castle' was the whole of the fortified enclosure; it was the whole of the motte-and-bailey, and not simply the lord's house on the motte.

Later, however, some mottes were by themselves as large as the whole of an early motte-and-bailey; their crests might be an acre in extent. Several of these larger mottes have been identified with the peels which were built by order of Edward I during the War of Independence, and the word 'peel' (derived from the old French *pel*, which came from the Latin *palus*, meaning a stake[1]) means simply a palisaded or stockaded enclosure. The peel, indeed, might be merely a timber stockade with no motte at all; and inside the peel there might be further stockades within the encircling stockade.

In Scotland, about the middle of the thirteenth century, wooden buildings began to give way to stone. The lord's house, the tower, was then built of stone, sometimes on the site of the old timber house, sometimes on an adjoining site. It might be called a *donjon*, purely because it was the lord's house, for the word *donjon* is related to *dominus*, a lord. The old timber stockade was then replaced by a stone wall – an enclosing wall: a curtain wall, or a wall of enceinte – and soon, within the wall, we begin to read of courts, of forecourts, and basse courts.

A tower, indeed, was the simplest way of arranging a group of rooms for the lord's quarters – for the lord, for his lady, for his son – with mural chambers which were privies with shutes opening out over the moat, or water-filled ditch. Also within the tower was the lord's hall and kitchen, and, in its lowest depths, the lord's prison or 'pit': for the lord liked to know that he was sitting safely in his house with his enemy securely immured in the pit below.[2]

At this stage, the end of the thirteenth century and early in the fourteenth century, the castle would probably have a stone wall of enceinte, a stone tower for the lord and his household, and wooden (often lean-to) buildings for the lord's immediate followers, for stables,

---

[1] From which comes our present word, *paling*. The later use of the word 'peel' to describe stone towers on the Borders is historically incorrect. Many Border strongholds, even at the beginning of the sixteenth century, were still timber built, often with timber outworks, and might properly be termed 'peels'. From the timber enclosure, or stockade, however, the word was apparently transferred to a stone house which might be built therein, and then a stone house without any 'peel' at all.

[2] So also *dungeon* comes from *donjon* because the dungeon is usually in the depths of the lord's tower-house.

store-houses and the like. But gradually these wooden buildings were themselves replaced by stone; then they were built round the castle's court, and many of them were inter-connected.

The gate, once approached by a wooden ladder defended at each end, was still of supreme importance. It was a ' hole in the wall ': and the new stone walls of enceinte were high to scale, thick to breach,[1] and surrounded by a moat. The gate was the weakest part of the defence, and there every ingenuity was contrived to make entry difficult. The ladder-bridge to the top of the mound had by this time been replaced by a drawbridge over the moat – a bridge that could be drawn up at night and in times of danger by means of chains, attached to its outer edges, which were wound up by a windlass in a room above the gate itself. And just as the old ladder-bridge might have had a gate at its foot, so the drawbridge might also have a gate at its outer end: a gate defending the drawbridge itself, but a gate that tended to be set in front of the drawbridge. This gate, now stone-built, was known as a barbican. At the inner end of the drawbridge were the gates of the castle itself, built of heavy timbers, iron-bound, and secured within by thick beams that were drawn across and held fast in slots in the stone-work on either side, while the drawbridge itself, when raised, formed an additional defence in front of the main gates.

Once through the castle gates the next defence was the portcullis – a cross-cross of strong timbers with iron spikes at the foot. It was dropped vertically, sliding down in two grooves cut in the stone-work on either side; and it could be dropped instantly, whereas the raising of the drawbridge was slow and laborious work.[2] The portcullis-chamber, into which it was drawn up, also often contained the draw-bridge windlass. Beyond the portcullis there was sometimes a second pair of gates or an ' iron yett '.[3] Only after passing these defences could entrance be gained to the castle-court.[4]

Because of the importance of these defences of the entrance to the

[1] The wall might be from twelve to fifteen feet thick, and from twenty-five to fifty feet high.

[2] In some later castles, however, the drawbridge was operated by beams (or ' gaffs ') and counterweights and so could be quickly raised or lowered.

[3] Sometimes there was a considerable distance, almost like a chamber, between the two pairs of gates; and in the roof of this ' chamber ' there was sometimes a ' murder-hole ' – an opening through which, presumably, the defenders could hurl missiles upon attackers who had breached the first line of defence: though the purpose of these openings is largely surmise.

[4] Edinburgh Castle, built on a steep rock, had three widely separate gates and a portcullis in the slow ascent round the rock face.

castle, the feudal lord sometimes had his own rooms over or by the gate. It is noticeable that in the fifteenth century some castles had their gateways altered to provide accommodation there for the lord and his immediate attendants. Such control of the entrance, by the lord himself, or his household, was doubly necessary when mercenaries were employed, or when the lord was doubtful of the loyalty of some of those who were within his stronghold.

Against an attack the defenders shot their arrows (from bows) and bolts (from cross-bows) from the parapet of the encircling wall (the wall-walk) and from the tops of the towers with which the gates and the angles of the wall were eventually strengthened. Such towers, with their staircases, provided quick access to the wall-walk; they facilitated lateral fire; and they also provided additional small rooms. The top of the wall and the tops of the towers were built with convenient openings (called embrasures) alternating with solid walling (called the merlons). They were crenellated, or embattled. The merlon protected the bowman while he was preparing for his next shot through the embrasure – and the embrasure itself might have swinging wooden shutters for further protection, while the merlon might have a slit for use as a peep-hole. The tops of the towers and the top of the wall might also be corbelled to provide an overhang, with openings (called machicolations) in the corbelling through which missiles could be dropped upon the attackers below.

The attackers used movable wooden shields (called *pavises*) to protect their archers and those who were trying to fill up the moat with bundles of faggots (called *fascines*) and earth and stones. If they succeeded in filling the moat, they might bring forward a ' belfry ', a tall wooden tower which overtopped the wall and from which they could try to ' board ' the castle by fighting their way on to the wall-walks. Or alternatively, or in conjunction with a belfry, they might bring up a ' sow ' to try to breach the wall or gates – a heavy battering ram with a wooden roof to protect those who were manning it, and sometimes also with a platform for archers who endeavoured to keep down the fire of the defenders. Here the machicolations in the corbelling came to the aid of the defenders, and, in addition, a wooden gallery (called a *bretasche* or *brattice*) might be built out from the wall to command its base. If the attackers did not succeed in getting close to the castle wall they might use mangonels, heavy catapults that could throw large stones. Edward I had many such siege engines for his siege of Stirling Castle in 1304: and it is said that, although the stones did little damage to the walls and towers, they did great damage when they broke through the roofs and vaults. To meet a long siege, and to frustrate attempts to mine the wall or gate, sally-ports were constructed.

Behind their strong and skilfully constructed defences a small garrison could put an army of besiegers to defiance, unless powerful siege-engines could be brought into play. In the siege of Stirling Castle, in 1304, already referred to, a garrison of less than two hundred men held out for three months against the assembled might of the English king until, at last, Edward's engines began to take effect. Two hundred men, moreover, was a large garrison; the usual number was between fifty and one hundred; and, more often than not, it was starvation, or the fouling of the castle well, that eventually let to surrender.

In normal times, the centre of life in the castle was the hall. There the lord and his household ate and drank, talked and entertained their guests; and the tables were trestle-tables which could easily be cleared to make more room. By the fifteenth century, however, the lord had his own ' solar ', or private chamber. Then the kitchens might be at one end of the hall, which by this time had become larger and longer, and the lord's own chamber, also much larger, at the other end; and the early tower had become a ' tower-house '. Or, indeed, the tower might now have become subordinate to the other buildings. By then, too, there would probably be a dais at the lord's end of the hall on which the lord, his family and his guests would sit, elevated and distinguished from mere followers and retainers.[1] The windows were often still narrow slits[2] – though sometimes splayed and with window-seats – but gradually they, too, were enlarged, and then the upper part would be glazed, while the lower part would consist of wooden shutters which could be opened wide. The walls of the hall, the solar, and other important rooms, though seen today as bare stone, were probably

[1] Later still, in the sixteenth century, the lord, his family and his guests could ' withdraw ' into a ' withdrawing-room ' which, in due course, became the modern ' drawing-room '. All these developments can be clearly seen at Dirleton Castle, East Lothian.

[2] Often wrongly called loop-holes. The defending archers sometimes shot through specially constructed slits that provided a controlled field of fire; but generally they shot from the ' wall-walks ' or ' battlements '. The windows were narrow slits to prevent the arrows of the enemy from finding the rooms, and to prevent the enemy from climbing into the rooms. Also they let in the minimum of cold air, for they were not glazed. Later, when larger windows were made, they were usually covered with iron grills to prevent entry.

painted in bright colours – possibly with heraldic designs – and they might even be hung with tapestries, ' to keep away the draughts and the spiders '.

The chambers were probably still few in number. Guests (other than very distinguished ones) would sleep on heather or straw on the floor of the hall, or with their horses in the stables – in both cases for warmth. The king, and also the more important lord, would now have a ' wardrobe ' – a room in which he kept his clothes,[1] his jewels, and his personal papers. But steadily the chambers increased in number with the increase in the buildings round the castle's court. More luxury was provided. There are more and more references to beds and bedclothes, cushions and pillows. And so the castle also had a ' doocot ', for the pigeons (or ' doos ') provided feathers for cushions and pillows as well as providing eggs and the contents of pies; and there was the added advantage that they fed indiscriminately on the lord's corn and the corn of his tenants.

Now, too, the kitchen became bigger, to cope with a larger establish-ment. It had an enormous fireplace, fully capable of roasting ' an ox whole ', together with ovens and smaller fireplaces. Usually there were separate brewhouses and bakehouses. The well, sometimes seen in the castle-court, was more usually near to the kitchen, sometimes within the kitchen. Water was used for cooking (and especially for soaking salted meat and fish), for the horses, and occasionally for washing the hands and face. Ale was the common drink, though the lord might be wealthy enough to afford wine which was imported from France. So the buttery (from an Old French word *boterie*) was the room where the wine was kept – and wine was usually imported in butts, or tuns, or barrels; the pantry was the bread-room (from the Latin *panis*); and the larder was the store-room for meat which was preserved by ' larding ' it with fat.

The meals must have been enormous, if we are to judge from the vast quantities referred to in ' provisionings '; and because of the great storage space that was required there were big vaults.[2] The heavy imports of spices of various kinds – pepper, mace, cloves, nutmegs, cinnamon, saffron and so forth – were necessary to offset the taste of long-stored food, of salted marts[3] and of meat and eggs which had

---

[1] Clothes were hung on ' perches ' jutting out from the wall, and which also acted as sleeping pegs for the lord's falcons.

[2] These vaults are sometimes mistaken for dungeons. The dungeons were usually quite small.

[3] For the meaning of this word see *supra*, p. 69.

become 'high'. Stale fish, however, was apparently handed to the poor at the castle-gate.[1]

But the lord preferred an open life to being cooped up in his castle. Like 'the good Sir James Douglas' he loved better to hear the lark sing than the mouse squeak. He was often out hunting or hawking or riding round his lands. He might be away from his castle for weeks or months at a time – fighting in the king's wars, or conducting a private war of his own, or accompanying the king as the king rode throughout the realm. For the king and the great lords who were with him moved about the kingdom to maintain the king's peace, to exercise the royal justice and the royal clemency, and to eat the king's rents which were often paid in kind. Then the king and his lords were accommodated in castles or monasteries (the only buildings capable of housing them); and they moved on from place to place, partly again to mete out justice and to consume the royal rents, but also because, after a few weeks' stay in a castle, the primitive sanitary arrangements had become so fouled that the king and his court were bound to move on, and, indeed, were glad to do so.[2]

Yet, although he loved war and fighting, the lord was still attentive to the church and its services. He usually had his own priest or chaplain; the buildings in the larger castles usually included a chapel; and frequently there was a private chapel or an oratory (or 'praying room') near to the lord's own chamber.

In an early French book on chivalry we are told that the lord had other 'delights' than hunting, hawking, jousting, riding to the wars, holding his court and hanging thieves; and these other delights are listed for us: they include listening to the minstrels, playing chess, talking with the ladies, warming himself before the fire, being bled, eating and drinking, having a good belch, and watching the snow fall.

---

[1] And it is noticeable that the eating of stale fish was thought to be one of the causes of leprosy.

[2] In the monastic houses, however, the sanitary arrangements were superior to those in the castles, and there the king might stay for long periods – with a considerable drain upon the individual abbey's resources and to the despair of the abbot and monks.

CHAPTER XI

Feudal Scotland - II

IN THEIR endeavours to hold down the outlying parts of their kingdom, or, perhaps we should say, in their endeavours to weld the outlying parts to the king's central authority, David I and his immediate successors did not rely solely upon grants of lands and powers to feudal lords. The king, too, built his castles here and there throughout his kingdom; and into his castles he put his own officers to hold and to administer their ' castle-areas ' in his name. So, in the reign of David I we hear for the first time of a new royal officer, the sheriff (*vicecomes*), and, under his control, and administered from a royal castle held by him, a castle-area which is called a sheriffdom (*vicecomitatus*) and which eventually became the modern shire.

From the records it would appear that these new units of government, these sheriffdoms, were first established in Lothian, the midland valley and the eastern coastal plain; then we find them in the south-west; and as late as 1293 Skye, Lorne and Kintyre were erected into sheriffdoms ' for the peace and stability of the kingdom '.[1] The reach of the sheriffdoms marked the reach of the new royal power. The king's castles, with sheriffdoms attached to them, held and administered by the king's sheriffs, were planted here and there throughout the kingdom just as trees are planted to hold firm a shifting soil. The sheriffdoms were new units for the government of the kingdom of Scotland; the feudal fiefs held of the king were the units of the sheriffdoms.

The sheriff was the strong hand of the king in the localities; and his duties were all-embracing – judicial, military, financial and administrative.

He held a court in the name of the king for the whole area of the sheriffdom,[2] a court which had both a civil and a criminal jurisdiction. From the evidence of charters of the thirteenth century, we know that by then (and undoubtedly earlier still) suit was paid to his court by those who held their lands direct of the king within the sheriffdom and that decisions made by lower courts within the sheriffdom could be

---

[1] Though these erections did not last, and a later attempt by James IV to establish sheriffs – depute for the Isles, both north and south, also failed.

[2] Though, later, the regalities were outside its jurisdiction (see *supra*, pp. 92-3.) When there were regalities within the sheriffdom the lands of the sheriffdom were differentiated as ' royalty ' and ' regality '.

reviewed, upon what we should now call appeal, by the court of the sheriff. In effect, the dissatisfied litigant could ' gainsay ' or ' false ' the doom of the baron court. In a later formula, he could denounce the doom as ' false, stinking and rotten '; he could refuse to accept it, and thereby his case would come before the sheriff court, and the sheriff court, in its decision, would state whether the doom in the baron court had been ' well said ' (the appeal failed) or had been ' evil given ' (the appeal succeeded). The sheriff, or his sergeand, was also at first required to supervise baronial justice in actions of ' life and limb ' – though this safeguard apparently soon lapsed.

The king's castle, held by the sheriff, was the king's strong-point for that locality. At the time of Hakon's expedition of 1263, the records show that the sheriff of Inverness strengthened his castle with additional outworks, the sheriff of Dumfries put his castle in repair, additional watchmen were enlisted at Stirling Castle, and the sheriff of Ayr increased both his military stores and his garrison. When the host was called out, the sheriff was the leader of the men of the sheriffdom.

Our earliest financial records (of the mid-thirteenth century) show that as a financial officer the sheriff collected all money and victual due to the king from the lands of sheriffdom – as rents, as feudal casualties, as escheats, and so forth – and, upon the king's instructions, he made out payment. For all his ingatherings (his *charge*) and for all his outgoings (his *discharge*) he was expected to make account once a year in the king's exchequer. When special taxes were imposed[1] the sheriff was usually made responsible for their collection.

In his administrative capacity the sheriff executed every order sent to him by the king, and in due course many and varied duties were placed upon him by the king's council or parliament. By the end of the fifteenth century we find that he had to hunt ' the wolfe and the whelps ', to destroy illegal fish-traps, to inspect weights and measures, to enforce sumptuary laws, to license beggars, and so forth. In addition he acted as the executive officer to the justiciar and the chamberlain when those royal officials visited his sheriffdom.

But, just as baronies and regalities descended heritably from father to son, so the office of sheriff tended to become heritable, son succeeding to father. As early as 1305 the office was heritable in Selkirk, Kinross and Cromarty; and Dumbarton and Roxburgh soon followed. More-over there grew up a tendency for the big local lord to become the local

---

[1] For example the ' tenth penny ' granted to Bruce in 1326 and the ' contribution for peace ' to raise the £20,000 due under the treaty of 1328 (*infra*, pp. 172, 187).

sheriff. And where then lay the sheriff's supervision of baronial justice, or what effectiveness was there in an appeal from the court of the lord as baron to the court of the lord as sheriff ?

Modern counties, like Peebles, Selkirk, Roxburgh, Stirling, Aberdeen, Banff, Inverness and so forth represent the old sheriffdoms; their names come from the royal castles (and from the burghs which, as we shall see, grew up beside them) which were the sheriffs' seats and from which the sheriffs exercised their authority. A few counties, like Sutherland, Ross and Fife, are real counties, in the true sense of the word, taking their names from territories once held by an earl (*comes*). Kirkcudbright, exceptionally, is still called a stewartry, a designation going back to 1369 when David II granted to Archibald, later third earl of Douglas, and his heirs, ' all our lands of Galloway between the Nith and the Cree ' (to be held for the render annually of a white rose at the castle of Dumfries), and when the Douglas put in a ' steward ' to administer the lands and to collect the revenues on his behalf.[1]

But the introduction of Anglo-Norman feudalism led not only to all these many changes in the local government of Scotland; it also led to many changes in the central government and in the administration of the law. Now, for the first time, we hear of the Chancellor, the Chamberlain, the Constable, the Justiciar and so forth – with offices and duties adopted from the administration of England.

The Chancellor was the most intimate counsellor of the king and the keeper of the king's seal. At first, one of his main duties was to examine every document carefully before it received the king's assent – that is, before the king's seal was attached to it. Later, with the growth of government and an increasing ' civil service ', the king's seal was called the ' Great Seal ', to distinguish it from the ' Privy Seal ' which appears on record in the thirteenth century. In the middle of the fourteenth century, we hear of the ' Signet ', the king's ' ring seal ', and, by the middle of the fifteenth century, there had emerged a whole system of checks, and payments at each check, whereby, for example, a royal grant of lands had to ' pass ' the Signet, and then the Privy Seal, before it could finally receive the appending of the Great Seal.

The Chamberlain was the chief financial officer of the king. He took his name (*camerarius*) from the *camera* which was the king's treasury. It was also his duty to supervise the king's burghs (which

---

[1] It should perhaps be noted that the names of certain districts, like Mar, Buchan and the Lennox, come from old earldoms ; others, like Kyle and Cunningham, come from extinct bailiaries (lands administered by a bailie).

were on the king's lands and which paid money rents to the king)[1] and, to carry out that duty, he went on circuit (he held an *iter* or an *ayre*) visiting the king's burghs to ensure that justice was being rightly administered, that each burgh's affairs were being well managed,[2] and, above all, that the king's revenue from his burghs was not suffering through fraud or maladministration. Theoretically the chamberlain went on this ayre round the king's burghs once a year, but practice often fell short of theory.

The Constable was responsible for maintaining peace in a wide area (called the ' verge ') around the king's presence, and for guarding the door of the king's chamber. He had under him twenty-four ' doorwards ' who took their stations at the king's door, and who rode before the king on his progress through his realm. The Marischal, on the other hand, maintained due order on the other side of the door – inside the king's hall and chamber.[3] And the king, the constable and the marischal might hold a ' court of chivalry ': before them, a knight might defend his honour with his own hand by battle in the lists.

Again, by mid-thirteenth century, our fuller records show that the Justiciars were itinerant officers providing, like the chamberlain, a close link between the centre and the localities. They travelled on ayre throughout the kingdom, moving from sheriffdom to sheriffdom, ensuring that each sheriff was efficiently carrying out his many duties and, in each sheriffdom, holding a court to hear appeals from the sheriff's court and also to hear those pleas, ' the pleas of the crown ', which were regarded as so serious that they were ' reserved ' for them.[4] These early records refer to several justiciars – for Lothian, for Galloway, for ' Scotland ' south of the ' Mounth ' and for ' Scotland ' north of the ' Mounth ';[5] but, early in the fourteenth century, there was a simple

[1] *Infra*, chap. xii.
[2] In a document of the latter part of the reign of Robert I, outlining the ' points ' to be enquired into by the chamberlain, he is to ascertain, among many other points, whether justice is done equally to rich and to poor, whether good weights and measures are used, whether the burgh's market privileges are maintained, and whether the rents and issues pertaining to the king are reaching the king. In a somewhat later document of a similar character, the chamberlain is to enquire, *inter alia*, whether the miller is using two measures, ' ane to tak with and ane uther to deliver with ', and whether the souters are using ' fals and rotten threid throu the quhilk the schone [shoes] ar tynt [lost: worn out] or [before] thai be half worn '.
[3] The domestic arrangements, however, were in the hands of the Steward under whom were the cup-bearers, the butlers, the pantlers, and all the servants of the royal household.
[4] Cf. *supra*, p. 93, n.1.
[5] See *supra*, p. 34, n. 2.

administrative arrangement of one justiciar for the sheriffdoms south of the Forth[1] and one justiciar for those north of the Forth. Theoretically, the justiciars went on ayre twice a year (in spring and autumn); but again intention was often better than practice, and in troublous times (and, following the outbreak of the War of Independence, the times were often troublous) the ayres tended to be few and infrequent. Nevertheless it cannot be too strongly stressed that the ayres of the chamberlain and the justiciars were of supreme importance: they ensured not only that the authority delegated by the king to his officers in the different parts of the realm was being rightly exercised but also that the final authority was still the king's.

The king, however, like any other feudal lord, could call upon his tenants to render suit and service to his court. And the tenants-in-chief whom the king called to give him ' aid and counsel ', together with the officers whom we have named,[2] formed the *curia regis*. This court of the king, like any other feudal court, was both judicial and administrative. The court of a feudal lord was concerned not only with justice but also with the well-being and orderly government of the people on his lands; and, in the case of the king, the lands were the kingdom.

As we have seen, this new administration brings in its train the concept that the king is lord of all the land and fountain of all justice. So, should there be a failure of heirs, the lands will return to the king; should there be a failure of justice, the plea will be heard by the king. Not only does the king reserve his own royal justice should there be a lack of justice in the court of the feudal lord, but, by the thirteenth century, we find there is a pyramid of appeal which rises from the baron court to the sheriff court, from the sheriff court to the court of the justiciar on his ayre, and from the court of the justiciar to the court of the king. Finally, in addition to hearing these appeals, the king's court will also hear important causes or the causes of important men.

At first, the king would sit in his court with the officers of his household and with those great men who happened to be with him at the time. In 1230 we have reference to such a sitting with one bishop, two earls, one prior, three barons, and ' many others ' (*cum multis aliis* – which probably means little or nothing, and is simply added as a good resounding phrase); in 1244 an ordinance was made with the

---

[1] That is, south of the narrow ' neck ' of the Forth-Clyde isthmus.
[2] They are called the officers of the king's ' household '; and the king's household of mediaeval times was the Whitehall of today.

counsel, advice and consent of two bishops, three abbots, seven earls, eight barons, and ' many other earls, barons and worthy men of the kingdom ' (which again probably means very little, if anything at all).

Then, to ensure a fuller attendance, the king began to summon others of his tenants-in-chief to come to his court to help him with their counsel. But still only the few and the great were summoned or attended; for naturally the king called only those whom he thought fit or necessary for the occasion; and attendance was always a burden. Nevertheless there were some upon whose advice the king regularly relied, and who were regularly asked for their counsel; these men, who were so often asked to give him counsel, became the king's council (and the Latin word *concilium* means both ' counsel ' and ' council '); and it is difficult to distinguish between the king's council and the king's court.

Like the king's court, the council might sit in various capacities and various ways; and at first there was apparently no distinction between its sittings for the various aspects of its work. It might sit as a court of justice or as a court of enquiry; it might sit for financial matters, or to give counsel in matters of state, including the general administration and government of the kingdom. Gradually, however, with increasing affairs of state, distinctions began to creep in. Thus, in the middle of the thirteenth century (if not earlier[1]), when the council, or a group of its members, sat for financial matters it was said to be sitting ' in exchequer ' (*in scaccario*).[2] About the same time, for important affairs of state the council might sit *in colloquio*. Finally, in 1293, we read of certain pleas which have been heard ' in the presence of the king [John Balliol] and his council in his first parliament ' (*in parliamento suo*).

At first, a *colloquium* or a *parliamentum* was probably a full and formal meeting of the council for a discussion, a ' talking ', about a matter that was regarded as being of particular importance, but, by the end of the thirteenth century, the surviving records show that a Scottish ' parliament ' had become primarily a sitting of the council in its capacity as the supreme court of law – the ' King's High Court of Parliament '. Moreover, and the point is important, this court of parliament declared the law. Feudal law was the law declared by the

[1] Unfortunately the earlier records have been lost.

[2] The word *scaccarium* means a chess-board, or a reckoning-board, chequered in squares. Until the introduction of the Arabic system of numbers such a reckoning-board, with counters, was the only way of carrying out addition and subtraction. The reader need only try to subtract xxxv from ccli, or to add xxix to xli, without recourse to the Arabic system, to realise the difficulties.

king's court. A case was heard by parliament – either a case of first instance, or a case which had risen on appeal from court to court until, finally, it had come to the highest court, the king's court of parliament; parliament gave its decision; and that decision became the law for all similar cases in time to come. By its decision parliament had laid down the law: indeed the dempster (doomster) of parliament, when declaring parliament's decision, used the phrase, ' This court of parliament shows for law '. Parliament might re-affirm the old law, or declare a change in the law to meet some changing need. Thus, although the king was the fountain of justice, his court was the fountain of the law. But the law, feudal law, was still largely a land-law. New laws, as opposed to the law that was determined by adjudication, tended to be concerned only with the details of government and administration, and with the maintenance of order in the realm.

Or again, the king, feeling the need for the advice of a large number of his great men, might increase the size of his council by inviting others to attend. The council was then said to be ' afforced '; it was strengthened. And from 1357 this larger gathering was called a ' general council '. But, although important decisions might be reached by either a parliament or a general council, it is clear from the records that the two bodies were different and distinguished.

Parliament was a court of law; a meeting of parliament had to be publicly proclaimed in advance; and those who were summoned to attend had to be given at least forty days' notice. Although parliament might do work other than that of a court of law, a sitting of parliament was always a much-advertised-in-advance occasion for all men to come to seek the king's justice in the king's own court, and to bring to him their petitions and complaints. In 1399 a general council even suggested that a parliament should be held each year for the next three years so that the king's subjects could be ' servit of the law ' – that is, could obtain justice. A general council, on the other hand, was not a court of law; its meeting was not publicly proclaimed in advance; it could be called together at short notice and there was no rule that at least forty days' notice had to be given. In every way it was easier to call a general council. Above all, the king called to a general council those whom he wanted to attend; he could pick and choose. For example, after the burghs had gained a right to send representatives to parliament, they yet had later to secure a right to be called to general councils.[1]

In all affairs of state, however, the king was still supreme. He was

----

[1] See *infra*, chap. xx.

supremus dominus noster Rex. He might, or might not, take the ' counsel ' offered to him. Not until the second half of the fourteenth century do we find a parliament opposing his wishes. Frequently, in the exchequer accounts, we find a marginal note, *consulendus rex* – the king must be asked about this: does he agree ? Everything was still dependent upon the king's decision and the king's writ. The king was a ' personal ' king; his actions were ' personal '. If David I had issued a charter confirming his gift of certain lands, it was as well to have that charter confirmed by Malcolm IV when he succeeded to the throne, and, when Malcolm IV died, to have the gift again confirmed by William. Even at the beginning of the fifteenth century a writ, issued in the king's name, could be called in question if, in the meantime, the king had died. The concept of an ' impersonal crown ' – that is, ' the government ', as we call it today – only slowly developed. Thus, and the point is important, homage was also personal. Homage to Edward I, for example, died with him, for it was personal; and, as we shall see, even a king's ransom might be regarded as a personal payment too.

Again, this new feudal administration, introduced by David I and developed by his immediate successors, was also accompanied by equally important changes in legal procedure. Already, in David's reign, we hear of the ' jury ', a body of local men who are sworn (*jurati*) to ascertain the truth which they must declare in a ' verdict ', a ' true-saying ' (*veredictum*). The jury might sit in judgment (*assisa*, and hence our modern ' assizes '), or they might sit as an ' inquest ' (*inquisicio*) to enquire (*inquirere*) into certain facts – as, for example, what was the boundary between these two holdings of land ?[1] who was the rightful heir to the lands of *X* of which the holder had just died ? was *A* taking so much water from the stream to work his mill-wheel that there was insufficient water to work the mill-wheel of *B* ?

Moreover, in the king's courts (such as the courts of his sheriffs and his justiciars), all these enquiries made by local juries, and also all civil actions, were initiated by the purchase of a ' brieve ' (a letter, a writ, in formal terms, *brevi manu*) from the king. The man worried about some infringement of his boundaries, or a lack of water for his mill-wheel, the prospective heir to lands, or the raiser of a civil action, purchased from the king's ' central office ' (his chancery) a brieve directed to the local sheriff, charging him to look into the matter by means of an inquest. In certain cases the brieve also charged the sheriff

---

[1] Called a ' perambulation ', for the jury walked round the boundary to define its line.

to report back to chancery. In those cases the finding of the jury was 'returned' to chancery; the jury made a *retour*. This was done, for example, when the jury decided who was the lawful heir to lands of which the holder had just died – and naturally so, for the king was interested. If the rightful heir were a minor, the king would enjoy wardship of the lands; and in all cases the king would want to know from whom was to come the payment of 'relief'. And, for any such payment to the king, the king's local officer, the sheriff, was responsible.

These brieves, with their standard wording and their standard directions, sent out to the king's officers in the different districts from a central office in the king's chancery, helped to ensure that the law should be uniform throughout the kingdom. Local and customary laws tended to disappear; and there was a steady approach to the ideal of one land, one people, one law, one king.

All these many changes and developments, however, were not achieved in a day and a night. Only slowly and gradually did the king's law and the king's authority reach the more distant parts of the realm. The king might build his castles at Inverness and Dumbarton and place his sheriffs there, but, west of the 'Highland line', feudal tenures and feudal incidents, baronies and regalities, sheriffs and justiciars were largely unknown. Even in the sixteenth century, when Campbells and Gordons held the flanks of this line, the sentries on the castle of Stirling saw the tops of distant peaks in a land that was known to few and where even fewer knew the way. In the Western Highlands and Islands the king's writ hardly ran until the beginning of the seventeenth century; until then the Highlanders obeyed the king only if they so chose. In the extreme south-west the Galwegians for long refused to accept the new Norman jury system, preferring a system of 'compurgation' in which 'oath-helpers' swore with a litigant that his cause was good and true. In the reign of Alexander II, in 1244, an order to the justiciar to 'enquire into the misdoers in the land' added 'except in Galloway which has special laws within it'. In 1324 Robert I partially extended the jury system there, though still allowing some continuance of the 'laws of Galloway'; and as late as 1384 it was noted in a meeting of the king's council that Galloway still had special laws of its own.

Nevertheless, the sources for the history of Scotland, under its new feudal administration in the twelfth and thirteenth centuries, reveal, in general, and apart from the 'heart of Gaeldom' in the far north-west, a country which was being gradually welded together, a country under law and order, with a strong central government ably served by an efficient local administration. Then came a sudden and disastrous change. Ten years after the death of Alexander III in 1286 came the War of Independence and the beginning of long centuries of resistance to English claims. In those years of war and disorder men looked back to the good government and to the peace and plenty of the thirteenth century as a 'golden age'. The earliest known piece of Scottish poetry, preserved for us by Andrew of Wyntoun, a chronicler writing in the opening years of the fifteenth century, records the change in a sad lament:

> Quhen Alysandyr oure Kyng was dede
> That Scotland led in luve and le,   [*peace*
> Away wes sons off ale and brede,   [*abundance*
> Off wyne and wax, off gamyn and gle;   [*enjoyment*
> Oure gold wes changyd in to lede;
> Chryst, borne in to Vyrgynyté,
> Succoure Scotland, and remede
> That stad is in perplexyté.   [*placed*

CHAPTER XII

The Early Burghs

IN THE twelfth century we also begin to read of ' burghs ' – the earliest
burghs known to us being those of Berwick and Roxburgh which are
referred to in a charter granted by David a few years before he became
king.

The burgh was a natural and necessary part of a mercantile revolution
which had swept through western Europe and had come belatedly to
Scotland. It was the concomitant of a change in economic life, a
change from a self-supporting and almost purely agricultural economy
(whether of pasture or arable) to one in which there were organised
manufactures (notably of cloth) and in which organised trading began
– a surplus of agricultural products, wool, wool-fells,[1] skins and
hides, for example, being exchanged in a new overseas commerce for
manufactured goods, for luxuries (such as wine and spices), or for raw
materials in which Scotland was deficient (such as iron). And this
trading was in the hands of the burgesses of the new burghs. Significantly, too, we now have, in David I's reign, our earliest known
Scottish coinage – silver pennies, minted at Berwick, Roxburgh,
Edinburgh and other centres – and a ' money economy ' is the basis of
the burghal system.

Undoubtedly there were towns and villages in Scotland before the
rise of the burghs in the twelfth century. Dunfermline, Berwick and
St Andrews, for example, at once spring to mind; and other centres
of settlement must have arisen at places which were important because
of their geographical situations – for example, Stirling, with its crossing
of the Forth – or places with good harbours at the mouths of navigable
rivers. But the burgh was not simply an earlier town or village which
had grown larger or more important. The burgh was something
entirely different. By royal grant, confirmed by royal charter, a
settlement was given a new status – the status of a burgh. It might be an
old settlement, or it might be (and often was) a new settlement which
had grown up by the new castle. Or the king might even ' plan ' an
entirely new burgh, to be built at the time of the building of his castle
(much as ' new towns ', like Glenrothes, were planned in the years

---

[1] The sheep's skin with the wool still on it.

following the second World War), and inducements might be offered to merchants to settle there. The burgh, in effect, did not arise or grow. The burgh was made. A place or a settlement became a burgh only when the king had made it one, only when he had 'erected' it into a burgh, only when he had conferred that status upon it. Then it was the king's burgh: it was on the king's land, its burgesses were the king's men, its rents were the king's rents, it was subject to the supervision of the king's officers. This new status of being a burgh was, moreover, largely a legal concept – for the burgesses of a burgh enjoyed special laws and privileges; the 'laws' of the burghs were different from the law of the land.

If we look at the erections of these early king's burghs (or 'royal burghs' as they later came to be called) we find that practically every one of them was adjacent to one of the king's new castles. This was only natural. The king's castle was an administrative centre: to it would be brought the surplus products from the royal lands as well as the royal rents that were levied in kind. But the king's castle also ensured the king's peace and could provide protection. Merchants and traders began to cluster beside it and soon formed a supply-centre for the castle's needs,[1] and, in due course, a market-centre for the castle's area, the sheriffdom. Thus, at first, there tended to be one royal castle and one royal burgh in each sheriffdom; and, in the reigns of William and Alexander II we find the king granting to a number of his burghs a monopoly of trade over the whole area of their respective sheriffdoms.[2]

At the end of the reign of David I at least fifteen of these new burghs had been erected in Scotland, and steadily their number increased – doubtless in royal endeavours to stimulate trade, for, from his burghs, and from trade, the king received a useful revenue in hard cash. Moreover, in addition to increasing the number of their 'royal' burghs, the kings, from David I onwards, gave leave to a number of abbeys, cathedrals and great lay lords to have burghs of their own. David I, for example, gave leave to the abbey of Holyrood to have its own burgh (Canongate) adjacent to the king's burgh (Edinburgh); he gave

[1] Many of the early plans of the burghs show the main street running direct to the castle, that is, to the centre which the burgh first served. This can be seen in the early 'lay-out' of, for example, Edinburgh, Banff, Berwick, Elgin, Forres and Inverness. In a like way the three main streets of St Andrews converge on the cathedral and priory.

[2] Possibly also to other burghs whose records have been lost. It may well be that all the 'head burghs' of sheriffdoms received such a privilege.

leave to the bishop of St Andrews to found a burgh there. Thus, in addition to the king's burghs there were soon episcopal burghs, abbatial burghs and baronial burghs – of which three groups typical examples are St Andrews and Glasgow, Arbroath and Kelso, Kirkintilloch and Dunbar. But for many centuries the king's burghs were the most important, while the other burghs merely provided local markets for local needs.

Both castle and burgh were new: and the new burghs were settlements of new men, or of men who had broken away from the feudal ties of lord and land.[1] William of Newburgh, writing in the closing years of the twelfth century, says that ' the towns and burghs of the Scottish realm are known to be inhabited by English '; but, from the records themselves, including lists of the names of burgesses, we know that these new burghs were inhabited also by Flemings (who were great mediaeval traders), Normans, Anglo-Danes, and Scots. And, like the castle, the burgh was a strong-point – its very name, derived from *burh*, *burg*, means a fortified enclosure.[2] For not only was it a settlement of new men but also its wealth lay in movable goods which could be easily looted and carried away. Like the castle it was ' timbered ' with its palisade, and it had a fosse or an earthen wall with ' ports ' or ' bows ' which could be securely closed at night or when danger threatened. We read that King William agreed with his burgesses of Inverness that, when he had made a fosse around the burgh, the burgesses would erect thereon a stout palisade which they would keep in sound repair to enclose their burgh. There are many other references to burgh defences, and ' watch and ward ' was a duty always imposed upon every burgess. Both castle and burgh were units in a new royal administration intended to colonise and to hold the land.[3]

Because the burgh was an enclosed strong-point, it was what we should call today a ' built-up area '. It was the duty of the new burgess

---

[1] Cf. *infra*, p. 115, where it is noted that the man who has lived in a burgh unchallenged for a year and a day cannot thereafter be claimed by a lord.

[2] Possibly the importance soon attached to ' The Four Burghs ' – Berwick, Roxburgh, Edinburgh and Stirling (*infra*, p. 119) – may reflect an importance that had formerly belonged to them as [Anglian] *burhs* built and fortified at an earlier time. All four stood at points of the highest strategic importance; two of them carry the word *burh* in their names; and two of them (Berwick and Roxburgh) are, as we have seen, the earliest Scottish burghs on record.

[3] The idea of the burgh as a colony to help to civilise a difficult part long continued. As late as 1597, for example, parliament ordered three burghs to be erected and built in Kintyre, Lochaber and Lewis for ' civility and policy ' in those parts. And ' policy ' here means what we would now call ' improvement '.

to build his ' tenement ' within a stated period of time (usually one year), and the ' back ' of his ' land ' (his ' burgage holding ') had also to be well secured so that it formed, with the ' backs ' of his neighbours, a further line of defence. Outside the burgh, however, there were cultivated lands (worked in run-rig) and common grazings – often later referred to in such phrases as ' the town's acres ', the ' burgh muir ', ' the burgess acres ', and so forth – and many a burgh, like Aberdeen, had ' burgh fishings '. These lands and fishings were granted to the burgesses and the burgh by the king. Often they are said to have been granted ' for the support of the burgh '; and it is amply evident that the early burgess was a farmer as well as a trader. And naturally so, for a group of people concentrated together in a settlement could not rely solely upon the victuals which might be brought to their market from the surrounding countryside.

From his burghs, as we have said, the king drew a revenue in hard cash. He drew a money-rent from each burgage holding, from each ' land ' held by a burgess, which was usually fixed at fivepence from every ' rood ',[1] though in some burghs other rents were prescribed, such as sixpence or a shilling. He drew the revenue from the tolls or ' petty customs ' paid by produce which was brought for sale at the burgh market, and, probably from the latter part of the thirteenth century, he drew the ' great customs ', or export dues, which, in the seaport burghs, were paid upon the wool, wool-fells, skins and hides that were traded overseas.[2] The issues of justice were the king's, and, because the burgh was the king's burgh on the king's lands, the burgesses might be called upon to pay *auxilia* to the king, special payments to meet the king's special needs.

In all this the king secured local control through his own officer – possibly, at first, the sheriff in the adjoining castle; central control was exercised by the Chamberlain who, in theory if not always in practice, passed on his ayre from burgh to burgh ascertaining that justice had been done in the burgh court ' alike to the poor and the rich ', hearing appeals from the decisions of the burgh court, and, above all, ensuring that the king's revenues from his burghs duly reached the royal coffers. So, while the castle was the centre of the royal authority in the sheriffdom, the burgh was the centre for the royal receipts from trade.

But, if the new burgh were to survive, to attract a population and

---

[1] Not the ' rood ' of agriculture, but the ' burgh rood ' which, according to an early ' law ', meant a frontage of twenty feet – though other differing frontages are to be found.   [2] But see *infra*, p. 117, n. 1.

to develop and grow, inducements were necessary. Partly the protection afforded by the neighbouring castle together with the enjoyment of the king's peace was in itself an attraction; in addition, the newcomer was offered a ' period of peaceful sitting ' (sometimes called *kirset*), usually one year,[1] which was allowed for the building of his tenement and during which he paid no rent. But more than this was necessary, particularly if the burgh were to attract men from the landward areas as well as ' new men ' of foreign origin. Above all, the burgh's trading activities (in sale and delivery of goods, settlement of debt, contracts and agreements, and so forth) required a law and a procedure far different from the feudal law of the land. So, because of their particular needs, the burghs were quickly given particular rights and special privileges; they were given their own ' customs ' which formed a burgh law. And in this Scotland borrowed much from England and the continent.[2]

In the burghs if, perchance, a man had lived there unchallenged for a year and a day, he could henceforth live there freely; no lord could claim him as his ' man '. In the burghs the burgess held his toft and tenement as freely as he held his goods. The only burden upon his land was the payment of his rent. A year-and-a-day's possession of a toft and tenement (a ' land ') without challenge gave him full right thereto. He could divide his holding. He could marry, and give his children in marriage, without seeking the leave of any lord or paying any feudal render. His heir paid no relief; if he died leaving his children minors, wardship was governed by the burgh customs and not by feudal law. He was free in his person and could come and go as he wished. Above all, he enjoyed and could claim the jurisdiction of his own burgh court which had special procedures and special laws to meet his own particular needs, and which imposed fixed monetary penalties to which he knew he was subject. The travelling merchant, for example, would want his action to be settled quickly so that he could move on to the next burgh he wished to visit. So the action of the travelling merchant

---

[1] Though in remote or dangerous parts a longer period of ' rent-free sitting ' might be offered: in Dumbarton, five years was offered, and, in Dingwall, ten years.

[2] Trading contacts not only provided knowledge of the laws and privileges of the burghs in other lands, but also necessitated some uniformity in a ' mercantile ' law. The travelling merchant, to be encouraged, must not be subject to arbitrary laws; he must be reasonably aware of the laws which govern his activities. Trade will be encouraged if the laws of trade are more or less the same in all burghs in all lands. Moreover, because the burghs had direct contacts with one another, when one burgh enjoyed a particular privilege other burghs would be quick to claim a like privilege for themselves.

had to be settled 'within three tides' (or thirty-six hours). Again, in the burgh court there was greater reliance upon the *witnesses* to a transaction: two witnesses were sufficient to prove the payment or receipt of any sum.

The possession of a court, with its own special laws and procedures (to which all the burgesses of the burgh were subject, and in which all, as suitors, at first took part), as well as the possession of a trading monopoly over the area of the sheriffdom and of lands and rights held in common, all bound the burgh together as a 'community'. Frequently the early burgh is referred to as a *communitas*. The new burgess, upon his admission, takes an oath to be 'leel and feel' to the king *and to* the community of the burgh. At the time of his oath he must possess a house (or find a pledge that he will build a house within a year); and his house becomes a 'gage' for his performance of common duties and for his observance of 'good neighbourhood' (*vicinitas*) towards his fellow burgesses. If he fails therein, his house may be destroyed, thus making it impossible for him to remain within the community.

Again, at the beginning of the thirteenth century we begin to read of burgh seals. The burgh seal could be affixed to a document in the name of the community; the burgh seal could bind the community to take certain action, or to pay a given sum. In 1296, when the treaty of alliance between Scotland and France was ratified, the seals of the communities of six burghs (Aberdeen, Perth, Stirling, Edinburgh, Roxburgh and Berwick) were affixed to the ratification, binding those burghs (and possibly through them all the king's burghs) to maintain and implement the treaty's terms.

This sense of a community, moreover, was strengthened by the fact that the burgh soon became self-governing. At first, as we have seen, it was apparently administered by a royal official, but, possibly as early as the reign of William, the officers of the burgh were elected annually by the burgesses themselves from among their own number. According to the 'laws' of the burgh, and certainly as early as the reign of Robert I, the election took place at the 'head court' held at Michaelmas, when all the burgesses were expected to be present; and at that 'head court' the burgh's 'acts' (its by-laws as we should call them today) were also confirmed by the community, and any new 'acts' were approved. The officers of the burgh, elected from among the burgesses themselves, usually came to include a provost, bailies, sergeands, liners, tasters of wine and ale, and apprisers of flesh. The liners were responsible for defining the boundaries of burgage holdings within the burgh (and in a burgh a 'land' was always defined and referred to by the street in which it lay and by the names of the owners of the 'lands' on either side of it); the tasters of wine and ale and the apprisers of flesh were appointed to ensure that the quality was maintained and that fair prices were charged. The provost (or alderman) was the head of the community; the bailies presided over the burgh court (having the sergeands to help them in making summons and in ensuring that the court's decisions were carried out) and were also responsible to the king for the burgh's finances.

In finance, too, the sense of a community was further strengthened when the burgh received what is known as 'feu-ferme' status. At first, all the issues or 'fermes' of a burgh – the individual rents of the burgages, the petty tolls and customs, the profits of justice, and so forth – were collected and accounted for separately. Then, in certain burghs, we find the chamberlain fixing a definite sum to be paid annually by the burgh for a stated number of years in place of all the individual rents and other issues, leaving the burgesses to make their own arrangements for the raising of the annual amount. Finally, the king began to grant charters to his burghs whereby in future, and *in perpetuity*, this or that burgh would pay an annual fixed sum in lieu of all its issues – except, however, the great customs on exports which were still to be collected and accounted for separately.[1] Under such a charter the burgh acquired 'feu-ferme' status; it paid a 'ferme' annually and in perpetuity for its 'feu' from the king. Aberdeen was the first to receive this privilege, in a charter granted by Robert I, in 1319, for a ferme of £213 6s. 8d. Berwick received a charter in 1320 (for a ferme of £333 6s. 8d.), and Edinburgh in 1329 (for a ferme of £34 13s. 4d.); and by the end of the fourteenth century most of the important burghs had been granted a like privilege. Sometimes, though not always, the fixed sum laid down in the charter was higher than the previous total of the separate issues,[2] for the king was allowing for growth and development; but, as we shall see, there was to be a rapid decrease in the value of money, mainly through debasement of the coinage,[3] and, with the fall in the value of money, the burghs that were fortunate enough to hold a charter of feu-ferme benefited enormously, with a correspondingly enormous loss to the royal exchequer.

[1] The great customs on the export of wool, woolfells and hides were always kept separate and distinct from the issues of the burgh and were accounted for in exchequer by special officers, for each seaport burgh, known as custumars (*custumarii*).

[2] Thus the amounts fixed in the charters of feu-ferme do not necessarily reflect the relative importance of the burghs concerned.   [3] Cf. *infra*, p. 231.

This burgh community, largely self-governing and, before long, often financially autonomous, included both the merchants who traded, buying locally and selling overseas, and the craftsmen who served the day-to-day needs of the burgh (such as the masons, wrights, skinners, weavers, bonnet-makers, tailors, bakers and fleshers[1]), together with their families, apprentices, and menial[2] servants. And, at first, both merchants and craftsmen were apparently equal members of the community. In the earliest burgh accounts rendered at exchequer we find soutars, tailors, dyers, weavers, bakers and so forth in office as *prepositi* or *ballivi* of burghs. But, in the reign of David II, all that was to change.

The charters of privilege granted in the reigns of William and Alexander II, whereby this or that burgh was given a monopoly of trade within the area of the sheriffdom in which it stood, were, strictly, charters to the *merchants* giving them a monopoly in the manufacture of, and trade in, cloth, and in the purchase and sale of hides and wool. In the latter half of the thirteenth century, however, the manufacture and trade in cloth declined; and early in the fourteenth century the *merchants* were claiming only a monopoly in buying and selling wool, woolfells and hides. But the overseas trade of the merchants increased the revenues of the king and the bullion of the kingdom – through the customs dues on their exports and the profits of their trade. Thus the craftsmen, who worked with their hands and merely served local needs, came to be regarded as men of lesser standing in the burghs and men of lesser importance in national affairs; and because of that, the merchants gradually gained more and more control in the affairs of the burghs and were granted more and more power in burghal administration – particularly when, in the middle of the fourteenth century, large sums of money had to be found for the ransom of David II. Then money could be raised from the burghs only through the activities of the merchants; because of that only the merchants mattered; and so the merchants became the real rulers in the burghs and the craftsmen soon had little or no voice in burgh affairs.[3]

Finally, because the ' law ' of the burghs was different from the law of the land, the burghs had their own ' parliament ' which, in hearing

---

[1] It is interesting to note how many modern surnames are derived from the exercise of a craft – Webster, a weaver; Cordiner, a shoemaker; Lorimer, a maker of horse-trappings; and Fuller, Mason, Wright, Skinner, Taylor, Baxter, Potter, Glover. It is also strange to note how the old Scottish term *Flesher* is giving way to the English *Family Butcher* – surely a murderous occupation.

[2] i.e. of his ' *mesnie* ', or household. [3] See *infra*, chap xxiv.

and deciding cases that came before it, declared the law of the burghs, just as the king's High Court of Parliament declared the law of the land. Before this 'parliament' of the burghs, known as the Court of the Four Burghs, and presided over by the chamberlain, went disputes between the burghs as well as appeals from the burgh courts and the chamberlain's ayre. The earliest record evidence for the Court of the Four Burghs is to be found in 1292[1] when a question relating to the interpretation of the 'law' of the burghs with regard to debt was referred to 'the four burghs'; and in 1296 the burgesses of Berwick, Edinburgh, Roxburgh and Stirling made a declaration with regard to the law of 'heirship goods'.[2]

The 'Four Burghs' were thus Berwick, Edinburgh, Roxburgh and Stirling; but in 1369, because of continued English occupation of Berwick and Roxburgh, those two burghs were replaced by Lanark and Linlithgow. Later, the Court of the Four Burghs was enlarged to include representatives of more than the Four Burghs, and, probably in emulation of it, there emerged the Convention of Royal Burghs.[3] But, whatever the constitution of the Court, it served to stress and to maintain the position of the burghs as communities which were somehow different and which were outside the feudal law and the feudal administration of the rest of the king's land.[4]

[1] That is was then functioning almost certainly indicates an earlier origin.

[2] That is, the goods to which the heir was entitled to succeed as of right.

[3] See *infra*, pp. 185-6.

[4] The various returns to the Exchequer at the end of the reign of Robert I show that at that time there were five important and relatively wealthy burghs – Berwick, Aberdeen, Edinburgh, Perth and Dundee – while all the others were a long way behind, much smaller and less prosperous.

The amount ingathered from the burghs towards the three annual payments of £6,666 13s. 4d. due under the treaty of 1328 (*infra*, p. 172) also provides an indication of the place of the burghs at that time in the national economy. The burghs as a whole compounded with the Chamberlain for three annual payments of £333 6s. 8d.; and this small sum (although a bargain for the burghs) is in striking contrast to, roughly, £5,000 annually from the lay holders of land and, roughly, £2,000 from the Church. (And for the contribution from the burghs to national taxations at a later period, see *infra*, p. 298, note.)

Thus the early Scottish burghs must have been small in size. We have few figures upon which to work, but it would appear that the population of Berwick in 1296, when it was sacked by Edward I, was only about 1,500. Edinburgh seems to have had about 400 houses in the reign of David II; and Stirling had only about 1,500 inhabitants in 1550. In most of the mediaeval burghs the population would probably number only a few hundreds, and in some cases only a hundred or less.

CHAPTER XIII

The Mediaeval Church - I

FOLLOWING THE decision at the Synod of Whitby[1] the church in northern Britain rapidly accepted obedience to Rome. The Roman usage was adopted by Nechtan, king of the Picts; Iona conformed; before 731 Candida Casa was erected into a bishopric subject to York; and in 735 Egbert, archbishop of York, received the *pallium*[2] from the Pope. Then came the Danish-Norwegian invasions. In the north, Orkney and Shetland, the Western Isles, and the modern counties of Caithness, Sutherland and Ross were seized and held by the Norse; to the south, a great pagan wedge soon stretched across northern England from sea to sea; to the west, in Ireland, a Danish kingdom, with its centre in Dublin, was established and consolidated. To a large extent Scotland was isolated. She was separated from southern England, and a pagan sea-power could cut her communications with Ireland and the continent. Towards the end of the ninth century we have a lone reference to the *ecclesia Scoticana*, but it was a church deprived of real contact with Western Christendom and Rome.

When we have fuller evidence of this ' Scottish church ' we find at St Andrews a community of clergy, maintained by family succession, whose members could hold personal property, and whose life was said to be shaped ' in accordance with their own ideas ' rather than with the ' precepts of the holy fathers '. The clergy serving this church were called Célidé[3] or ' Culdees '; there were also known Culdee communities at Lochleven, Monifieth, Brechin, Muthill, Monymusk, Abernethy and Iona; and it was some of the ' traditions ' of the Culdees that Margaret, the Saxon queen of Malcolm III, strove to correct.

The Célidé were the descendants of an eighth-century anchorite movement, in the Celtic (Irish) church, which was a movement for revival and reform, and led to the drawing up of ' rules ' defining the

---

[1] *Supra*, p. 48.

[2] A band of white lamb's wool (from lambs presented by the nuns of the Convent of St Agnes at Rome) adorned with purple crosses, and consecrated at St Peter's. At first granted by the popes as a mark of honour, it was in due course conferred upon all metropolitans, primates and archbishops as a symbol of the jurisdiction delegated to them by the Holy See, and an archbishop was not allowed to exercise the functions pertaining to his office until he had applied for, and received, the *pallium*.

[3] Servants of God.

true monastic way of life. Thus the Célidé exercised a disciplined life (with the possibility of greater seclusion by the withdrawal of individual members into solitary places and the living of an eremitic life), and their monasteries became more properly colleges of secular priests, somewhat similar to the minsters in England. By the time of Margaret, however, there were certainly other clergy in the Celtic church, individual priests who were not Célidé (Culdees), and in the time of Margaret's sons the whole corporate framework of the Culdees began to collapse.

The importance of Margaret's work, however, does not lie in the changes she secured, for they were few and touched neither the organisation nor the administration of the church – though we know she was in correspondence with Lanfranc (the exponent of reform in England), and at Dunfermline she founded the first Benedictine house in Scotland. Yet there is no indication that she called for reforms such as clerical celibacy or the dispossession of the lay holders of church property.[1] Indeed, one of Margaret's own sons, Ethelred, became abbot of Dunkeld ; and both Margaret and Malcolm gave benefactions to the Culdee community of Lochleven. If we are to trust the contemporary account of her confessor, Turgot, Margaret concerned herself mainly with certain points of observance, such as the date of the beginning of Lent, the use of certain ' barbarous rites ' in the celebration of mass, and the scruples of the Scottish clergy who regarded themselves as ' unworthy ' to take the sacrament on Easter Day – all observances in which the Scottish church differed from Rome, and every difference probably arising only from the long severance of contact with Rome.

But Margaret's ' reforms', arising from her contacts with England, were important in that they marked the beginning of a change – a change to be continued and expedited by her sons, and notably by David I, whereby in every way, in organisation, in administration and in observances, the church in Scotland was brought into line with the churches of England and the continent. And, under David, the reformed, reorganised church was used to further and to support the royal reorganisation of the state.

In his reform of the church David adopted a two-fold policy: he encouraged the foundation of new religious houses which were within the great continental orders, principally Cistercian monasteries and

---

[1] Indeed, the Celtic church in Scotland had now become so largely laicised that probably those of the clergy who still continued the services of the church in the various monasteries were now called Culdees, and the name may even have been applied to groups of clergy who had never been true Célidé.

Augustinian priories; and he restored old episcopal seats, and founded new ones.

Side by side with certain old Culdee communities David promoted new communities of Augustinian canons,[1] and there the new communities gradually supplanted the old. Under David, Augustinians were established at St Andrews and St Serf's (Lochleven) – where there were Culdee communities – and at Holyrood, Jedburgh and Cambuskenneth; while in the thirteenth century Augustinians were established in place of the Culdee communities at Monymusk and Abernethy. At St Andrews, for example, an Augustinian priory was founded, with David's support, in 1144, and in 1147 the Pope granted the canons the right to elect the bishops of St Andrews while at the same time he decreed that upon the death of any Culdee his place was to be taken by an Austin canon.[2] To the Culdees of Lochleven David offered the choice either of accepting the Augustinian rule and becoming canons, or of being expelled from the island. At other ecclesiastical centres, like Dunblane, Dunkeld and Brechin (which also may have had Culdee communities), David seems to have restored bishops' seats and, with the restoration or the new erection of other sees, the kingdom of Scotland was divided into ten dioceses[3] with bishops elected by the cathedral ' chapters ', or by the local clergy, but in both cases almost certainly under royal influence.[4]

In addition to canons regular, who might serve as the clergy of a cathedral (as they did at St Andrews and Whithorn[5]), and who combined the disciplined life of a ' rule '[6] with their work as clergy, David

[1] The Augustinian (Austin) canons were probably the nearest Roman parallel to the Culdees for, although living according to a rule, they were not cloistered monks but canons who could go outside their precinct to serve neighbouring churches. Their first priories in Scotland were founded by Alexander I at Scone and, possibly at Inchcolm.

[2] These provisions were not fully carried out. The Culdees of St Andrews were transformed into the collegiate church of St Mary of the Rock and, as such, claimed some share in episcopal elections until the middle of the thirteenth century.

[3] About 1190 the number became eleven, when Lismore (Argyll) was separated from Dunkeld. In 1472, when St Andrews was erected into an archbishopric, Whithorn (Galloway) was transferred from the province of York to that of St Andrews, and the bishopric of Orkney and the bishopric of the Isles were also transferred from the province of Nidaros (Trondheim, Norway) to St Andrews. Thereby the Scottish dioceses, numbering thirteen, all came within the obedience of St Andrews. In 1492 when Glasgow was erected into an archbishopric, Whithorn, Dunkeld, Dunblane and Lismore were transferred from St Andrews to the province of Glasgow (Cf. infra, p. 273). [4] See infra, pp. 138-40.

[5] At St Andrews, Augustinians; at Whithorn, Premonstratensians, a reformed branch of the Augustinians. [6] See infra, pp. 128-9.

also encouraged the foundation of houses of the great monastic orders, houses of cloistered monks. He himself founded the second[1] of such houses in Scotland, at Selkirk, persuading twelve monks from Tiron, together with their abbot, to come there[2]; and during his reign, mainly through his initiative and always with his support, houses of Cistercians (White Monks) were founded at Melrose, Newbattle, Dundrennan, Kinloss and Holmecultram (now in Cumberland). In the words of Wyntoun,

> He illumynyd in his dayis
> His landys wyth Kyrkys and wyth abbayis,

and the number and nature of his foundations 'must rank as the most remarkable of any Scottish monarch, or indeed of any monarch of the age'. Under his immediate successors, moreover, further abbeys were founded (in two instances by the king himself) at Paisley and Crossraguel (both Cluniac houses), at Coupar-Angus, Culross, Glenluce, Balmerino, Sweetheart and Deer (all Cistercian houses), and at Arbroath, Lindores and Kilwinning (all Tironensian houses); while at Ardchattan, Pluscarden and Beauly priories were founded of the Order of Vallis Caulium.

In all this, although there was much piety, there was also much political wisdom. While the sheriff's castle displayed the strength of the king, the strength of the secular arm, the cathedral churches and the monastic houses were indicative of the power of God; with the humbler parish churches they exerted a spiritual influence towards the maintenance of order and stability. The bishops' seats and the new monastic houses were counterparts to the king's castles in helping to weld Scotland together. The bishop and the abbot or prior were the 'king's men' supporting the king's policy in the outlying parts of his kingdom[3]; like the king's sheriffs and officers of state, they tended to be Anglo-Normans; and many of the religious houses were 'colonised' from England.[4] Moreover, bishops, abbots and priors were all im-

---

[1] Bearing in mind Margaret's earlier foundation of a Benedictine house at Dunfermline.

[2] In 1128 the abbey was moved from Selkirk to Kelso.

[3] Though it is doubtful whether the bishops of far-distant Caithness or Argyll could exert much influence on behalf of the Scottish king. John, bishop of Caithness, had his tongue cut out (and according to the *Orkneyinga Saga*, was also blinded) on the orders of the Earl of Orkney and Caithness in 1200 or 1201; and Adam, his successor, was murdered at his episcopal manor of Halkirk in 1222.

[4] The Augustinian houses of Holyrood, Scone, and possibly St Andrews were founded from Merton (Surrey) and Nostell (Yorkshire); the Premonstratensian house

portant members of the king's council (and later of parliament) and, as men of learning, they could fill important offices of state and they could be sent on embassies abroad. So it was important in every way that they should be men who saw eye-to-eye with the king; so, in due course, we shall see that an earlier indefinite royal control became regularised, and that whenever a vacancy occurred in a bishopric the king's permission had to be obtained before the cathedral chapter could proceed to an election, and the king's approval of the bishop-elect had to be given before consecration was sought.

Within the dioceses, the smaller divisions of parishes, each under a parish priest, gradually took shape. As churches were built, so they served areas around them, and in due course, those areas became parishes – that is, the district served by a 'baptismal church', a church with a priest who could administer the sacraments of baptism and marriage and perform the rites of burial, and who was subject to the 'visitation' of the bishop of the diocese within which the parish lay. Often the feudal baron would build a church on his lands, would endow it, and, acting as its patron, would himself appoint the priest. In the spirit of the times he would do this almost automatically – for the weal of his soul and the souls of his ancestors and his family. He himself would be buried there, and masses for his soul would be said there. His wife, his son, his son's son, and so forth would also be buried there and masses said for their souls. In due course that particular feudal holding of lands tended to become a parish; and later we often find that barony and parish are identical. But, although the dioceses had taken definite shape in the reign of David I, the building of churches, the growth of the parish system and the provision of parochial clergy were slow and sporadic; a new parish system had to be fitted into, or to supersede, and older organisation that was possibly based upon the Celtic monasteries; and parishes emerged and became defined more rapidly in Lothian and the eastern coastal plain than elsewhere.

The exaction of tithes from a particular area for a particular church (enforced by David I and Malcolm IV) undoubtedly helped to define the early parishes. For, in addition to any endowment of lands that a church might enjoy, together with the offerings (oblations) of the faithful, it was also supported by the payment of tithes (or teinds) – a

at Dryburgh was a 'daughter' of Alnwick (Northumberland); and all the Cistercian houses were founded either direct from Rievaulx (Yorkshire) or through Melrose or Dundrennan.

payment of one-tenth of all 'increase', for while man planted it was God who gave the increase. So payment was made (and could be enforced) of a tithe of all crops, a tithe of the offspring of animals (calculated according to a monetary scale), a tithe of milk, butter, cheese and eggs and, with the growth of trade, a tithe of the profits of merchandise and craftsmanship. And the area of exaction for the support of a church was the area of its parish.

Yet, just when the new parochial system was taking shape, and the church was becoming organised in dioceses and parishes, there arose a passion to support the monasteries and other religious houses and, as it happened, they were supported at the expense of the parishes. Lands, rights (fishing rights, hunting rights, trading rights), exemptions (from tolls, from customs and so forth), and monetary grants (from the king's treasury, from the rents of burghs and from the profits of justice) were showered upon the monasteries; the great nobles followed the example of the kings; and these grants to abbeys and priories included also many grants of parish churches.

David I's charter to Holyrood, given between 1128 and 1136, included, in its grants to the abbey, lands in Broughton, Inverleith, Pittendreich and Whitekirk; tofts in the burghs of Stirling, Edinburgh, Berwick and Renfrew; forty shillings a year from the burgh fermes of Edinburgh, a hundred shillings a year from the customs of Perth, and £10 a year from the royal treasury; fishing rights at Stirling, Berwick and Renfrew; freedom from toll and custom in trading throughout the realm; a right to have its own burgh (Canongate); *and also certain churches* (the church of the castle of Edinburgh, the church of St Cuthbert with its chapels at Corstorphine and Liberton, and the church of Airth). In the reign of William, the abbey of Arbroath (founded by that king) was given no less than thirty-four churches; and by 1265 the abbeys of Kelso, Paisley, Holyrood and Arbroath held among them 126 churches. Or again, we find Gilbert, earl of Strathearn, granting to the abbey of Inchaffray (which he had then founded) the [parish] church of Aberuthven (Perthshire) with its tithes, oblations, and other income, and with the land with which it had been endowed by the earl's father and mother – and the church of Aberuthven was only one of five churches given at that time (c. 1200) by Earl Gilbert to Inchaffray for its support.

In assigning a church, a lay patron may have been moved not only by an endeavour to secure the weal of his soul, but also by a feeling that the priest could more appropriately be appointed by the religious house; and in a number of early instances only the right of patronage was assigned. But the practice of 'assigning' or 'appropriating' churches to abbeys and priories quickly developed into an assignment to the religious house for its benefit (*ad proprios usus*). All this was not peculiar to Scotland, but in Scotland it became so common that a definite system of independent parish churches – if such a system had indeed been envisaged – was everywhere frustrated. A monastery might now hold parish churches in far distant parts; Holyrood, for example, held churches in Galloway, and Inchaffray held churches in Argyll. Also, and in a like way, parish churches were frequently assigned to the bishops' seats – perhaps to support a canonry, or for the general support of the cathedral chapter – and, later, to collegiate churches and academic colleges. So what might have been a simple administrative system of church government through dioceses and parishes was rendered complex. More than that, the parish churches soon began to suffer.

Admittedly an 'appropriated' parish church was still served by a priest, but the tithes and endowments all went to the cathedral, abbey, priory or college to which it had been assigned, and out of them the priest was paid a stipend, so becoming a vicar,[1] or deputy. Moreover, while the assignment of a parish church had to receive the consent of the bishop of the diocese within which it lay, and while it was the duty of the bishop to ensure that 'a decent maintenance' (in the thirteenth century fixed at a minimum of ten merks a year[2]) was provided for the priest, the records reveal that often this minimum payment was not provided, even when the revenues of the church were amply sufficient. The cathedral, abbey or priory was tempted to enrich itself at the expense of the parish. Gradually the appropriated churches were regarded more and more as the yielders of revenue; their priests were underpaid,[3] and all too often they were men of small ability. So, while the parishes were neglected or ill-served, the cathedrals, abbeys and priories, with their many endowments and their enjoyment of many assigned churches, became possessed of enormous wealth.

On the eve of the Reformation, in the middle of the sixteenth

[1] In some cases vicars received the 'lesser tithes' or 'vicarage tithes' in place of a stipend; always they received the oblations – and hence, to some extent, the later rapacity in their demands.

[2] Ten merks, or £6 13s. 4d., was probably a sufficient maintenance at that time, for the exchequer accounts show that then a cow could be bought for 4s., a pig for 2s., and a hen for a penny.

[3] In 1549 the minimum stipend was raised to twenty merks, and in 1559 to

century, nearly nine-tenths of the parish churches in Scotland had been assigned to religious houses, to bishops' seats, and to collegiate churches and academic colleges. Then many a parish church, often in ill repair, and often served by an illiterate underpaid priest, had long since ceased to meet the spiritual needs of the people, while, on the other hand, many prelacies, too well endowed, were enjoyed by men who were unworthy and who had sought promotion to high office largely through a desire to live in luxury and ease. So arose two of the many causes which led to the call for reform in the church.

twenty-four merks; but these belated increases were far from sufficient to meet the greatly increased cost of living. Moreover, on the eve of the Reformation some vicarages still had less than the old minimum of ten merks.

CHAPTER XIV

Monks and Friars

THE FOUNDING of the monasteries of Subiaco and Monte Cassino by St Benedict early in the sixth century marked the beginning of a monastic movement which rapidly spread throughout western Europe. When the barbarians were overrunning the west, the monasteries were ' retreats ' into which men could go to lead a Christian life away from the ills and evils of the world.

The Benedictine monks, having taken the vows of poverty, chastity and obedience, and living a corporate life within their own community, followed a ' rule ' laid down by St Benedict.[1] Their house was ' a school for the service of God '; their first duty was worship, which was ' the work of God '; thereafter their hours were to be employed in manual labour or study, and in manual labour they became ardent agriculturalists. The monk and the community were bound together; a monk, once admitted to a monastery, lived and died there. In this the Benedictines differed from the Irish monks who went out from their monasteries to act as missionaries or to lead hermit lives.

Later, when Europe had become more settled, monasteries were still founded as houses of God – a very profusion of foundations took place in the eleventh and twelfth centuries – and they still attracted men with the same idea of a retreat from the world. Then, in addition to ' the work of God ', they became centres of education and scholarship, and much of our knowledge of mediaeval times comes from the chronicles kept by monastic houses – as, for example, in Scotland, the chronicle kept by the abbey of Melrose. The monks also encouraged the crafts of masonry, woodcarving, metal work and pottery; they improved agricultural methods and cultivated ' waste ' (as at Coupar-Angus and Kinloss); and they provided hospitality for both rich and poor.[2]

[1] So, in the ranks of the clergy, the ' regulars ' were those who were members of an order observing a ' rule ' (as, for example, the Augustinians, or ' canons regular ', and the cloistered monks), while the ' secular clergy ' were those ' living in the world ' (as, for example, the bishops and the parish priests).

[2] Not all monasteries kept a chronicle, maintained a school, and encouraged the arts and learning; and the Cistercians never provided education for the lay brothers. Moreover, in all this there was soon a serious decline. The Scottish evidence, which shows how little was done by the monasteries after the first fervour had died out, is examined in G. G. Coulton, *Scottish Abbeys and Social Life.*

In this more settled period most of the monasteries were at first Cluniac houses, tied to the mother-house of Cluny; but, in the early years of the twelfth century, the Cistercians, with a mother-house at Cîteaux, broke away, observing more strictly the rule of St Benedict and becoming a separate ' Order ' with a different constitution from that of Cluny and a different method of government. There were other differences too. While the Cluniac monks occupied themselves solely with the services in their church, the Cistercians, on the other hand, laid more and more stress on field work and, because they were forbidden to use serf-labour, introduced ' lay-brothers ' (*conversi*) to help with agriculture and sheep-farming and to manage their outlying ' granges '.

The Augustinian Order (Canons Regular) which arose in the middle of the eleventh century was not a monastic order; its members did not live a cloistered life apart from the world. The Augustinians, although they obeyed the so-called ' Rule of St Augustine ', took vows, and lived in a community, were clergy (sometimes of a cathedral – as at St Andrews), and might go outside their community to serve churches within their neighbourhood or churches which had been ' assigned ' to the community. The Premonstratensians (founded in 1120 by St Norbert) were also canons regular who had added their own supplementary statutes to the ' Rule of St Augustine ' in order to follow a life of greater austerity. They too might go outside their community to serve neighbouring churches, and at Whithorn were the clergy of the cathedral.

In Scotland, as we have seen, many of the abbeys belonged to the Cistercian Order; and it is noticeable that they were situated on good agricultural land – in the Tweed valley (Melrose), in the south-west (Dundrennan, Glenluce and Sweetheart), along the Forth (Newbattle and Culross) and in Strathmore (Coupar Angus). What, then, did one of these monasteries look like ? And what was the life led by a Cistercian monk ?

In the first place, the monks were *cloistered*, they were shut in.[1] Their monastery was surrounded by a precinct wall which cut them off from the world. They were ' out of the world ' and all its evil; and within their wall they prayed in their church that their own sins and the sins of the world might be forgiven. These prayers (' choir services ') were their daily task and their chief duty; and the church and the precinct wall were two outward signs and visible tokens of a monastic house.

---

[1] The word *cloister* comes from the Latin *claustra*, from *claudere*, to enclose, to shut in, to cut off.

The Cistercians (observing the rule of St Benedict) praised and prayed seven times a day and had also a service at midnight – so fulfilling two verses of the 119th Psalm, ' At midnight I will rise to give thanks unto thee because of thy righteous judgments ', and ' Seven times a day do I praise thee because of thy righteous judgments '.[1] And because of the midnight service there was a stair-case (the ' night-stair ') leading from the long dormitory (the ' dorter '), in which the monks slept, down into the church, into one of the transepts by the choir. Also because of this midnight service the monks slept clad and girdled.

The plan of one monastery might vary slightly from that of another, but, in general, the plan of every Cistercian house was the same. Within the precinct wall was the church, the monks' dorter and the lay-brothers' dorter (both with their night-stairs, leading into the choir and the nave respectively), the monks' frater and the lay-brothers' frater (the refectories where they ate together), the infirmary, the kitchens, the bakehouse, the malthouse and brewery, the vegetable gardens (mainly peas, beans and herbs) and the orchards. In addition, the monks had a cloister (an enclosed open space with a sheltered walk around it, usually on the south, or sunny side, of the church[2]), a chapter-house for the discussion of business (and so called because every day they met there to hear a chapter of their rule read to them), a parlour where they could talk to one another (for elsewhere, and even at meals, the monks were expected to be sparing in their conversation), and a warming-room, the only room in the monastery where there was a fire – save for the necessary fires in kitchens and bakehouse, and save for a fire in the guest house and possibly also one in the abbot's chamber.[3]

At midnight, then, the monk rose for a service in the church (Vigils, or Nocturns); at dawn he rose again for the service called Matins, or Lauds; and thereafter there were services at roughly three-hour intervals – at the first hour (Prime, 6 a.m. or sunrise), at the third hour (Tierce, 9 a.m.), at Sext (12 o'clock), at None (3 p.m.), at Vespers (6 p.m.) and Compline just before bedtime. The hours, however, might vary at particular seasons or on particular days; and, in general, they were gradually anticipated so that the service of None eventually moved back towards midday and thus gave us our modern word ' noon '.

---

[1] Verses 62, 164. The Psalm is no. 118 in the Vulgate.

[2] At Melrose, owing to the configuration of the ground, the cloister is on the north side of the church. The cloister walk was often used for study.

[3] Though, later, fireplaces are sometimes to be found in the monks' dorters.

In all, these services might take up some six hours of the monks' day.[1]

After Prime, there was an early Mass. After Tierce, the monks assembled in the Chapter House where first of all there was a reading, from the Martyrology, of the account of the saint and martyr commemorated on that particular day, then the reading of a chapter of the Rule, then, if there were one, the hearing of some case of discipline, some instance of a brother who had broken the Rule, and finally, if necessary, a discussion of some business matter that required decision. Thereafter, about 10 a.m., High Mass was celebrated, and, after Mass, the monks sat down to dinner in their frater – though during the autumn and winter the strict Cistercians fasted by omitting dinner and taking only the one other meal of the day, namely supper, which came immediately after Vespers.[2] After supper came Collation, a reading from a work by Johannes Cassianus called *Collationes Patrum*[3]; and thereafter came the last service (Compline) and then bed.

During their free time the monks were expected to work in their gardens or orchards, or at building or woodwork, or perhaps in their scriptorium writing music for their services or adding to their chronicle, or perhaps simply making a copy of some manuscript book. Partly they had to be self-supporting; partly the founder of their order believed in a balance of work and prayer: to him ' idleness was the enemy of the soul '. So the early Cistercians became expert farmers and agricultural improvers, and the different houses exchanged notes with one another, as well as exchanging seeds and cuttings. They were also good craftsmen. Gradually, however, the work within the monastic precinct, as well as the work of the outlying granges (the management of the sheep runs and of the farms on lands conferred upon the monks by the generosity of kings and nobles), was done more and more by the lay-brothers. Thereby the monks lost the balance of prayer and work, and tended to become lazy and corrupt.

[1] The services were in the choir of the church; Mass was celebrated in the presbytery. The lay-brothers had their own shorter services in the nave – usually little more than a repetition of the *Pater Noster* and the *Ave Maria*. In most Scottish houses the laity of the neighbourhood were admitted to the nave, which served as a parish church, and one of the monks, or a secular priest, conducted the parish services there. The nave was separated from the choir by the pulpitum and rood-screen.

[2] A practice grew up, however, of taking an early ' breakfast ' of bread and ale – which was probably necessary for reasons of health.

[3] A series of dialogues showing the way in which the dangers of monastic life (gluttony, unchastity, pride, avarice, apathy, etc.) might be avoided or overcome. Because it later became common for ale and bread to be taken during this reading, the word ' collation ' took its modern meaning of a light meal at an odd hour.

But the monks, cut off from the world and living cloistered lives behind their precinct wall, did nothing to meet the spiritual needs of the people. Nor was the church organisation, by diocese and parish, able at first to meet the needs of the new burghs which were multiplying in number and expanding in size. Moreover, the generosity of kings and nobles had made the monastic houses wealthy and, with their wealth, they had become more closely identified with the rich than with the poor.

Because of all this, early in the thirteenth century the popes blessed the new orders of *friars* who did not cut themselves off from the world, who lived among the people and with the people, who embraced poverty, who preached in the streets and markets, who tended the sick and heard confession, and who gave both spiritual and temporal help to the ordinary folk. In addition, although the orders of friars had their ' houses ' in the burghs, the individual friar could always be sent here, there and everywhere to carry out his work. As opposed to the monk, the friar had ' the whole world for his cloister '.

At first, the friars, embracing poverty, held no possessions either individually or as an order. Unlike the monastic houses, they had at first no corporate endowments. They were entirely dependent upon alms, and so were often called *mendicants*.[1] The most important of these new mendicant orders were the Franciscans (or Grey Friars, or Friars Minor), founded in 1209; the Dominicans (or Black Friars, or Friars Preachers), founded in 1215; and the Carmelites (or White Friars) who, at first eremites, became in the middle of the thirteenth century an order analogous to the Franciscans and Dominicans.[2] The Trinitarians (often called Red Friars), founded in 1198, were more properly canons regular who devoted themselves to the raising of money for ransoming Christians who had been taken captive by the Moors and Saracens – sometimes even offering themselves as captives in exchange.

These orders of friars reached Scotland in the reign of Alexander II,[3] and soon both the Franciscans and Dominicans had houses in

---

[1] Later, however, they began to hold worldly wealth, and, with wealth, corruption tended to creep in.

[2] Likewise the Augustinian Friars, at first eremites, later moved into the towns and became one of the mendicant orders.

[3] The Black Friars were established in Edinburgh in 1230, and the Grey Friars in Berwick in 1231. The first Scottish house of Carmelites, however, was not founded until the reign of Alexander III – at Tullilum, near Perth, 1262 – and there was one house of Augustinian Friars, at Berwick, founded before 1299.

many Scottish burghs. Because the Trinitarians devoted themselves to the release of Christian captives (and also to meeting the needs of pilgrims) their houses were often in important seaport burghs like Aberdeen, Berwick and Dunbar.

If the wealthy lord could grant an endowment of lands to this or that monastery and thereby secure masses for his soul, now even the humblest dweller in the towns could receive the ministrations of a friar. The work of both the monks and the friars was supplementary to that of the secular clergy in parish and diocese.[1]

[1] It should perhaps be added that the nuns, like the monks, lived in a closed community and took vows of observance, but, being debarred from exercising any priestly office, devoted themselves to a life of contemplation. The Scottish nunneries were small, and most of them were of the Cistercian Order.

CHAPTER XV

The Mediaeval Church - II

IN A CHURCH council at Windsor, in 1072, it was agreed between Lanfranc, archbishop of Canterbury, and Thomas, archbishop of York, that all churches from the shores of the Humber to the furthermost limits of Scotland should be within the province of York and their bishops subject to the archbishop of York as their metropolitan.[1] As far as we know, no representative from Scotland was present at this council, though later, in the fourteenth century, it was stated by a chronicler of York that, following the council, Malcolm and Margaret sent Fothad, the last of the Celtic bishops of St Andrews, to Archbishop Thomas at York to profess his obedience to him. Whether or not that statement was an invention of the chronicler (and it probably was),[2] Alexander I (1107-24) definitely rejected the claims of York, and thereafter there ensued a long struggle by the Scottish church, supported by the Scottish kings, to establish and to maintain its independence and its freedom from obedience to the archbishop of York.

The line of Celtic bishops of St Andrews came to an end in 1093 with the death of Fothad. For nearly fifteen years the see remained vacant until, soon after his accession, Alexander I invited Turgot, prior of Durham, and formerly Queen Margaret's confessor, to be bishop of St Andrews. But who was to consecrate the new bishop ? – for canon law required the consecration of a bishop either by his metropolitan or by a papal legate. According to the contemporary chronicler, Symeon of Durham, ' dissensions ' at once arose ' between the church of York and the church of St Andrew of Scotland; for the former demands for herself as by a certain right the ordination and subjection of the primate of the Scots, but the latter on the contrary asserts that she owes nothing by any right of antiquity or custom '. Then, in 1109, a new archbishop of York, Thomas, was consecrated. He at once claimed a right to consecrate Turgot, and, in the same year, Turgot was consecrated by him, though with agreement that the consecration should be without ' subjection, saving the authority of both

---

[1] In the organisation of the Roman church an archbishop who was metropolitan of a province had jurisdiction over all the bishops within his province.

[2] See Alexander I's letter to Ralph, archbishop of Canterbury, in which he says that the agreement was made ' in the absence of us and ours ' (*infra*, p. 135).

churches, so that later a just conclusion should decide the controversy '. With Turgot now consecrated bishop of St Andrews, and now in Scotland, however ' quarrels ' soon arose between the bishop and the king. We do not know what these quarrels were – possibly they were connected with the relation of St Andrews to York, possibly they arose out of the relationship of the church to the king – but apparently they were irreconcilable, and Turgot finally left Scotland, retiring to Durham where he died in 1115.

At this time the see of York was again vacant,[1] and Alexander I at once wrote to Archbishop Ralph of Canterbury asking for his advice and assistance. In this letter, the king declared that ' the bishops of the church of St Andrews in ancient times used not to be consecrated save by the Roman pontiff himself or by the archbishop of Canterbury. This we have adhered to, and have established by authority ' though Archbishop Lanfranc, ' by what agreement we know not, and in the absence of us and ours ', placed the church in obedience to York; ' but we permit that by no means to continue any longer, being supported, if it please you, by your authority '. Finally, in 1120, at Alexander I's request, and despite a letter addressed to the bishops of Scotland in 1119 by Pope Calixtus II ordering them to give canonical obedience to the archbishop of York and commanding that ' no one henceforth be consecrated as bishop in your churches save by your metropolitan the archbishop of York, or by his permission ', Archbishop Ralph of Canterbury, with the agreement of King Henry I, sent Eadmer, a monk of Canterbury, to Scotland where he was elected as bishop of St Andrews. But again difficulties arose over the bishop's consecration. Eadmer wished to be consecrated by the archbishop of Canterbury; the archbishop of York insisted upon his right; while Alexander I was determined to be king in all things in his kingdom and would not agree to any other authority having any power therein.[2] And within a year Eadmer had returned to Canterbury.

Upon Eadmer's death in 1124, Alexander I promptly chose as his successor Robert, who, although a Yorkshireman, was prior of the Augustinian house at Scone.[3] This was clearly a choice of a Scottish churchman, and Robert was duly elected. But again, who was to consecrate the new bishop? Alexander I died a few months after

[1] Archbishop Thomas had died in 1114 and Archbishop Thurstan was not consecrated until 1119.

[2] This is a rough paraphrase of the attitude of the King of Scots as explained to Eadmer by John, bishop of Glasgow.

[3] See *supra*, p. 122, n. 1.

Robert's election, and David I, who succeeded his brother on the throne, was equally determined that the Scottish church should be independent and free. Robert, too, refused to acknowledge the archbishop of York as his metropolitan. There were four years of argument and when, finally, Robert was consecrated by Thurstan, archbishop of York, the consecration was ' without profession of obedience, saving the claim of the church of York and saving the just right of the church of St Andrew '.

Meantime, in 1126, David I had endeavoured to solve the whole problem with a request to the Pope that St Andrews should be erected into a metropolitan see with Scotland as its province; but, owing to English opposition, the request was refused.

In all this the issues were far deeper than the obedience of the Scottish church to York. Alexander I, David I, and their immediate successors were insistent upon the independence of the Scottish church because, under the new feudal administration in Scotland, church and state were closely inter-related. The cathedral chapters and the monastic houses held vast extents of lands; they had jurisdiction over the tenants on their lands. No king could allow a lord, lay or spiritual, holding many lands within his realm, to be too greatly subject to an overlord in another realm. More than that, the church, through its spiritual work, had a great influence over the lives and thoughts of the people; while its bishops, abbots and priors, by virtue of their office, had voice in the king's council and, as learned men, frequently filled high offices in the state. How then could the Scottish king allow the Scottish church to be subject to the directions of an English metro-politan ? Even if Scotland and England enjoyed friendly relations, there was still the danger that the churchmen might be influenced by England; if Scotland and England were in opposition, it was vital that the church should support the state.

Under Alexander I this struggle for the independence of the Scottish church had taken place in relation to St Andrews; under David I there was a long and similar struggle with regard to Glasgow. There, the bishop, John, who had been consecreted by Pope Paschal II, consistently refused to acknowledge the claims of York despite all papal commands and admonitions; and, upon his death in 1147, the claims of York were still evaded when his successor, Herbert, was consecrated by Pope Eugenius III.

In the reign of Malcolm IV, however, we find what appears to be a change in papal policy. Early in Malcolm's reign, in 1155, Adrian IV had written to the bishops of Scotland enjoining them ' to love and

honour ' the archbishop of York as their metropolitan and to ' offer him
the obedience and reverence due to him by metropolitan right '; but in
1159 Pope Alexander III, while regretting his inability to grant a
petition from St Andrews (almost certainly a petition for freedom from
the claims of York and for the erection of St Andrews into an archbishopric and metropolitan see – for St Andrews was then vacant),
nevertheless appointed William, bishop of Moray, to be legate of the
Apostolic See in Scotland, and it was by William, acting as papal legate,
that the new bishop of St Andrews was consecrated in 1160. Then,
in 1164, Engelram, bishop of Glasgow, was consecrated by Pope
Alexander III himself, ' although the messengers of Roger, archbishop
of York, very greatly opposed it ', while in his bull informing the church
of Glasgow of the consecration of Engelram, the Pope referred to
Glasgow as being ' special ' to him; and in 1165 Richard, who succeeded
Arnold in St Andrews, is said to have been consecrated by the other
bishops of Scotland by papal authority.

This change in papal policy was undoubtedly influenced by Henry
II's attack on the jurisdiction of the church courts in England – culminating in 1164 in the Constitutions of Clarendon; and papal willingness to help the Scottish church was further increased by the murder
of Thomas à Becket, archbishop of Canterbury, in 1170.

Then came the capture of King William and the treaty of Falaise.[1]
Under that treaty the bishops and abbots of Scotland swore fealty to
Henry II and swore also that they would make to the church of England
' the same subjection as their predecessors were wont to make and which
they ought to make ', conceding that the church of England was to have
' that right in the church of Scotland which by right she ought to have ';
but when, at a council held at Northampton in January 1176 and
attended by King William and many of the Scottish bishops, abbots
and priors, Henry II demanded the subjection which the Scottish
church ' ought to make ', he was met with the blunt reply from the
Scottish bishops that ' their predecessors never made any subjection
to the church of England, neither ought they to make any subjection to
her '.[2] Then an unseemly dispute arose between the archbishop of

[1] See *supra*, p. 78.
[2] Jocelyn, bishop of Glasgow, is said further to have claimed that his church was
a special daughter of Rome, exempt from all subjection to archbishops or bishops;
and, in a *Life of Kentigern*, probably written about this time, the author is careful to
state that after the Pope had confirmed in person Kentigern's election and consecration, and had sent him back to Scotland, the Pope later conferred upon him a special
privilege to the effect that he was to be subject to no other bishop but was to be the
Pope's own vicar and chaplain.

York and the archbishop of Canterbury, each claiming the subjection of the Scottish church, ' and thus ended that conference '.

King William and the Scottish bishops now sent ambassadors to Pope Alexander III, requesting him to receive the Scottish church into his own protection. In March or April of the same year (1176) the see of York sent to the Pope what can only be regarded as a forged letter purporting to have been written by William, admitting the claims of York and asking the Pope to confirm them.[1] And in July the Pope wrote to the bishops of Scotland condemning the oath to obey the English church which Henry had exacted from them,[2] informing them that he had enjoined the archbishop of York not to exercise any metropolitan right over them, and commanding them to obey only the Pope himself until the Pope had reached his own conclusion with regard to the claims of York. Then, just when the Scottish church, under the favour of Rome, appeared likely to secure its independence and freedom from the metropolitan claims of York, King William entered into a violent quarrel with the papacy over an election to the see of St Andrews.

We know little about the early methods of episcopal appointment. Turgot, we are told, was appointed ' by the king and by the clergy and people '; Eadmer was ' elected by the clergy and the people, the king consenting '; and, in the case of Robert, the *Chronicle of Melrose* states that the king, Alexander I, ' caused Robert to be elected bishop of St Andrews '. The king, as we have noted, had an undoubted interest in any election to a vacant bishopric; and, although *formal* election by cathedral chapters was now becoming the rule, the king undoubtedly had considerable influence, while his consent to an election appears to have been regarded as necessary.[3]

As we have already seen, Pope Eugenius III, in 1147, had given to the chapter of St Andrews the right of electing its bishop; and in 1178,

---

[1] The messengers of York were persistent in asking for William's letter to be given back to them, but the Pope carefully kept the letter and sent back to York an authenticated copy.

[2] Again an attempt to protect the church in general against the invasion of its liberties by Henry II for, as the Pope's letter maintained, ' it is not for any king or prince to exercise control over churches or ecclesiastics '.

[3] Cathedral chapters were, moreover, slow in taking shape. The Chapter of Glasgow was in existence in the reign of David I, but, in other cases, the ' chapter ' may at first have consisted of the clergy of the see. In the dioceses of Dunkeld and Dunblane, the ' chapter ' consisted of the archdeacon and certain parish clergy, especially the rural deans, until early in the thirteenth century; and the local clergy, headed by the archdeacon, preserved a claim to some say in episcopal elections at Sodor, Lismore, Whithorn and Aberdeen. This was in accord with canon law, and was not a legacy from ' Celtic ' practices.

on the death of Bishop Richard, the chapter unanimously elected John, called the Scot, to succeed him. It seems clear that John had been elected without King William's knowledge; certainly William refused to recognise the election. But then the king went beyond all his rights. He intruded his own chaplain, Hugh, secured his consecration, and expelled John from the kingdom. At once John took his appeal to Rome. The Pope wrote a stern letter to the king and sent a legate to Scotland who, following a church council at Holyrood, deposed Hugh, confirmed the election of John, and caused John to be consecrated by four of the Scottish bishops. But William was still obdurate. In the resultant struggle, first John was again banished by the king; then Hugh was excommunicated and Scotland laid under an interdict; and finally, when the king had banished those of the clergy who supported John, the king himself was excommunicated.[1]

At this stage Pope Alexander III died (1181) and his successor, Lucius III, at once made gestures of reconciliation. He released King William from his excommunication and Scotland from its interdict; he also sent to William, as a mark of grace, the Golden Rose.[2] But the situation was not finally resolved until 1188 when, Hugh having died and John the Scot having been elected bishop of Dunkeld (an election to which William agreed), the chapter of St Andrews, sitting at Perth, elected as bishop Roger, the king's cousin and chancellor.

The election of Roger[3] at Perth, and not at St Andrews, is significant. Perth was a royal residence, and royal influence could be

---

[1] An *interdict* was a ' forbidding '. It forbade, as a punishment (i) the celebration of divine service (though particular dispensations might be granted for the celebration of Mass behind closed doors); (ii) the administration of certain of the sacraments – Baptism and Confirmation were usually permitted, but neither Marriage nor Extreme Unction; (iii) Holy Burial. It was directed against a community of people rather than against an individual.

Excommunication was a ' cutting off from all communication with other Christians '. The excommunicated was outside the church and all Christian society. He was excluded from the sacraments and the prayers of the faithful. He was denied holy burial. He could not plead in a civil or ecclesiastical court – though actions could be brought against him. No one could have business or social relationships with him. This punishment was usually directed against an individual though it could also be directed against a whole community.

[2] ' On the Sunday which falls in the middle of Lent, the Pope is wont to bear in his hand a rose of gold, enamelled red, and perfumed. This he may bestow as a mark of grace, sometimes on the most favoured of his attendants, at other times on a foreign prince. By the rose, Christ is figured; by the gold, His kingly office; by the colour red, His passion and death; and by the perfume, His resurrection.'

[3] According to one chronicler, Roger was not even in holy orders at the time of his election. Certainly he was not consecrated until some nine or ten years later.

exercised there more easily. Moreover in England, by the Constitutions of Clarendon (1164), Henry II had secured that elections to bishoprics and abbacies had to take place in the royal chapel and were to be subject to the approval of the king and his council. The king's interests had to be secured, and those interests were now recognised. In 1239, in a papal mandate relating to the election of David de Bernham as bishop of St Andrews, we read that the chapter had first sought from the king leave to elect (*eligendi licentia*), according to custom (*juxta morem*), and that the king had subsequently given his assent to the election of David.

Soon the evidence suggests that royal pressure was brought to bear upon cathedral chapters to induce them to elect bishops acceptable to the king, perhaps even the king's nominee. And it may be that, while the king wanted bishops who were acceptable to him, the cathedral chapters were not unwilling to see eye to eye with the king. After all, a bishop who enjoyed the royal favour would be able to further the interests of his cathedral at the royal court, perhaps even to secure for its benefit further gifts of lands and privileges.

We have noted that, in 1176, all the Scottish bishops were made subject only to Rome until a decision had been reached on the claims of York. Then, in 1188, the dispute over St Andrews was finally settled, and, in 1189, the quit-claim of Canterbury released Scotland and its king from feudal subjection to England.[1] Scotland was once more a free and independent kingdom. And, in 1192, Pope Celestine III made the Scottish church a ' special daughter ' of Rome. By the Bull *Cum Universi*[2] the Scottish church[3] was to be subject only to Rome, ' with no intermediary ' (such as Canterbury or York); henceforth no one save the Pope, or a legate *a latere*,[4] could publish a sentence of interdict or of excommunication within the kingdom of Scotland; and no one who was not ' of the kingdom of Scotland ' could exercise the office of papal legate in Scotland unless he were sent for that purpose direct from the apostolic see.

[1] *Supra*, p. 78.

[2] Although this Bull is sometimes called the *Filia Specialis* Bull, it is more correct to cite papal Bulls by the opening words that follow the address – in this case the Bull opened by saying, *Cum universi Christi jugo subjecti apud Sedem Apostolicam patrocinium invenire debeant et honorem ac favorem* . . . .

[3] In the Bull, only the episcopal sees of St Andrews, Glasgow, Dunkeld, Dunblane, Brechin, Aberdeen, Moray, Ross and Caithness are mentioned. Argyll (Lismore) is strangely omitted; so too is Whithorn which, until 1472, gave obedience to York (see *supra*, p. 122, n. 3).

[4] A legate *a latere* is one sent by the Pope from the Holy See (originally from the Pope's own ' household ') and possessing full papal authority.

Confirmations of this Bull, whereby the Scottish church was brought into a direct relationship with Rome, and owed obedience only to Rome, were made by succeeding popes.[1] But Scotland was still not a province; its church had no internal head, no metropolitan archbishop. Yet the need for an internal head arose soon after the granting of the Bull *Cum Universi*; and then a new and unusual arrangement was made whereby the Scottish church was given a unity of its own.

At the fourth Lateran Council,[2] convened by Innocent III in 1215, and at which four bishops, an abbot,[3] and representatives of the other prelates of Scotland were present, it was decreed that metropolitans should hold annual provincial councils or synods of their clergy to review the state of the church within their provinces, to ensure that papal decrees were being observed, and to pass provincial statutes. But Scotland had no metropolitan. Moreover, according to canon law, no body of clergy could hold a council among themselves without the consent of their metropolitan. How then could the church in Scotland observe and obey this decree ? Nor can it be taken for granted that there was still a desire for St Andrews to be erected into a metropolitan see. So far as the Scottish king was concerned, he had seen, in England, that an archbishop could oppose the king and the king's council; so far as the Scottish bishops were concerned, probably not one of them was anxious to see the bishop of St Andrews raised in authority over them all.

Some representations (of which we have no record) must have been made to Rome. They resulted, in 1225, in the Bull *Quidam Vestrum*,[4] granted by Pope Honorius III, whereby the Scottish church was commanded to hold a provincial council by authority of the apostolic see. But, again, who was to preside over the council when no one bishop had authority over the rest, and when doubtless each bishop was jealous of his independence ? Here the expedient was adopted of choosing a ' Conservator ' for each council – at first called the ' Conservator of the Statutes of the Council '; later called the ' Conservator

[1] At a later date, in the reign of Alexander III, there is some evidence that the religious orders were likewise striving to escape from the jursidiction of the higher authorities in England.

[2] When a General Council of the Church met in Rome itself, the Council was called a ' Lateran Council ' because it was customary for it to meet in the cathedral church of St John in Laterano. The fourth Lateran Council was the twelfth General Council.

[3] The Bishops of St Andrews, Glasgow, Caithness and Moray, and the Abbot of Kelso.

[4] *Quidam vestrum nuper auribus nostris intimaverunt quod cum non haberetis Archiepiscopum cujus auctoritate possitis Concilium Provinciale celebrare . . .*

of the Privileges of the Scottish Church'. The Conservator was chosen from among the whole body of bishops; he presided over the council; it was his duty to enforce its statutes and decrees; but he held office only from the one council to the next. In this way parity was still secured.

The Bull *Quidam Vestrum* maintained the direct relationship between Rome and her 'special daughter'. But now the Scottish church could meet in its own councils; now it was given a coherence and a unity that would have been otherwise denied.[1]

Moreover, some distrust of Rome had already begun to make itself manifest – at first in a distrust of papal legates. A papal legate might endeavour to secure a policy which was unwelcome to the king and council. In the Bull *Cum Universi* the Pope had granted that in future the office of legate should be exercised in Scotland only by one who was 'of the kingdom of Scotland' or who was sent direct by the Pope from the Holy See. But even then, was there not a danger that a legate might act in the interests of Rome rather than in the interests of 'the kingdom of Scotland'? Some such distrust might be felt by the king and his council. Yet we should also note that, according to the *Scotichronicon*, the Scottish clergy in 1269 wholly rejected certain statutes, pertaining particularly to Scotland, which were passed by a legatine council held in London – a council at which the Bishops of Dunkeld and Dunblane, the Abbot of Dunfermline and the Prior of Lindores had been present but, apparently, present only to ensure that nothing was there done to the prejudice of the Scottish church. We can sense that the Scottish church is moving towards the position a number of its leading prelates were to take when they supported Bruce in defiance of Rome.

---

[1] Annual councils, however, were not held. Although a few councils may have escaped record, we know of only some thirty councils between 1225 and 1560. Even on the eve of the Reformation, when councils to secure internal reform were assuredly necessary, we find the Scottish church holding provincial councils only in 1549, 1552, 1555 and 1559.

CHAPTER XVI

The Competition for the Crown

ALEXANDER III's first wife, Margaret, sister of Edward I of England, died in February 1275, and in October 1285 Alexander married, as his second wife, Yolande, daughter of the Comte de Dreux. Less than six months later, on the night of 18-19 March 1286, in a storm of wind and rain, the king, riding from Edinburgh to join his wife at Kinghorn, apparently lost touch with his guides and, near Kinghorn, was thrown from his horse and killed.[1]

Of Alexander's children, the younger son, David, had died in 1281 when he was eight years old; the elder son, Alexander, had died in January 1284 when he had just reached the age of twenty; and the king's daughter, Margaret, who had married Eric II, king of Norway, had died in 1283 leaving an infant daughter, Margaret. In February 1284, a week after the death of Alexander, the king's only surviving son, the magnates of the realm, called together at Scone, had acknowledged the king's grand-daughter, Margaret, as heiress to the kingdom of Scotland should the king have no other issue.[2] Alexander III had no other issue, and thus the infant Margaret, ' The Maid of Norway ', became full heiress to the throne. She was about three years old; and in April 1286, a month after the death of the king, six guardians were appointed to administer the realm in her name: three deputed from the country north of the Forth – William Fraser, bishop of St Andrews, Duncan, earl of Fife, and Alexander Comyn, earl of Buchan; and three deputed from the country south of the Forth – Robert Wishart, bishop of Glasgow, James, the High Steward, and John Comyn (the 'Black Comyn').

Here we should note that, according to Robert Bruce, when Alexander II, still childless, was about to make an expedition to the Isles, the magnates of the realm, at the request of the king, had named his successor to the throne – and, as his successor, they had named Bruce. In this decision the magnates are said to have preferred Bruce, as the *son* of the second daughter of the king's uncle, David, earl of Huntingdon, rather than Devorguilla, the *daughter* of the eldest daughter.

---

[1] According to local tradition the king's horse plunged with its rider over the cliffs at Kinghorn Ness, near Pettycur.
[2] See *supra*, p. 57.

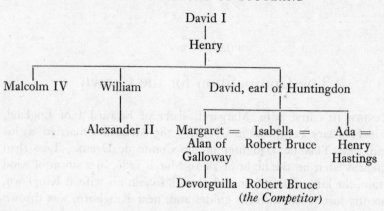

David I
|
Henry
|

| | |
Malcolm IV | William | David, earl of Huntingdon

Alexander II   Margaret =   Isabella =   Ada =
                Alan of   Robert Bruce   Henry
                Galloway   Hastings
                | |
                Devorguilla Robert Bruce
                             (*the Competitor*)

If such a decision was made, however, it was nullified by the birth of
Alexander III in 1241 (by Alexander II's second wife, Marie de Coucy);
and, moreover, there was now (in 1286) a male descendant of the
eldest daughter of David, earl of Huntingdon, – for Devorguilla had
married John Balliol by whom she had a son, John Balliol, born about
1250. Nevertheless, although Robert Bruce was one of the magnates
who, in 1284, had acknowledged the infant Margaret as heir to the
kingdom, it appears that, on the death of Alexander III, Bruce and his
son, the earl of Carrick, made some show of force in a claim to the
throne. The account of the Sheriff of Wigtown refers to ' war stirred
up by the Earl of Carrick after the death of the king '; the ' danger of
war ', ' the time of war ', and measures taken for strengthening certain
royal castles are also referred to in other accounts. And that the
succession was still regarded as uncertain is clear from a pact, entered
into by Bruce's adherents at Turnberry in September 1286, which
speaks of the man ' who by reason of the blood of the late King Alexander
and by ancient usages ', ought to occupy the throne.

We do not know how serious these disturbances were, or for how
long they lasted. We do know that in May 1289 Eric of Norway sent
ambassadors to Edward I to discuss the position of Margaret and the
kingdom of Scotland[1]; that in October 1289, at Edward's request, the
guardians appointed representatives to join in discussions with the
Norwegian ambassadors and with Edward's own representatives,
' saving in all things the liberty and honour of Scotland '; and that in

[1] Probably Eric approached Edward I because of the recent (and possibly still
continuing) disturbed state of Scotland. Moreover Edward was the grand-uncle of
the Maid, and Eric had recently been in diplomatic correspondence with him over
other matters.

November 1289 the discussions concluded with the treaty of Salisbury. By that treaty the Norwegian envoys promised to send Margaret to England before 1 November 1290 ' free and quit of all contract of marriage '; Edward promised that, if Margaret came to England, and if the kingdom of Scotland were then ' fully settled in quietness and peace ' so that she could safely stay there, he would, when requested by the Scots, send her to Scotland ' as free and quit of all contract of marriage as when he received her '; and the Scots representatives promised to establish quietness in their land before Margaret came there, and, further, that they would not contract her in marriage save with ' the ordinance, will and counsel of Edward ', and save with the assent of the King of Norway, her father.

Much stress was here laid upon the freedom of the Maid from marriage contracts; but Edward, in anticipation, had already sent messengers to Pope Nicholas IV applying for a dispensation for the marriage of Margaret to his son Edward (later Edward II) since they were within the forbidden degrees of the canon law –

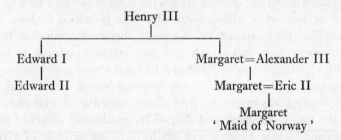

The dispensation was granted ten days after the conclusion of the treaty; and the Scots, when later they heard of its granting, accepted it as joyful news and agreed wholeheartedly to the proposed marriage. In what must have been a well-nigh unanimous letter sent from Birgham in March 1290, the four surviving guardians (the Bishops of St Andrews and Glasgow, John Comyn and James the High Steward[1]), the eight other bishops of Scotland (and also the Bishops of Galloway and Man[2]), twelve earls, twenty-three abbots, eleven priors and forty-eight barons spoke of the joyous news of the dispensation and cordially agreed to the marriage, ' subject to such reasonable conditions as they might put forward '; and another letter, sent by the Scots to Eric, urged him to send his daughter to England.

[1] Duncan, earl of Fife, had been murdered in 1289; and Alexander Comyn, earl of Buchan, had died in 1289.   [2] i.e. The Isles and Man.

In the following July a new treaty, the treaty of Birgham,[1] was concluded between Scotland and England – a marriage treaty, but one in which the ' rights, laws, liberties and customs of Scotland ' were for all time to be ' wholly and inviolably preserved '. The kingdom of Scotland was to remain ' separate and divided from the kingdom of England ' and to be ' free in itself and without subjection '; failing heirs to Edward and Margaret, or either of them, the kingdom of Scotland was to return to the nearest heirs ' wholly, freely, absolutely, and without any subjection ' so that the king of England, his heirs, or any others should neither gain nor lose thereby; while other clauses preserved the separate character of the Scottish parliament, the independence of the Scottish courts, and the freedom of Scottish chapter elections.

All these were ' reasonable conditions ', and, on the face of it, the treaty of Birgham was both fair and statesmanlike. Nevertheless in each of the two clauses guaranteeing the rights, laws, liberties and customs of Scotland, and the separateness of the kingdom, there was an added sentence, ' Saving always the right of our lord king [of England] and of any other whomsoever, that has pertained to him, or to any other, on the marches, or elsewhere, before the time of the present agreement, or which in any just way ought to pertain to him in the future '. Undoubtedly Edward I had not abandoned English claims[2] – claims which he was later to advance and extend – but, for the present, the wording was cautious. And when, immediately upon the conclusion of the treaty, he demanded that all the castles and places of strength in Scotland should be delivered up to him ' on account of a rumour of some dangers and suspicions of which he had heard ', was that purely with a desire to secure internal order in Scotland on behalf of Margaret and her chosen husband, his son ? The demand was refused; and Edward bided his time.

A ' great ship ' had already been freighted at Yarmouth to bring over the Maid, its stores including such childish delights as sugar-loaves, gingerbread, raisins and figs. It sailed in May 1290, but returned without her, for Eric apparently preferred to entrust his daughter only to a ship of Norway. The ' great ship ' sailed to Norway a second time; but we do not know whether Margaret now embarked in it or in a Norwegian ship. She sailed from Norway in September 1290, but never reached her kingdom. Somewhere in the islands of Orkney she died ' between the hands of Bishop Narve [of Bergen] and in the

[1] Confirmed at Northampton in August 1290.   [2] Cf. *infra*, p. 148.

presence of the best men who accompanied her from Norway ' – possibly of excessive sea-sickness, or possibly because the ship was wrecked: both likely events on such a voyage at the time of the autumnal equinox. Her corpse was taken to Bergen where she was buried, beside her mother, in the choir of Christ's Kirk.

The death of the Maid of Norway upset all Edward's plans, which, with certain reservations, had been statesmanlike, and had looked to a future peaceful union of Scotland and England. Moreover, the decision of February 1284 with regard to the succession to the Scottish throne had looked no further than the Maid. Who now was the rightful claimant to the throne ? A letter from William Fraser, bishop of St Andrews, addressed to Edward I on 7 October, reported that, upon a ' sorrowful rumour ' of the death of the queen reaching the people, the kingdom of Scotland had become disturbed; Robert Bruce had come with a great following to Perth; his supporters, the Earls of Mar and Atholl, were collecting their forces; parties were beginning to form, and there was fear of general war which could be averted only by Edward's good services. The bishop's letter, however, did not end there. ' If ', he continued, ' Sir John of Balliol should come to your presence we advise you to take care so to treat with him that in any event your honour and your advantage may be preserved '; and, if indeed the queen be dead, then let Edward come to the Border to console the people, to save the shedding of blood, and to set up ' for king the man who ought to have the succession, provided he will follow your counsel '.

Here was a double hint – that Balliol ought to succeed to the kingdom, and that Balliol would follow Edward's counsel to Edward's own honour and advantage. Here too was the situation that Edward now sought to exploit in his own interests; and what his interests were, time was soon to show.

Fordun, writing in the second half of the fourteenth century, says that the magnates, not knowing how to decide the succession, asked for Edward's help. Certainly the surviving guardians might well doubt their ability to prevent civil war between the Bruce and Balliol factions: Bruce was strongly supported by most of the magnates, while Balliol, as early as 16 November, had declared himself to be ' heir of the kingdom of Scotland '. Certainly, too, the recent close and friendly relationships with England would encourage an approach to England for aid and counsel.

An approach to Edward was made; but we can be sure that it was not an approach to a superior lord. Edward agreed to help Scotland in her difficulties, and that agreement to help almost certainly averted civil war. But also Edward now proceeded to take advantage of Scotland's difficulties to further his own interests. He invited the Scottish clergy and nobility to meet him at Norham on 10 May 1291, and, possibly significantly, he also summoned the northern levies of England to be at Norham on 3 June 1291.[1] Thereafter his moves were clever – revealing a *subtilitas* to which Fordun later bitterly referred.

Assembled at Norham, the Scots were at once informed that Edward had come to do justice to all ' as the superior and lord paramount of the kingdom of Scotland ', and that before he could act as judge in the cause of the succession his position and competence as lord superior must first be recognised. But whatever may have been the earlier relationships between English and Scottish kings in the reigns of William the Conqueror, Rufus, and Henry I, it is clear that ever since the quit-claim of Canterbury in 1189, and the treaty of York in 1237,[2] the Scottish kings had regarded their homage paid to English kings as homage solely for the lands which they held in England; nor had recent English kings pressed for more, although at times ' reserving their rights '. Indeed, upon the occasion of his homage in 1278, Alexander III, doubtless schooled by his councillors, is reported to have declared, ' speaking openly, " To homage for my kingdom of Scotland, no one has right, save God alone, nor do I hold it, save of God alone." '[3] Moreover, from 1286 to 1290 Edward had never claimed the feudal superior's rights of wardship and marriage, although the Maid of Norway was then under age. Not only had he not claimed the rights of a feudal superior, but he had even entered into a treaty, on equal terms with the Scots, for the marriage of his son to the infant queen.

Clearly the demand which he now made took the Scots by surprise; and Edward graciously granted an adjournment for three weeks to 2 June – and the feudal levies of northern England had been summoned to meet in arms at Norham on 3 June.

We are told, in one of the English accounts, that only the *communitas* made answer to Edward's claim; and that the answer put forward by the *communitas* was not to the point (*nihil tamen efficax*). The text of this answer, however, has recently been discovered. The

---

[1] Though this may have been purely a precautionary measure by Edward to ensure the maintenance of law and order during the determination of the succession (and perhaps even thereafter). [2] *Supra*, pp. 78, 81.

[3] See *Source Book of Scottish History*, VOL. 1 (2nd edn.), p. 89. There is no reason to doubt this report and the English version, contained in the Close Rolls, is little different.

communitas was not the common people (as was at one time supposed): it was the ' good men ' of the realm (*la bone gent Descoce*), the ' community of the realm ' – phrases which were then in use to mean the whole body of prelates, lords and important men. And their answer, if partly astute, was certainly to the point. Such a claim, they declared, was new to them; they had no knowledge of any previous claim by Edward, or by any of his predecessors, for recognition as ' supreme lord of the realm '. Moreover, how could they admit Edward's claim when they had no king, to whom alone such a claim should be made and who alone could answer it ? And did they not put themselves in jeopardy were they so to commit in advance their future king ?

Nor was Edward apparently fully content with his claim to be lord paramount of Scotland. On 3 June he spoke of his hereditary right to the kingdom of Scotland; there was a threat that Scotland might be held to be a male fief which, failing male heirs, would return into the hands of the superior (and the three principal claimants, as we shall see, all claimed through females); and, at a later date, Edward protested that, although of grace he had consented to judge the cause of the succession, he had never intended thereby to prejudice his own rights.

And now, on 5 and 6 June 1291, and probably quite apart from Edward's show of force, Bruce, Balliol and seven other ' competitors ' for the crown set their seals to documents acknowledging Edward's right to the ' sovereign lordship ' of the ' kingdom of Scotland ' (and, thereby, his right of determining the cause), agreeing to stand by his award, and also granting that sasine of the land and castles of Scotland should be given to him so that, when judgment was given, they could be delivered by him to the man adjudged to have the right to the crown. All the competitors, it would appear, were prepared to accept Edward as a direct overlord to whom the realm should pass during a vacancy in the throne. Did they all believe his claim to be firmly based on the preceding relations of English and Scottish kings ? Or did the more important competitors (Bruce, Balliol, Hastings, the Count of Holland and John Comyn) recognise this direct lordship, each in the hope that his lord would award him the crown and support him thereafter in wearing it ? Or, to put the most generous interpretation upon it, did they feel that only by such a recognition could their competing claims be decided and civil war (or perhaps even an assertion of the English claims by force)[1] be avoided ?

[1] It should be remembered, that both Bruce and Balliol held lands in England of the English king. A breach with Edward would mean the forfeiture of their English

So, despite the protest of 'la bone gent Descoce', the kingdom of Scotland was now in Edward's hands as supreme lord. He re-appointed the four surviving guardians (possibly in the hope of governing Scotland by Scots); a number of English officials were appointed to act in co-operation with Scottish colleagues; certain administrative re-arrangements were carried out; an oath of fealty was taken from the bishops, earls, magnates, freeholders *et aliis universis*; and, in turn, Edward swore to govern the realm in accordance with its laws and customs.

The nine competitors had now grown in number to thirteen – six claimed through illegitimate children of William 'the Lion' or Alexander II, and their claims were ruled out. Eric, king of Norway, claimed by ascent, not descent: he was the father of the 'Maid' – a good claim, but it, too, was ruled out. In effect, according to descent by heir of line, the only three possible claimants were John Balliol, Robert Bruce and John Hastings, the three descendants of the three daughters of David, earl of Huntingdon, the younger brother of Malcolm IV and William. On the other hand, Florence, count of Holland, claimed that David, earl of Huntingdon, had resigned all claim he might have to the Scottish throne in favour of his sister Ada, from whom Florence was in direct descent: a claim that was so strong (ruling out Balliol, Bruce and Hastings alike) that it led to a postponement of the hearing of the cause so that the resignation could be found and produced. In the end, after nearly a year's delay, the resignation was not forthcoming and Florence appears to have abandoned his claim.[1]

The abandonment of Florence's claim meant a return once more to the claims of Balliol, Bruce and Hastings. Balliol claimed as direct heir of line – he was the descendant of the eldest daughter, Margaret. Bruce, although the descendant of the second daughter, Isabella, claimed as a grandson of Earl David, whereas Balliol was only a great-grandson; moreover he claimed he had been chosen to succeed in the time of Alexander II.[2] Hastings claimed that the 'fief' of Scotland should be divided between the three descendants of the three co-heiresses, with the descendant of the eldest co-heiress, Balliol, receiving the crown.

The first decision was that although in feudal law lands could be equally partitioned among co-heiresses, the eldest co-heiress receiving

lands. Later, when war broke out, many an Anglo-Norman who held lands in both England and Scotland had to decide where his allegiance lay – to the King of Scotland or to the King of England. Then came complete severance between the two kingdoms and many Norman names disappeared from Scottish history.

[1] See *Scottish Historical Review*, VOL. XXXVI (1957), pp. 111-24.
[2] *Supra*, p. 143.

THE THIRTEEN CLAIMANTS FOR THE CROWN

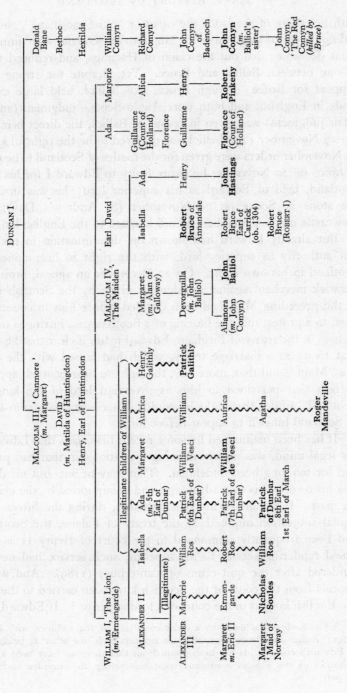

with her share of the lands the *caput* or ' chief messuage ', such a rule did not apply to kingdoms: the kingdom of Scotland was ' impartible '. That decision ruled out the claim of Hastings, and reduced the issue to one between Balliol and Bruce. Yet, despite the strong Scottish support for Bruce – though Bruce, like Balliol, held large extents of lands in England, and both were Anglo-Scots – judgment (and it was a fair judgment) was given in favour of Balliol, the direct heir of line.[1] On 17 November 1292 Balliol was declared to be the rightful king; on 19 November orders were given for the castles of Scotland to be rendered to him; on 20 November he swore fealty to Edward I for his realm of Scotland, held of Edward as his superior lord; he was installed on the stone at Scone on 30 November (St Andrew's Day); and at Newcastle on 26 December, he did homage to the English king.

But already Edward had shown his determination to exercise his full authority as superior lord, with the right to hear appeals from Scotland in his own court. On 22 December an appeal, brought by a Berwick merchant against a judgment given by the Scottish justiciars in the preceding May, had been decided before him in council. And now, to a protest that the hearing of a Scottish case infringed one of the clauses of the treaty of Birgham, Edward made it clear that he regarded that treaty as a marriage treaty, which had lapsed with the death of the ' Maid ', and that, moreover, the right to hear Scottish appeals was a right that pertained to him as sovereign lord of the kingdom of Scotland: under that right he could, if necessary, summon the King of Scotland himself to appear before him.

It has been maintained by some recent historians that Edward, with his legal mind, was merely defining a relationship that had previously and for too long been undefined. That may be so; but his definition was his own, to his own advantage, and unsupported by the evidence of the past. It is noteworthy that although, during the fifteen years of feudal subjection imposed by the treaty of Falaise, the Scottish king had been frequently summoned to the court of Henry II as a feudal vassal rendering service to his superior, such service had never been rendered after the quit-claim of Canterbury (1189). And when had appeals from the court of the Scottish king been carried to the court of the English king as to the court of a lord superior ? If Edward, indeed,

[1] The finding was made by a court consisting of 104 auditors, with Edward as judge: Balliol and Bruce nominating 40 auditors each, the other 24 being members of Edward's council. It has been pointed out that this may have been a deliberate imitation of the Roman *centumviri* who, numbering 105, decided successions to property.

was ' sovereign lord ' of the kingdom of Scotland, for what had Scotland paid 10,000 merks of silver in 1189 ? And of what worth was the treaty of York? To Edward, however, a legalist who believed in his own interpretations, Balliol and Scotland were a vassal king and a vassal state; and Balliol (who had already accepted Edward as his sovereign lord and had thereby prejudiced the Scottish case), further strengthened Edward's hand by formally releasing him of all agreements, promises and obligations undertaken by him to the people of Scotland[1] – and that included a formal release from the safeguarding clauses of Birgham.

A little later, indeed, Balliol made some endeavour to resist Edward's unprecedented demands. Summoned to London to maintain there a judgment that had been given in the parliament of Scotland against Macduff (an uncle of the deceased Earl of Fife), he ignored the summons. Summoned a second time, he appeared before Edward and, asked what defence he had to offer, is reported to have replied: ' I am King of Scotland. To the complaint of Macduff, or to aught else respecting my kingdom, I dare not make answer without the advice of my people.' But events were moving rapidly to a crisis. Could the same Scots who had insisted upon the independence of their kingdom in the treaty of Birgham in 1290 accept the new order imposed by the English king ? Could they even accept a king who might obey a summons to answer for his actions before another and superior king ?

In the early summer of 1294, when Edward mobilised his army for the defence of Gascony, he demanded from Scotland the military service of her king, and of a number of her earls and barons. Balliol, faced with a stiffening Scottish opposition to Edward, was constrained to refuse the demand. Indeed, early in July 1295 a special council consisting of four bishops, four earls and four barons was set up to be responsible for all public affairs – probably an indication of a patriotic and popular move in defence of the realm rather than the appointment of a representative council to strengthen the hand of the king. Through this council, an alliance was concluded with France, Edward's enemy (October 1295).

Faced with this situation, Edward marched north ' to seek remedy '. The Scottish leaders, leaving Balliol behind them, gathered their forces to meet him. On 28 March 1296 Edward's army crossed the

---

[1] Also confirming and recognising all acts done by Edward and his officials during the time that the kingdom of Scotland was in Edward's hands – a necessary step to secure continuity in government, and notably in finance and the administration of justice.

Tweed. Scotland's long struggle for independence had begun. Whatever earlier ambiguities there may have been, Edward's attempt to 'secure his fief' and to crush his 'rebellious vassal' was to lead to the final independence of a united Scottish kingdom.

NOTE A

Edward I's 'Legalitas'

It is interesting to note that Edward I's actions, once he had been accepted by the 'Competitors' as 'sovereign lord of the land of Scotland', were the legally correct actions of a feudal superior hearing a case of disputed succession to lands that were held of him. It was a clear rule of feudal law that an action relating to land should come before the court of the lord of whom the land was held. So Edward, as lord superior of Scotland, was judge competent. Again, should the action be one of disputed succession, the lands had to be in the superior's hands so that, when he had decided the succession, the rightful successor could swear fealty to the superior before he was given sasine of the lands. Hence Edward demanded, and was given, sasine of the kingdom and the castles of Scotland; hence, immediately after the award, Balliol swore fealty to Edward and received sasine of the kingdom and its castles.

But in his subsequent actions Edward failed to realise that Scotland was more than a feudal fief. The 'reasonable conditions' demanded by the Scots in the treaty of Birgham and the answer of 'la bone gent Descoce' should have warned him that Scotland was also a kingdom with an emergent national spirit.

NOTE B

Edward I's personal interest in the Succession to the Scottish Throne

Possibly Edward I was personally interested in the formal and ceremonial decision that the kingdom of Scotland was impartible and that succession to the throne was to the direct heir of line. In April 1290 in the presence of a number of important bishops he had defined by ordinance the succession to the kingdom of England: first to the young Edward and his heirs; if Edward died without heirs, to any son who might yet be born to the king; failing such heirs and such son, to Eleanor, the king's eldest daughter and her heirs; whom failing to Joan and her heirs; whom failing to the king's younger daughters and their heirs in strict order. Here, failing male heirs, was succession according to the heir of line. Here it was clearly shown that the kingdom was impartible, and that there was to be no division of its lands among the king's daughters as equal co-heiresses. And when, immediately afterwards, Edward married his daughter Joan to the powerful Earl of Gloucester, he bound the Earl by solemn oath to maintain the order of the ordinance and therewith to maintain the order of Eleanor before Joan.

This was an important move on Edward's part. If we look at the succession of English kings we note that—

William of Normandy was a Conqueror, though he also relied on the gift of Edward the Confessor and Harold's oath.

Rufus relied upon election and the support of the people – for Robert Curthose was the Conqueror's eldest son.

Henry I likewise relied upon election and the support of the people – Robert Curthose was still alive – and also, perhaps significantly in view of the rising concept of primogeniture, upon the argument that, while Robert Curthose was the Conqueror's eldest son before he became King of England, he (Henry) was the Conqueror's eldest son after he became King of England.

Stephen had excluded the heiress of line, Matilda, and asserted a title by election.

John excluded (and later murdered) Arthur of Britanny (the son of John's elder brother, Geoffrey)[1] and claimed by the support of the barons and election from within the nearest of kin.

Henry III was the direct male heir, and, moreover, succeeded as a boy of nine and in a time of trouble. His succession was important as stressing the concept of primogeniture and hereditary succession.

Edward I was the direct male heir, and, moreover, reigned before he was crowned. He was absent from England, on crusade, when his father, Henry III, died, but no one questioned his right to succeed, and the Council proclaimed that the kingdom had devolved on him by hereditary right and by the will and fealty of the *proceres*.

Already, in 1290, Edward, looking to the future, had defined the succession in favour of his son, Edward, whom failing, to the strict heir of line. There was to be no attempt in favour of Joan, the second daughter. The decision of 1292 in favour of Balliol, in the ' Great Cause ' of Scotland, strengthened not only the position of the young Edward (who was only eight years old in 1292) as Edward I's heir to the English throne, but also, failing the young Edward, the position of Eleanor, the King's eldest daughter.

[1] See the Table on p. 79.

CHAPTER XVII

The War of Independence - I

IT MAY be that Balliol deserves some credit for delaying a war that Edward I had made inevitable. His position as King of Scotland from 1292 to 1296 was unenviable, caught as he was between Edward's interpretation of his rights as lord superior on the one hand and, on the other hand, a new and rising spirit of Scottish patriotism. Despised by the Scots nobility, and virtually deprived of authority, he was of use neither to Edward nor to the Scots. Within a few months he was to disappear from the scene.

Faced by Scotland's alliance with France, Edward marched north to punish his weakling vassal and to secure his rebellious fief. Berwick was taken by storm on 30 March 1296, and its inhabitants, men, women and children, were mercilessly massacred; on 27 April the Scottish army was overwhelmed at Dunbar; and on 10 July, at Brechin, the spineless Balliol formally repeated to Edward the surrender of his realm, his people and his kingship which he had already made at Kincardine.[1] Making a triumphal progress northwards, Edward reached Elgin on 26 July and then turned southwards again by a slightly different route, From Scone he took the stone said to be that on which the Scottish kings were enthroned (the so-called ' Coronation Stone '), and from Edinburgh he took the ' Black Rood ' of St Margaret. Returning to Berwick (which was replanned and rebuilt), he held a parliament there; and there from Scottish bishops and earls, barons and priests, freeholders and burgesses, he received homage and the oath of fealty.[2] English officials were installed, the castle were ' stuffit ' with English garrisons, and the government of Scotland was entrusted to John de Warenne, earl of Surrey, and Hugh Cressingham. To all appearances, Edward had ' secured his fief '. Many of the Scots leaders had been captured at Dunbar; most of the important castles were in English hands; and homage and fealty had been exacted from lords and commons alike. But ' not all the substantial free tenants of Scotland went to Berwick

---

[1] The nickname ' Toom Tabard ', *Empty Jacket*, later given to Balliol, may come from this surrender when the heraldic insignia on his tabard were probably ripped off.
    Balliol was sent to England where he remained until 1299 when he was allowed to retire to his estate at Bailleul in France. He died at Bailleul in 1313.
[2] The record is known as the ' Ragman Rolls '.

to do homage; some never did homage; one of these was biding his time near Paisley; and there were others in Moray '.

It may be that the English officials were too exacting in the discharge of their duties, or too overbearing in their office; undoubtedly they were ' foreigners ' and unwelcome, as likewise were the soldiers who gave them armed support. Certainly when opposition arose to the English administration, it arose in the localities, and the opposition came mainly from the ' middle folk ' and the people. Of these middle folk, William Wallace soon stood out; but it is well to remember that before Wallace slew the English Sheriff of Lanark (May 1297) there had already been trouble in other parts, in Ross, Argyll, Moray and Aberdeen. In the west, too, certain lords were making some show of resistance. Robert Bruce (whose father, the competitor, had died in 1294), James, the High Steward, William, lord of Douglas, and Bishop Wishart of Glasgow had assembled in arms but, when faced by an English force under the command of Percy and Clifford, and unable to agree among themselves, most of them had capitulated at Irvine (July 1297). Nevertheless, in that same month (July 1297) Cressingham was reporting to Edward that the whole land was in turmoil, that in many shires the Scots had set up officials of their own, and that proper order existed only in the shires of Berwick and Roxburgh.

William Wallace, a younger son of Sir Malcolm Wallace of Elderslie, had suddenly ' lifted up his head ' (in the words of Fordun) when he had killed the Sheriff of Lanark, and now, under him, the scattered risings against the English domination gradually took the shape of a national resistance. We next hear of Wallace at Perth, in a surprise attack on Edward's justiciar, William de Ormesby, who barely escaped; in July 1297 Cressingham reported him as ' lying with a large company in the Forest of Selkirk '; and in August he was apparently besieging the castle of Dundee. Moreover he was ' bestriding ' the land ' not in secret, as before, but openly '.

Meanwhile, in the north, the castles of Aberdeen, Urquhart and Inverness had fallen to Scottish forces led by Andrew de Moray (the son of Sir Andrew de Moray of Petty), and the fall of Montrose, Brechin and Forfar quickly followed. Wallace and de Moray joined forces; they became, in their own words, ' leaders of the army of Scotland '; and the greater part of the land to the north of the Forth was now under their control.

Edward, however, intent upon a campaign against France, and refusing to believe the alarming reports of Cressingham, sailed for

Flanders on 22 August 1297. But both Warenne and Cressingham, despite the capitulation of certain of the Scottish lords at Irvine, were under no illusions. The threat from the north was too serious. Realising that Wallace, de Moray, and their ' band ' had to be crushed without delay, the English leaders advanced northwards with a strong force of heavy cavalry, some northern English levies and a contingent of Welsh archers. They reached the Forth at Stirling, intending to cross there; instead they found the Scots under Wallace and de Moray barring the way, with their forces drawn up on the foothills of the Ochils, to the north of the bridge,[1] and with the swampy carse protecting their front.[2] Despite the strength of the Scottish position, Cressingham is said to have succeeded in bringing about an immediate attack – ' Why,' he is reported to have asked, ' should the king's treasure be wasted in prolonging the war ? ' But the bridge was narrow, and the English mounted knights, the spearmen and the Welsh archers could cross only slowly and two or three abreast. And when ' as many of the enemy as he believed he could overcome ' had crossed, Wallace gave the order to attack. His men cut off those who had crossed and then seized and held the northern bridge-head. All was at once confusion. Those who had crossed were attacked on both flanks; those who had not crossed were unable to move to the support of their fellows; the cavalry were unable to manoeuvre on the swampy ground; the Welsh foot fled; Cressingham was killed; and Warenne barely escaped to Berwick. The Scottish triumph was complete (11 September 1297). The castle of Stirling surrendered; and soon the only important castles holding out for England were those of Edinburgh, Dunbar, Roxburgh and Berwick. In October the Scots were over the Border, raiding North-umberland and Cumberland.

For ten months the government of Scotland was in Wallace's hands. On 11 October 1297 Wallace and de Moray wrote triumphantly to Lübeck and Hamburg that trade with Scotland could now be resumed, ' because the kingdom of Scotland, thanks be to God, has been recovered by war from the power of the English '. And they wrote from Hadding-ton, south of the Forth. De Moray, however, who was probably wounded in the battle of Stirling bridge, died soon after this letter, leaving Wallace to lead alone.

[1] A wooden bridge situated about sixty-five yards upstream from the present fifteenth-century stone bridge.
[2] It is probable that a firm but narrow causeway led northwards from the bridge across the carse.

But Wallace was fighting in the name of Balliol; the Bruces and their supporters could hardly fight in such a cause; and there were undoubtedly many others who regarded Balliol as not worth fighting for. Moreover, although Wallace had now won a large measure of support, some of the great men still stood aloof. Finally, on 31 January 1298, Philip of France made truce with Edward and deserted his Scottish allies.

Edward returned to England in March 1298 and at once took action. He moved the seat of government from London to York, and on 3 July he crossed the Tweed at Coldstream with a strong force which had been assembling prior to his return. By mid-July he was approaching Edinburgh. Prudence would have dictated a retreat before him and the use of guerilla tactics. On the other hand it was known that Edward's army was suffering from lack of supplies and that the Welsh, who formed a large part of his footmen, were on the verge of mutiny; moreover there was the danger that as harvest-time approached many of those in the Scots army might slip away. Wallace decided to stand and meet the English threat forthwith. He awaited Edward's force near Falkirk – only to suffer a disastrous defeat (22 July 1298).

Wallace's tactics at Falkirk were perfectly sound. The spearmen, his main strength, were drawn up, like bristling hedgehogs, in four rounded compact groups, each probably three-deep, called *schiltrons*[1]; his few archers were ranged in the intervals between these schiltrons; and his cavalry, few in number and of doubtful quality, were in the rear. But, despite the gallantry of the thick-grouped spearmen, who broke the first English charge, the English archers soon took a heavy toll; the close formations were broken up; and then the English knights rode in. Wallace, alas, possessed no heavy ' covered horse ' to meet those of England, nor even sufficient light horse to disperse the English archers; as it was, most of his small force of mounted men had fled the field at the beginning of the fight.

Falkirk was never a rout – the spearmen stood their ground to the last; but it was a heavy and grievous defeat, and it marked the end of Wallace's brief but glorious career. His subsequent moves are not easy to trace, though there is evidence that he went to France in an endeavour to secure French support and that he received letters from Philip recommending him to the Pope and to Hakon of Norway.

[1] An interesting use of this word in mediaeval anatomy, to indicate the *rounded three-deep* joints in the hand and the foot, is noted in *The Scottish Antiquary*, VOL. XIV, 185-8.

But Falkirk, seemingly decisive, was not decisive. Edward had won a battle, but his subsequent campaign was ineffective. Scotland was still in revolt and still unconquered. Moreover, Wallace had shown that something could be done, and, probably significantly, as early as December 1298 his place as guardian had been taken by two magnates – Robert Bruce, earl of Carrick (and later to be King Robert I), and John Comyn, the ' Red Comyn ', Lord of Badenoch.[1] Bruce may have been already thinking of a crown and a kingdom that had been yielded to Edward by Balliol[2]; but Comyn was the son of Balliol's sister, Alianora, and his cause was bound to be that of Balliol. It is possible that in the appointment of these two guardians there may have been some hope of uniting forces and of sinking all differences in the face of a common foe but, as was soon to be proved, old antipathies and old jealousies were too hard in dying. At a council of war at Peebles, in August 1299, accusations of treason were made, and Comyn seized Bruce by the throat. The quarrel was patched up, and William de Lamberton, bishop of St Andrews, was appointed as principal guardian – possibly in an endeavour to hold the opposition together; but the conflict of interests was still too strong, and the feud between Bruce and Comyn became irreconcilable. Bruce resigned his guardianship in 1300 and, later, fearing the possible return of John Balliol as a vassal king, and therewith the loss of the Bruce lands, came for a while (1302) into Edward's peace. His place as guardian was first taken by Ingram de Umfraville, while later, we find John de Soules acting as sole guardian in the name of Balliol.

Nevertheless, the English control, such as it was, was virtually limited to Lothian and the Borders; all the land to the north of the Forth was held by the guardians. A campaign by Edward in the summer of 1300 was a fiasco, achieving nothing save the capture of the castle of Caerlaverock. A second campaign in the summer of 1301 achieved little more – though another castle, Bothwell, was captured; and although Edward wintered at Linlithgow from 1301 to 1302 his efforts were proving fruitless. Even without a king (and the person of a king was of supreme importance in times such as these), the Scots, under guardians, or a guardian, were more than holding their own. Soon there were to be setbacks; but also, soon thereafter, the Scots were to be fighting under a king.

The year 1303 opened with the rout at Roslin of an English light

[1] Son of John Comyn (the ' Black Comyn '), the ' Competitor '.
[2] Bruce was the grandson of the Competitor (died 1294); his father, who died in 1304, had earlier transferred to him the Bruce claim to the Scottish throne.

cavalry force under John Segrave; but that proved to be a solitary Scottish success. Philip of France again deserted the Scots[1]; and in May 1303 Edward invaded Scotland once more – but for the last time. As in 1296 he again made an armed progress through the realm, as far as Kinloss, and returned to winter at Dunfermline. In March 1304 he held a Scottish parliament at St Andrews, when most of the nobility and men of note once more came into his allegiance; in July 1304, after a siege of three months, Stirling Castle (which alone was holding out and which had been in Scottish hands since November 1299) surrendered; and in August 1305 Wallace (who had been captured) was ' tried ' in London and suffered an agonising death as a traitor to a king whom he had never acknowledged and to whom he had never sworn fealty and allegiance.

Edward might well think that his troubles in Scotland were now over. Admittedly there was discontent in almost every part of the land, and these obstinate Scots never seemed to know when they were beaten, but, if the Scottish nobility remained true to the allegiance they had newly sworn, peace and quiet might yet be assured. After functioning for seven years at York, the royal administration returned to Westminster. In September 1305 Edward approved an Ordinance for the Government of Scotland, a statesmanlike document according to which, while the principal offices were to be held by Englishmen, authority was to be largely shared between Scottish and English officials – though its whole framework of government still stressed that Scotland was subject to the English king.[2] And, in a mood of content and satisfaction, Edward granted generous terms to the Scottish lords who had come into his will. Given time, surely all would now be well. But time was not given. On 10 February 1306 Bruce and his companions slew the ' Red Comyn ' in the Franciscan church at Dumfries. Possibly Bruce had already planned a new revolt; possibly the

[1] The treaty of Paris (May 1303) was probably inevitable after the French defeat at Courtrai, but it left Edward free to concentrate all his forces against Scotland.

[2] Scotland was to be governed by a Lieutenant, with a Chancellor, a Chamberlain and a Comptroller. The Lieutenant was to have a Council consisting of the officers of the Crown together with four bishops, four abbots, five earls and nine magnates of Scotland. Two Justiciars (one an Englishman, and one a Scot) were to be appointed for each of four regions (Lothian, Galloway, ' Scotland ' south of the Mounth, and ' Scotland ' north of the Mounth); sheriffs were to be appointed who were ' fittest for the maintenance of good order ' irrespective of whether they were Scots or Englishmen, and, indeed, many of those named were Scots. Finally the laws of David I were to be revised in an assembly of the people and thereafter proclaimed and observed.

All this was a distinct and statesmanlike advance on the *ad hoc* arrangements that had prevailed since 1296; to be at once defeated by the march of events early in 1306.

meeting with Comyn was arranged in a vain attempt to secure his support.[1] Certainly the murder was unpremeditated – for no one would choose a consecreted place for the murder of an enemy: thereby committing sacrilege of the deepest kind. Equally certainly the murder hastened whatever plans may have been taking shape. Although one of the romantic stories of Scottish history,[2] the murder of the Red Comyn committed Bruce to an assertion of his claim to the throne. The claim made by his grandfather in 1291-92 was now to be advanced by force of arms. Whatever Bruce's previous vacillations may have been – and it is probable that, despite the opposition of Comyn, and the possibility of the return of Balliol, he had never abandoned hope of the crown – now it was essential for his success that he should lead the Scottish revolt as a Scottish king. Moreover, would not Scottish support rally to a king at last ? On 25 March 1306 Bruce was crowned; and on 27 March Isabella, countess of Buchan, the sister of Duncan earl of Fife, placed a gold circlet on the king's head at Scone.[3] Those who were present included the Bishops of St Andrews, Glasgow and Moray, the Abbots of Scone and Inchaffray, and the Earls of Menteith, Atholl and Lennox. The new king, raised to kingship at the beginning of a new year,[4] was to lead his people to a new fortune.

Yet the auspices were far from favourable. His following had still to be built up, and he had to face not only Edward of England but also the feud of the Comyns and those of kin or alliance with them – notably John Comyn, earl of Buchan, Alexander of Argyll and his son, John of Lorne, and the MacDowells of Galloway.[5] And on 18 May 1306 sentence of excommunication for sacrilege was passed upon him by Pope Clement V.

Almost at once he was defeated with great loss at Methven, near

[1] For Comyn, whose father had died in 1304 and who was the son of Balliol's sister, might be said to be ' heir presumptive ' to Balliol's claim to the throne. He was bound to be in opposition to the claim of Bruce.

[2] The story of Bruce's words, ' I doubt I've slain the Red Comyn ', and Kirkpatrick's answer, ' Doubt ye ? I'll mak siccar ', is of late date.

[3] The Earl of Fife enjoyed the right of placing the new king upon the royal stone at Scone; but the royal stone could no longer be used, and in 1306 Duncan, earl of Fife, was in ward in Edward's hands.

[4] The new year then began on Lady Day (Annunciation), 25 March. Lamberton, bishop of St Andrews, stated in August 1306 that he had given communion at Mass to Bruce ' on Palm Sunday [27 March], the third day after his coronation '.

[5] Comyn, earl of Buchan, was of kin to the murdered ' Red Comyn '; the ' Red Comyn ' was a nephew by marriage to Alexander of Argyll; and while Dougal MacDowell is said to have married one of Red Comyn's aunts, the MacDowells were bound to follow Alexander of Argyll as the head of their line.

Perth, (19 June 1306) by the earl of Pembroke, Edward's commander in Scotland. Retiring to Atholl, and later to the west, he was again defeated, this time at Dalry (near Tyndrum), by the Lord of Lorne (July or August 1306). Sending his queen and his young brother Nigel to the castle of Kildrummy in Aberdeenshire, he found refuge for a brief space in Dunaverty; but when the castle was taken Bruce had gone – no one knew where: possibly somewhere in the Western Isles, and probably thence to Rathlin off the north coast of Ireland. ' For the next four and a half months Scotland knew him not.'

Meantime Edward, whose dream of a settled Scotland had been so rudely shattered, and whose recent trust in the Scottish lords had been so ill rewarded, showed no mercy. Upon his orders, William de Lamberton, bishop of St Andrews, and Robert Wishart, bishop of Glasgow, were imprisoned in irons; others of Bruce's supporters (including his brother Nigel and the Earl of Atholl) who were unlucky enough to be captured were hanged; and Bruce's wife, his sisters and his daughter, who had fled from Kildrummy upon the approach of an English siege-force, were dragged from the sanctuary of St Duthac, at Tain, and imprisoned.[1] Nor did Edward propose to leave the new troubles in Scotland solely to the care of his lieutenants. Old and ill, and unable to ride, he was already being carried slowly northwards in a litter until, reaching the priory of Lanercost, near Carlisle, in September 1306, he was compelled by illness to stay there for a period of nearly six months.

Yet, despite these seemingly overwhelming reverses, Bruce returned to Scotland early in February 1307, landing in Arran, and then crossing over to his own lands in Carrick; and about the same time his brothers, Thomas and Alexander, landed in Loch Ryan with a small Irish force. Again disaster ensued. His brothers, defeated by Dougal MacDowell, were taken prisoner and a week later executed at Carlisle. Deprived of their support, the new king, with only a small company, was again compelled to take to the hills; yet there, by choosing his ground well, and already showing that military genius which was later to decide the battle of Bannockburn, he mauled and baffled an English force in Glentrool, and later (10 May 1307), at Loudoun Hill, he defeated another force under the Earl of Pembroke himself.

Roused by the news of Pembroke's defeat, and hearing reports of

---

[1] Possibly they had hoped to reach Norway via Orkney. Bruce's sister, Isobel, had married Eric, king of Norway. She was Eric's second wife; his first wife was Margaret, daughter of Alexander III and mother of the ' Maid of Norway '.

the tenuous nature of the English hold in the different parts of Scotland, Edward determined to lead his army in person. He had moved from Lanercost to Carlisle, and now, abandoning his litter, he rode on horseback towards the Solway; but he was so weak that in four or five days he had advanced only some six miles. Grim, determined, striving to force his body to obey his will, he died at Burgh-on-Sands on 7 July 1307.

From that moment the tide turned in Bruce's favour. Edward II, weak and intemperate, neither soldier nor statesman, was an unworthy son and successor to Edward I.

CHAPTER XVIII

The War of Independence - II

WITH HIS dying breath Edward I is said to have ordered that his bones were to be carried at the head of his army until Scotland had been wholly subdued. Such an order would be in keeping with the old king's character. Bruce is reported to have said that he feared the bones of the father more than he feared the living son. The statement, if made, was amply proved by the course of events.

Edward II did not obey his father's dying injunction. Turning south with Edward I's body he entrusted it to the care of the Archbishop of York at Richmond; then, marching northwards again, he made a futile advance into Scotland through Upper Nithsdale, and promptly returned to England, leading back the great army that had been assembled to crush the rebellious Scots. Perhaps more important, though its significance for Scotland was not at once apparent, on 6 August 1307 Edward II, by one of his earliest acts of royalty and within a month of his accession, granted the earldom of Cornwall to his favourite, Piers Gaveston.

Edward II's inglorious retreat was an immediate encouragement to Bruce. Moreover, it left him free to fight his personal enemies in Scotland (mainly those who had embraced the blood-feud of the murdered Comyn) and it deprived his enemies of English support.

So, in a campaign over the winter of 1307-08, John Comyn, earl of Buchan, was finally routed at Inverurie; his lands were wasted with fire and sword (the 'Herschip of Buchan'); and the power of the Comyns was completely destroyed. Turning now to the west and south-west, Bruce, with the help of Douglas, defeated John of Lorne in the battle of the Pass of Brander and, during the winter of 1308-09, his brother, Edward Bruce, ravaged in Galloway – though not until 1313 was the south-west finally subdued with the surrender of the castle of Dumfries.

Having secured himself against attack from his personal enemies, Robert I was now able to attempt the greater task of winning back his kingdom from the power of the English. But already much had been done. Already, following the overthrow of the Earl of Buchan, Bruce himself had helped the burgesses of Aberdeen to take the castle that

165

dominated their burgh; and thereafter most of the other castles in the north were quickly captured. Moreover, men in every part now began to range themselves openly on the side of Bruce, and with every success his following grew. By March 1309, the King had so established himself that he was able to hold a parliament at St Andrews, and a letter, sent from that parliament to the King of France, and sealed by a large number of lords and barons, affirmed that Bruce was recognised by them as their ' leader and prince '. Added to that, by the summer of 1309, in all Scotland north of the Tay, only Dundee and Banff were still held by England; while between the Tay and the Firths of Forth and Clyde the only important castles still in English hands were those of Stirling and Perth. Even those castles, moreover, were probably able to hold out only because they could receive occasional supplies by sea: for all the land-routes north of the Forth were now commanded by the Scots.[1]

Meantime Edward II, in constant financial difficulties and in strife with his magnates, was unable to give any attention to Scotland. Undermanned and under-supplied castles fell to the Scots one by one; and each, as it was captured, was razed to the ground – a deliberate policy to prevent the English forces from re-establishing themselves in fortified positions. So, in Barbour's epic poem, we may read that at this castle or that

> And syne gert brek doune the wall
> And fordid well and castell all   [*destroyed*

or

> Tour and wall rycht to the ground
> War tumlyt in ane litill stound   [*a moment*

And when, in the autumn of 1310, Edward II led an unhappy English army through the southern counties of Scotland, achieving nothing, and suffering hardship from the weather and inadequate supplies, Bruce retaliated, in 1311, with a devastating raid into Durham.

Then, in June 1312, Piers Gaveston, Edward II's hated favourite, was seized and hanged, without trial, by a number of the Lords Ordainers,[2] and for nearly a year there was danger of civil war in England. Neither party had time or thought for Scotland. The

---

[1] Also, we should remember that Edward I, beset by financial difficulties, had never been able to build in Scotland strong castles like those which he had built in Wales. Nor was he able to do much to strengthen the Scottish castles which he captured.

[2] In effect a group of barons, appointed by the Council, to reform Edward II's ineffective government.

Chronicle of Lanercost regretfully records, ' Now, while the aforesaid things were being done with Piers, the march of England had no defender against the Scots, and therefore they rendered tribute to Robert in order to have peace for a while '. And the chronicler then tells of an invasion by Bruce as far as Durham when the people paid £2,000 for a ten months' truce, at the same time agreeing to give the Scots unopposed passage through their lands whenever they wished to raid in England; whereupon ' the Northumbrians, fearing that the Scots would visit them, gave them other two thousand pounds ', and the people of Westmorland and Cumberland ' redeemed themselves in a similar way '. Truces, indeed, continued to be bought for a number of years; they were bought for lands as far south as Ripon and Richmond; and it has been calculated that Bruce must have collected some £20,000 in various payments exacted from the northern counties of England.

Yet Bruce did not allow the harrying of northern England (or the welcome payments *pro pace habenda* or *ad tributum Roberto Brus* or for *souffrance de guerre*) to take precedence of the important work still to be done in Scotland. The castles of Perth, Dumfries, Roxburgh and Edinburgh were all recaptured in 1313 and the early months of 1314 − all tributes to the daring and inventiveness of the besiegers, for, through-out his campaigns, Bruce never possessed the massive siege engines which were almost essential for the reduction of any strongly built mediaeval stone castle. Stirling and Berwick were now the only important castles still held by England, and at Stirling Edward Bruce, despairing of its capture, entered into an agreement with its constable, De Mowbray, whereby De Mowbray, too, would surrender unless he were relieved within a year, that is by Midsummer Day (24 June) 1314. The agreement, though well in accord with the chivalrous practice of the time, was rash and foolish. Edward II and the Lords Ordainers had come to terms; the relief of a major castle in the heart of Scotland, still held by England touched English pride; the agreement made a determined effort by England inevitable, and at the same time gave England time to mobilise her might. Above all, in resisting relief by an English force Bruce would be committed to a pitched battle in which he would be confronted by England's superiority in knights and archers.

All that happened. Edward II led into Scotland a large army perhaps 20,000 strong and including some 3,000 heavy cavalry. He reached Edinburgh on 21 June 1314, with only three days to spare. The Scots, about one-third in number to the English, were already assembled in the Torwood, to the south of Stirling, to bar his way.

Any reconstruction of the subsequent movements of the English army and of the battle itself is far from easy. Advancing from Edinburgh, Edward's army apparently reached the Bannock burn towards the evening of 23 June. A body of horse, under Clifford, made a dash to reach Stirling Castle but, challenged by Randolph's spearmen, was severely handled and compelled to withdraw. Nearer to the Scottish lines, De Bohun was killed in single combat with Bruce. Probably the whole army (but not its baggage train) now crossed the Bannock and took up its position for the night somewhere in the angle formed by the Bannock and the loops of the Forth. They were within easy distance of the castle for its relief next day; and, although their position was wet and uncomfortable, they were well protected by the nature of the ground. The Bannock and marshy ground guarded their left; bog and marsh, interspersed with pools of water, guarded their right; the Forth guarded their rear.

But, so far as we can reconstruct events, on the morning of the next day – Midsummer Day, 24 June 1314 – the English commanders, greatly to their surprise, saw the Scots boldly advancing to the attack. Great general that he was, Bruce had noted the cramped position of the English host and its inability to deploy and to manoeuvre; if it could be ' contained ' in the position where it had passed the night, with marshy and impassable ground on both its flanks, and with only a narrow front[1] on which to fight, its very numbers would be a hindrance rather than a help. His well trained spearmen, in their schiltrons, stopped, and then pushed back, the first challenge of the English knights under the Earl of Gloucester; the English archers could not fan out to harass the Scottish schiltrons from the flanks (and those who strove to do so were dispersed by Bruce's light cavalry under Sir Robert Keith); the English knights, discomfited, were slowly and inexorably driven back into the ranks of those behind them, thus masking the footmen, and, finally, throwing them into disorder. The battle quickly became one between the Scots in ordered formation and the English crowded together in complete confusion and disarray; its end was the total rout of the impressive might of England. Many of those who strove to escape were drowned in the Forth; the Bannock was ' so filled with horses and men ' that others passed over them as over a bridge; wandering small groups of fugitives were at the mercy of the countryside; and Edward II, accompanied by a few horsemen, was lucky to escape to Dunbar. Nor should we forget the spoil, which was enormous, and

---

[1] Barbour speaks of ' the gret strathes of the plas ' (*The Bruce*, BOOK XII, line 430).

which included jewels, vestments, rich furniture and dress, as well as military stores and equipment. In addition, the ransoms of those English barons who were fortunate to be taken prisoner helped to fill many an empty Scottish purse. ' Scotland ', it was said, ' became rich in one day.'

The victory of Bannockburn secured Scotland's independence – for a time. And on 6 November 1314 a parliament, sitting at the Abbey of Cambuskenneth (near the field of the recent battle), passed sentence of forfeiture on all those who had fought for England in the preceding years of struggle and who did not now ' stand forth ' and declare their loyalty to King Robert.[1] The King, now secure from England, was to be assured of the faith of all men in his own kingdom.

Nor was that all. In the following year (1315) a further important question was decided – that of the succession to the throne. Bruce had as yet no son, for David, later to reign as David II, was not born until 1324; and the recent long struggle with England discouraged any thought of the succession of Bruce's daughter, Marjorie. Accordingly, in a national assembly at Ayr, and with the consent of Marjorie Bruce, it was agreed that Edward Bruce, the king's brother, and Edward Bruce's male heirs should succeed to the throne should King Robert leave no son. Failing male heirs to the king and to Edward Bruce, then the succession was to revert to Marjorie and her heirs; and failing all heirs to the king, to Edward and to Marjorie, the prelates, earls, barons and others of the community of the kingdom were to assemble to decide upon the succession to the throne. The lesson of 1291-92 was not to be forgotten; the decision of 1284 had not looked beyond the infant Margaret; and her premature death, with no declared successor, lay in the background of all the ills that had followed. Here, too, was a reversion to something like the old law of succession: the king-to-be was the king's brother, and he was named as successor because of his suitability to reign – Edward Bruce was chosen *tanquam vir strenuus et in actibus bellicis pro defensione juris et libertatis regni Scotie quam plurimum expertus*.

Edward Bruce, however, was killed in Ireland, in 1318, fighting against the English; he left no lawful son; and accordingly the succession to the throne had again to be defined. In December 1318, in a parliament held at Scone, Robert, the son of Marjorie Bruce and

---

[1] Barbour (*The Bruce*, BOOK XIII, lines 722-31) says that all who claimed to hold lands in Scotland were to do their right to the king within twelve months; and a number of lords were later restored by Bruce.

Walter the High Steward, was declared to be the heir to the throne
should Robert I leave no son; if Robert, or a son born to the king, was
of minor age at the time of the king's death, then Randolph was to be
guardian of the young king and the realm, and if, perchance, Randolph
was dead, James, lord of Douglas, was to be the guardian.   In 1324,
however, the king had a son, David (who succeeded as David II) and, in
1326, again to define the succession, an act of entail laid down that the
crown was to pass to Robert Stewart and his heirs should David leave
no lawful heir of his body.

With England heavily defeated and in no position to renew the
conflict, with Robert Bruce the acknowledged King of Scots, with those
who had previously opposed him either forfeited or now on his side,
and with the succession settled, the next step was to secure the recognition of Bruce's kingship by both England and the Pope.

While the English church had supported Edward's policy (although
resisting his financial demands), the more important Scottish churchmen (and notably the Bishops of St Andrews, Glasgow and Moray)
had consistently supported Bruce, even in defiance of the Pope who
equally consistently had refused to recognise Bruce's kingship.   Only a
few days after the killing of the Red Comyn, Robert Wishart, bishop of
Glasgow, had absolved Bruce.   When Bruce was crowned at Scone, the
Bishops of St Andrews, Glasgow and Moray and the Abbots of Scone
and Inchaffray took part in the ceremony.   In 1309 a number of the
clergy issued a declaration (which was accompanied by a declaration,
possibly in identical terms, by the nobles and community) in which they
proclaimed that Robert I had been ' solemnly made King of Scots ' and
that ' with him the faithful people of the Kingdom will live and die as
with one who, possessing the right of blood, and endowed with the
other cardinal virtues, is fitted to rule, and worthy of the name of King
and the honour of the Kingdom, since, by the grace of the Saviour . . .
he has by the sword restored the realm '.   And in 1320, when, at the
instance of Edward II, the Pope (John XXII) cited four of the Scottish
bishops to answer at the papal court, and sent two legates to publish a
further sentence of excommunication against Bruce (for continuing the
war), the letter sent by the barons to the Pope (the ' Declaration of
Arbroath '), was almost certainly drafted by Bernard de Linton, abbot
of Arbroath, Bruce's chancellor.   There the position of Bruce, and what
he meant to his people, were made abundantly clear.   There it was boldly
affirmed that all were bound to him ' both of right and by the service
he has rendered '; there it was declared that never would there be

submission to the yoke of England; there, in noble words the Scottish barons proclaimed that they fought ' not for glory, or riches or honours, but only for liberty, which no true man would yield save with his life.'[1]

But papal opposition to Bruce still persisted; the Pope refused to recognise his kingship; and papal letters were addressed to him as ' the noble man who at present governs Scotland ', or as ' Robert Bruce, calling himself king '; or as, simply, ' Robert Bruce '. In 1318 the Pope granted Edward II permission to devote towards an attack on Scotland part of a tithe collected in England for the purpose of a crusade[2]; and in 1324 he was still insisting upon a recognition of the English king's superiority over Scotland as a prerequisite to lifting the ban of excommunication and recognising Bruce as King of Scots.

In May 1323, however, a truce for thirteen years was concluded between Scotland and England, and with renewed tension between England and France over the question of Gascony (1324), and with the conclusion of the treaty of Corbeil (1326) between Bruce and Charles IV of France – a treaty under which neither country was to make peace or truce with England if the other country were still at war with England – the Pope, anxious for an end of the war, became more favourable to the Scots. Yet in the end, it was the troubles in England leading to the fall of Edward II which led also to the full recognition of Robert I by both England and the papacy.

In January 1327 Edward II was compelled to abdicate, and for a time the government of England was in the hands of his queen, Isabella, and her lover, Mortimer. Edward III was only fourteen years old. But if Edward II had been blamed for the loss of Scotland, Isabella and Mortimer were now to ratify that loss.

It is clear that the Scots regarded the truce of 1323 as expiring with the deposition of Edward II. In the summer of 1327 they were ravaging over the Border and Bruce was even making grants of lands in North-umberland – as though he aimed at its annexation. After a disastrous campaign against seasoned Scots troops led by Randolph and Douglas (who nearly captured the young Edward III in his tent), Isabella and Mortimer decided to sue for peace. Ambassadors with full power were

[1] Though the propagandist aspect of these Declarations must be kept in mind.

[2] To complete the story, the attack (made in 1319) was a miserable failure. The English army laid siege to Berwick, which had just been recaptured by the Scots after being held by England for twenty years; the Scots, leaving Berwick to defend itself, penetrated as far south as Yorkshire, harrying as they went and hoping to seize the English queen who was staying near York; a hastily assembled English force was routed at Myton-on-Swale; and the English magnates abandoned their siege of Berwick in an endeavour to protect their own lands from the Scottish invaders.

sent to Scotland; the terms of a treaty were concluded with Bruce (now suffering from a grave disease which may have been paralytic leprosy) in his chamber at Holyrood Abbey (March 1328); and, exceptionally, and more binding, the treaty was confirmed in an English parliament at Northampton (May 1328).

It is important to note that the final discussions were preceded by a renunciation by England of all claims to superiority over Scotland, and by a recognition by England of Robert Bruce as King of Scotland. Thus the treaty itself was concluded between two kings of two independent kingdoms. By the treaty, Bruce was again recognised as King of Scotland; there was to be ' good peace, final and perpetual ' between the two kingdoms, ' saving on the part of the king of Scotland the alliance made between him and the king of France ' (an important exception, dictated by virtue of the treaty of Corbeil, continuing the alliance of 1295-6, and, at times, to lead Scotland into disaster); all documents that could be found in England touching the subjection of the people or land of Scotland to the king of England, or touching the freedom of Scotland, were to be returned to Scotland[1]; Scotland was to pay (and did pay) to England the sum of £20,000 by three annual instalments[2]; for assuring the peace, David, the son of Bruce, was to marry Joan, the sister of Edward III; and, finally, the English were to use their endeavours to secure the removal of the papal ban on Bruce and any other Scots. The treaty did not include any mention of the return of the ' Coronation Stone ' nor any mention of the restoration to their lands of those who had been forfeited by Bruce and who, with others, were later to cause trouble in the reign of David II.

The marriage of David and Joan took place at Berwick on 12 July 1328. We have record of the arrangements for the wedding and of the food provided for the guests; and that the wall of the churchyard ' was broken down to the ground at the time of the marriage ' may be some

---

[1] It is to be noted that not *all* the Scottish records removed by Edward I were to be restored; but, so far as we know, not even those records touching the freedom of Scotland were returned. In August 1937, 600 years after the treaty, nine solitary Scottish documents, out of the vast mass of record removed by Edward I, were solemnly transferred from the Record Office in London to the Record Office in Edinburgh, and later a number of other Scottish documents, of little importance, were similarly handed over. All the many rolls of financial, judicial and executive affairs which Edward had carried away were lost in English keeping, and we possess only lists of the records that have been lost and that would have enabled a fuller history of Scotland to be written.

[2] This seems an ' Alice through the Looking Glass ' arrangement, whereby those who came to sue for peace were paid reparations by the victors.

indication of the throng of people who crowded to see the event. Bruce was not present – possibly through his illness: more likely because Edward III refused to be there. But the Queen Mother, Isabella, attended her daughter's wedding, and the evidence of the English records suggests that there she promised to return the ' Coronation Stone ' to Scotland, while the Scottish magnates agreed to restore Wake, Percy and Beaumont to their forfeited Scottish lands, to which, in fact, their claim rested mainly on recent English grants. Although Bruce was strongly opposed to the restoration of the ' disinherited ', he seems to have been willing to restore Percy's lands; but, in the result, neither the ' Stone ' nor the lands were restored.

With this treaty of ' final and perpetual peace ', Pope John XXII released Bruce from the ban of excommunication (October 1328), and addressed him as, ' Our dearest son, Robert, illustrious King of Scotland '. More than that, less than a year later he issued a Bull authorising Robert I and his successors to be crowned and anointed as Kings of Scotland – a clear recognition of their independent status as rulers of an independent kingdom.[1] The Bull was dated from Avignon, 13 June 1329; but Bruce, who, in the words of the Declaration of Arbroath, had ' cheerfully endured all manner of toil, fatigue, hardship and hazard ' that ' he might deliver his people and his heritage from the hands of enemies ', had died at Cardross a week earlier and never knew of this final recognition of his kingship and, with it, the independence of his kingdom.

Nor had Bruce striven for that alone. The full legislation of only one of his parliaments (that of 1318) has been preserved, but that legislation bears every mark of a determined effort to restore law and order within the realm and to strengthen the executive and the judiciary, as well as to provide for future defence. There we find enactments relating to the land law, to the criminal law, and to the arming of the lieges; we even find an act proscribing the sale or transfer of arms to ' our enemies of England '. The preamble to the acts states that the parliament had concerned itself with the ' amending of the land and the defence of the people, together with the peace of the land to be maintained and assured '; the work was one of reconstruction after war; and, indeed, in one respect the statutes of this parliament have been aptly termed the ' First Law Reform (Miscellaneous Provisions) Act ' for Scotland.

Scotland's independence had been acknowledged – for a while.

---

[1] By virtue of the Bull of 1329, David II was the first King of Scots to be anointed and crowned.

But something more than independence had been gained. The long struggle with England had completed the task that both the state and the church, working hand-in-hand, had earlier striven to achieve. A country had been moulded into a nation. Men from all corners of the land fought side by side at Bannockburn.[1] The bitterness of long and destructive war, however, and, immediately upon Bruce's death, its renewal by England and therewith Scotland's continuing struggle to maintain her independence, turned a new patriotism into a hostility to England that endured for centuries. England became the ' auld enemy '. In these succeeding years of warfare with England, invasion and counter-invasion, raiding and harrying became accepted as part of the Scot's inheritance, but also that inheritance now included a fierce spirit of independence which, in this and in other ways, became part and parcel of the Scottish character.

NOTE

Some Reasons for England's Failure in the ' Scots War '

In the War of Independence from 1296 to 1314 England had a number of factors in her favour. Many of the Scottish magnates, including both Bruce and Balliol, were of Anglo-Norman descent, holding lands in England as well as in Scotland. Hence, some were at first openly on the side of England and a few continued to fight on that side during the whole of the struggle. Others, however, who had at first supported the English king gradually came over to the side of Bruce, and, even after the forfeitures of 1314 (*supra*, p. 169), Bruce was generous to those who were willing to come into his peace. Again, at first, Edward I could play upon disunity. The Bruces would not fight for Balliol – nor would many others who regarded him as not worth fighting for. Later, when Bruce became king, the Comyns and their allies fought *against* Bruce but *not for* the English king. In general, Scotland, a much smaller country, could raise no fighting force comparable with that of England. She was particularly weak in knights and ' covered ' horse; and the bows of her archers were not equal to the English ' long bow '. She could not afford to hire mercenaries, and, despite the alliance with Philip IV, she received no real help from France. On the contrary,

---

[1] Though it should perhaps be noted that in the west the bitterness of the blood-feud still persisted, and some of the MacDowells, dispossessed because of continuing enmity, became soldiers of fortune as ' gallowglasses ' in Ireland. So, too, did some of the Sweyns of Knapdale (who had consistently opposed Bruce); and the Comyns disappeared from Buchan.

174

France twice deserted the Scots by making truce with Edward in 1297 and 1303.

On the other hand England suffered from a number of disadvantages. With simultaneous wars in Scotland and France (until 1303), Edward I could not concentrate his forces on one front only; and his frequent demands for fighting service to be rendered by his feudal tenants-in-chief in continual campaigns outside England led to trouble between the King and the magnates. Because of this, and because of protracted military operations in Scotland, mercenaries had to be paid. But the English treasury was empty; and Edward's use of high-handed methods to secure the necessary finance led to further opposition from the clergy and the merchants, and to borrowing instead of taxing. Edward II's difficulties accordingly arose from the heavy burden of debt which he had inherited from his father, and from baronial opposition – at first directed against his favourite, Piers Gaveston. Domestic strife in England enabled Bruce to consolidate his position in Scotland.

In the actual warfare itself, the physical geography of Scotland made conquest difficult and guerilla warfare easy; and Bruce's policy of destroying the castles prevented the English from holding any strong-points. All this, in turn, faced the English with constant difficulties in supply. When lines of communication could be cut, it was impossible to maintain a large army inland for any length of time, and the outlying castles were difficult to supply. Moreover there were no roads worthy of the name. Thus, in the end, only those castles which could be supplied by sea were able to continue to resist; and supplies by sea were dependent upon favourable winds. Feeding an army, moreover, meant feeding horses as well as men – notably the ' covered ' horses of the knights and the sumpter horses of the baggage train – and there was always a dearth of fodder in Scotland. This meant that real campaigning could be carried on only during the summer months; and the cessation of movement during the winter months gave the Scots opportunities for recovery. Even when Edward wintered at Linlithgow, in fertile Lothian, in 1301-2, he lost many horses through lack of feed.

But the English effort failed principally because Edward I failed to appreciate the determination of Scottish opposition to English rule – a determination revealed in one sentence in the ' Declaration of Arbroath ': ' so long as but one hundred of us shall remain alive, we shall never consent to bow beneath the yoke of English domination '. And that fervent spirit was fostered by the leading churchmen who had a strong hold over the lives and thoughts of the people.

CHAPTER XIX

' Dark and Drublie Days '

ALTHOUGH THE treaty of 1328 was accompanied by the marriage of David and Joan – a marriage ' for the assurance and confirming ' of peace between Scotland and England – the treaty was unstable. It was unpopular in England, where it was called ' the shameful peace ', and it was ascribed to treachery and cowardice on the part of Isabella and Mortimer who, it was argued, had sold to Scotland her independence for the paltry sum of £20,000, and moreover, at a time when Bruce was dying. Above all, once Edward III had established himself as a personal king (1330), he soon found an agent willing to help him to imitate the Scottish designs of his grandfather, Edward I. So the reign of Bruce's son, David II, was to be one of much misery and distress: unfortunate or incompetent regents were succeeded by a king who lacked his father's character; internal dissensions accompanied a renewed struggle with England, leading to great economic distress; and, in the midst of it all, the plague of the Black Death afflicted Scotland in 1349 and 1350, recurring with equal violence in 1361 and 1362.

David II, the son of King Robert I, was just over five years old when he became king. In accordance with the act of 1318 settling the succession to the crown, Thomas Randolph, earl of Moray, assumed the regency; and, in accordance with the papal Bull of 1329, David was anointed and crowned at Scone on 24 November 1331. But within a year thereafter Scotland was again fighting for her independence against a new threat from England.

Randolph, ' a man to be remembered while integrity, prudence and valour are held in esteem ', died on 20 July 1332. According to the act of 1318 he should have been succeeded in the regency by Sir James Douglas, but Douglas, taking the heart of Bruce to the Holy Land, had been killed in Spain when fighting against the Moors (August 1330). The new regent, chosen by the magnates (2 August 1332), was Donald, earl of Mar, a nephew of King Robert I; and, within the next few days, on 6 August 1332, Edward Balliol, son of John Balliol, landed with a small force at Kinghorn in Fife. On 12 August 1332 the new regent was defeated and slain at Dupplin, near Perth.[1] The struggle had begun anew.

[1] It is said that Balliol's force was guided to a ford over the river Earn by a

It is customary to refer to those who had landed with Edward Balliol as 'The Disinherited'. Certainly his followers included a number of those who, because of their adherence to the side of England, had been deprived of their lands in Scotland; but there were others in Balliol's following – some English who hoped to gain Scottish lands and, ere long, some Scots who sided with him for various motives of their own. Moreover there can be little doubt that from the very outset Balliol received the support and encouragement of Edward III, who had already received Balliol's homage and fealty as king of Scotland.

Following his victory at Dupplin, Balliol was crowned at Scone (24 September 1332). There are indications that the defeat of Mar's army – the defeat of a large Scots force by a mere 'handful' under Balliol – was regarded by some as a 'judgment of God' and a vindication of Balliol's 'right' to the crown. This might account for the presence, at the coronation, of former loyalists including William Sinclair, Bruce's 'fighting bishop' of Dunkeld[1]; though, according to one chronicler, all who were there 'were armed save for their helmets, since people and nobles inclined to Balliol more from fear than from love'. Within three months, indeed, Balliol, was surprised at Annan by the Earl of Moray (a son of Randolph) and by Archibald Douglas (a younger brother of the 'good Sir James'), and was compelled to seek refuge over the Border, fleeing, it was said, 'with one leg booted, the other naked'.

Hitherto Edward III, although secretly supporting Balliol, had preserved an outward neutrality; but now a few minor Scottish raids over the Border enabled the English king to declare that the treaty of 1328 had been broken. Balliol, with English support, once more entered Scotland and made his way towards Berwick; in May 1333 Edward III and Balliol began a combined siege of Berwick; and in July 1333 the Scots, under Archibald Douglas as regent, attempting to raise the siege, were massacred in trying to come to grips with the English army which was posted behind a marsh and on the rising ground of Halidon Hill. Although it was vital to prevent Berwick from falling into English hands and so becoming an English base on

---

Murray of Tullibardine, and was thus able to make a surprise attack on the sleeping Scots in the hours of darkness. But the defeat of the Scottish army by a much smaller English force was due, partly to Mar's military incompetence, partly to distrust and jealousy of his leadership, and partly to the English archers who, spread out on the flanks, poured a murderous rain of arrows on to the massed Scots.

[1] Bower relates how the Bishop had led an attack against the English at Donibristle and how Bruce had called him 'my bishop'.

the Scottish side of the Tweed, the regent's strategy and tactics were both at fault. The English archers ' won the battle at a distance ' and were already perfecting the use of the ' long bow ' that was soon to decide the field of Crécy.

' And now ', writes an English chronicler, ' it was the general opinion that the Scottish wars were over; for no man remained of that nation who had either the influence to assemble or the skill to lead an army.' In two disastrous defeats – at Dupplin and at Halidon Hill – Scotland had suffered enormous casualties and the loss of most of her important men.

In February 1334 Balliol and his supporters, Scots and English, held a parliament at Edinburgh in which, acknowledging the help he had received from Edward III as Lord Paramount of Scotland, Balliol surrendered the castle, town and county of Berwick to be forever annexed to the kingdom of England. The record of that ' parliament ', moreover, shows how the ' disinherited ' had been restored to their lands and how others who had come north from England had received their rewards from Balliol. There we read of Henry de Beaumont, earl of Buchan; David of Strathbogie, earl of Atholl; Richard Talbot, lord of Mar; while elsewhere we read that John de Warenne had been granted the earldom of Strathearn, that Percy claimed Annandale, and that Wake held Liddesdale. In the following June, at Newcastle, Balliol, again acknowledging the ' great assistance ' he had received from his ' dearest lord ', granted by charter to Edward III the southern counties of Scotland from Haddington in the east to Dumfries in the west, to be annexed and united ' to the royal dignity, crown and kingdom of England in all times to come '. Into these southern counties, although treated separately from England, Edward III promptly put his own sheriffs; in their castles he placed English garrisons; over them he appointed an English chamberlain and an English justiciar.

By these surrenders in return for Edward's help, Balliol committed Scotland to more than a hundred years of warfare in the recovery of her southern lands. Not until 1460 was Roxburgh castle finally regained from the English hold (in a siege which cost the life of James II); and not until 1461 was the castle of Berwick regained – only to be lost again, for ever, in 1482. But also by these surrenders, Balliol, emphasising the position of Edward as his overlord, stiffened a national resistance that had suffered but had not yielded. And, to complete the story of Edward Balliol's ' gratitude ' to Edward III, six days after granting away so rich a part of the realm, he did homage to his liege

lord for his kingdom of Scotland – or, perhaps more correctly, for what
was left of that kingdom.

The situation seemed so black that already the young King David II
and his queen had been sent for safety to France (May 1334). Yet,
here and there, those who were loyal to the house of Bruce were winning
small successes, and Balliol once more apparently found it advisable
to retire into northern England.[1] In the autumn of 1334 and the
summer of 1335 Edward III led large English forces into southern
Scotland in support of his puppet king, when, according to Wyntoun,
so many Scottish lords submitted to him that only the children dared
to own that they were on the side of David.

But Balliol still returned to winter in England, and even an English
chronicler records that ' he possessed no castle or town in Scotland
in which he could live in safety '. In the winter of 1335, moreover,
Sir Andrew Moray of Bothwell, Patrick, earl of Dunbar, and William
Douglas of Liddesdale defeated and slew his lieutenant, David, earl of
Atholl, in the forest of Culblean in Mar. Once more Edward III
intervened. In the summer of 1336 he made a ' progress in strength '
as far north as Lochindorb[2] where he relieved Catherine de Beaumont
(the widow of the Earl of Atholl) who was holding the castle against an
attack by loyal Scots. Forres, Elgin and Aberdeen were burned, and
new defences were made at Perth and Stirling. But Sir Andrew Moray
of Bothwell, the new guardian of the realm, wiser than his predecessors,
refused to be drawn into battle, and, as soon as Edward had returned
to England, he began to reduce one by one the castles that were held
for Balliol. Nevertheless the hold of England was still strong, particularly in all the southern parts; and many Scots, through attachment to
Balliol, or through ambition and self-interest, still adhered to the
English side.

For a short time in the summer of 1337 Edward was back in Scotland,
compelling Moray to abandon his siege of Stirling castle; and then, in
1338, he sailed to the Low Countries to advance his claim to the throne
of France. So began the Hundred Years War – ' happily for Scotland ',
as Bower records, ' for if the King of England had continued his warfare

---

[1] It is not easy to ascertain to what extent Balliol's frequent departures from
Scotland into northern England were due to difficulties facing him in Scotland. Some
visits to northern England were probably necessary in that Edward III had entrusted
to him the command of certain English forces there.

[2] On the border of the counties of Elgin and Nairn. The castle, on an island in
the loch, was protected by very deep water and was regarded as being well-nigh
impregnable.

in Scotland, he would have gained possession of the whole land, without difficulty, as far as it is humanly possible to judge '.

Certainly, with Edward III's new commitments in France, the whole picture in Scotland began to change. Already, prior to Edward's departure, ' Black Agnes ', wife of Patrick, earl of Dunbar, had successfully held Dunbar castle against a five months' siege by the Earl of Salisbury who is said to have complained that

> Came I early, came I late,
> I found Agnes at the gate.

Already, too, in the west, Sir William Douglas, the ' Knight of Liddesdale ', was driving out the English forces. Before long, the castles of Perth and Edinburgh were recaptured from their English garrisons; in the summer of 1341 it was deemed safe for David II and his queen to return from France; and in 1342 Stirling castle was starved into surrender. Balliol had again retired to England.

But the troubles of Scotland were not ended. In 1346, while Edward (whose archers had won the battle of Crécy) was investing Calais, the young David II (he was then twenty-two), partly in response to an appeal from France (and in fulfilment of the treaty of Corbeil of 1326), and partly anxious to display his military prowess in the field of battle, invaded England as far south as Durham, wasting as he went. At Neville's Cross, near Durham, he was met by an army that had been assembled by the northern lords still in England and was defeated and taken prisoner. The King, as befitted the son of Bruce, had fought bravely and, when at last overpowered, had been twice wounded. Robert, the High Steward,[1] who, according to the English chroniclers, had virtually fled the field, escaped with the remnant of the Scottish army and now became regent of the realm. David II was to be a closely guarded prisoner in England, and the Steward was to be regent in Scotland, for almost exactly eleven years.

As early as 1348 negotiations were begun for the release of David, the payment of his ransom, and the settlement of a treaty of peace. The negotiations dragged on, however, until 1354 when, by a treaty concluded at Newcastle, the Scots King was to be ransomed for 90,000 merks to be paid in nine annual instalments of 10,000 merks each, and during that time there was to be a truce between the two realms. As

---

[1] It is perhaps important to remember that the Steward, although David II's nephew (he was the son of David's sister, Marjorie), was older than the King. In 1346 the Steward was thirty years of age.

soon as the French heard of this, however, they at once sent to Scotland a small force of knights and men-at-arms and, with them, a sum of money[1] to be distributed among the nobility to persuade them to renew the war. Whereupon the Scots, who, according to Fordun, ' will frequently lose a shilling to gain a penny ', tempted by the French gold, ravaged the Border and, with the help of the French troops, seized Berwick. This was promptly followed by the ' Burnt Candlemas ' of 1356 when Edward III, who had returned from France, regained Berwick and thereafter ravaged and burned the whole countryside between Roxburgh and Edinburgh.[2] And meantime, in January 1356, at Roxburgh, Edward Balliol had surrendered to the English king the crown and kingdom of Scotland – though that, as one chronicler remarks, meant little, for he had no right to either the kingdom or the crown. For Scotland, it simply meant that Edward Balliol was heard of no more; but, for Edward III, it made possible new designs which were to take final shape in 1363-4.

By a treaty concluded at Berwick (October 1357), David II was released from his eleven years' captivity for a ransom of 100,000 merks to be paid in ten annual instalments of 10,000 merks each during a ten-year truce – terms that were virtually identical with those of the treaty of Newcastle, save that now the Scots had to pay a further 10,000 merks for breaking that treaty. But, from the Exchequer accounts that have been preserved, it would appear that at this period the royal receipts and the royal expenditure barely balanced; and now Scotland had to find, somehow, for the next ten years, an additional £6,666 a year (an additional annual sum which seems to have been about equal to the total of the gross annual revenue of the crown), as well as supporting the costs of twenty noble hostages who were to be maintained in England as security for the ransom payments.[3]

During the many negotiations, from 1348 to 1357, which preceded the treaty of Berwick, it is twice reported by the chroniclers that David had been willing to barter the independence of his kingdom in return for his release. During the winter of 1351-2 he appears to have been allowed to go to Scotland to try to negotiate some such terms, but, according to Wyntoun, ' spede noucht at his likynge '. Certainly, in a

---

[1] Variously stated to be 10,000 merks or as much as 17,000 merks.

[2] Particularly mourned by Fordun was the burning of the church of the Friars Minor of Haddington, of which the choir, on account of its singular beauty and the clearness of its light, was known as ' The Lamp of Lothian '.

[3] It is necessary to stress, however, that the Exchequer accounts, in addition to being fragmentary, do not give an exact or complete picture of the national finances

petition to the Pope in 1350, David had declared that the King of England would grant him his freedom if he would do homage to him, would be willing to be cited as a vassal to the parliaments and councils of England, and would be ready to concur in an agreement under which, if he died without a lawful heir, the King of England or one of his sons should succeed him on the Scottish throne. And finally, in 1363-4, six years after his release, David and Edward III came to a somewhat similar agreement – undoubtedly put forward by the English king, and this time solely as a bargain for the cancellation of the unpaid part of the ransom.

David II was childless. His queen, Joan, had died in 1362; and, although he married Margaret Drummond in 1363, she, too, was to bear him no children. His successor, according to the settlement of 1318, would be the Steward – Robert, the son of Marjorie Bruce; and David hated the Steward. He could not forget that his long captivity had been due in part to the Steward's conduct on the field of Neville's Cross; and, during his long captivity, the Steward had ruled the realm. Moreover, the heavy burden of the ransom (although by 1362 only two instalments had been paid in full), apparently made it impossible for the king to live as he desired, or thought to be consonant with his dignity. In 1363 the Earl of Douglas, with Robert the Steward and the Earl of March, had even risen in revolt on a cry that the king, ransomed at great cost to his people, was squandering in the gratification of his own pleasures the monies collected for the ransom payments to England. Yet it is to be noted that, immediately after that rising had collapsed, and new oaths of fealty had been exacted, David II proceeded to London where, in November 1363, he entered into an agreement with Edward III under which, in return for the cancellation of all the arrears of the ransom and the release of the Scottish hostages, the King of England, or one of his sons, was to succeed to the kingdom of Scotland – though the name and title of the realm of Scotland and all its laws and customs were to be maintained.

According to this agreement, David was to ' sound the inclinations ' of his people, upon his return to Scotland, and to report back to Edward before 7 April 1364. David did sound the inclinations of his people, in a parliament held at Scone on 4 March 1364. We do not know what the king said to his parliament; but we know what parliament said to the king. ' It was there expressly replied by the three estates that they were in no way willing to comply with, nor in any wise willing to assent to those points ' which had been put before them: and the

Latin of the record has the ring of finality – *Nullo modo voluerunt concedere nec eis aliqualiter assentire*. The people of Scotland preferred the burden of the ransom to the rule of an English king.

And what did that mean ? Already heavy taxations had been laid upon those holding land; already the great customs had been doubled and then trebled, with the result that these exceptionally heavy export duties seemed likely to affect adversely the exports of wool, skins and hides; and already the crown had been authorised to buy the staple products of wool and skins at fixed prices so that it could sell them abroad at higher rates. Already, too, all land-holdings had been revalued and a census had been taken of all livestock and goods, so that a ' willing grant ' or a ' capital levy ' could be imposed – though there is no record of its exaction.

In 1369, however, when, after nine years of peace, the French war broke out again, Edward III, completely without allies, and anxious to have a quiet Scotland in his rear, agreed that, since 44,000 merks had now been paid, the balance of the ransom should be paid off by reduced annual instalments of 4,000 merks over a period of truce lasting fourteen years. Under that arrangement Scotland regularly paid her 4,000 merks a year from 1369 until the death of Edward III in 1377,[1] when she ceased to pay.[2] Possibly she took advantage of the troubled state of England on the accession of Richard II; possibly, having learned legal arguments from Edward I, she could argue that the ransom was a personal payment to Edward III, and not an impersonal payment to the government of England, and that, as a personal payment, it was automatically cancelled with Edward III's demise.

David II died in 1371. He was only forty-six years old. The records prove that he strove to strengthen the authority of the crown and the administration of the law which had languished under the Steward; his reply to the rising led by the Steward and the earls of Douglas and March reveals energy, spirit and purpose; and, to Wyntoun, his chief characteristic was his ' radure ' – his rigour, or severity.[3] Nevertheless, although he was undoubtedly influenced by a hatred of the Steward, the negotiations with Edward III were unworthy of the son of Robert Bruce.

---

[1] The treaty of 1357 had provided for the payment of the whole ransom even if David died before complete payment had been made. David had died in 1371, and that part of the treaty was thus observed.

[2] The outstanding balance of 24,000 merks was never paid.

[3] If, at times, there was also irascibility, it may be that he endured constant pain from an arrow-barb (a legacy of Neville's Cross) which for many years could not be removed from his head: though the story is to be found only in the *Scotichronicon*.

It is perhaps easy to forget his long imprisonment and its effect upon him; equally easy to underrate his difficulties. The burden of the ransom and of the support of the hostages in England, coming so soon after crippling years of war and devastation, was bound to weaken the royal authority. Laws have need of arms, and arms need money. The royal exchequer was probably incapable of meeting the essential royal needs – quite apart from any extravagances of the king. The task of ' government ' was thus doubly difficult. Significantly, certain lords had shown in 1363 that they could try to put the king to defiance: under David's immediate successors such defiance was to be more successful.

It would appear that David II tried to improve the efficiency of Parliament,[1] and there is evidence that he strove to combat the cumbrous and slow machinery of the courts of law. On the other hand it is clear that, apart from its forthright reply in 1364, the king's council in parliament was beginning to act as a check upon the king. In 1357, for example, immediately upon the conclusion of the treaty of Berwick, it was enacted that the King must not alienate the crown lands and rents, but that they must be retained with the crown to provide the crown with its essential revenues, so that ' the community of the kingdom, already burdened with the payment of the king's ransom, may not be further burdened with his expenses '.[2] Finally, the difficulty of raising the ransom payments eventually gave the burghs (which could contribute through their overseas trade) definite and regular representation in parliament. In the reign of David II we read, for the first time, of ' the Three Estates '.

[1] Cf. *infra*, pp. 192-3.

[2] But much the same thing was said again with greater emphasis in the Parliament of 1366, which suggests that the earlier enactment had not been effective. Parliament might pass good laws, but, in the absence of a strong executive to enforce them, they remained little more than expressions of good intent.

CHAPTER XX

The Burgesses Come to Parliament

WE HAVE already seen the burghs as new colonies of new men concerned with trade. We have seen them as strong-points helping to hold for the king the outlying parts of the king's lands: for trade is dependent upon peace. We have seen the kings granting charters to their burghs (the king's burghs, later known as ' royal burghs '), by which the burgh adjacent to the sheriff's castle was given a monopoly of trade over the area of the sheriffdom. And we have noted that the burgh was essentially a trading community.

We have seen, too, that because trade requires special laws of its own, different from the feudal law which is largely a land law, the burghs, in consequence, had a separate central court, the ' Court of the Four Burghs ', which, sitting under the Chamberlain, heard appeals and determined burgh law.[1] Indeed, this court was sometimes called the ' Parliament ' of the Four Burghs; and naturally so, for at first it was essentially a court of law: it declared the law of the burghs just as the other and better-known Parliament declared the law of the land.

Gradually, however, the Court of the Four Burghs became concerned with the trade of the burghs rather than with burgh law; and its membership increased. For example, it was apparently decided in 1405[2] that henceforth two or three burgesses from *every* burgh south of the Spey should attend the Court of the Four Burghs annually so that there they could ' treat, ordain and determine upon all things concerning the utility of the common weal of the king's burghs '. Certainly in 1487 Parliament enacted that representatives of all the burghs, both north and south, should meet yearly to treat of ' the welfare of merchants ' and ' the common profit of burghs '. In effect, representatives of the burghs were to meet together regularly, so that they could consider how to advance their prosperity through the advancement of trade.

The Court of the Four Burghs, although by then more broadly based, disappeared in the early years of the sixteenth century, but its place was soon taken by other, informal, meetings of representatives of the more important burghs. Common discussion, leading to common action to protect and further burgh trade, was too desirable to be allowed

---

[1] *Supra*, pp. 118-19.　　　　[2] Though 1455 would appear a more likely date.

to fall into desuetude. And from about 1552 these irregular and informal meetings became regular and formal: they became meetings of the Convention of Royal Burghs, which, from 1587 (if not earlier), sat annually and which still sits annually, to discuss burgh privileges, burgh trade and burgh policy.

The Convention of Royal Burghs contained representatives of all the important royal burghs; so, too, did Parliament. And towards the end of the sixteenth century it was apparently customary for a Convention of Royal Burghs to meet just before a meeting of Parliament. This was doubly convenient. In their Convention the burghs could decide upon a common policy which they would adopt in Parliament; also (and a great saving in travelling expenses), the representatives of the burghs who were attending the Convention could stay on to attend the Parliament. But how did the burghs become one of the ' Estates ' in Parliament ?

There is no reference to the burghs in the early negotiations with Edward I. The letter sent from Birgham in 1290, agreeing to the marriage of the ' Maid of Norway ' with Edward I's son, bore the names of twelve bishops, twelve earls, twenty-three abbots, eleven priors, and all the important barons in the land; but there is no mention of burghs or burgh representatives. Yet in 1296 the seals of six leading burghs (Edinburgh, Berwick, Roxburgh, Stirling, Perth and Aberdeen) were appended to the ratification of the alliance with France ' in token of their consent and approval '. This was something new. Six of the leading burghs were associated with an important step in national affairs, though we do not know whether they were participators in the deliberations which preceded that step.

The next stage was reached in 1326 when we find the ' burgesses ' (and that must mean burgesses from the king's burghs) agreeing that they, with the earls, barons and freeholders, would pay one-tenth (a ' tenth penny ') of their annual revenues to King Robert I to enable him to maintain his royal state – the crown lands and rents having been sadly diminished by war. This agreement was made at Cambuskenneth when the King was holding his Parliament there, and it was in the form of an indenture – a duplicate agreement, of which one part, sealed by the King, was to be held by the earls, barons, freeholders and burgesses, and the other part, sealed by the earls, barons, freeholders and burghs, was to be held by the King. It was a bargain as well as an agreement. The King was granted a tenth penny; he, in turn, promised, among other things, to pay, in ready cash, the market price for anything requisitioned by his officers for his own personal needs when on his journeyings through his kingdom.

All the evidence indicates that burgesses, equally with the prelates and barons, had been called to a Parliament to agree there to a financial burden that was to be imposed upon all of them; and, since the burgesses were the king's men and the land of the burgh was the king's land, the presence of burgesses of the king's burghs at the king's court was compatible with feudal theory: though how far the king would have strict regard to feudal theory when finance was required is another matter. Again, in 1328, when the treaty of 'perpetual peace' was drawn up at Edinburgh and when again the burghs would have to contribute towards the payment of £20,000 to England,[1] the records show that the burgesses were called to the Parliament that agreed the treaty.

But while, in 1326 and 1328, and probably, too, in 1340 and 1341, burgesses were called to Parliament when the burghs were involved in Parliament's financial decisions, there is no evidence that they were called to other Parliaments at which no such financial decisions were made. Thirty years later, however, the necessity of finding largs sums of money for the payment of David II's ransom not only again brought the burgesses into Parliament, but also led to the regular attendance of burgh representatives at all subsequent Parliaments where they sat as an 'Estate' of the realm. That is to say, out of the endeavours to meet David II's ransom the Scottish Parliament became a body of 'Three Estates' – Prelates, Nobles, Burgesses.

Here it is essential to bear in mind the characteristics that by now distinguished a meeting of Parliament from other meetings of the King's Council.[2] A Parliament was now publicly proclaimed; it was summoned by precept; and both the proclamation and the precepts had to give at least forty days' notice in advance. And those characteristics were now emphasised in the confirmation of the treaty for the release of David II and the payment of his ransom.

In September 1357 the Steward, as lieutenant of the King, the clergy, the magnates, and seventeen named royal burghs, had empowered plenipotentiaries to negotiate for the ransoming of the King. The treaty of release and ransom was finally concluded at Berwick on 3 October, and was ratified there on 5 October by the King and the Scottish plenipotentiaries, but confirmation by David II under the great seal had to reach Berwick on 11 November, or within eight days there-

[1] *Supra*, p. 119, n. 172.   [2] *Supra*, p. 107.

187

after. Such a short interval, however, made it impossible to summon a Parliament: there was not sufficient time to prepare all the precepts and to give the requisite forty days' notice. Accordingly David confirmed the treaty in a Council held at Scone on 6 November 1357. And in the proceedings of that Council (as recorded in a near-contemporary transcript called ' The Black Book ': for unfortunately the original record has not survived) we find the phrase ' The Three Estates ' (*tres communitates*) used for the first time. Apart from the use of this phrase, the proceedings, as they have come down to us, provide no clear indication of the attendance of burgh representatives; but confirmation of the treaty meant finding the money for the ransom payments. In the account of the proceedings of the Council at Scone it is significant that the trading privileges of the burghs are expressly confirmed and it is laid down that foreign merchants are to be allowed to enter peacefully to buy and to sell – which suggests not only the presence of burgesses but even some representations by the burghs that if they were to contribute to heavy ransom payments they could do so only if their trade was protected by the Crown. That is, the evidence indicates that some representatives of the burghs were present at the Council at Scone in November 1357; and the use of the phrase ' The Three Estates ' may mean that the burgh representatives took a full part, with the prelates and the nobility, in the council's deliberations – thus turning a council into a General Council.

Then, in March 1364, it is just possible that burgh representatives were present in the Parliament to which David II presented the agreement he had made with Edward III.[1] Again we have to rely upon the ' Black Book ', and there, although those present are said to be the prelates and the nobility (*proceres*), the rejection of the agreement is stated to have been made ' by the three estates '. Possibly the prelates and the nobility thought that they, and they alone, were concerned in such a high matter as the succession to the throne; but the rejection of David's scheme meant continuing to pay the ransom – a matter in which the burghs also had a lively concern.

In addition to the possibility that burgh representatives were present in the Parliament of March 1364, the proceedings of that Parliament are interesting in another way. As we have seen, the burden of the ransom was preferred to an English king on the Scottish throne[2]; but, nevertheless, it was decided to send an embassy to

[1] *Supra*, pp. 182-3.
[2] *Supra*, pp. 182-3.

England to try to negotiate easier ransom payments. We then read that the prelates and the nobles (again there is no mention of the burghs) undertook to meet again immediately upon the return of the ambassadors; more than that, they agreed that they would meet in response to royal letters under whatsoever seal, that they would come together ' as if they were lawfully summoned upon forty days as to a parliament ', and that they would raise no objection to a shorter summons. A clear proof that Parliament was summoned upon forty days' notice and that the precepts summoning the prelates and nobles to parliament were issued under a particular seal.

So far we have been dependent largely upon indirect evidence, but there is direct and definite evidence that representatives of the burghs were present in the Parliament of 1366. In the Parliament held in July 1366 – again mainly to devise ways and means of paying the king's ransom – we read that the bishops, abbots, priors, earls, barons and tenants-in-chief of the king had been summoned in the manner due and wont (*more debito et solito*), and that from each burgh certain burgesses had been summoned for the purpose and cause then on hand (*qui ad hoc fuerunt ex causa summoniti*). The ' purpose and cause then on hand ' was simply the raising of money for the ransom. Finance, as in 1326, 1328, 1357 and 1364, was the controlling factor. The burghs had money; the burghs had to contribute to the ransom; therefore the burghs could claim and were given a right to take part in the discussions. And in 1367 burgh representatives were again in Parliament, and we read ' Statutum est per tres communitates in parliamento '.

Admittedly the burgesses were in Parliament only for a special purpose; they were present *ad hoc* and *ex causa*. But, from now onwards, they stayed in. The limiting phrases *ad hoc* and *ex causa* disappeared early in the fifteenth century, and then we find that from every burgh ' three or four of the more sufficient burgesses, holding sufficient commission ', were to be summoned to each Parliament. That is, the burgess-representatives were to come with authenticated documents (their commissions) showing that they had been duly appointed by their fellow burgesses and were capable of speaking and acting for them.

At the same time we should note that not all the royal burghs took advantage of their new privilege and right, and, until the second half of the sixteenth century, the presence of representatives from this or that burgh tended to be somewhat haphazard. The burghs might wish to have a say in matters that affected them, but attendance could be

189

burdensome and was always expensive. During the fifteenth century we can trace irregular attendance from various burghs numbering some thirty-four in all, but in the second half of the sixteenth century there was fairly regular attendance from about fifty burghs. By then, too, the burghs had come to an agreement among themselves that Edinburgh should send two representatives to Parliament while the remaining burghs should send one each. But, until the second half of the sixteenth century, the new ' Third Estate ' was never strong. Moreover, the burgh representatives came into Parliament to give their consent to a policy that entailed taxation – and, to the very end, burgh representation in Parliament was closely associated with the burghs' contributions to national taxations. As a result, there was a tendency for the burgh representatives to think mainly of the protection of their purses and the maintenance of their trading rights.

This attitude was aggravated in other ways. For example, the burghs had their own assembly to discuss their own affairs, and when, as we have seen, the practice grew up of holding a Convention of Royal Burghs immediately prior to a sitting of Parliament, the Convention could ' instruct ' the burgess representatives. Naturally this accentuated a concern with matters touching ' the common weal ' of the burghs, rather than a concern with matters touching the welfare of the whole realm. In due course, the Convention of Royal Burghs even endeavoured to ensure that no individual burgh representative should raise any matter in Parliament without the previous consent of the Convention. Again, when the burgh representatives came into parliament they were a lone group, and, isolated from the prelates and the nobles, but sitting in the same chamber with them (for the Scottish Parliament was always unicameral), they would be apt to suffer from an inferiority complex. Until the very end of the sixteenth century there were no representatives of the shires, as there were in England; and thus the mediaeval Scottish Parliament, unlike that of England, had no real Third Estate composed of burgesses and knights of the shire. In the Scottish Parliament influence and power still lay with the great lords, spiritual and temporal. Some burgesses there might be, but they were there to help with the finding of money, and they were expected not to interfere too much in important matters of state.

Further, we should note that although, from 1366 onwards, there were some burgh representatives in Parliament, and until about 1450 some burgh representatives in General Councils, by the close of the fifteenth century the king was holding General Councils to which, apparently, he invited lords spiritual and temporal, barons and lairds but not burgesses. But, and of importance to the burghs, General Councils, as we have seen, could, and did, impose taxations. Indeed, taxation in due course tended to be closely associated with the work of a General Council. Gradually the burghs, becoming more politically conscious, and realising that the presence of burgesses at General Councils would be to their advantage, began to struggle for a right to take part in the work of a General Council, and notably when the General Council was concerned with finance. In 1504 it was conceded that the burghs were to be warned when ' taxes or contributions ' were to be imposed so that their advice could be had ' as one of the three estates of the realm '. In 1563 they gained a right to be called when ' peace or war ' (which might well mean taxation) was under consideration; and in 1567 a right to take part in discussions touching ' weighty affairs ' of the realm. Soon after 1504, indeed, a General Council began to be called a ' Convention of Estates ' – a coming-together-by-invitation of the Three Estates, as compared with a formal summoning to Parliament; and early in the seventeenth century there was little difference in membership between a Convention of Estates and a Parliament.

Again, with the financial burdens falling upon the realm to meet the ransom of the king, it was vital that burgh privileges (the source of much money) should be protected, and also that law and order should be maintained, so that trade could flourish. As we have seen, when the first arrangements for raising the ransom money were made in 1357, it was enacted that the burghs and burgesses were freely to enjoy all their wonted rights, liberties and privileges. Then, in 1364, when the agreement entered into between David II and Edward III was rejected, and there was a continuing need to find money for the ransom payments, the King issued a general charter to all his burghs granting that trade with foreign merchants was to be limited to the king's burghs, and that the buying and selling of wool, skins, hides and other merchandise was to be conducted only through the burgh merchants.[1] At this time, too, each succeeding Parliament and General Council emphasised the necessity for maintaining peace throughout the realm; the king's officers were to be men capable of giving ' justice to every man ' with ' one common justice ' which was to be done ' without exception of person '. Yet the constant re-enactment that law and order must be

[1] That is, confirming the trading monopolies granted by earlier charters (see *supra*, pp. 112, 118).

maintained is in itself proof that enactment was not enough; and although there was some attempt to secure better justice with more efficient judges in the local courts, it was already becoming clear that the executive was too weak. Good laws might be passed for good justice; but the machinery to put the good laws and good justice into effect was not there.

NOTE

Committees and Commissions of Parliament

Because of the continuing lack of good justice in the local courts men began to seek justice more and more in the king's own court of Parliament – sometimes on appeal to the highest court, sometimes on petition for the remedy of some wrong or the enforcement of some right. But Parliaments, to which all the great lords, spiritual and temporal, were summoned, could be neither frequent nor of long duration, and, when sitting, had increasingly important matters of state to demand their attention. To ease this situation, we find, in the reign of David II, that Parliament had begun to appoint two small committees for judicial work: one committee for falsed dooms (*ad judicia contradicta*), and one committee for causes, complaints and petitions (*ad causas et querelas* or *supplicationes*). This development enabled Parliament to get on with the work of government while the committees were dealing with its judicial work; and the committees reported their findings to Parliament for Parliament's confirmation. Later, as we shall see, James I set up a new court to try to secure better justice for his lieges (and again to relieve Parliament of the burden of appeals and complaints); but a final solution to the problem of a central court for civil justice was not found until the establishment of the College of Justice (Court of Session) in the reign of James V.

Also, beginning in the reign of David II, and possibly because of the difficulty of keeping a large number of people together in one place for any length of time, we find the Estates electing certain of their number to 'hold' the Parliament, while leave is given to all the rest to go home. The chosen members, holding Parliament by commission, had the full power of Parliament; they could decide and act; they were, in fact, the Parliament. While a smaller parliament could be conducive to greater expedition – perhaps even to greater efficiency – the membership of each 'commission' was of considerable importance. The expedient, valuable in itself, could become subject to abuse. The king's Council, or a feudal faction then in power, might put forward the names of the members. Again, when we find a commission dividing itself into committees for judicial work and for ' secret affairs of the king and kingdom ', and when we note that there are no burgess members among those who are to consider the ' secret affairs ', it begins to look as though the burghs had gained little by their admission to Parliament and that effective power was still in the hands of the big lords.[1]

[1] See *Source Book of Scottish History*, VOL. I (2nd edn.), pp. 194-208.

CHAPTER XXI

The Early Stewarts

DAVID II had died without issue, and accordingly he was succeeded on the throne by Robert, the High Steward, who became Robert II, the first king of the Stewart dynasty, by virtue of the ' Acts of Settlement ' of 1318 and 1326.[1] But, once more, there was need to define the succession to the throne. Not only was Robert II nearly fifty-five years old, but also there was some dubiety about the legitimacy of his children by his first wife, Elizabeth Mure, daughter of Sir Adam Mure of Rowallan. The Steward had been granted a papal dispensation in 1347 for his marriage to Elizabeth Mure, but, on the other hand, his eldest son John, earl of Carrick (and later Robert III), had been born some ten years before the dispensation was granted. Admittedly the canon law laid down that children who were born out of wedlock were made legitimate by the subsequent marriage (*per subsequens matri- monium*) of their parents; but there were those who argued that no subsequent marriage under a papal dispensation could make legitimate the children already born to parents who were within the forbidden degrees. If the parents were not ignorant of their relationship, were not such children born in incest ? Were they not debarred from every legal right ? Was John, earl of Carrick, born ten years before the dispensation for the marriage of his parents, made legitimate by that dispensation ? Could he, indeed, claim to be the lawful and legitimate heir to the Scottish throne ? And, if all the children of Elizabeth Mure who were born before the granting of the dispensation were not legi- timate, was not the rightful heir to the throne David, earl of Strathearn, the eldest son of Robert II by his second wife, Euphemia, daughter of Hugh, earl of Ross ?

Thus, with the accession of Robert II in February 1371, it was essential, in view of the King's advanced age, that the succession to the throne should be put beyond question. Accordingly, at Scone, in March 1371, and on the day following the King's coronation, it was declared ' for greater certainty ' that John, earl of Carrick, the eldest son of Robert II and Elizabeth Mure, was the rightful heir to the

---

[1] *Supra*, pp. 169-70. A settlement of the throne which Parliament had refused to alter when it rejected the proposals of 1364 (*supra*, pp. 182-3).

throne[1] – a declaration to which the prelates and nobles assented and which they swore, individually, to maintain, and to which, when written on parchment, they affixed their seals; and the whole nature of this declaration, which, with its many seals, has fortunately survived, indicates the serious nature of the decision that had to be made. Again, two years later, in 1373, and to avoid ' the uncertainty of the succession ', Parliament reaffirmed the right of John, earl of Carrick, and his heirs male, and thereafter defined the order of succession *nominatim*. In the event of the failure of the line of John, earl of Carrick, and his heirs male, the crown was to pass to Robert, earl of Fife, and his heirs male; whom failing, to Alexander, lord of Badenoch, and his heirs male – all these being the three surviving sons of Robert II by Elizabeth Mure. Only if all those lines were to fail was the crown to pass to David, earl of Strathearn, and his heirs male; whom failing, to Walter, his brother, and his heirs male – these being the two sons of Robert II by Euphemia Ross.

Nevertheless, there were still some who felt that the sons whose legitimacy was dubious had been preferred to the sons whose legitimacy was unquestioned; and the possibility of a claim to the throne being made by the House of Strathearn is reflected, much later, in the steps taken by James I to consolidate his position immediately upon his return from captivity,[2] and in the plot that culminated in his assassination.[3] Even as late as 1632, when, in the reign of Charles I, the Earl of Menteith had successfully claimed the earldom of Strathearn, it was felt that there might be a challenge to the throne, and the Earl was stated by his enemies to have boasted that he had ' the reddest blood in Scotland' with a better right to the crown than Charles himself, who could claim descent only from John, earl of Carrick, the eldest son of Robert II and Elizabeth Mure.

Of Robert II's own right to the throne there could be no doubt; but his ability to rule was another matter. Throughout his reign his rule was weak and inefficient, and that of his son, John, who succeeded as Robert III,[4] was even weaker still. And the weakness of the royal rule was revealed in the unfettered strength of the nobility. To the more powerful among the nobility these Stewarts were merely a noble house raised to kingship by a lucky marriage in the dim and distant

---

[1] And thereby the canon law doctrine of legitimation *per subsequens matrimonium* apparently became accepted in Scottish law. Only in modern times was it accepted in English law.

[2] *Infra*, p. 211.   [3] *Infra*, p. 218.

[4] The name of John was possibly considered to be one of ill omen for a king; also, would the new king be John I or John II?

THE EARLY STEWARTS

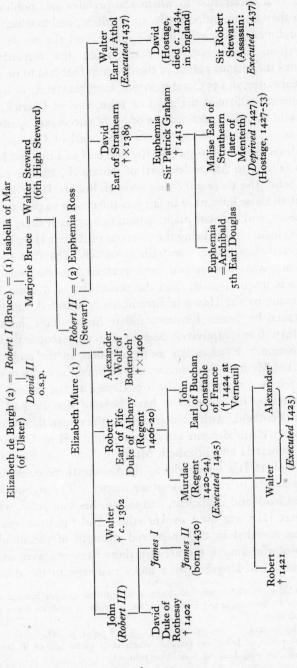

Elizabeth de Burgh (2) = *Robert I* (Bruce) = (1) Isabella of Mar
(of Ulster) |
|
David II
o.s.p.

Marjorie Bruce = Walter Steward
(6th High Steward)
|
Elizabeth Mure (1) = *Robert II* = (2) Euphemia Ross
(Stewart)

Walter
† *c.* 1362

John
(*Robert III*)
|
David
Duke of
Rothesay
† 1402

Robert
Earl of Fife
Duke of Albany
(Regent
1406–20)
|
Murdac
(Regent
1420–24)
(*Executed* 1425)
|
Walter
|
James I
|
James II
(born 1430)

Alexander
'Wolf of
Badenoch'
† × 1406

John
Earl of Buchan
Constable
of France
(† 1424 at
Verneuil)

Alexander
|
Robert
† 1421

(*Executed* 1425)

David
Earl of Strathearn
† × 1389
|
Euphemia
= Sir Patrick Graham
† 1413
|
Malise Earl of
Strathearn
(later of
Menteith)
(*Deprived* 1427)
(Hostage, 1427–53)

Walter
Earl of Athol
(*Executed* 1437)
|
David
(Hostage,
died *c.* 1434,
in England)
|
Sir Robert
Stewart
(Assassin:
Executed 1437)

Euphemia
= Archibald
5th Earl Douglas

past.[1] Where, in them, lay the ' divinity that doth hedge a King ' ? So began a grim struggle between the Scottish kings and their over-mighty subjects[2]: a struggle that was prolonged partly because of the feudal power enjoyed by the great lords in their own localities, and partly because of an unhappy sequence of minorities in the Stewart line.[3] Now, when the king was weak, the strong magnate assumed in his locality powers which were subject to no royal control; in the locality of this or that great feudatory, smaller men found it necessary to submit to the lord's authority in order to obtain a protection that the king was impotent to give, and thereby the lord became more powerful still with further followers. When the king was a minor, there had perforce to be a regent[4]; then there were lords who were jealous of the regent's power; there were lords who supported him and lords who put him to defiance. Factions arose; this or that lord would join this or that faction as he was moved by family loyalties or his own inclination; and the regent in power might be overthrown and suc-ceeded by another regent of an opposing faction. In these unhappy times names like Albany or Douglas seem to take precedence over the name of the king; and the chroniclers speak of lords who ' worked their will outwith the law '. On the other hand, the king was soon to find a new weapon against rebellious lords. In the Chamberlain's account rendered in 1385, we find a payment of £4 ' pro uno instrumento, dicto gun ' for Edinburgh Castle[5]; in the reign of James II we read of the king's guns; and it was only the king who could put into the field a train of heavy artillery.

Now the truce with England, secured by the treaty of Berwick in 1357, had no firm foundation. It was purchased by tardy payments, always in arrears and never paid in full. Moreover, part of southern Scotland (to the south and west of the Lothians) was still in English

---

[1] The marriage of Walter, 6th High Steward, to Marjorie Bruce in 1315.

[2] And already in David II's reign there had been signs that the King could not control the lords. One outstanding example was the seizure, imprisonment and death of Sir Alexander Ramsay of Dalhousie (sheriff of Roxburghshire and hero of the recapture of Roxburgh Castle from the English in 1342) at the hands of Sir William Douglas of Liddesdale who was even given Ramsay's offices instead of a different and juster award.

[3] James I was eleven years old at his accession; James II was six years old; James III was eight years old; James V was one year old; Mary was one *week* old; and James VI was one year old.

[4] Between 1406 (the accession of James I) and 1587 (when James VI attained his majority) there were nearly one hundred years of minority rule and government by regents.

[5] If £4 was the purchase price, the gun must have been a very small one.

hands – a legacy of Edward Balliol's surrender of 1334.[1] In France, too, much territory was still held by England. Scotland had succeeded in regaining some of her land. So, too, had France. Not unnaturally both countries (allied in opposition to England since 1295-6) hoped to work together to break the English hold.

With the accession of Robert II in 1371 the alliance with France was promptly renewed – as it was renewed again in 1390 with the accession of Robert III. Moreover, despite the truce for fourteen years which had been agreed in 1369,[2] border warfare had still continued. Berwick had been recaptured by the Scots in 1378; only to be forthwith lost again. In 1380 John of Gaunt had led an English army to the Borders, but had done little more than renew the truce for its remaining period of three years. In 1384 he had again led an army northwards, and had advanced as far as Edinburgh; but he had acted with such restraint (refusing to allow Edinburgh to be burned) that his enemies declared he had inflicted more hardship on his own men than on the Scots.[3]

In 1385, however, with an intensification of French efforts against England, a small force of French knights and men-at-arms, and a fairly large subsidy in gold, were brought to Scotland by John de Vienne. But the French found Scotland poor and backward; there were few comforts, and little save ' hard beds and ill nights '. Nor was their coming wholly popular; and some of the Scots are said to have asked, ' Who needs them ? Can we not fight our battles ourselves ? ' The succeeding campaign, indeed, gave the answer to those questions. There was a typical Border raid into England, in which the French took part; but when Richard II, fearing the threat from the north, led an army into Scotland, the differences between the French and the Scots were clearly revealed. The French knights wanted the glory of war in pitched battle with the enemy; but the Scots, knowing better how to recover their southern lands, preferred harassing tactics and the certainty of regaining a little here and then a little there. In disgust the French had watched the English burn down Melrose Abbey while the Scots, under Douglas, had held aloof and had done nothing; but Douglas, in avoiding battle, had followed the better plan. Although Richard II marched on to burn Dryburgh, Newbattle, Holyrood and Edinburgh, his invasion (which had taxed his resources to the utmost)

---

[1] *Supra*, p. 178.   [2] *Supra*, p. 183.
[3] But at the time of the Peasants' Revolt in England (1381) he had been given temporary asylum and hospitality in Holyrood, and he had not forgotten.

brought no military advantages; and meantime the Scots were recovering Teviotdale from English control.

So the struggle went on. At Otterburn, in 1388, a ' dead Douglas ' (James, second earl of Douglas) won the field[1]; but in 1402 a body of Border raiders was defeated on Nisbet Moor and, three months later, at Homildon Hill, in Northumberland, a Scottish army, forgetting the lessons of the past, was heavily defeated when the English archers again won the battle at a distance.

Six months after their arrival the French knights of de Vienne's force, unhappy and disillusioned, had been glad to return to their own country, and, to Scotland's disgrace, had been compelled to pay for all their expenses during their stay in Scotland, leaving behind, as surety for payment, their own leader, de Vienne. In effect, French knights were of little use to Scotland in her well-tried methods of meeting English aggression; though, by contrast, Scottish soldiers, fighting against England in the armies of France on French soil, won everlasting renown.[2] Scots companies played a large part in helping France to win the battles of Liege (1408) and Baugé (1421), and when, at Verneuil (1424), they were cut to pieces, their dead included John Stewart, earl of Buchan (nephew of King Robert III), and Archibald, fourth earl of Douglas. Later, they fought under the banner of Joan of Arc, and, later still, formed the ' Scots Guard ' of French kings. Scotland and France, together, were proving too much for the English armies in France; and England's difficulties both at home and in France enabled Scotland at home, despite set-backs such as those of Homildon Hill and the ' Foul Raid ' of 1417,[3] steadily to regain her southern lands.

But Scotland's problem was no longer that of resisting England or of striving to regain her southern lands. Now the problem was that of internal order within Scotland itself. The realm was ' nocht governit '. In these mediaeval times, when members of the nobility played a leading

---

[1] Cf. *infra*, p. 252.

[2] Though, like the French in Scotland, the Scots in France were not always popular. If, in Scotland, it was feared that the French would plunder and spoil the land, in France the Scots were accused of robbing nobles and peasants alike. It was even argued that, however well-disciplined they might be, the Scottish men-at-arms would be the ruin of the land through their large appetites. In 1385 the French knights under de Vienne had hoped to win fame by knightly deeds; the Scots soldiers in France fought partly to be in active arms against England, but partly also in the hope of winning tangible rewards in pay, booty and ransoms.

[3] When Albany and Douglas collected an army to capture both Berwick and Roxburgh but met with so little success that their attempt was called the ' Foul Raid '.

part in government, in both the executive and the judiciary, much depended upon the character of the king. But these early Stewarts were strong neither in body nor in character. In 1384, because the King (Robert II, who was then 68) could not himself secure 'the execution of government and law', his son, the Earl of Carrick, was invested with authority to enforce the law ' everywhere throughout the realm ',[1] and to give justice to all who were suffering grievance or wrong. Four years later, however, in 1388, the Earl of Carrick was likewise relieved of authority because of *his* bodily weakness. And yet, two years later, in 1390, this same Earl of Carrick was to become King, at the age of fifty-three, as Robert III.[2]

Now, indeed, under these first two Stewart kings, both old and of little force of character, and both unfitted for strong and active rule, chroniclers and records alike speak of ' horrible destructions, burnings and slaughters commonly done through all the kingdom ', and of a government that cannot govern. In 1389, for example, it is recorded that the king's rents from his burgh of Inverness had not been paid for the last six years owing to disorder in those parts. There, too, in the north, Alexander, a younger son of Robert II, earned the title of ' The Wolf of Badenoch ': having incurred the censures of the Bishop of Moray for his many and various misdeeds, he retaliated by burning down the bishop's cathedral at Elgin and, for good measure, the burgh as well (1390); and in the preceding month he had burned the burgh of Forres and the church of St Laurence. Plaintively, under the year 1398, a brief chronicle in the *Register of Moray* has the entry, ' In those days there was no law in Scotland, but the strong oppressed the weak, and the whole kingdom was one den of thieves. Homicides, robberies, fire-raisings and other evil deeds went unpunished, and justice, outlawed, was in exile, beyond the bounds of the kingdom '. And the ordinances of a General Council held in 1404 appear to have been concerned solely with attempts to strengthen the courts of justice and the administration of the law.[3]

In Highlands and Lowlands alike, disorder was rampant, but two

---

[1] Wording which suggests that the king was still expected to ride throughout his kingdom to execute the royal justice.

[2] It should be added, however, that his bodily weakness was due mainly to an injury received from the kick of a horse, though the injury appears also to have affected his character and to have made him timid and retreating.

[3] The ordinances of this General Council were recently discovered in a manuscript in the National Library of Scotland and are printed in *Scottish Historical Review*, VOL. XXXV (1956), pp. 132-41.

events of this time, in relation to the Highlands, stand out. In 1396, in an attempt to settle one Highland dispute, a judicial combat on the grand scale was fought on the Inch of Perth between thirty men of the Clan Hay (Yha) or Kay and thirty of the Clan Quele.[1] The story has been immortalised by Scott in *The Fair Maid of Perth*; but we know little of the background and nature of the dispute. The Exchequer Rolls contain an entry of the expenditure of £14 2s. 11d. ' for wood, iron, and making the enclosure for sixty persons fighting on the Inch of Perth '; but we are ignorant of the outcome of the resulting shambles.[2] The chronicler Bower says that thereafter ' for a long time the north was at peace '; but in truth the ' long time ' was very short. In 1411 Donald, lord of the Isles, claiming the earldom of Ross by right of his wife, and possibly fearing the designs of Robert, duke of Albany – who, indeed, awarded the earldom to his son, John, earl of Buchan – advanced with a large force towards Aberdeen, intending to secure the lands of the earldom in the sheriffdoms of Banff, Aberdeen and Kincardine. Knowing that already he had seized Dingwall and burned Inverness, and knowing that the plunder of Aberdeen was to be a reward for his followers, the burgesses of the burgh, together with the local lairds (Forbeses, Keiths and Leslies), led by Alexander Stewart, earl of Mar, met Donald's army at Harlaw where, after a bloody battle with great loss on both sides (and the battle became known as the ' Red Harlaw '), they compelled him to withdraw. It has sometimes been maintained that Harlaw was a fight between the civilised parts and the Highland caterans. But Highlanders fought on both sides. Moreover, Donald, lord of the Isles, was no Highland cateran: his mother was a daughter of Robert II, he was an acknowledged scholar, and he had attended the court of Henry IV of England. On the other hand, the Earl of Mar could hardly claim ' civility ' and is even described by contemporary chroniclers as being himself a ' leader of caterans '.

Into this picture of lawlessness and lack of rule must now be fitted the enigmatic figure of the Earl of Fife, the second surviving son of Robert II, the brother of Robert III, and better known by his later title of Duke of Albany.[3] In 1388, when the Earl of Carrick was

---

[1] We do not know what this clan was. It occurs as Clanqwheril in 1392 (*Acts, Parl. Scot.*, i, 579). In effect neither clan has as yet been identified with certainty.

[2] The accounts of the chroniclers vary. Wyntoun says fifty or more were slain; the *Book of Pluscarden* says seven, wounded, survived; and an entry in the *Register of Moray* says eleven, wounded, survived.

[3] In 1398 Robert III's eldest son, David, was created Duke of Rothesay, while the King's brother, Robert, earl of Fife, was created Duke of Albany. These were the first creations of Scottish dukes.

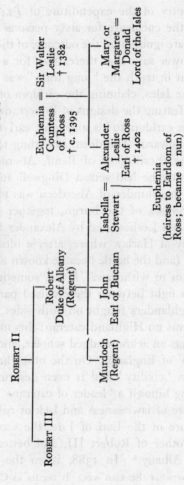

HARLAW AND THE EARLDOM OF ROSS

ROBERT II

Euphemia = Sir Walter Leslie † 1382
Countess of Ross † c. 1395

Mary or Margaret = Donald Lord of the Isles

Alexander Leslie Earl of Ross † 1402 = Isabella Stewart

Euphemia (heiress to Earldom of Ross; became a nun)

Robert Duke of Albany (Regent)

John Earl of Buchan

Murdoch (Regent)

ROBERT III

relieved of his authority because of bodily weakness, the Earl of Fife was made Governor of the realm, to have the power of the king to do justice and maintain the laws: and already he was the Chamberlain (the chief financial officer) and the keeper of Stirling Castle. Moreover, in 1390, when the enfeebled Earl of Carrick became King, as Robert III, the earl of Fife still continued to act as Governor. In 1393, however, he ceased to hold office, and Robert III apparently took the government into his own hands. Certainly in 1399 a General Council openly attributed the ' misgovernance of the realm ' to the failure of the King and the officers of the law; and it then appointed David, duke of Rothesay, Robert III's eldest son, to be Lieutenant throughout the kingdom, ' with full power and commission of the king ', for a period of three years. The Earl of Fife (now Duke of Albany) may well have expected re-appointment to an office he had formerly held for so long; and he may have been embittered and jealous of Rothesay. Moreover, Rothesay, who had married[1] Elizabeth, daughter of the Earl of March, repudiated her, and ' married ' Mary (or Marjory), a daughter of Archibald, third earl of Douglas,[2] only to neglect her and to continue to lead a life of vice and folly. It may be that he abused his authority as Lieutenant, and possibly Robert III did agree to some steps being taken to curb the licence of his eldest son. But it was left to the romantic Boece to tell the story of his starvation and death in Falkland castle at the hands of Albany and the young Earl of Douglas (1402)[3].

Once more Albany was made Lieutenant, to rule and govern the realm in the name of the king – a commission which was again renewed in 1404. At the same time it is also obvious that, with the death of Rothesay, only the king's second son, the seven-years-old James, now stood between Albany and the throne. And it is not difficult to guess what was in Robert III's mind when, in 1406, he arranged for the young James to be sent to France; though unluckily the prince, on his way to France, was captured at sea and remained a prisoner in England until 1424.

James's capture took place in March 1406; and in April 1406

---

[1] See *Scots Peerage*, III, 279 note.

[2] The Earl of March, in anger, deserted to England, became high in the favour of Henry IV from whom he received various grants of land, and fought against the Scots at Nisbet Moor (June 1402) and Homildon Hill (September 1402).

[3] Archibald, fourth earl of Douglas, brother of the unfortunate Mary or Marjory, had succeeded to the earldom about Christmas 1400. For an analysis of the stories of Rothesay's death, see *Source Book of Scottish History*, VOL. I (2nd edn.), pp. 188-9.

Robert III died, giving to those around him his own epitaph: 'Here lies the worst of kings and the most miserable of men'.

We have no official record of the steps taken to form a government after the death of the king; but an entry in the burgh records of Aberdeen reveals that a General Council held at Perth appointed Albany as *generalis gubernator*. The terms of his regency are unknown. The situation was unique, for the heir to the throne was held captive and could neither be crowned nor take the coronation oath. Certainly Albany at once assumed royal powers and a royal style – and even the title of his dukedom (1398) had been royal, for Albany, or Albania, was the old Alba, the united kingdom of the Picts and Scots. A new Great Seal was struck, bearing the legend 'Sigillum Roberti ducis Albanie gubernatoris Scocie'; charters issued under the Great Seal ran in Albany's name and not in the name of James, and were dated, not by the year of the king's reign, but by the year of Albany's regency; and General Councils and Exchequers were held in the name of 'domini Roberti ducis Albanie, Comitis de Fife et de Menteith, regni Scocie gubernatoris'. In 1409, in the Exchequer Rolls, James is referred to, not as king, but as 'the prince, son of the king, now in England'; and in 1410, in a letter to Henry IV, Albany speaks of *his* subjects of Scotland.

It is possible to exaggerate the importance of all this. Wyntoun, writing contemporaneously, seems to stress that although James was recognised as his father's heir he could not be King James I until he had been crowned as such – though Wyntoun may have been striving to explain the unique situation which led to Albany's assumption of royal prerogatives. Nevertheless, when, in 1409, Albany entered into a 'band' with Archibald, fourth earl of Douglas – a band for mutual support and defence – one clause of the band ran, 'and if it happens the said Lord the Duke [Albany] to grow in time to come to the estate of King, this band, as touching even [equal] fellowship and estate shall expire from henceforth, but all kindness and friendship shall be kept between them in time to come'; and that clause may well reflect Albany's ambitions and hopes.

At the same time the very fact that Albany, the Governor of the realm, should deem it advisable to enter into a band with the Earl of Douglas is in itself a clear indication of the Douglas's power. And, if the great feudatories had regarded the first two Stewarts as a feudal house raised to kingship by a lucky chance, what regard could they have for a Stewart acting as Governor in the absence of an uncrowned king ? In the reigns of Robert II and Robert III these aged Stewarts, striving in vain to govern the realm, had attempted to buy quietness and peace among the barons, partly by gifts of crown lands, mainly by gifts of pensions from the crown revenues – some of these pensions even being granted heritably. Individually, these grants and pensions were usually too small to achieve their object: instead they merely served to create a desire for more. Collectively, however, they were a heavy drain on the finances of the crown. Albany not only continued this weak and unwise policy, but now, in his regency, we find some of the nobility calmly helping themselves to the crown's revenues; and the Governor was too weak to bring them to book. More than once we find a Douglas seizing the customs that have been collected in Edinburgh and in Linlithgow, and there are references to barons who were flagrant evaders of custom payments. It is evident on all hands that Albany, like Robert II and Robert III, was unable to hold the nobility in check, and it is clear that the House of Douglas was becoming over-mighty.

Albany died in 1420 and was succeeded as Governor by his son, Murdac – we do not know how, or under what authority. Under Murdac, however, lawlessness grew apace; and even the Governor's own sons are said to have been impudent in their contempt of the law. The pillaging of the crown's revenues went from bad to worse. In 1422, for example, only a miserable £50 out of a total collection of £1,150 from the customs of Edinburgh reached the royal exchequer; and other, though less extensive, losses were recorded from various parts of the realm. Not only was there a growing tide of discontent among the burgesses and the smaller barons and lairds, but even among the more important lords and barons there was apparently a growing hatred of Murdac and his arrogance in authority. Moreover the English council governing in the name of the infant Henry VI was not unwilling to allow James to return to Scotland – a ransom would be useful, and possibly Scotland could be weaned from her alliance with France.

So, at last, by the treaty of London (December 1423) James was ransomed for 60,000 merks (euphemistically called the ' maintenance and expenses ' of his stay in England) to be paid in six annual instalments of 10,000 merks each, though 10,000 merks were remitted as the dowry of Joan Beaufort whom James married in the February preceding his return to Scotland in April 1424.[1] And the new King's return

[1] Although certain taxes (which would yield much more than 10,000 merks a year) were imposed in James's first Parliament for the raising of the ransom payments,

was one to a grievous inheritance. He returned to find a weak central authority, over-mighty barons, crippled crown finances, and lawlessness rampant throughout the whole realm.

In conclusion we should note that during the period of Albany's regency the University of St Andrews, Scotland's first university, was founded, and also that at this time we begin to read of ' heresy '.

One result of the war of independence had been that Scottish students had tended to go to the University of Paris rather than to Oxford or Cambridge. With the Great Schism (1378-1417), moreover, when England remained within the obedience of the Pope in Rome, and when Scotland and France adhered to the anti-Pope in Avignon, Scottish students, more than ever, had gone to Paris or Orleans – for the mediaeval universities were largely training-centres for appointment and promotion in the Church. In 1408, however, France abandoned the anti-Pope, Benedict XIII, and he was compelled to move to Peniscola in Aragon. Only Scotland and part of Spain remained faithful to him. But the schools of learning in Spain were both undistinguished and far-distant; moreover, in the opening years of the fifteenth century appreciable and growing numbers of Scottish students were attending universities abroad, and there was probably an increasing desire and enthusiasm for the benefits of higher education at home.

There is evidence that as early as 1410 a number of masters had begun to teach in St Andrews. There they were joined by other masters who had felt compelled to leave Paris when France abandoned the anti-Pope. These masters soon attracted students, and the new school in St Andrews quickly prospered. In 1412 the masters and students were granted a charter of incorporation by Henry Wardlaw bishop of St Andrews; and in 1413, at the request of the Church of St Andrews, of Scotland's prisoner-king, James I, and of the Estates of the realm, the incorporation of masters and students was granted Bulls of privilege and protection, as a university, from the anti-Pope, Benedict XIII. These Bulls gave St Andrews recognition as a university with a right to teach and to examine in theology, canon and civil law, arts, medicine, and ' other lawful faculties .' The Bulls arrived in St Andrews in February 1414, and were solemnly promulgated; a *Te Deum* was sung in the Cathedral; and the University of St Andrews had been founded.

Yet, little more than four years later, in 1418, the young University of St Andrews took the initiative in persuading the Scottish Estates and

the taxes were apparently collected for only two years, and England received in all only 9,500 merks of ransom money (*infra*, p. 218, n. 1).

the Scottish Church to desert Benedict XIII (who had been deposed by the Council of Constance in 1417) and to come within the obedience of Pope Martin V at Rome. This might appear to be ingratitude, as indeed it was; but we must again remember that masters and students in the universities looked for appointments in the Church, and that by now the anti-Pope had practically no benefices in his patronage for, apart from Scotland and Aragon, the whole of Western Christendom was adhering to the Pope in Rome. Undoubtedly the masters and students of St Andrews were influenced by the hard fact that the Pope in Rome would be more useful to them than their deserted, isolated and deposed founder, Benedict XIII.

Turning to ' heresy ', we read that when Rothesay was appointed to be Lieutenant, in 1399, the oath he was to take, which was based upon the sovereign's coronation oath, included a promise to ' restrain cursit men and heretics '. In 1406 or 1407 a certain James Resby was burned at Perth for preaching the doctrines of Wycliffe. We hear, too, of Lollards – the people who had embraced Wycliffe's doctrines. Those doctrines, moreover, called for social as well as religious change. There was denunciation of the wealth of the church and the scandalous lives led by some of the churchmen, and there was the argument that no man could be pope or priest unless he led a holy life; but there was also a vague theory that the possession of worldly goods was dependent upon ' grace ' – a theory that, for rulers and lords, had dangerous possibilities. Wyntoun, writing of Albany's appointment as Governor, in 1406, includes in his praises

> He wes a constant Catholike
> All Lollard he hatyt and heretike.

And in 1416 we find a Congregation[1] of the new University of St Andrews enacting that henceforth its Masters of Arts were to swear to ' defend the Church against the insult of the Lollards and to resist with all their power any who adhered to that sect '.

But the Reformation of the Scottish church was to come only after another century and a half had passed away. The cloud on the horizon was still no bigger than a man's hand.

---

[1] The ' Congregation ' was then the governing body of the University.

CHAPTER XXII

The Reign of James I

JAMES I, released in March 1424 from his long captivity, was crowned
at Scone on 21 May 1424. He was nearly thirty years old, in the prime
of life, and full of vigour; and, in a Parliament which he held at Perth
within a week of his coronation, he at once revealed his determination
to remedy the evils that had recently passed unchecked. Indeed, the
opening Acts of this Parliament are eloquent of the resolve traditionally
said to have been made by the King immediately upon his return – ' If
God grant me life, though it be but the life of a dog, there shall be no
place in my realm where the key shall not keep the castle and the
bracken-bush the cow '. One after another the enactments of James's
first Parliament laid down –

That firm and sure peace be kept and held throughout the realm among
all subjects of the king; and if any man presume to make war against another,
he shall suffer the full penalties of the law.

That if any man presume to rebel against the king he shall suffer the pain
of forfeiture of life, lands and goods.

That any man who refuses to help the king against his rebels shall himself
be accounted a rebel.

That no men shall ride throughout the country with excessive followings;
and all who move through the land shall make full and ready payment for all
they need.

That officers of the law shall be appointed who can and may hold the
law to the people; that they shall be persons of substance who can be punished
in their own goods if they fail to do their duty; and that any now holding
office who are incapable shall be replaced by others.

That the sheriffs shall arrest any men who move about the country in
bands, squatting upon other men's lands and demanding sustenance [in other
words, ' valiant beggars '].

That all the great and small customs and all the rents of the burghs are
the king's for his support. If any man has a claim to any payment from the
customs, let him state his claim, and the king will give an answer.

That enquiry be made as to the lands and rents which pertained to the
crown in the reign of David II; that the king be informed of those lands,
possessions and rents which have fallen into other hands; and that, if he so

desire, the king may summon all his tenants to give proof of their right to their holdings.[1]

Here there is a determination to secure a firm administration of the law under strong royal officials, and an equal determination to ensure that the revenues of the crown reach the crown for crown needs. James realised that his immediate task was to restore the authority and the resources of the crown; and he knew that the two went together. Authority must have resources for its enforcement.

The strengthening of the resources of the crown is at once revealed in the rolls of the exchequer. For the exchequer audit of 1425 only the accounts of the burghs and of the custumars have survived; but there we see that, with the exception of certain long-standing royal grants made to religious houses, practically no grants or pensions from the customs and the burgh fermes were allowed – and of the few that were allowed more than one was stated to be ' at the risk ' of the officer rendering the account, while other entries demanded the production of charters as a prerequisite to any payment or allowance from the royal revenues. Nor are there any references to interference with the custom payments: the customs were apparently reaching the royal exchequer. As a result, the customs revenue for this first year of James's reign was almost exactly the same as the customs revenue for the *two* years of the audit in 1420; and it may be inferred that the King's strong hand would have like results in respect of those other sources of the crown revenue for which, unfortunately, the accounts have perished.

At the same time James apparently decided to reduce the power possessed by the Chamberlain as the principal financial officer of the realm. Since 1382 the office of Chamberlain had been held first by Albany and then by his son John, earl of Buchan: and during their tenure of office heavy encroachments had been made upon the patrimony of the crown. The death of the Earl of Buchan at Verneuil (August 1424) gave the king his opportunity. He promoted the chamberlain-depute, Sir John Forrester (not a great noble, and, from all the evidence, a man in whom James placed considerable trust), to be Chamberlain, while at the same time he appointed two new and additional financial officers – a Comptroller and a Treasurer. Over

---

[1] It is significant, too, that this first Parliament of James I enacted that all men should learn and practise archery. Bow-marks were to be erected near parish kirks; all men were to shoot there regularly ' thrice about '; and football was proscribed under the pain of fourpence for each offence. As recently as Homildon Hill (1402) the English archers had demonstrated their superiority.

the next few years there appear to have been experiments and adjustments in relation to the duties pertaining to the three officers; but, in the final division of duties, and the one that prevailed, the Comptroller was made responsible for all revenue arising from the king's ' property ', mainly the rents of crown lands, the burgh fermes and the receipts of the great customs, while the Treasurer was made responsible for all the king's ' casualty ', that is, chance or casual revenue such as that coming in from the feudal casualties of ward and relief, from judicial amercements and escheats, from payments for respites and remissions, and so forth. In effect, the Comptroller and the Treasurer soon ingathered all the royal revenue, and the Chamberlain did little more than preside over the Court of the Four Burghs and pass round the burghs on his ayre.

Turning from resources to authority, we find James's hands strengthened at the very outset through the absence of a number of the Scottish nobility who were fighting, and dying, in France in war against England. Also, under the treaty for his release, a number of nobles and sons of nobles had to be sent to England as hostages for the payment of his ransom: and, in the exchanges of the hostages, James could send those who opposed him. Nor did the King hesitate to take positive action against certain of the nobility. Late in 1424 he imprisoned Sir Robert Graham in Dunbar, though apparently Graham soon escaped to become thereafter the King's inveterate enemy and to be the chief of his assassins. In May 1425, Murdac, duke of Albany (the recent regent), his two sons, Walter and Alexander, and the aged Duncan, earl of Lennox, Murdac's father-in-law (all of whom had been earlier imprisoned), were beheaded – possibly for opposition to the strong measures of the new king. In 1427, in an exchange of hostages, Malise, earl of Strathearn, was deprived of his earldom and sent to England where he remained a hostage for twenty-six years. In 1428, in a display of strength at Inverness, some fifty highland chiefs were arrested and imprisoned: only three appear to have been executed, while the rest were released after a short imprisonment; but the king had shown that his authority was to be felt even in the far north.[1] In 1430, Archibald, fifth earl of Douglas, and his cousin Sir John

[1] In the following year, 1429, however, Alexander, lord of the Isles, who had been arrested in 1428 but soon released, burned the burgh of Inverness. James immediately marched north again and, somewhere in Lochaber, Alexander was constrained to surrender unconditionally. He was committed to imprisonment in Tantallon and remained a prisoner until after Michaelmas 1431 when he was restored to his freedom, dignities and possessions.

Kennedy were imprisoned *ob certas causas*; Douglas was released in the autumn of 1431, but Kennedy was certainly still in prison in 1434.[1] And, in 1434, George, earl of March (who had been imprisoned in the previous year), was sentenced by Parliament to forfeit his earldom and estates, on the grounds of his father's treason.[2]

Possibly, in the case of the Albanies, James may have been moved by revenge – had they made any real effort to secure his release during the long period from 1406 to 1424 ?[3] Possibly, in the case of Malise, earl of Strathearn, who was deprived of his earldom and who remained a hostage in England from 1427 to 1453, James may have feared some support for Strathearn as a claimant to the throne – a 'legitimist' claimant, the descendant of the elder son of the marriage of Robert II and Euphemia Ross[4], even though through a *female* line – and it is important to note that the King's son (later James II) was not born until 1430, and that James II's son (later James III), was not born until 1452. Possibly, too, as one contemporary said, there was some avarice on the part of the King: a greed for lands and money.

Yet James I clearly realised that a strong assertion of the royal authority was Scotland's prime need, and in his efforts to secure law and order he did not rely solely upon suppression and forefeiture. He made definite and constructive attempts to improve the 'government' of the realm and the administration of the king's justice.

We have already seen in the acts of his first Parliament (acts which, we are told, were initiated by the King himself) a clear enunciation of the principle that the king's judges must be strong enough to 'hold the law' to the people. Two years later, in 1426, Parliament enacted that all the king's subjects were to live and be governed by the king's own laws and not by particular laws or particular privileges.[5] Moreover,

---

[1] Douglas and his wife (who was the sister of Malise Graham, earl of Strathearn) had been conducting a secret correspondence with the Earl of Salisbury, Warden of the West March, who was the custodian of Malise; and again there may have been a background of the legitimist claims of the descendants of Euphemia Ross (cf. *infra*, p. 254).

[2] *Supra*, p. 203, n. 2. Though in 1408 or 1409 his father had apparently been rehabilitated by Albany and restored to his earldom.

[3] And James probably remembered that in 1415 Robert, duke of Albany, had secured the release of his son, Murdac, who had been taken prisoner at Homildon Hill in 1402.

[4] See the Table on p.196.

[5] And as recently as 1384, in the reign of Robert II, and in a General Council, the Earl of Fife (later the Regent Albany) and Archibald Douglas, Lord of Galloway, had claimed rights to certain special laws within their lands.

the statutes of this Parliament, and of the preceding Parliaments of 1424 and 1425 (and clearly of succeeding Parliaments also), were to be registered in the king's Register,[1] and copies were to be given to the sheriffs who were to proclaim the laws in all notable places within their sheriffdoms and to provide copies for any prelates, barons and burghs who might ask for them – so that ' no one might have cause to pretend or allege ignorance ' of the law. The laws in general, ' the books of the law ', were to be examined by six wise and discreet men so that they could be ' mended ' if in need of amendment; and although one modern historian has commented, ' precisely as if laws could be cobbled like boots ', James realised that all laws are in constant need of ' mending ' to meet the constantly changing needs of society. Finally, this Parliament of 1426 set up a new royal court of justice.

The preceding Parliament of 1425 had re-affirmed that all judges, including those within regalities, were to do ' full law and justice ' as well ' to poor as to rich, without fraud or favour '. But the local courts were apparently still far from being efficient and impartial, and causes, petitions and complaints were still pouring in to the King in Council and Parliament. Hence, in 1426, Parliament, on the initiative of the King, set up a special court to hear these many causes and complaints. The court was to consist of the Chancellor and ' certain discreet persons of the Three Estates chosen by the King '; it was to sit three times a year in centres that were to be determined by the King; and it was to ' examine, conclude, and finally determine ' all causes and complaints that might otherwise come before the King in Council – that is, there was to be no appeal from its judgments.

Partly this was an attempt to meet the old difficulty presented by a host of causes and complaints coming before the King in Council and in Parliament which hindered the progress of the more important work of government.[2] Partly it eased the burden of seeking the King and Council ' wherever they might happen to be '. But also this new court could sit when Parliament was not in session; it could sit in different parts of the realm with prior notice of its sittings; its members were to be chosen by the King and not by the Estates; and, lastly, its judgments were not subject to the confirmation of the court of Parliament and were to be final.

In persuading Parliament to confer these wider powers upon his

---

[1] Some record was certainly kept but, like many others, it has unfortunately been lost.

[2] Cf. *supra*, p. 192.

new court, James I may have been moved by varying motives: a desire to meet the grievances of his people and to give them justice (and in mediaeval times the 'good king' was the king who ensured 'good justice'); a desire to limit the powers of the great lords in their localities (for the new court was to sit 'where the King likes to command'); and a desire to overcome the rigid rules and procedure of the ordinary courts by providing a court which could proceed to justice more speedily, less formally, and with regard to equity rather than to a strict interpretation of the common law. Unfortunately we have no record of the work of the court, and we do not know to what extent it was effective.[1]

This new court was one for civil causes, civil justice. James's energies were almost certainly directed towards criminal justice also; but all the records that would throw light on the work of the justice-ayres have unfortunately perished. We know that in the reign of David II the ayres of the justiciars had been held only intermittently, and that, at times, several years had elapsed during which no justice-ayres had been held at all. The ayres, however, were not only the main courts for criminal justice, administered by officers directly responsible to the King, they were also, through their amercements, escheats and forfeitures, a source of much revenue. That is, the justice-ayres strengthened both the authority and the resources of the crown: as such they would not be neglected by James I.

Again, in relation to the power of the great lords in Parliament (which, as we have seen, was still essentially a feudal gathering of the great), James strove to establish an Estate of 'Commons' similar to that which he had seen at work in England. In 1426 it was enacted that all who held direct of the king – prelates, earls, barons and freeholders – must attend Parliaments and General Councils personally and were to be allowed to send procurators only if they could adduce lawful reasons for their personal absence.[2] Here there was emphasis on the personal attendance of all, including barons and freeholder.

---

[1] Under James II, in 1439, its sittings were cut down to 'two sessions' a year, and from that the court acquired its name of 'the Session'. It is clear, however, that the 'sessions' were not held 'ilk yere'. In the reign of James III, enactments made from time to time ordaining the sessions to be held have an *ad hoc* appearance, and the King's Council was again burdened with 'causes and complaints'. Indeed, in 1488, it was even enacted that it would be a deferment of justice if parties were to be denied access to the king and council.

The problem was not finally solved until the establishment of the College of Justice (the Court of Session) in the Reign of James V (*infra*, pp. 306-7).

[2] Lawful excuses (*essoins*) for personal absence included bed-sickness, an engagement on the king's service, and passing on a pilgrimage.

This was in strict accord with the feudal law of rendering service to the superior's court; but James may have had in mind that the attendance of small barons and freeholders might help him to check the power of the large feudatories. Possibly, however, the smaller men found the burden (and expense) too heavy for them; possibly there was even some murmuring. We do not know. Certainly on 1428 there was a further Act by which the small barons and freeholders were released from personal attendance at Parliaments and General Councils provided that, in each sheriffdom, according to its size, they elected two or more ' wise men ', to represent them.[1] These commissioners of the shires were to be elected at the head court of the sheriffdom[2]; they were to bring with them their commissions attesting their election, sealed with the sheriff's seal and the seals of the barons of the shire; they were to have full power ' to hear, treat and finally determine ' – that is, they were to be definite representatives, with full powers, whose decisions would be binding on those who elected them; and their expenses were to be met proportionately by those who, by electing commissioners, were thus excused from attendance.[3] Moreover, when they came to Parliament, the commissioners of the shires were to choose ' a wise and expert man ' to be ' the common speaker of the Parliament ' to put forward all the ' needs and causes pertaining to the commons '. And, finally, the Act concluded by saying that all others – bishops, abbots, priors, dukes, earls and lords, according to the king's choice – were to be summoned to Councils and Parliaments by special precept.

This final clause was clearly necessary. Some distinction had to be made between those whose attendance would be excused because they were represented by their elected commissioners, and those who were still bound to attend personally: there had to be a distinction between those who were ' small barons and freeholders ' and those who were of higher rank. And that distinction was made by personal summons, by precept, to those of higher rank.

It is possible that James I had in mind a bi-cameral Parliament

---

[1] In each of the small sheriffdoms of Clackmannan and Kinross, however, only one representative was to be elected.

[2] In each sheriffdom there were three ' head courts ' a year – at Yule, Easter and Michaelmas. These were full assemblies of all those in the sheriffdom who held direct of the king and owed attendance at the court. Thus, at a head court, all the small barons and freeholders would be present to elect their representatives.

[3] This arrangement for meeting the expenses of the ' commissioners ' may provide a clue to the failure of the Act of 1426.

similar to that which he had seen at work in England – the Commons, with their ' Speaker ', containing representatives of the shires and the burghs; and the Lords, summoned by special precept. It is certain that he was striving to make Parliament something other than a gathering of the few and the great.

In the second half of the fifteenth century there is evidence that a few barons and lairds came to Parliament, though there is no evidence that they came as commissioners of the shires; and in the first half of the sixteenth century fewer still, if any, attended. In that respect, then, the Act of 1428 apparently was, or became, a dead letter. On the other hand, because certain of the greater barons were now summoned by special precept, a ' parliamentary peerage ' arose – barons who, because they received a personal writ, became known as ' Lords of Parliament '. They were something more than barons, but something less than earls; soon the words ' of Parliament ' were dropped, and they became Lords. So, for the first time, we begin to read of Lord Crichton, Lord Livingston, Lord Seton, Lord Boyd, and so forth. Moreover, although the Act of 1428 had clearly stated that precepts were to be sent out according to the king's choice, it is clear that these new peerages quickly became hereditary – probably inevitably so, for the simple reason that it was easier for the ' writing office ' in Chancery to have a standing list of barons to whom writs would be sent automatically for each and every Parliament.

Finally, in relation to Parliament, it is probable that James's constitutional experiments included something in the nature of a small committee to prepare the business before it was considered by the whole House – a small committee which later developed into the ' Committee of the Articles '.

We have already seen that the major difficulty in relation to mediaeval parliaments was that of keeping a large number of people together in one place for any length of time. Because of that difficulty Parliament strove to expedite its work by appointing committees to attend to its judicial business; because of that difficulty, Parliament had adopted the device of electing a small number of its members to ' hold ' the parliament and allowing all the rest to go home.[1] To meet the same difficulty, there was now an attempt to accelerate the work of Parliament so that all the members might have some say in its decisions and yet all the members would not be kept ' in the Parliament ' for too long a period of time. And the work of Parliament could be accelerated if

[1] *Supra*, pp. 192-3.

the business had been considered beforehand and was put before Parliament in a prepared form.

So, in the first Parliament of James I (1424) we read of certain ' articles ' (*articuli*, ' points ') presented by the King; in his third Parliament (1426) we read that the articles had been put forward by the King to be ' determined by certain persons thereto chosen by the Three Estates ', and thereafter apparently the whole Parliament ' answered, ordained, statute and decreed '. It would appear that the king (probably in consultation with his Council) had drawn up certain points for consideration by Parliament; these points had then been considered by a committee; and Parliament had finally legislated according to the committee's recommendations.

From now onwards, indeed, the amount of legislation passed by Parliament in a very few days clearly indicates that the ' articles ' must have been brought before the House in a fully prepared form. In 1467 we have record of a committee, nine in number, chosen from the Three Estates *ad formandos articulos* – to put the articles into shape. In 1469 Parliament met on 20 November, elected a ' committee of the articles ' on 21 November, and passed its legislation on 27 November. Evidently expedition has been achieved. But, as the decades pass, it is borne in upon us that expedition has been achieved at a price: the price of Parliament's initiative. The step from ' putting the articles into shape ' to ' deciding upon the articles ' has been only too easy. In due course we find that Parliament meets and elects the ' Lords of the Articles ' – a certain number from each estate; it then disperses and, say, a fortnight later meets again to say ' yes ' to the legislation that is placed before it. Parliament, in effect, has become little more than a rubber stamp to endorse conclusions reached by its committee. There is no debate, there is no legislation other than that which is drafted by the Committee of the Articles. In 1587 Parliament elected the Committee of the Articles on 13 July, and on 29 July (sixteen days later) gave its assent to no less than 136 Acts, some of which were both lengthy and involved.[1] We know, however, that by then it was customary for the king's Privy Council to draft the legislation for the Lords of the Articles to consider; and thus, if the king (or the faction that was in power) could control the membership of both the Privy Council and the Committee of the Articles, the king (or the faction) had complete control over all legislation – as was to happen in the reign of James VI

---

[1] Charles I's Parliament of 1633 met on 20 June and elected the Committee of the Articles, and on 28 June (only eight days later) passed 168 statutes *en bloc*.

after the Union of the Crowns. The Committee of the Articles which had begun as a convenient device was in the end to be denounced as a ' great grievance to the nation '.

Owing to the loss of the national records – already so often referred to – it is difficult to know the full tale of James's efforts to improve the government of the realm or to estimate their success. That he secured good justice for his people appears to be beyond doubt, and it is notable that to him must be given the credit of instituting ' the poor man's advocate ' – one of his early enactments laying down that a ' lele and a wys advocate ' was to be given to ' ony pur creatur ' to plead on his behalf. To support his authority we find him buying ' bombards ' and engines of war, and there is evidence in the Exchequer rolls of his interest in ship-building and of the emergence of a small fleet of ' king's ships '. An early attempt to call a halt to the debasement of the coinage[1] had to be abandoned; regulations to secure uniformity in weights and measures[2] were probably more successful through the co-operation of the burghs. His endeavours to secure law and order at home were seconded by endeavours to avoid warfare with England[3] – despite the non-payment of his ransom[4] and despite the continuance of the alliance with France which was strengthened in 1436 by the marriage of his eldest daughter, Margaret, to the Dauphin. As for his personal accomplishments, he was a musician, a poet[5], and a lover of all arts.

As we shall see, James I's efforts to conserve the resources of the realm led to a conflict with the papacy.[6] His attempts to establish his own authority and to enforce law and order throughout the whole kingdom possibly played some part in his murder in the Blackfriars of Perth on the night of 20/21 February 1437. Certainly to one contemporary James died a martyr for justice; though to another it seemed that his cupidity in seizing the lands of noble houses, in retaining in his own hands the monies raised by taxation for his ransom (and thereby abandoning the noble hostages in England), and in failing to repay loans that had been made to him had aroused the hostility of too many people. It is worthy of note that Bower describes him as ' acquisitive ',

[1] See *infra*, pp. 230-1.

[2] Including the provision that the ' pint ' should hold forty-one ounces of clear water from the river Tay.

[3] Though in 1435 there was a minor Border clash at Piperden (near Berwick), and in 1436 James himself conducted a futile siege of Roxburgh.

[4] *Infra*, p. 218, n. 1.

[5] His authorship of *The Kingis Quair*, however, is still a matter of dispute, though the poem must either have been written by James himself or composed from materials supplied by him.   [6] *Infra*, pp. 264-6.

and undoubtedly the taxation collected for the two years 1424-25 to meet the king's ransom was not wholly devoted to that purpose[1] – James I being in this respect no better than David II – and was highly unpopular coming after a long period of freedom from all taxes.[2] Yet there was also a dynastic background to the murder of the King.

According to Bower, Walter, earl of Atholl, was the moving conspirator, hoping for the crown. Certainly he was the surviving son of Robert II's marriage to Euphemia Ross, and, according to the settlement of the crown in 1373, only James, and James's young son, stood between him and the throne.[3] It is said that he hoped to be hailed by the rest of the nobility as their liberator from a tyrant's rule; apparently he also hoped that, once James was dead, a Parliament, dominated by the nobility, would set aside James's six-year-old son and place him on a throne that had been usurped by the illegitimate line of Elizabeth Mure. It may be, too, that Atholl was spurred to action by his grandson, Sir Robert Stewart who, in view of Atholl's advanced age (he was about seventy-five), might hope to be King himself within a few years.

But the ' fiery Graham '[4] was undoubtedly the chief enemy of the King and chief member of the murderous band. To the end he declared that he had slain a tyrant, and that posterity would bless his deed. The feeling of the people, however, was expressed in the rhyme

> Sir Robert Graham,
> That slew our king:
> God give him shame.

And that must be our judgment too. James brought law and order to his realm; he was a great innovator in administration; he was fearless and just.

Nobles and commons alike rallied to the support of the widowed

---

[1] 10,000 merks were to be paid annually to England for five years (*supra*, p. 205). Unfortunately there is no record of the full accounts of the receipts from the taxations imposed in James's first parliament and collected for only two years. It would appear that the proportion to be paid by the burghs brought in about 20,000 merks; but we have no record of what came in from the clergy and the barons. The *total* amount paid to England, however, came to only some 9,500 merks (instead of the 50,000 merks due under the treaty), and the excess of the receipts was used by James for other purposes, including some personal expenditure on jewels and luxuries.

[2] According to Bower, Albany had declared that as Governor he would never consent to the imposition of a taxation ' lest the poor should curse him '. Albany's real motives may have been somewhat different; but, whatever his motives were, his financial policies merely stored up troubles for the future.

[3] See *supra*, p. 193 and the table on p. 196.

[4] *Supra*, p. 210.

queen, and none hailed the murder of James I as a liberation. Her young son was anointed and crowned as James II on 25 March 1437, and the conspirators were ruthlessly hunted down and put to death with cruelly devised tortures. But, with the death of the strong king, and the accession of his six-year-old son, all that James I had done to bring order into the realm was quickly undone. Faction and feud once more became the order of the day, and over-mighty subjects were still to be a danger to more than one Scottish king.

CHAPTER XXIII

The Fifteenth Century

AFTER THE murder of King James I the Queen had hurried with her young son to the safety of the castle of Edinburgh. Four weeks later, on 25 March 1437, James II, aged six, was crowned at Holyrood. Edinburgh was safer than Perth; and the long tradition of inaugurating the new king at Scone had been broken. The rule of law that had been established by James I had been broken also.

Although Archibald, fifth earl of Douglas, was appointed as Lieutenant-General of the kingdom, and Bishop Cameron of Glasgow was confirmed as Chancellor, the promise of strong government under the Queen (as custodian of the young King), Douglas and Cameron was not fulfilled. Almost at once faction and feud arose to disturb the land, and the magnates who had been curbed by James I again returned to strife and disorder in their own parts. As early as March 1439 we find a General Council ordering Douglas, as Lieutenant-General, to ' raise the country ' and proceed in strength against ' rebels and unruleful men '; and already Sir Alan Stewart of Darnley had been killed by Sir Thomas Boyd of Kilmarnock who, in turn, was later slain by the Stewarts. But Douglas was either incapable of office, or unable to make his office felt; and what little restraint he may have been able to impose was removed by his sudden death, while still in the prime of life, in June 1439.[1]

Almost at once Sir Alexander Livingston, the keeper of Stirling castle, and Sir William Crichton, the keeper of Edinburgh castle, strove against each other for the possession of the young King: Crichton endeavouring to maintain the government, Livingston greedy for power. Temporarily coming together in alliance against the Douglas, they accused the new Earl, William (aged about sixteen), of treasonable intentions,[2] and murdered him, together with his only brother David, at the ' Black Dinner ' in Edinburgh Castle – a deed denounced in the popular rhyme

---

[1] He died of the plague that was called ' the pestilence but [without] mercy ', for those who contracted it never recovered and died within twenty-four hours.

[2] His mother was Euphemia Graham, sister of Malise Graham, and a direct descendant of Robert II and Euphemia Ross. (See the table on p. 196; and see *infra*, pp. 253-4.)

Edinburgh Castle, Toune and Towre
God grant thou sinke for sinne,
And that even for the black dinoir
Earl Douglas gat therin.

While Crichton and Livingston were undoubtedly in a stronger position with the removal of the young and powerful Earl of Douglas, there is a suspicion that one or both of them had acted in secret agreement with James Douglas, earl of Avondale, brother of Archibald, fourth earl of Douglas, who now fell heir to the Douglas earldom.[1] If that is so, James, seventh earl of Douglas, did not long enjoy the fruits of his perfidy; he died three years later, in 1443, and was succeeded in the earldom by his son William.

William, eighth earl of Douglas, now allied with Livingston against Crichton. Crichtons and Livingstons harried each other's lands; Crichtons ravaged the Douglas lands in Lothian, and Douglases burned Crichton's castle of Barnton. Bishop Kennedy of St Andrews, ' whose singleness of purpose and purity of character stand out in bright relief in an age when such qualities were rare ', but who was still a man of his time, fearing the growing power of Douglas, his alliance with the Livingstons, and their friendship with the Earl of Crawford, gave his strong support to the Crichtons. The followers of Crawford and Livingston ravaged and looted the Bishop's lands; in turn, Kennedy excommunicated the Earl of Crawford and all his adherents.

Disorder was now rampant. Hepburn of Hailes seized Dunbar and carried off the Prior of Coldingham to imprisonment there. Stewarts and Ruthvens fought at Perth, and Sir William Ruthven, the sheriff, was slain. Lindsays and Ogilvies did battle at Arbroath, and the Earl of Crawford was mortally wounded when trying to make peace between the contenders.[2] On the Borders, the Douglases enhanced their prestige by routing an English army at Gretna on the banks of the Sark in 1448, and in the following year the English burned Dunbar and Dumfries while the Scots burned Alnwick and Wark.

Then, in July 1449, James II, nearly nineteen years old, married

[1] See the Table, *infra*, p. 253. James Douglas, earl of Avondale, had lived a life of violence in his younger days, but had now become so excessively corpulent as to be incapable of action or exertion of any kind. Thus it is also possible that Crichton and Livingston may have thought they would suffer from less interference if James ' the Gross ' were Earl of Douglas.

[2] It is said that his death took place exactly a year after his excommunication by Bishop Kennedy, and was popularly regarded as a judgment of God. Also, because he died excommunicate, his body is said to have remained unburied until Kennedy lifted his excommunication.

Mary of Gueldres, and, with his marriage, appears to have assumed the government of his kingdom. The Livingstons were forfeited in the autumn of the same year – partly, it would appear, because the King discovered their appropriations of crown finances, but also, and certainly, because of their former ill-treatment of the King's mother and her second husband, the ' Black Knight of Lorne '. And yet, on the other hand, the Earl of Douglas, already too powerful, was given a share of the forfeited lands.

In the following year, however, when Douglas visited Rome (and on his outward journey, talked secretly with the Duke of Burgundy and, on his return journey, stayed some weeks with the King of England) James apparently took some action against his over-mighty subject. We do not know to what extent, at this juncture, the King strove to suppress the great power of the Douglases in the south-west; all we know is that upon Douglas's return in 1451 he made a formal submission in Parliament, was restored to all his lordships (except the earldom of Wigtown),[1] and received a ' free remission ' from the King. But the shadow had already fallen upon the house of Douglas. In 1452 James II stabbed the Douglas in Stirling castle because ' he mycht nocht nor wald nocht ' break his ' band ' with the Earl of Crawford; and Alexander, first earl of Huntly, overthrew the rebellious Crawford in battle near Brechin. There was an illusory reconciliation between the King and James, ninth earl of Douglas; John of the Isles, earl of Ross, who had leagued with Crawford and Douglas and had daunted Huntly, was brought over to the side of the King by fair words and grants of royal lands; and when the Douglases were finally overthrown in 1455[2] they virtually fought and fell alone.

James II had now made himself master in his own kingdom. But if domestic strife had been settled, relations with England grew steadily worse. Partly England arrogantly renewed the old claim to the over-lordship of Scotland; partly Scotland, renewing the auld alliance with France, was determined to regain Berwick and Roxburgh. Periods of uneasy truce alternated with Border raids and forays; but England was torn between Lancaster and York, and the initiative lay with James. Unhappily, when besieging Roxburgh castle in August 1460, he was accidentally killed by one of his own guns which ' brak in the fyring ' (3 August 1460).

For the last ten years of his reign James II had followed policies

[1] Which also was restored a few months later.
[2] *Infra*, p. 256.

much similar to those of his father. He had striven to strengthen the authority of the Crown; he had chosen important ministers from the clerical estate; and his name had become associated with equity and justice. He was only in his thirtieth year when his sudden death fulfilled an old prophecy that a dead king would win the castle of Marchmont (or Roxburgh) from the hands of the English – for, after the death of the King, the siege was still continued and, on 8 August, the castle surrendered and was destroyed. Two days later (10 August 1460) the new King, James III, was crowned in the near-by abbey of Kelso.

Once more Scotland was faced with a long minority, for James III was only eight years old; once more the nobles were freed from the control of a strong and determined king; and once more self-interest was placed before service to the realm.

It is sometimes said that James II had attacked Roxburgh castle ' in the Lancastrian interest '. It would be truer to say that he had attacked it in the interests of Scotland. Be that as it may, in December of the same year (1460), Margaret of Anjou, the queen of Henry VI, arrived in Scotland to seek help against her opponents of York. Early in 1461 she led southwards a motley army of ' Scots, Welsh and other strangers and Northernmen ', which, plundering as it went, met the Yorkists near St Albans, won the victory there, and regained possession of the King's person. The way to London lay open; yet, unaccountably, Margaret did not take it. Yorkist forces were able to enter and hold the city; the Duke of York assumed the crown as Edward IV; and, in March 1461, the Yorkist king made his title effective by defeating the Lancastrians at Towton near York. Margaret had again to cross the Border into Scotland, this time in company with Henry VI.

Desperate for help, Margaret now surrendered Berwick to the Scots, and made a promise to cede Carlisle. For a brief twenty-one years the gateway of the eastern march returned to Scottish possession. In reply Edward IV used the forfeited and exiled Black Douglas to enter into negotiations with John of the Isles to try to ' stab Scotland in the back with the Celtic dirk '. Early in 1462, by a treaty (which has come to be known as the treaty of Westminster-Ardtornish[1]), John of the Isles, earl of Ross, and his kinsman, Donald Balloch, bound themselves to become and remain liegemen of the King of England and to co-operate with Douglas to conquer and subdue the realm of Scotland. If

---

[1] Ardtornish in Morvern was a stronghold of the Lords of the Isles and the meeting-place of their assemblies.

they were successful, then all Scotland north of the Forth was to be held by them and to be divided equally between the MacDonalds and Douglas as vassals of the Crown of England, while Douglas was to enjoy his former possessions in the south-west, to be held in a like way of the English king.

The treaty of Westminster-Ardtornish, however, was of little or no effect. For a time the Earl of Ross was able to usurp the royal authority in the north, gathering in the King's rents and assuming regal powers; but Douglas's sole success on the Borders appears to have been the capture of the Earl of Crawford, Lord Maxwell, and ' other noble men ' in a raid of March 1463. A little later in the same year another raid by Douglas was repulsed and his brother John, Lord Balvany, was captured and executed; and when, in 1464, a truce for fifteen years was signed with England, the Earl of Ross apparently deemed it expedient to return to his proper allegiance to the Scottish king, though that allegiance was to be of short duration.

During this period the government of the country had been largely directed by the Queen Mother, Mary of Gueldres, and Bishop Kennedy. The Queen Mother died in December 1463, however, and James Kennedy, a great churchman, a great statesman, and the founder of St Salvator's College at St Andrews university, died in May 1465. Then, in the following year, the young King, aged fourteen, was suddenly seized by a group of lesser nobles headed by the Boyds of Kilmarnock.

This seizure of James III, and the hope of power to come thereby, was much like the work of Livingston during the minority of James II. And the Boyds were mere upstarts, as the Livingstons had been before them. Nevertheless for some three years they held all power in their own hands.

At Edinburgh, in October 1466, at a meeting of the Estates following the King's seizure, James III, in what must have been a prearranged scene, stated that all that had been done by the Boyds had been done at his command. More than that, by an act of the Estates, ratified by charter under the Great Seal, Robert, Lord Boyd was made Governor of the King's person and keeper of the fortresses of the kingdom, until the King should reach the age of twenty-one. The Estates, as we have seen before, still tended to be a gathering of those who supported the faction that was in power.

There is no evidence that Lord Boyd abused his newly-won power save, perhaps, in seeking the aggrandisement of his family – as when, early in 1467, his eldest son, Sir Thomas Boyd, received in marriage the Lady Mary, the King's sister, and was created Earl of Arran.

In the following year (1468) Lord Boyd concluded the treaty under which James III married Margaret, the daughter of Christian I of Denmark, and through which Orkney and Shetland eventually became part of the Scottish realm.[1] He sent his son, the Earl of Arran, to bring the Princess to Scotland, and, during Arran's absence, with many of his friends and followers, and also during the absence of Lord Boyd himself, on an embassy to England, the enemies of the Boyds, jealous of their sudden rise to power, apparently gained the ear of the King. When Arran reached Leith with the royal bride, his wife met him on board ship with the news that the King ' had conceived great hatred against him '. The royal bride disembarked with her train, and Arran and his wife at once sailed back to Denmark. At Bruges they were joined by Lord Boyd who had crossed to the Low Countries direct from England; and in Scotland another meeting of the Estates, held by the opposing faction, found the Boyds guilty of treason and in their absence forfeited them in life, lands and goods (November 1469).[2]

Whether or not James III had been captivated by Sir Alexander Boyd, ' a mirror of chivalry ', who had been his instructor in knightly exercises, and whether or not he had truly agreed in 1466 to the power assumed by the Boyds – who were ' great ' in neither lands nor ' following ' – certainly the King was now showing little inclination to rely upon the advice of the older nobility. In this he may have been in advance of the time, as also in his patronage of music, poetry and architecture. Nevertheless it is clear that law and order were not kept.

The enactments of his Parliaments now recall very similar enactments during the weak reigns of Robert II and Robert III. Thus, in 1473 the King was exhorted to cease granting remissions and respites for crime and was urged to travel throughout his realm to ensure that justice was done; in 1478 he was again exhorted to cease granting remissions and respites for slaughter and other crimes; and in 1479 it was piously hoped that James would diligently ' put forth justice ' throughout all his realm and would hold and set justice-ayres in every

[1] See supra, p. 42.

[2] Sir Alexander Boyd, who alone appeared to answer the charge, was attainted, and executed.

The Earl of Arran subsequently took service with the Duke of Burgundy. His wife, the Lady Mary, who was greatly attached to him, apparently returned to Scotland in an attempt to secure a pardon for him from her brother, the King. In this she was unsuccessful; she was not allowed to return to him; and early in 1474 she was married to James, Lord Hamilton – a marriage which brought the Hamiltons into the position of heirs presumptive to the Scottish crown (see infra, pp. 260-3).

part. Moreover the need for royal justice, and the failure of the King to hold the law to the people, is amply revealed in the record for the Parliament of 1479 which lists feuds between the Earls of Buchan and Erroll, between the Master of Crawford and Lord Glamis, and between Rutherfords and Turnbulls, and which also speaks of ' great trouble ' in Ross, Caithness and Sutherland.

In his love of the arts James was now surrounding himself with men who, to the nobles, were simply ' fiddlers and masons '; and in his failure to govern,[1] and his contempt of warlike exercises and manly sports, he was contrasted, to his disadvantage, with his brothers the Duke of Albany and the Earl of Mar. Becoming superstitious and introspective, and fearing some kind of intrigue between his brothers and the nobility, James placed Albany and Mar in ward. Mar died, possibly of a fever, but Albany escaped to France (1479).[2]

From France, Albany crossed to England where, by treaties concluded with Edward IV at Fotheringhay in June 1482, he was acknowledged as King of Scotland, holding his kingdom of the English King; he was to break the old alliance with France, and to hand over to England, Berwick and Lochmaben and the lands of Liddesdale, Eskdale and Annandale; he was to marry Edward's daughter Cecilia (already pledged, in 1474, to James III's eldest son, later James IV); and, in all this, he was to have English aid and support. In fulfilment of the treaty an English army marched towards the Border. James assembled a Scottish army to meet it; but the Scottish nobles, encouraged by Archibald, earl of Angus (henceforth to be known as ' Bell-the-Cat '),[3] hanged some of the King's favourites over Lauder bridge in preference to marching to the defence of Berwick. They then seized the King and led him back to Edinburgh where he was placed in the castle and held prisoner (July 1482).

Hatred of the King's favourites is evident in all the accounts of the chroniclers, and yet James's favourites do not seem to have played any part in the affairs of state. Possibly the King spent too much time in their company, which he preferred to that of his lords. Possibly some

---

[1] Successive Parliaments reminded him of his duty to govern and to hold the law to his people, and were particularly outspoken in 1473, 1478, 1479, 1484, 1485 and 1487.

[2] The story of Albany's escape from Edinburgh castle, and of his courage in carrying his injured page to safety, is to be read in Pitscottie at his best.

[3] According to Pitscottie, one of the nobles told the story of the mice who wished to hang a warning bell round the cat's neck, and Angus promptly declared his willingness to ' bell the cat '.

of them, like Cochrane, may have been overbearing in manner. But there was also general discontent due to a recent outbreak of plague and to successive bad harvests in 1480 and 1481. There was famine and dearth, with their accompanying hunger and high prices; and the high prices were attributed (not without some justification) to the ' black money ', a debased coinage for which Cochrane was held to be responsible and which, immediately after the executions at Lauder Bridge, was ' cryit doun '.[1] In effect the King and his favourites were blamed for much for which they had little responsibility.

The English, unopposed, recaptured Berwick (which thereafter remained in English hands and is still part of England), and marched on to Edinburgh, withdrawing after a few days at the request of Albany.

Albany, however, was suspected of being little more than an English agent, and, although he was restored to his lands and honours, and made Lieutenant-General of the realm, his continuing intrigues with England gave the King a chance to reassert his own authority. Albany was compelled once more to take refuge over the Border and, in his absence, was forfeited (1483). But Richard III, beset with troubles of his own, made terms of peace with Scotland; and although, in the summer of 1484, Albany and the ageing Douglas led a small force into Scotland in the hope of finding friends and allies who would support them against the King, they were easily routed. Albany escaped and succeeded in reaching France where he died in 1485. Douglas, who was taken prisoner, was sent into confinement in the Abbey of Lindores and died there, probably in 1491.

But James's troubles were far from over. He was now to find himself in conflict with the Humes, a powerful Border family that was in close alliance with the Hepburns. And both the Humes and the Hepburns had been friends of the Boyds.

At the request of James, the Pope had suppressed the Priory of Coldingham and had assigned half its revenues to the Chapel Royal at St Andrews. But the Priory of Coldingham had become virtually an appanage of the Humes, who claimed that its revenues were theirs by hereditary right. The quarrel soon spread. Old antipathies, old fears and old allegiances moved a number of the nobility to side with the Humes. The Earls of Angus and Argyll, the Lords Gray, Hailes and Lyle, the Bishop of Glasgow, the Humes and the Hepburns secured possession of the King's son, the sixteen-year-old James, and put the King to defiance. The northern Earls – Huntly, Crawford, Erroll and

---

[1] See *infra*, pp. 230-1.

Buchan – Lord Glamis, Lord Forbes, William Scheves, archbishop of St Andrews, and William Elphinstone, bishop of Aberdeen, remained loyal to the King, as also did the great sea-captain Sir Andrew Wood and, in general, the ' commons and burghs '.

Following an indecisive skirmish at Blackness, both sides agreed to an interchange of their ' debates and causes '; but the Pacification of Blackness, which was then accepted, was unstable. James was of opinion that he had yielded too much to men who were in arms against their King, and, in particular, he disliked leaving the young prince in the hands of 'wise lords and honourable persons of wisdom and discretion ' – namely, those who had put him to defiance.

On 11 June 1488 the two sides met again near Stirling. Without waiting for the loyal northern lords to join him, James gave fight to his enemies forthwith. But, carried away by his horse which possibly bolted from the battle, the King was thrown and, taken to a nearby cottage or mill, was there murdered by a ' pretendit priest ' – though how ' the king happened to be slain ' was never discovered.

All this tangled story of politics, of Lauder Bridge, the King's favourites, the ' black money ' and so forth, partly hides and partly reveals important changes and developments that were taking place in Scotland at this period in her history. Not only was a ' civil service ' emerging – quite separate from the nobility (' the born counsellors of the realm '), but also the second half of the fifteenth century was a time of expanding economy and changing standards of living, helped, perhaps, to some extent, by the respite afforded to Scotland through England's pre-occupation with the Wars of the Roses.

Signs of increasing wealth are to be seen, for example, in the many foundations by laymen of collegiate churches,[1] chantries and chapels. One stupendous example of the collegiate church has survived in Roslin Chapel, founded by Sir William Sinclair about 1450, where, although only the choir was completed, the building is overwhelming in the intricacy of its mason-work; another interesting and unusually complete example has survived at Seton, near Prestonpans. Within the burghs there was also much beautiful church-work, to which St

---

[1] The years between 1440 and 1460 saw many such foundations, and by 1500, in Lothian alone, no less than twelve collegiate churches had been founded. The wealthy Lord anxious to secure prayers for his soul, no longer gave some large endowment to a monastic house; instead he erected and endowed his own collegiate church. While the clergy of the church celebrated mass and observed the canonical hours, their main task was to pray for the souls of the founder and his kin. Moreover, and symptomatic of the times, the erection of a collegiate church was a status symbol.

John's at Perth, St Michael's at Linlithgow, and the Church of the Holy Rood at Stirling are witnesses; while within the burgh-churches many altars were founded by merchant burgesses and craft associations.[1]

There was also much secular building. To the fifteenth century belongs imposing work at important castles like those of Doune, Borthwick and Craigmillar. James III, interested in architecture, had begun to improve and beautify the royal residences at Linlithgow and Stirling. Many of the small castles and towers of Scotland were erected at this time, as also were many of the ' halls ' that were added to earlier, purely military, structures. In the burghs, more houses were being built of stone.

Increasing wealth, and changing ideas of importance and prestige are also to be seen in the many charters of erection of new burghs of barony – baron apparently vying with baron, and at least fifty new burghs of barony being erected during the period 1450-1513.

Increasing wealth, and the example set by James III, led also to a new interest in the arts. If the collegiate church at Roslin is astonishing in its mason-work, Trinity College Church, founded by Mary of Gueldres, possessed a beautiful altar-piece, painted by Hugo van der Goes,[2] bearing portraits of James III, and of his Queen, Margaret of Denmark, and a third portrait, which is probably that of Alexander, duke of Albany. In literature, Henryson's best work was done in the time of James III, and Dunbar's *Lament for the Makars* enumerates a number of poets whose work has perished but who, by their naming, were appreciated in their time. The Treasurer's accounts also reveal the King's love of music,[3] particularly that of the lute, and church music at this time in Scotland is said to have been outstanding.

In the realm of learning, a second university, that of Glasgow, had already been founded (1451) through the initiative of William Turnbull, bishop of Glasgow – though for many years it was to remain a small and struggling foundation.

Increasing wealth, better standards of living and an interest in the arts, were all part and parcel of an expanding economy which, however, was almost inevitably accompanied by inflation. Because of that, the governments of James III, like the British governments in the years

---

[1] In the Church of the Holy Trinity, St Andrews, there were thirty-two or thirty-three altars, and in St Giles, Edinburgh, forty-four altars of which in both cases the greater number were fifteenth-century foundations.

[2] Now in the Scottish National Gallery.

[3] The assignment of part of the revenues of Coldingham to the Chapel Royal (of St Mary the Virgin) at St Andrews was apparently to provide an increase in the choir.

following the second World War, passed from one economic crisis to another. Control and restraint were urged upon the people in the second half of the fifteenth century much as they were again urged in the mid-twentieth century. Sumptuary laws were passed to prevent luxury spending on costly clothes, and also to limit the amount of material that could be used in any one dress. Too many holidays were denounced, and in 1469 it was enacted that masons, wrights and other craftsmen were to work on Saturdays until 4 o'clock in the afternoon. Excessive spending and a shorter working-week were both dangers to the national economy, and the realm was likely to be impoverished thereby.

But the main problem was that of ' the money '. All Europe was short of bullion, and yet, with increasing trade,[1] coined money was in greater and greater demand. Scotland herself was especially short of bullion owing to the drain upon her gold and silver for the payment of the ransom of David II, followed by the much smaller payment for the ransom of James I. And the shortage of bullion in fifteenth-century Scotland was much like our twentieth-century shortage of foreign exchange.

Practically every Council and Parliament of James III's reign concerned itself with the problem of the ' cunzie '. More than once a ' royal commission ' was appointed to investigate and report. But, as Parliament lamented in 1474, ' the matter of the money ' remained ' right subtle and great '. To meet the shortage of bullion there were constant enactments designed to prevent money leaving the realm – including one, in 1466, that persons going abroad were to take with them only their reasonable expenses: again very much like mid-twentieth century restrictions upon those taking holidays abroad. There were equally constant enactments hopefully designed to bring bullion in. Finally, there was debasement, the coinage of black money, and thereby the provision of a large number of coins to meet a multiplicity of small transactions.

Throughout the whole of the fifteenth and sixteenth centuries there was steady debasement of the coinage, each recoinage being baser than the one before; and naturally each recoinage led to further hoarding of the earlier and more valuable coins. Steadily more and more pennies were coined from the pound of silver; an alloy called ' billon ' was soon used; finally the penny contained no silver at all.

[1] And trade increased despite the maintenance of old mediaeval concepts, such as the ' monopoly precincts ' of the burghs and exports to a ' staple port ' (Middelburg, Bruges, and finally Veere) in the Low Countries.

In a perfectly pure coinage the pound of silver would be coined into 240 pennies (the 240 pennyweights to the pound of Troy measure), but, as early as David I's initial coinages, the King had coined more than 240 pennies out of each pound of silver – partly to cover the cost of minting the coins, partly to meet the loss through wear, and partly to make a small profit from the work of the royal mint. In 1150 David I had coined 252 pennies out of the pound of silver; but real debasement began in 1367, in the reign of David II, when the number of pennies to the pound of silver was increased to 352.[1] Thereafter further debasement (and the resultant inflation) was rapid. Exact calculations are impossible, but roughly we may say that in 1393 a pound of silver was worth 528 pennies; in 1440 it was worth 768 pennies; in 1451 it was worth 1,152 pennies; and in 1483, the year following Lauder Bridge, 1,680 pennies. And debasement still continued. Other countries, including England, were likewise faced with the same problem of a shortage of bullion in a time of expanding economy; other countries likewise debased their coinages; but Scotland's debasement was much heavier than that of England with the result that, whereas up to 1367 the coinages of the two countries had probably been on a parity, in the reign of James III four Scots pounds became equated with one English pound, and by the time of the Union of the Crowns in 1603 one English pound was worth twelve Scots pounds. Nevertheless, the Scottish mint was apparently well run. Its methods, and its coin-types, weights and denominations all show continental influences – whereas, until the fourteenth century, it had followed English practice.

Continuing debasement of the coinage, however, with its accompanying inflation, meant continually rising prices which affected all classes in the realm. Moreover, the coinage itself became suspect – and we know that the craftsmen of Edinburgh complained that they were paid in ' black pennies ' but no one would accept the ' black pennies ' when they tried to buy with them.

Finally, it should be noted that Edinburgh, with its ready access to the port of Leith, was coming to be accepted as the principal burgh and capital of the kingdom. James II was born, crowned, married and buried in the Abbey of Holyrood. A number of important privileges were granted to the burgh of Edinburgh by James III, and, in one of these charters of privilege, it is described as ' the principal burgh of our kingdom '.

[1] Of which nineteen pennies were to be retained for seigniorage and minting.

CHAPTER XXIV

Merchants and Craftsmen

WE HAVE already seen that, in the middle of the fourteenth century, when the burghs had to find large sums of money to help to meet the payment of the ransom of David II, the merchants tended to become more important than the craftsmen.[1] Large sums of money could be raised only through the trading activities of the merchants, whereas the craftsmen did little more than serve and satisfy local needs. Thus the merchants, who furnished the greater part of the burghs' contributions to national needs, gradually gained more influence than the craftsmen in the day-to-day administration of burgh affairs. And this influential position of the merchants was strengthened in the second half of the fifteenth century when, through certain parliamentary enactments, they gained practically all authority and power in burgh government.

According to the early 'laws' of the burghs the magistrates and officers of the burgh were to be elected annually by the burgesses at the head court held at Michaelmas[2]; and we know that such elections took place in the time of Robert I. By the beginning of the fifteenth century, however, in many burghs the merchants had gained control of the town council to the exclusion of the craftsmen; and in those burghs where the merchants were associated together in a merchant guild, the town council (largely, if not entirely composed of merchants) naturally favoured the interests of the guild. Moreover, in some burghs the guild and the town council worked together so closely that eventually the town council was chosen from the guild and by the guild; and often it becomes difficult to differentiate between council and guild. Thereby the merchants gained an even greater control over burgh affairs to the exclusion of the craftsmen.

Looking at the records, we find that in Edinburgh, in the middle of the fifteenth century, the officers of the burgh were sometimes called officers of the guild, and a sitting of the burgh court was sometimes called a sitting of the guild. In Aberdeen, about the same time, the town council was elected by the merchant guild on the Friday following the holding of the Michaelmas head court: and consequently the

[1] *Supra*, p. 118.　　　　[2] *Supra*, p. 116.

craftsmen could have had no voice in the election. At this time, too, in Aberdeen, we find the *council* making burgh regulations (or ' bye-laws ') at meetings of the *guild*. Perhaps even more important, we find that the merchants in their guild had complete control over the admission of new burgesses, and that apparently only ' worthy ' craftsmen, few in number, were being admitted to burgess-ship.

By this time, however, opposition to such a merchant oligarchy had apparently begun to make itself heard. An act of 1469, referring to ' great trouble and contention . . . through the multitude and clamour of common simple persons ' at the time of burgh elections, laid down that henceforth the new town council was to be elected by the old town council, and that both councils, sitting together, were to choose the burgh officers – though, as a concession to the craftsmen, each craft was to be allowed to appoint one member to have a voice in the election of the officers. How far such a minority voice, accorded to the crafts, lessened their ' clamour ' (and the ' common simple persons ' were undoubtedly the craftsmen), we do not know; but, and of importance in another way, the appointment of one member from each craft to have voice in the election of the officers necessarily meant some form of craft organisation. Following the act of 1469 a number of crafts in the different burghs obtained from the town councils what were virtually charters of incorporation, and which were popularly called ' seals of cause '[1]; and, as we shall see, such ' seals of cause ' gave strength and unity to the individual crafts,[2] and increased their bargaining powers.

Then, in 1474, Parliament further enacted that four members of the old council were to be chosen to serve on the new council; and in 1504 it enacted that all provosts, bailies and others ' having office of jurisdiction within burgh ' were to be changed yearly, and that no one was to exercise jurisdiction within a burgh unless he ' used merchandise ', that is, was a merchant engaged in overseas trade.[3]

These successive acts of parliament, although their intent may have been laudable, and although they did not at once become operative in every burgh, and were in some ways evaded, nevertheless confirmed the powers already gained by the merchants, and also concentrated

[1] They were so called because they were sealed, not with the burgh's common seal, but with its court seal, its seal of causes.

[2] There is evidence that in some burghs some of the crafts were already well organised at the time of the act of 1469, but, after that act, seals of cause followed thick and fast.

[3] This act was re-enacted in 1535. It has been argued that it was directed against the holding of office by local lords and lairds, but, even if that were so, the act still placed office in the hands of the merchants and excluded the craftsmen.

power in each burgh in the hands of a small merchant group. In Aberdeen, for example, the act of 1504, prescribing that the burgh officers were to be changed yearly, was disregarded until 1590. Moreover it was easy to argue that the act of 1474 did not say that 'four *and four only*' of the old council were to be elected to the new council; the act said 'four', which could mean 'at least four'. And if at least four members of the old council were to be elected to the new council, why should not the whole of the old council, or at any rate a majority of the old council, be elected to the new? From that, the final step was easy. In some burghs, the council re-elected itself to office, year by year; in other burghs, the old council (council *A*) elected the new council (council *B*), and then, at the end of its year of office, council *B* elected council *A* to serve again – and so on, thereafter, year by year. Thus a small group of merchants could gather and retain all power in its own hands, and burgh offices could be held by the same men, or at least the same families, year after year. In 1590, for example, complaint was made to the Privy Council that in Aberdeen the provostry and chief offices had been held by the same men, their kin, friends and allies 'these fourscore years bygone', and it was notorious that in most of the burghs the retiring council, in choosing the new council, tended more and more to re-elect a majority of themselves.

Such a monopoly of power, moreover, inevitably led to corruption. The burgh's common lands or common fishings, for example, could be leased, or even set in feu-ferme, to a councillor, or some member of his family, or even some friend, at a figure much below the real value[1]; indeed, the small clique who had secured control of the town council could manage to its own advantage the whole of the ' Common Good ' of the burgh – that is, all the property and all the funds belonging in common to all the burgesses. This is well illustrated in a complaint made to the Privy Council by the burgesses of Cupar in 1567 which reveals what had happened in that burgh and was undoubtedly happening elsewhere: 'The old council having always faculty to elect the new, they choose men of their faction and so hold the public offices and the council among a certain [number] of particular men, from hand to hand, using and disponing the common good of the burgh at their pleasure '.

Quite apart from the control of burgh government and burgh

---

[1] The burghs had long been leasing or setting part of their common lands in private holdings and placing the revenues derived therefrom to their ' common good ', and it is apparent that this setting or disponing of the ' common geir ' was known to be liable to grave abuse. The setting of common lands or common fishings in feu-ferme (a heritable *perpetual* tenure) was particularly ill-advised and liable to abuse.

property which, in each burgh, was thus gained by a small group of merchants, Parliament had attempted in other ways to place the craftsmen under the direction of the merchants. In the reign of James I, in 1426 and 1427, craft meetings had been denounced as ' conspiracies '; craft organisations had been condemned as tending to raise prices to the hurt of the lieges; and power had been given to the town councils (already, as we have seen, largely composed of merchants) to fix the prices to be put upon craftsmen's work, and the wages to be paid to craftsmen who, like wrights and masons, used materials supplied by others. Steadily, moreover, there had been legislation throughout the fifteenth century against craftsmen ' using merchandise ' unless they had ' renounced ' their craft.

Occasionally, but only occasionally, there is record of a craftsman renouncing his craft and being admitted to the ranks of the merchants. Sometimes this occurs because of some special service rendered to the burgh – perhaps the craftsman had put new windows into the town church, or had been particularly helpful in repairs to the tolbooth. But transition from craftsman to merchant was apparently rare; and it became more difficult still as the distinction between merchant and craftsman became a social one. To rise from craftsman to merchant was to climb the social ladder. In 1588, for example, when an Edinburgh skinner was admitted as a guild brother he not only renounced his ' trade ' but also he undertook that his wife and servants would use ' no point of common cookery outwith his house ', would not carry ' meat dishes or courses through the town ', and would not appear in the streets ' with their aprons and serviettes '.

But, although in the reign of James I Parliament had denounced craft organisations, the act of 1469, as we have seen, had encouraged incorporation under seals of cause; and, although from time to time the government still forbade craft associations, incorporations under seals of cause quickly multiplied. Under its seal of cause a craft could now draw up rules to ensure good workmanship for the honour of the craft, to regularise apprenticeships, and to exercise discipline over its members. In addition, the incorporated craft could raise funds from its members (usually in the form of a ' weekly penny ' from each craftsman) to maintain an altar to its patron saint and to care for ' decayed brethren ' and for the widows and orphans of brethren who had untimely deceased.[1] So arose the ' Incorporated Trades ', of

---

[1] In this the craft incorporations closely followed the pattern of the merchant guilds.

which the numbers varied in the different burghs: in Edinburgh and Glasgow there were finally fourteen incorporated trades[1]; in Renfrew there was only one. Each incorporated trade, with its deacon, could hold an assembly, or court, to enforce the rules and regulations of the craft; and, in due course, in the case of disputes between different crafts a decision could be given by an assembly or court consisting of representatives of all the incorporated trades within the burgh sitting under a ' deacon-convener '.

Such incorporations enabled each craft to ensure that, within the burgh, the work of the craft was done only by its own members: a position similar to the ' closed shop '; and James VI was later to complain in his *Basilikon Doron* that ' the craftsmen think we should be content with their work, how bad and dear soever it be, and if they in anything be controlled, up goeth the blue blanket [the Edinburgh craftsmen's banner]'. But such incorporations also increased the ' bargaining power ' of the crafts and placed them in a stronger position to contend with the merchants for a share in burgh government and administration.

The many references to ' risings ' and ' commotions ' within the burghs in the first half of the sixteenth century possibly indicate agitation by the crafts for a fuller participation in burgh affairs – both in administration and in trade – and in 1555 Parliament returned to the repressive policy of the reign of James I. The choosing of deacons of crafts (which had proved to be ' right dangerous ') was forbidden, and craft meetings and the drawing up of craft rules were proscribed; but the act also laid down that two craftsmen were to be admitted to the council of every burgh and were to take part in the auditing of the burgh's common good.[2] In the following year, however, the Queen Regent, Mary of Guise, granted a general charter to the craftsmen which, after referring to ' dissensions and contentions ' between merchants and craftsmen in all burghs, virtually revoked the act of 1555, restored to the crafts the right to choose deacons (who, in accordance with the act of 1469, were to take part in the election of the burgh officers), gave them a right to meet and to make craft rules, and even empowered the craftsmen to ' use merchandise '.[3]

---

[1] The number of incorporated trades (crafts) in both Edinburgh and Glasgow varied from time to time but, with amalgamations and other changes, the final number appears to have been fourteen.

[2] Three years earlier the Convention of Royal Burghs had ordered the constitutions of all the royal burghs to be modelled upon that of Edinburgh; and in Edinburgh two craftsmen sat on the town council.

[3] This general charter was confirmed by Mary in 1564 and by James VI in 1581.

It is probably significant that the craftsmen do not appear to have taken advantage of this last privilege, and almost the only reference to it comes from a complaint of the craftsmen of Stirling in 1579. More generally, ' common agreements ' were now being reached between merchants and craftsmen, in the different burghs, under which ' merchandise ' (overseas trade) was reserved to the merchants while the craftsmen were given a local liberty to trade freely in their own wares. In effect, the craftsmen, again in a position of strength, and in many cases prosperous, were apparently content to leave overseas trade in the hands of the merchants and were more intent upon gaining a share in burgh administration.

Matters came to a head in 1582. A riot in Edinburgh, at the time of a burgh election in that year, was followed by an enquiry, presided over by the precocious sixteen-year-old James VI; and the findings of the enquiry were confirmed by an act of parliament in 1584. Edinburgh was given a ' set ' (or constitution) of a provost, four bailies, a dean of guild and a treasurer (all of whom, according to the act of 1504, were to be merchants), together with eighteen other town councillors of whom ten were to be merchants and eight craftsmen. Merchants and craftsmen were to share in the administration and auditing of the common good, and they were to share the privilege of representing the burgh in parliament and in the Convention of Royal Burghs.

Somewhat similar sets were gradually adopted by the other royal burghs; but it is noticeable that the merchants still retained their control. Merchants still filled all the offices, and merchants outnumbered the craftsmen on the town council.

Above all, corruption still continued. Theoretically, there was supervision – for what it was worth. By acts of 1535 and 1567 the administration of the common good of the burghs was placed under Exchequer control, and Books of the Common Good were certainly produced in Exchequer; but it is evident on all hands that that was little more than a formality. In 1590, for example, there was a complaint in the Convention of Royal Burghs that for the last thirty years the common lands of Aberdeen had been held in the hands of the magistrates and their friends; and later reports, down even to the nineteenth century and the era of burgh reform, reveal a sorry tale of private bargains at the expense of the common lands, fraudulent contracts for the carrying out of common works, and deliberate disregard of the welfare and solvency of the community in the selfish interests of the magistrates and councillors themselves.

CHAPTER XXV

Burgh Life in the Fifteenth and Sixteenth Centuries

DAVID I's charter to the Abbey of Holyrood, granted early in his reign, refers to a ' communio vendendi et emendi ' enjoyed by the burgesses of a burgh. Later charters, granted to their burghs by William ' the Lion ' and Alexander II, use the Latin word *communicare* when saying that the burgesses who ' participate together ' in buying and selling must also ' participate together ' in rendering their ' aids ' to the king. In Exchequer, we frequently find the *communitas burgi* rendering its account. In the records of any burgh the words ' the community ' occur on practically every page. Finally, the early burgh court, a gathering of ' all the good men of the community ', drew up rules and regulations for the orderly administration and well-being of the community, and enforced judicial sanctions against the transgressor whose actions had hurt the community of his burgh or one of its members.

Throughout, the stress is upon ' the community '. The newly admitted burgess had to take an oath to be ' leel and feel ' to the king and also to ' the community of his burgh '; he had to be a ' good neighbour ' and observe *vicinitas*. More than that, he had to build his house within a given period of time (usually a year and a day) so that he resided in the burgh – ' sleeping there and rising there ' as it is sometimes put – in order that he might carry out his duties in return for enjoying his privileges. And, if he offended against the community, his house might be pulled down, so that it became impossible for him to continue to live within the community.

This idea of a community can also be seen in other ways. Outside the burgh there were the ' town's acres ', or the ' burgess acres ', and the ' burgh muir ' – arable land cultivated in runrig by the burgesses and common grazing land upon which they put their cattle to be watched by the ' common herd '. There were ' common ' rights of pulling heather (for thatching) and of cutting peats. A burgh on a good river, as, for example, Aberdeen or Ayr, had its ' common fishings '. The burgh had its own burgh mill. And the profits that were made from ' setting ' the fishings, the mill, and so forth, and from the ' burgess silver ' (which was paid by new burgesses upon their admission),

238

became the 'common good' of the burgh – a fund to be expended upon common causes and common affairs (*communia negotia*).

This burgh community was a trading community, and its trading privileges were likewise enjoyed in common. In the burgh's trade there had to be equal opportunities for every member of the community who had been admitted to trading rights; no one burgess might enjoy special liberties or encroach on the liberties of others. If an unexpected ship arrived in the burgh's haven, the cargo was to be 'loosed' by the burgh officers in such a way that all might have equal opportunities to buy. If the burgh decided upon some 'wild aventure' (the usual term for a ship sailing forth with export goods), the freighting of the ship was done publicly (often at the tolbooth stair) so that all might know and have an equal chance of participating – and, if the offers of freight exceeded the vessel's capacity, then each had to cut his offer proportionately. For both imports and exports, no private bargains could be struck by individual burgesses with the master or crew of a ship.

Again, goods for sale had to be displayed openly for all the burgesses to see; there was to be no secret selling in lofts or cellars, whereby particular persons might benefit. The forestaller, who bought up goods before they reached the market for general sale, and the regrater, who bought more than he required in order to sell again at a higher price, were enemies to the community. At Elgin, Alexander Williamson was found to have done wrong in passing to the sea coast and buying from a French vessel twenty iron pots which had not been offered for sale in the burgh; in Inverness, Robert Reid was found guilty of 'making shoes in quiet places' and selling them to landward 'in hurt of the burgh'. All burgesses had to have an equal chance of any bargain – though one canny exception is to be found in Peebles where, in 1464, it was agreed that burgesses might make private bargains if the chance arose 'suddenly, in time of ganging to the kirk, or on other needful errand'.

The necessity for an open market for all arose particularly in the case of victuals. Although the burgesses were for long farmers (or at least small-holders) as well as traders, growing their crops on the burgess-acres, pasturing their cattle on the burgh muir and cultivating their own plots (and 'heirship goods', which could not be alienated and which had to descend to the heir, included ploughs, wains and carts, and the crop from any ground already sown with seed), the concentration of so many people in one centre naturally led to a large dependence upon the neighbouring countryside. So arose many regulations to ensure that all foodstuffs were made available in the burgh market and that no one bought before the ringing of the bell. General buying and selling was allowed only when the needs of the burgesses themselves had been met. No burgess was to buy more victual than he required for his own household; the fleshers were not to keep extra meat in their cellars and the bakers were not to buy more flour than they needed for their bakings. Maximum prices for grain and malt were fixed at regular intervals by ' the assize of bread and ale '; tasters of ale and wine (to test the quality) and apprisers of flesh were appointed; and there was strict supervision over measures – the ell-wand, the ' stane wecht ', the pint stoup and the firlot.

In every aspect of its life and work the burgh was always a community. In Dundee, the community was awakened with the hautboy at 6 a.m. in summer; it was put to sleep at ' the usual time of night ' by the town's piper, with bagpipe and drum. In Aberdeen this was done with the ' Almany whistle '. The community worked and played between sunrise and sunset. And, after sunset, let no man be found walking the street unless he were an ' honest neighbour ' on ' lawful errand ', and bearing a light in token thereof – otherwise he would be seized by the watch and ' thrust in the netherhole, incontinent '.

If the community had its common piper, so also it had its common minstrels for holidays and for special occasions. Dunbar wrote of the common minstrels of Edinburgh that they knew two tunes only; but James IV paid them fourteen shillings for playing before Mons Meg as she was drawn down the High Street on her way to the Raid of Norham. That was an extra payment; for usually common pipers and common minstrels received their ' meitt ' (or a small payment in lieu thereof) from the honest burgesses turn and turn about, or, as the Aberdeen records put it, ' circulale throw the nichtbouris '. When James IV left the burgh of Aberdeen in January 1498 he paid that burgh's common pipers twenty-eight shillings. We must not assume therefrom that the pipers of Aberdeen were twice as good as those of Edinburgh; but Aberdeen was certainly famed for its minstrels and its pageants, which are praised by Dunbar in *Blyth Aberdein*. And already in 1496, that they might not lag behind the other burghs of the realm, the Town Council of Aberdeen had caused enquiries to be made into the pageants and processions held in Edinburgh and elsewhere. The answers they received are not recorded; but in Edinburgh, in 1554, the ' play gear ' that was then the property of the town included ' 8 play hats, a king's crown, a mitre, a fool's hood, a sceptre, a pair of angel's wings and hair for two angels'. Dundee was even wealthier, with, among other properties, sixty crowns, six pairs of angel's wings, Abraham's hat, and twenty-three heads of hair.

Apart from pageants like that of Corpus Christi or of the Day of the Holy Rood, summer was brought in by the follies of an Abbot of Unreason, or by Robin Hood and Little John. In Aberdeen, in 1508, the town council ordered all the burgesses to be ' reddy with thair array-ment maid in grene and yallow, [with] bowis, arrowis, brass, and all uther convenient thingis according thairto ', so that they could be true ' foresters ' to Robin Hood. And although an Act of 1555 prohibited the May games of Robin Hood – which often led to ' perturbation ' of the burgh's tranquility – the Act was not really effective. Edinburgh, we know, still observed its ' Robin Hood ' in 1572; and in that same year, John Knox, aged and enfeebled, watched a play in St Andrews picturing the siege and fall of Edinburgh castle and the (prophetic) hanging of Kirkcaldy of Grange.[1]

But while Dunbar in *Blyth Aberdein*, which was written to com-memorate Queen Margaret's visit there, in 1511, on her pilgrimage to Tain, tells us that their Cross, in honour of the Queen, ' abundantly ran wine ', the evidence of the records soon checks our vivid imagina-tion. In Edinburgh, in 1566, to celebrate the birth of James VI, only one puncheon of wine was run at the Cross – its cost being entered in the records at £10 (Scots[2]); and in Aberdeen, at the birth of a son to James VI,[3] the amount of wine to be run at the Cross is entered as five gallons – which would certainly not run for long; and, moreover, the provost, the bailies and the town council would always be first in the queue.

But the burgh was not only a community; it was a close community. At first, because the burgh was largely a settlement of new men, or of men who had broken away from the feudal ties of lord and land, the burgesses naturally found their protection only in their own unity and solidarity. The new member had to be *admitted* by the other members and, as we have seen, he had to take the oath of good neighbourhood. There was no automatic succession of son to father, and the early

---

[1] It is perhaps as well to record that the Roman Church on the eve of the Reforma-tion tried to suppress plays and pageants because they had become too biting in their criticism of ecclesiastical corruption and clerical pretensions. The Reformed Church did not denounce them until the seventeenth century when their growing lewdness called for condemnation.　　　　　　　　　[2] Roughly 33s. 4d. sterling.
[3] Henry, born in February 1594; predeceased his father in 1612.

royal writs are addressed, not to the burgesses and their heirs, but to the burgesses and their *successors*. Later, under more settled conditions, this closeness, this exclusiveness, was further by jealousy – jealousy of the town's privileges, and notably its privileges of trade, which were to be enjoyed only by the burgess merchants themselves. Only those could have a share in the burgh's trade, only those could 'pack and peel', who resided in the burgh, who did 'watch and ward', who paid 'scot and lot', and who held 'stob and staik'.

Because of this, there was always deep distrust of the stranger. In the so-called 'Laws of the Four Burghs' no burgess could harbour a stranger for more than one night, unless he were willing to become pledge for him. In the Aberdeen records, in 1402, pledges are to be found that certain English sailors, whose ship had come to trade, would not be allowed to spy out 'the secrets of the town or the state and converse of the burgesses'; and, again in the Aberdeen records, in 1442, we read that 'no man of this town, whatever he be, harbour any man of without the town, but incontinent he shall come to the Alderman, and let him wit of how many persons and what persons they are, under the pain of law and banishing'. Above all, there was deep distrust of 'outside lords'. No member of the community could solicit the support of a lord 'dwelling to landward', or support the request of a lord for a place in the town.[1] In Aberdeen, in 1447, when the town council agreed that a burgess could assign his lease of one of the burgh fishings, it was careful to add, 'except [to] lordis'. And, if there were to be no outside lords poking their noses into burgh affairs, there were to be no outside lawyers either. In Peebles, in 1555, it was laid down that in all time coming no neighbour, under pain of losing his freedom for ever, was to solicit or cause men of law to come into the burgh to act as procurators, save only for brieves of heritage.

Always, and in all things, the burgh was a community – protecting its own interests in its own court (which had special laws and special procedures to meet its own special needs) and protecting itself by its own defences and by the watch and ward of its own burgesses. In this latter respect the Scottish burgess was for long a man-at-arms as well as a merchant or craftsman; and in many burghs one of the conditions of admission of a burgess was the possession of suitable and sufficient armour and weapons 'for serving the king's grace and the town'. In Peebles, in 1462 and 1463, we find newly admitted bur-

[1] This, moreover, was to be carefully enquired into and enforced by the Chamberlain on his ayre.

gesses paying ' a bow and a sheaf of arrows ' for the town's armoury, in place of the usual burgess silver; and in Edinburgh, as late as 1565, an English arrow-maker was admitted to burgess-ship in order that he might stay within the burgh to instruct others in his craft.

In Aberdeen, in 1412 (when the ordeal of Harlaw was still fresh in the memory of the burgh), it was laid down that every burgess must ' stand guaird ' and help to protect his neighbours ' fra schaith and surprice ' under pain of banishment and the destruction of his house. In Edinburgh, in 1513, when the rumour of Flodden reached the burgh, we read in the records that those burgesses who were still left in the burgh were ordered to look to their weapons of war and to be ready to gather at the sound of the common bell for the defence of the town; and, continues the order, sternly, let no women be seen clamouring and crying in the streets, but let them pass to church for prayer or busy themselves at home with their domestic tasks.

Upon such occasions many a worthy burgess doing his watch must have felt, as honest Simon Glover felt on the walls of Perth, ' a strange breathlessness and some desire to go home for a glass of distilled waters '. But such occasions became less and less frequent – save perhaps on the Borders where, for example, as late as 1540 a charter granted by James V to the burgh of Selkirk spoke of it as ' often burned, harried and destroyed ' because of its proximity ' to England, Liddesdale, and other broken parts ', and granted to it a right to have ' muros fossas et stagna '; while upon another occasion the king enjoined it to choose a ' warlike ' man to be its provost.

With more settled times, however, many a burgh had allowed its early defences to fall into disrepair. In Edinburgh, in 1559, three of the gates were reported to be ' auld and failyeit '; in Dundee, as in many other burghs, fines were prescribed for those who entered the burgh by climbing over the back-dykes of the tenements; and at Peebles, in 1572, the defences were in such a state that punishments were laid down for those found guilty of leaping the wall.

By now, too, the burgesses frequently paid out sums of money to be relieved of their military services. In national mobilisations, when the king's host was called out, many a burgh secured an arrangement whereby the burgesses could ' bide at hame ' by paying a fixed sum to the Lord High Treasurer or by furnishing a quota of mercenaries (' wageouris ') who were to be paid by a local stent[1] upon the town. In 1494 the burgesses of Aberdeen were allowed to ' reman at hame fra

[1] That is, a local taxation.

243

the passage in Ingland ' by paying a lump sum of £100 and providing five shillings and fourpence a day for the space of a month for the maintenance of eight Englishmen in Perkin Warbeck's force. For the Raid of Norham, in 1497, the community of Perth paid £150 and the community of Dundee £225 for the right to ' bide at hame ' – and James IV appears to have preferred the money (which he could use for the ' forthcoming of the artillery ') to the somewhat doubtful military prowess of the burgesses. It is to be noted, however, that occasionally some burgesses, bolder than their fellows, preferred to serve personally rather than contribute to the local stent. In Aberdeen, for example, in 1522, six burgesses refused to pay their share of a local stent for a licence to ' bide at hame ' from the muster at Roslin Muir and declared that, instead of paying, they would themselves ' pass furth to the said oist '.

Another picture, of a somewhat different kind, comes from Edinburgh, in 1559, when the Town Council, hearing of the approach of the Army of the Congregation, and remembering what had happened at Perth and Dundee, dispersed the vestments and the precious altar vessels of St Giles among individual burgesses for safe-keeping, hid the town's evidents,[1] and also hired three score ' men of war ', paying each man thirty pence a day, to defend St Giles and its choir-stalls. A little later we read that the walls and gates were hastily repaired; six gunners ' well qualified and of good practice ' were hired ' to handle the town's artillery '; ' cut-throats ' (weapons, not assassins) were placed in position; and six shillings and eightpence was ordered to be paid to Willie Thompson, the whistler, for his labours in playing for two nights upon his whistle at the watch – doubtless to keep up their spirits when the danger was most threatening.

The general plan of almost every Scottish burgh was one main street – the High Street, or Market Street – with a number of smaller and narrower streets, or perhaps only closes or vennels, running off it at right angles. This plan, as we have seen, goes back to the time when the burgh served the castle: when it was a supply-centre for the castle and a market-centre for the sheriffdom. Then the main street of the burgh ran direct to the castle-gate. When Perth was ' re-planned ', however, probably in the reign of William ' the Lion ', it was given two main streets – a High Street and a South Street; and in St Andrews, possibly also ' re-planned ', there were three main streets, all converging on the Priory and the Cathedral.

[1] That is, its legal documents which were ' evidence ' of its possessions.

In this High Street, everyone tried to keep to the crown of the causeway – for middens would be piled high on either side; forestairs jutted out; and, to add to the strong scent, the forestairs of the furriers and skinners would be hung with what the records aptly term their ' stinking goods '; while dogs and swine would be roaming freely around. Where the street widened out for the markets, these conditions were only intensified: the wider the street the more refuse it could hold. The fleshers and fish-dealers threw their trimmings on to the street and, despite many statutes of the town to the contrary, it was apparently difficult to say them nay. In Edinburgh, in 1511, it was even deemed necessary to enact that, whenever the bailies visited the fishmarket ' for the execution of the statutes of the town ' (presumably on this very matter of trimmings), one or two of the sergeants were always to accompany them so that, in the mild words of the record, the bailies would not ' be destitute in time of need '.

Admittedly from time to time the mess in the streets would be cleared: labourers would be hired and paid by the rood; but, in general, it was safer, and more comfortable, to keep to the ' crown of the causeway '. And, since everybody wished to do the same, one result, in the words of Dunbar, was ' cries and debates ' – or, in the words of the records, ' tulyies '. Hence all merchants and craftsmen had to keep their weapons ready by them in their booths, to come to the aid of the burgh officers in time of ' sudden tulye or bargaining ' – and the weapons were to be sufficient in number for themselves and all their servants. An act to this effect is to be found in the records of almost every burgh; though with frequent re-enactments we gradually notice a tendency to prescribe ' long weapons ' such as ' pike, spear, and other fencible long armour ' – the most useless type of weapon for close fighting in the street, but possibly the ideal type of weapon for separating contestants.

Naturally, too, this general filth and squalor, and also the primitive materials used for the construction of most of the houses (encouraging rats and vermin to flourish there), resulted in frequent outbreaks of plague. Then, remarkably, the burgh adopted measures which were advanced and efficient in their nature and comprehensiveness. A standstill order was placed on all persons and cattle; severe penalties, such as branding, were decreed for any who entered the burgh by back posterns or open places in the wall; children were to be kept off the streets; markets were closed; dogs and swine were to be kept ' in band '; special places were laid down for the washing of clothes, and special cleansers were appointed for the affected streets and houses. But also, and with a failure to understand the real nature of the outbreak, we generally find that all doors and windows were to be ' steikit up ' and opened ' only upon reasonable cause '.

In the High Street were usually to be found the tolbooth, the church, and the market-cross. The cross was the symbol of the burgh's jurisdiction and its market peace, and was thus its legal centre: the usual place for proclamations, for executions, and for the display of the dismembered limbs of traitors and criminals, At the market-cross the enemy to the community might be condemned to sit, with a paper on his head bearing the nature of his offence – as in Edinburgh, in 1585, when two fleshers were so punished for ' misusing ' an honest woman who had criticised their meat.[1] That may sound vastly different from today, but in other respects many traders' tricks of today were known in earlier times. In Dundee, in the reign of Mary, cadgers were not to sell their fish in bundles, so that good and big fish showed on the outside, whilst within there were only rotten fish, or small codlings and ling. Similarly, no man was to sell victual which showed good in the mouth of the sack, but which was bad and worse in the middle and bottom thereof. Nor was a black market in cattle and poultry unknown. Because of the many cattle that were stolen, killed, and then brought to market, the fleshers were forbidden to buy carcases unless in the hide, with the head thereon, and the lugs with the head[2]; nor were geese to be bought if they had been plucked and were wanting the head.

Usually the church was in fairly good repair, for the merchants took pride in keeping it so. The Dean of Guild was sometimes ' kirk-master ', or master of the kirk fabric, and it was common for each craft to maintain an altar to its patron saint. But the tolbooth was another matter; there are constant references in all records to the necessity for repairs. At Edinburgh, in 1555, the Lords of Council, sitting in the tolbooth, took ' ane effray ', and masons and wrights were quickly called in; but their repairs were apparently not extensive enough for, seven years later, in 1562, we find the Queen writing to the Town Council, calling their attention to the condition of the tolbooth as being ruinous and ' abill haistelie to dekay and fall doun ', and ordering its immediate demolition.

[1] And as late as 1738 a ' fishwife ' was condemned to stand there with two dozen herrings about her neck and with a label, noting her offence, on her breast.
[2] Possibly indicating an early use of ear-markings.

The tolbooth served the burgh for all its public affairs – the burgh court was held there, the council sat there, it was used as the burgh prison, and public intimation to the burgesses might be made at the tolbooth stair or at the market cross. Here, however, we must distinguish between two kinds of imprisonment – warding in the tolbooth being vastly different from being put into 'the netherhole, incontinent'. The distinction was partly a social one and partly one between civil and criminal offences. A person 'entered himself into ward' – he was not *put* there. Admittedly, like a baker of Canongate, he might answer that 'devil a foot wald he gang to his waird'; but the records do not suggest that that was a common reply. Warding was often 'open and free ward', when the door was not locked; and in the Paisley and Stirling records we read of the offender being given the key of the tolbooth and told to go and lock himself in. At Elgin a man warded in the tolbooth was later pursued 'for taking away the lock of the tolbooth', and presumably departing with it; and at Inverness an unfreeman, warded for trafficking in timber, was reported to have kept himself warm by burning the common firlot (the wooden standard measure) which was kept in the Council house – thus showing that he could pass freely about the building from one room to another.

But the tolbooth was so often in disrepair that it was common for the church to be pressed into service for public business. The court might be held in it (despite all canons to the contrary), and its steeple might be used as a prison. In Dundee the steeple was generally used for offenders against ecclesiastical discipline; and this was also the case in St Andrews where, in 1582, a woman who had been placed in solitary confinement in the steeple, by order of the Kirk Session, was released before the completion of her term 'in respect of the vehemency of the storm of weather' which made the steeple so to rock as to put her in terror of her life. In Peebles, as late as 1652, the town miller, who had rejected the Council's scale of payments with the opprobrious words 'Deill nor he break his neck if that he served upon those terms', was ordered into 'close prison within the steeple for abusing the magistrates and council to their face'.

While the 'kirk dykes and kirk yard' provided convenient places for the fullers to 'hang their gear', the kirk and the kirkyard were also the haunt of beggars (of whom there were always plenty), lovers, mischief-makers, and the general rag-tag and bob-tail of the town. The kirkyard was regarded not only as a common meeting-place for sports and dancing, but also as a common pasture, and a common dumping-ground and sanitary convenience. At Peebles, in 1468, in an attempt to protect the decency of the graves, the parish clerk was authorised to take 4d. for every head of cattle found pasturing there, and to kill all swine. But that was the least of the abuses. If the middens in the street tended to grow too quickly, the kirkyard provided a convenient place for the overflow, and a place of large capacity. This was particularly the case after the Reformation, and the general decay of most of the ecclesiastical buildings not used as parish churches. Then the vast utility of old kirkyards is aptly revealed by an entry in the Aberdeen records in 1606, when a certain Alexander Davidson asked for permission to build a ship in the kirkyard of the Trinitarians, arguing that it was a most suitable and convenient place for ' bigging of the said bark ', and that at present it was merely ' filthilie abusit be middingis '. The Council granted his request, finding the desire ' verie reasonable ', and ordered all those who had middens in the said yard to remove them within eight days.

In his strictures upon Edinburgh, Dunbar complains of the many ' fensum flyttingis of defame '. And certainly, if we are to trust the records, outspokenness was a characteristic of the burgesses, and, apparently, particularly the women. Acts innumerable were passed against flyting, backbiting, slandering, oaths, and opprobrious words; and the punishments included the pillory, the stocks, the cuck-stool, the branks,[1] and whipping. In Stirling and in Ayr, the unfortunate culprit might be ' creeled ', which meant suspension in a creel or cage hung by a rope from a projecting beam near the top of the tolbooth – much like the washing hung out from high tenements even today.

These ' acts innumerable ' were acts of the Town Council – our modern bye-laws – and, later issued as ' proclamations ', they covered every phase of burgh life. Some of them, such as those relating to prices and to trading regulations, or against forestalling and regrating, or against flyting and oaths, were passed annually; others were passed as the need occurred. For example, in Dundee, parents of children were to see that their bairns did not play, cry, or otherwise disquiet the preacher in the Kirk and, above all, that they did not break the glass windows; and, in the period immediately following the Reformation, the acts of almost every burgh included one against leaving the Kirk before the end of the sermon and prayers.

In all records, however, the entries that predominate are those relating to trade; for the burgh was essentially a community organised

---

[1] Scold's bridle.

for trade. Yet the burgh court also exercised an ordinary civil and criminal jurisdiction, and it was a court of record, that is, registration could be made in the court books and the authority of the court interponed for enforcement. Usually registration was that of some contract or agreement; one, in Edinburgh, in 1491, relating to the work of the masons on St Giles, reveals the long hours then worked in the building trade. But registration might also take other forms. In Inverness, in 1560, a burgess registered an entry that he would no longer be responsible for debts that were incurred by his wife, and the record was thereafter proclaimed by the bell-man throughout the burgh that none might pretend ignorance thereof. In Peebles, in 1559, we find a wager solemnly recorded – ten merks to a tar-barrel against Queen Elizabeth marrying the King of Sweden within a year.

In its civil jurisdiction the court could impose fines or the loss of burghal privileges; in criminal causes it could, in some burghs, impose the death penalty, though banishment from the burgh, often to the accompaniment of whipping or branding, or nailing by the ear to the tron[1] (with other variations) was more frequent. Here, again, we have the idea of a close community. As long as the burgh got rid of the undesirable, that was all that mattered: let others look out for themselves. But, when we constantly find this or that undesirable person sentenced to be banished perpetually ' like as she was of before ', or to be banished ' because she has been oft banished before ' (and it is usually a woman), we begin to wonder how effective banishment from the burgh really was.

Probably banishment was more popular with burgh bailies and town councils because it was simpler, and also cheaper, than the penalty of death. Hanging an undesirable was a costly business with little or nothing to be gained in return by way of escheats or otherwise. In 1593 ' Jonet Smyth the hussie that was execute ' cost the burgh of Ayr £1 11s. 4d.; and the burning of a witch in 1587 had cost the same community £7 3s. 8d. in ' candles, her meat and drink, pitch-barrels, coals, resin, heather, trees and other necessaries '. But both those executions were cheap. In Edinburgh, the new-fangled Maiden[2] was an expensive luxury – always needing to be sharpened, or to be oiled (the usual entry is 6s. 8d. for oil and soap to ' cresche ' her); and whenever she was brought into action a scaffold, resting on puncheons, had

---

[1] The public weighing-beam.

[2] A type of guillotine (now in the National Museum of Antiquities) popularly said to have been introduced into Scotland by the Earl of Morton who himself perished by it in 1581.

to be constructed at varying cost – the nobler the victim, the higher the scaffold – ranging from a humble 7s. to as much as £4 10s. for Patrick Stewart, second earl of Orkney, executed in 1615. Nor did the expenses end there. In 1619, the cost of the execution of two simple Highlanders, ' born thieves ' we are told, came to more than £30, which included their winding-sheets and payment ' to the women that wind thame '.

But what the burgh lost through criminal justice it more than made up in the general business coming before its court. And here again we see how all the activities of the burgh were woven together. For fines went to the common good (that is, the general funds of the burgh), or to specific common works, such as the repair of the tolbooth, the upkeep of the haven, buying a new town clock, or repairing a bridge. And sometimes it is impossible to avoid the suspicion that fines were always more strictly imposed whenever the burgh had some new and expensive common work on hand for which otherwise it would have been difficult to find the necessary funds. And, if the unfortunate had no money to pay his fine, then, more often than not, he was sentenced to give his labour, for perhaps a week or ten days, at the common work then on hand. So, in the end, the offender against the community assoiled himself by a community service.

CHAPTER XXVI

The Crown and the Nobility

AS WE have already seen, the weak rules of Robert II and Robert III, followed by the regencies of the Albanies, enabled the great barons to govern much as they wished within their own lands, and, upon occasion, to put the crown to defiance. Then, with the return of James I, the King strove to break the power of his overmighty subjects; but still, for some 150 years, the history of Scotland was too often the story of some noble house, or some baronial faction, that had too much power. Too often, and for too long, the crown was worn by a child and regents ruled the realm. Names like Douglas and Hamilton, or titles like Angus, Arran, Lennox, Moray and Morton, could often be chapter-headings in a history of the time.

Scotland was a small country with a small population which had risen to, say, about 750,000 at the opening of the sixteenth century. In this small country, many of the important noble houses were related to one another by marriage; and, out of such marriages, certain noble houses became too great in lands and powers and in alliances and followers. Some of the important noble houses, moreover, married into the royal house – itself a baronial family raised to kingship – and for the greater part of the sixteenth century this or that noble house was too near the throne. The king's life, indeed, might be all that prevented another noble family from wearing the crown which the Stewarts wore through the distant marriage of a Lord High Steward to a daughter of Robert Bruce.

From time to time the power of the ' Black ' Douglases has been referred to, and their final overthrow in the reign of James II has already been briefly recorded.[1] Nevertheless, any survey of the relations between the crown and the nobility should perforce begin with an account of the rise and fall of the house of Douglas; essentially, too, such a survey should end by explaining how the proximity of the houses of Arran and Lennox to the Scottish throne influenced the parts that were played by Hamiltons and Lennox-Stewarts in the decades that followed the death of James V. Indeed, it must have already become apparent to the discerning reader that much of the history of Scotland

[1] *Supra*, p. 222.

can be understood only through a knowledge of family history and family relationships.

The rise of the house of Douglas first began with the grants of lands and powers that were made to the ' good Sir James ' by a grateful Bruce. The earldom itself dates from 1358; and William, first earl of Douglas, then added the earldom of Mar to the Douglas lands by his marriage to Margaret of Mar. His son, James, the second earl, was the hero of Otterburn (1388) when, as told in one of the noblest of our ballads, a dead man won a field:

> But I hae dreamed a dreary dream,
> Beyond the Isle of Skye;
> I saw a dead man win a fight,
> And I think that man was I.
>
> My wound is deep; I fain would sleep
> Take thou the vanguard of the three,
> And hide me by the bracken bush
> That grows on yonder lily lee.

And, when the proud ' Hotspur ' was compelled to yield –

> Thou shalt not yield to lord nor loun,
> Nor yet shalt thou yield to me;
> But yield thee to the bracken bush,
> That grows upon yon lily lee!

With the death of the second Earl, the title and lands descended to Archibald ' the Grim ', a natural son of the ' good Sir James ', who already held all Galloway between the Nith and the Cree (granted to him by David II in 1369, and making him ' Lord of Galloway '), the earldom of Wigtown (which he had purchased from Thomas Fleming, earl of Wigtown, in 1372), and the Lordship of Bothwell (which he gained from his wife, the widow of Sir Thomas Moray of Bothwell). When he was succeeded by his son, Archibald, fourth earl of Douglas, about Christmas 1400, the house of Douglas held the whole of south-west Scotland together with lands in the north and the east, and the power of the ' Black ' Douglas in possessions and in followers had become enormous.

Archibald ' the Grim ' founded the collegiate church of Lincluden, restored Sweetheart Abbey, founded and began to build a collegiate church at Bothwell, and died in the strong castle of Threave which he had built on an island in the Kirkcudbright Dee. His son, Archibald,

THE 'BLACK' DOUGLASES

EARLS OF DOUGLAS

Sir William, 'le Hardi', Lord of Douglas † 1298

The 'Good Sir James' † 1330 (Bruce's heart)

Hugh † c. 1347

Sir Archibald Regent killed at Halidon Hill 1333

William killed at Halidon Hill 1333

Archibald 'The Grim', Lord of Galloway 3rd Earl Douglas † 1400

William 1st Earl Douglas † 1384

William = Egidia dau. of Robert II

George 1st Earl of Angus = Mary dau. of Robert III † 1403 (see Table of 'Red' Douglases)

James 2nd Earl Douglas killed at Otterburn 1388 = Isabel dau. of Robert II

Archibald 4th Earl Douglas killed at Verneuil 1424 = Margaret dau. of Robert III

Mary = David Duke of Rothesay

James 'The Gross' 7th Earl Douglas † 1443

Archibald 5th Earl Douglas † 1439 = Euphemia, dau. of Patrick Graham (see Table of Early Stewarts)

William 8th Earl Douglas assass. 1452 s.p. = Margaret 'Fair Maid of Galloway'

James 9th Earl Douglas attainted 1455; † 1488 s.p. = 'Fair Maid of Galloway'

Archibald Earl of Moray † 1455

Hugh Earl of Ormond ex. 1455

John of Balvany ex. 1463

William 6th Earl Douglas ex. 1440

David ex. 1440

fourth Earl, played a leading part in the warfare against England, both on the Borders and in France. When, on the Borders, the Earl of March, angered by Rothesay's treatment of his daughter, went over to England,[1] Douglas was given his lands and the Lordship of Dunbar; and when the Earl of March was rehabilitated by Albany, Douglas still retained the lands of Annandale. In France, Charles VII appointed him Lieutenant-General of the French armies and created him Duke of Touraine; but, together with his second son, James, and with John Stewart, earl of Buchan (son of the regent Albany), he was killed in the battle of Verneuil (1424).

Archibald, fourth earl, had married Margaret Stewart, the eldest daughter of John, earl of Carrick, afterwards King Robert III. His son, Archibald, fifth earl of Douglas, married, in 1424 or 1425, Euphemia, the elder daughter of Sir Patrick Graham, and sister of Malise Graham, earl of Strathearn, a possible claimant to the throne.[2] In 1427, James I, who was 'touchy' on the question of the descendants of Robert II and Euphemia Ross, deprived Malise of the earldom of Strathearn (creating him, instead, Earl of Menteith) and, two months later, sent him to England as a royal hostage; and, about Whitsuntide 1430, Douglas and his wife were in communication with the Earl of Salisbury, custodian of the imprisoned Malise. It may be that all they sought was the release of Malise, and their negotiations may have had no treasonable intent. It is to be remembered, however, that James I's son, James (later James II), was not born until the following October (1430), and that Malise Graham, though not an heir male, could be regarded as next in succession to the throne. Thus, when their negotiations came to the knowledge of the King, it is not surprising that the Earl was arrested and imprisoned in Lochleven Castle, from which he was not released until the autumn of 1431, when the King had a surviving direct heir.[3] After the assassination of James I, Douglas was appointed Lieutenant-General of the kingdom, but his government appears to have been ineffective and, little more than two years later, he died of plague.

The murder of William, sixth earl of Douglas, and the accession to the earldom of James 'the Gross', have already been described[4]; but, with the death of Earl William, the large Douglas territories were

[1] *Supra*, p. 203, and note.

[2] See *supra*, pp. 194-5, and the Table of Early Stewarts (p. 196).

[3] Twin sons were born to Joan Beaufort, James I's Queen, on 16 October 1430. Alexander, the elder twin, died in infancy; James, the younger twin, lived to become James II.   [4] *Supra*, pp. 220-1.

for a time divided. James, the seventh earl, the second son of Archibald 'the Grim', succeeded to the original Douglas lands, while Margaret, the daughter of Archibald, fifth earl, and sister of the murdered Earl William, succeeded to Galloway and to all the lands which had been acquired through the marriage of Archibald, 'the Grim', to Joanna Moray, and so became popularly known as 'The Fair Maid of Galloway'. The Earl of March recovered Annandale; and an ungrateful French king had already disposed of the duchy of Touraine.

Yet the vast Douglas territories were once more united under William, the eighth earl, who married the 'Fair Maid', probably about 1444; and when, after falling under suspicion in 1450, the Earl was confirmed in all his lands, offices and castle, in 1451, the charters of confirmation show that he held: the earldom of Douglas, the earldom of Wigtown, the lordship of Galloway, the forests of Ettrick and Selkirk, the lordship of Bothwell, large estates in the sheriffdoms of Edinburgh, Haddington, Lanark, Roxburgh, Linlithgow, Peebles, and Aberdeen, and the offices of sheriff of Lanark and Warden of the West and Middle Marches. Nor should it be forgotten that his brothers, Archibald, earl of Moray, Hugh, earl of Ormond, and John of Balvany, held large extents of lands in the north and northeast. The house of Douglas, indeed, bestrode Scotland like a Colossus. Thus, when the Douglas 'banded' with Alexander, fourth earl of Crawford (the 'Tiger' earl),[1] and John of the Isles, earl of Ross, who had already put the King to defiance, James II was not blind to the dangers that faced him – though Douglas, on his part, had reason to fear the King.

The King invited the Earl to Stirling Castle, under a royal safe-conduct, and there, together, they dined and supped. After their meal, the King bespoke the Douglas, asking him to 'break his band'. When Douglas replied that he 'might not nor would not', James, in sudden anger, stabbed him, and the royal attendants, rushing in, made sure that the Earl was dead (22 February 1452).[2] The story is well known; less well known, perhaps, is the fact that, in the following June, Parliament exonerated James from all blame, since the Earl had entered into treasonable conspiracies against the King and was guilty of his own death. Whether or not the King acted in sudden passion, James realised that if he was to rule his own realm, and not simply rule that part of it which lay outside the Douglas lands (and perhaps also the

[1] And Crawford, it should be noted, was a descendant of a daughter of Robert II and Euphemia Ross.

[2] And the Earl of Crawford was defeated by the Earl of Huntly, fighting under the king's banner, at Brechin (18 May 1452).

lands of those in band with Douglas), then it was vital to break the Douglas's power.

Following the murder of Earl William, James, his brother, the ninth and last earl of Douglas, came to Stirling with some six hundred men, denounced the King as a breaker of his word, dragged the violated safe-conduct through the town at the tail of a horse, and then burned and looted at will. He also made approaches to the English king, and declared his defiance of Parliament. In reply, James marched in force through the Douglas lands and, at Douglas castle, in August 1452, received the submission of the Earl and his adherents, together with an assurance that Douglas would abandon all rancour and feud for the death of his brother, and would make no band or league against the King in time to come. In January 1453, when the Earl bound himself to be faithful to the King, James, perhaps foolishly, promised to further a petition for a papal dispensation for the marriage of Earl James to his brother's widow, the Fair Maid of Galloway. The marriage took place, and the vast Douglas lands were united again.

In April 1453, however, when the ninth earl of Douglas went to London as a member of a commission seeking to arrange a truce with England, he secured the release of Malise Graham. This release of the man whose right to the throne was still considered by many to be better than that of the reigning King, was apparently obtained without James's knowledge or consent, and may well have been the ' treason ' which led James II to assemble his forces and march against the earl.[1] Douglas showed a singular lack of resolution and, deserted by his more important adherents, fled to England. His brothers were defeated in battle at Arkinholme – Archibald was killed, Hugh was taken prisoner and executed, and John fled to join his brother, the Earl, in England. In June 1455 the last Earl of Douglas was attainted, and the vast Douglas estates were forfeited to the crown.

Following the forfeiture of the Douglases, and the escheat of their lands, Parliament, in August 1455, proceeded to pass a number of important acts. Beginning with a general declaration that, since ' the poverty of the crown is oft-times the cause of the poverty of the realm ' leading to many ' inconvenients ' (including, certainly, taxation),therefore, in order to enable the king ' to live of his own ',[2] certain ' lordships

[1] Moreover, James's son (later James III) was still an infant and was apparently a sickly child.

[2] That is, to support the expenses of government, and his own personal expenses, out of the revenues of the crown lands and rents, the customs, the profits of justice and so forth, without recourse to taxation.

and castles ' were henceforth to be ' annexed ' to the crown and were to be inalienable save with the consent of Parliament, and then only for ' great and reasonable causes '. Thereafter the annexed lordships and castles are fully listed. The list opens with ' The whole customs of Scotland ', it includes the strategic castle of Edinburgh and Stirling, and in it appear many of the now forfeited Douglas lands.

Previous attempts to prevent the alienation of crown lands had been made in the reign of David II at the time when the realm was suffering the ' inconvenience ' of taxation to meet the king's ransom. Those attempts had covered *all* the crown lands, none of which were to be alienated without ' mature advice ' or, in a second attempt, without ' the consent of the three estates '; but they had been inoperative. Henceforth, however, the crown lands were to be of two categories – ' annexed lands ', which were to be inalienable and were to be retained with the crown for the support of the crown, and ' unannexed lands ', of which the king could dispose at his pleasure. Moreover, James II was now to swear, and his successors at the time of their coronations were to swear, to observe and keep this act.

In addition to this act prescribing the annexation of lands to the crown, parliament passed other acts which, had they been enforced, would also have strengthened the royal authority. It was decreed, for example, that in future no regality was to be erected without the consent of the Three Estates – that is, there were to be no more petty kings excluding the royal officers and the royal writ from their lands; and no offices were in future to be granted heritably, the office of Warden on the Border with England being expressly named.

Unfortunately, however, like too many acts of the Scottish Parliament, these acts of 1455 were little more than acts of good intention. Although one or two references to the ' annexing ' of lands to the crown are later to be found, it is clear that by the beginning of the sixteenth century the principles laid down in 1455 were not being observed. Moreover regalities were still erected without any reference to the Estates, and heritable grants of offices were still made.

After the fall of the house of Douglas James II ruled Scotland with a firm hand, but, when he was accidentally killed at the siege of Roxburgh castle (1460), his son and successor, James III, was unfortunately only eight years old. Almost at once there was again a threat to the throne. Early in 1462 MacDonald of the Isles concluded the treaty of Westminster-Ardtornish with Edward IV of England, a treaty under which the exiled Earl of Douglas was to enjoy all his former possessions in the south-west, John of the Isles, earl of Ross, and Douglas were to rule all Scotland north of the Forth, and both were to acknowledge the English King as their lord superior.[1] This grandiose scheme came to nothing; but there were to be later, and different, threats to James III.

As we have seen, it is exceedingly difficult to assess the character and aims of James III, but, in his reign, the struggle between the crown and the nobility assumed a new form. The Boyds might gain control of the King and, in a brief period of passing glory, might hope to establish their house through royal favour and by a royal marriage; but the Boyds were great in neither lands nor following. No over-mighty house now threatened the royal authority. Feud and faction still prevailed, as this or that noble house strove for power greater than that of its neighbour. But now, in the next struggle between the crown and the nobility, there was opposition by a group of lords who were dissatisfied with the King's policy and the King's actions – even with the King himself. Now, too, this group was aided and abetted by the King's own brother, Albany, whom James had banished, and who hoped to take James's place on the throne. Some of the King's favourites were hanged at Lauder Bridge – possibly as men who enjoyed too much of the King's attention – and the King was made a prisoner. But Albany was too closely associated with an England that had acknowledged him as King of Scots. The nobility might imprison their anointed King, but they would have naught to do with England.[2] And when, in 1484, Albany, accompanied by the exiled Douglas, rode into Lochmaben at the head of 500 men, making one last effort to supplant the King, the complete absence of support that met them in lands which had long pertained to the Douglases revealed that the struggle between the King and his nobles was different from that of former times.

A second struggle soon followed; and this time the barons who were in opposition to the King succeeded through his murder after a running fight near Stirling. Yet, as we have already noted, the northern barons and the wise Elphinstone supported James III in those final months; the death of the King was neither aimed at nor expected; and the successful faction apparently deemed it advisable to issue an immediate declaration justifying, if not excusing, their armed rebellion. Both struggles in the reign of James III were directed against a king

---

[1] *Supra*, pp. 223-4.
[2] *Supra*, pp. 226-7.

who was regarded as unfit to rule; neither struggle was an attempt by over-mighty subjects to contest the authority of the crown. The fiery Graham had boasted of his murder of James I; the ' Black ' Douglas had daunted James II; but when James III ' happened to be slain ' those who had fought against him issued an ' apologetical declaration '.

James IV was fifteen years old when he succeeded to the throne and, in two years, had rid himself of the baronial faction that had opposed his father. Ruling as a strong and well-loved King he met with little opposition from the nobility, and his forfeiture of the Lord of the Isles in 1493,[1] together with his subsequent Highland policy, helped to bring some stability to the difficult north-west. Almost every noble family fought by the side of the King on the fatal field of Flodden.

Then, once again, the new King was a child; and faction and feud were hardly held in check by a regent who was none other than the Duke of Albany, son of the traitor-Albany of the reign of James III, and who, after the death of the King's infant brother, was next in succession to the throne. These early years of the reign of James V were further troubled by the marriage of the Queen Mother to Archibald, sixth earl of Angus, the head of the ' Red ' Douglases, and once more there were those who showed contempt for the royal authority and the person of the King.

The ' Red ' Douglases, earls of Angus, had sprung from the ' Black ' Douglases, earls of Douglas. George Douglas, who was created Earl of Angus in 1397, at the time of his marriage to Mary, daughter of Robert III, was an illegitimate son of William, first earl of Douglas. After the overthrow of the ' Black ' Douglases in 1455, George, fourth earl of Angus, received a grant of the lands of Douglasdale, and the house of Angus began to assume importance and power. Archibald, fifth earl of Angus (' Bell the Cat '), played a leading part in the hanging of James III's favourites at Lauder Bridge, and was prominent among the nobility who were in opposition to the King in 1488. In the early years of the reign of James IV he was at one time in treasonable correspondence with England, and in 1501 was apparently again under suspicion; but his two eldest sons were killed at Flodden, and it is said that only a taunt from James IV kept the Earl himself from the battle.

Archibald, fifth earl, died about three months after Flodden and was succeeded by his grandson, Archibald, sixth earl, who, in August 1514, married Margaret Tudor, the widowed Queen of James IV. A period of intrigue, rivalry and faction ended with the Earl of Angus

[1] *Infra*, p. 276.

holding the fourteen-year-old James V in his hands and virtually ruling the country from 1526 to 1528[1] – a time when, according to Pitscottie, ' None durst strive against a Douglas, nor yet a Douglas man '. The ' Red ' Douglas was merely emulating Crichton and Livingston, and, later, Lord Boyd; and, like them, he was playing solely for his own hand. Twice other nobles strove to free the King from his custody, and the third Earl of Lennox was killed in the attempt. In the spring of 1528, however, James V escaped from his keeper; the ' Red ' Douglases were forfeited; and Angus fled to England.

Now began a new phase and the emergence of two parties – a party supporting the French alliance and the Roman faith, and a party advocating the Protestant faith and a new alliance with England. But while the Reformation, as we shall see, was also a rebellion in which a number of the nobility waged open warfare against the regent of the realm, the weakness of the Stewart line also influenced the parts then played by certain noble houses. From 1515 to 1594 the direct Stewart line depended upon the life of the reigning monarch, and, during nearly the whole of that period, the heir to the throne had to be sought from one of the descendants of James II.

The table of the Royal Stewarts, the Hamiltons and the Lennox Stewarts shows that, after the death of James V's infant brother, probably in 1515, John, duke of Albany, was next in succession to the throne. After the death of the Duke of Albany in 1536, James, Lord Hamilton, second earl of Arran, was heir presumptive to the crown until the birth of Mary in 1542; and, with the death of James V a week after the birth of Mary, he was next in succession during almost the whole of Mary's reign, for James VI, Mary's son, was not born until 1566. Again, when Mary was deposed in 1567, her son, James VI, was only one year old, and James VI's son, Henry, was not born until 1594. That is to say, a Hamilton was heir presumptive to the Scottish throne for virtually the whole of the period 1536 to 1594.

The table shows, however, that this proximity of the Hamiltons to the Scottish crown came through their descent from the *son* of the marriage of Mary, daughter of James II, whereas the Lennox Stewarts were only the descendants of the *daughter* of that marriage. On the other hand, James, first earl of Arran (who died in 1529), had been married twice – firstly to Elizabeth Home, and secondly to Janet Beaton. He was married to Elizabeth Home from about 1490 until 1504, when he secured a divorce; but he still lived with Elizabeth

[1] *Infra*, p. 305.

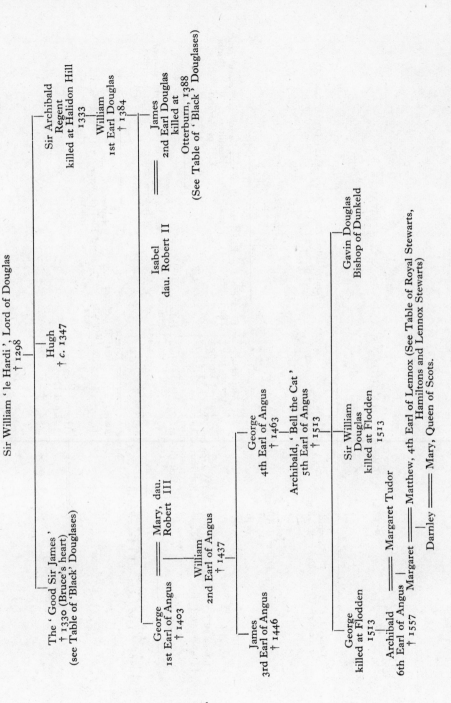

Sir William 'le Hardi', Lord of Douglas
† 1298

The 'Good Sir James'
† 1330 (Bruce's heart)
(see Table of 'Black' Douglases)

Hugh
† c. 1347

Sir Archibald
Regent
killed at Halidon Hill
1333

William
1st Earl Douglas
† 1384

James
2nd Earl Douglas
killed at
Otterburn, 1388
(See Table of 'Black' Douglases)

Isabel
dau. Robert II

George
1st Earl of Angus
† 1403
═══ Mary, dau.
Robert III

William
2nd Earl of Angus
† 1437

James
3rd Earl of Angus
† 1446

George
4th Earl of Angus
† 1463

Archibald, 'Bell the Cat'
5th Earl of Angus
† 1513

George
killed at Flodden
1513

Sir William
Douglas
killed at Flodden
1513

Gavin Douglas
Bishop of Dunkeld

Archibald
6th Earl of Angus
† 1557
═══ Margaret Tudor
│
Margaret ═══ Matthew, 4th Earl of Lennox (See Table of Royal Stewarts,
              Hamiltons and Lennox Stewarts)

Darnley ═══ Mary, Queen of Scots.

261

ROYAL STEWARTS, HAMILTONS, AND LENNOX STEWARTS

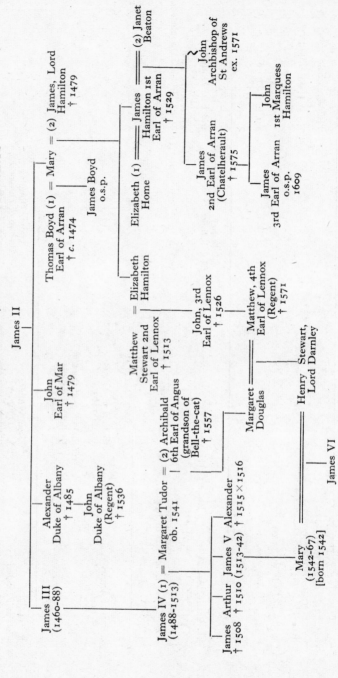

Home until 1510, when the sentence of divorce was renewed; and, six years later, in 1516, he married his second wife, Janet Beaton. James, second earl of Arran, the heir presumptive to the throne from 1536 until his death in 1575, was the son of the second marriage. If, however, as the Lennox Stewarts maintained, the first earl of Arran's divorce and his second marriage were unlawful,[1] then James, second earl of Arran, was illegitimate; and, in that event, the heir presumptive to the Scottish throne was a Lennox Stewart, namely Matthew, fourth earl of Lennox (1526-71).

This nearness of the Hamiltons and the Lennox Stewarts to the Scottish throne, and the question of the legitimacy of James, second earl of Arran, explains, to some extent, the policies followed by Arran and Lennox during the period 1542 to 1567 – and even thereafter. If, indeed, the Reformation and the establishment of the Protestant faith were to result in the deposition of Mary, a Roman Catholic queen, then James, second earl of Arran, could expect to wear the Scottish crown. Perhaps we need not be surprised that he became the titular head of the Protestant forces during the brief struggle of the Scottish reformation-rebellion. During the course of that struggle he was more than once accused of aiming at the throne; though, quite apart from the question of his legitimacy, there was also the possibility that another of the Protestant leaders, the Lord James Stewart, Mary's half-brother, might claim the throne, and Cecil, in the diplomatic correspondence of the time, regarded the Lord James Stewart as having more ' the personality and qualities ' of a king than the Earl of Arran.

After the success of the reformation-rebellion in 1560, the Scottish ' Reformation Parliament ' offered the hand of the young James, third earl of Arran,[2] to Queen Elizabeth, undoubtedly with the intention of effecting a Protestant marriage to unite two Protestant kingdoms to the exclusion of Mary, then Queen of Roman Catholic France. Elizabeth, however, declined the offer; and the death of Mary's husband, Francis II, in December 1560, and Mary's return to Scotland in August 1561, upset any other plans that may then have been taking shape. Finally, in 1565, Mary's marriage to Henry, Lord Darnley, the son of Matthew, fourth earl of Lennox, seemed to the Hamiltons to mean an end to all their hopes of kingship.

[1] The divorce of 1504, the earl's continued co-habitation with Elizabeth Home, and the renewal of the sentence of divorce in 1510, certainly suggest that the circumstances were unusual and peculiar.

[2] The second Earl of Arran became Duke of Châtelherault in 1549 and sometime thereafter resigned the title of Earl of Arran in favour of his son.

CHAPTER XXVII

The Church in Decline

WE HAVE already seen that in Scotland towards the end of the twelfth century or early in the thirteenth century a cathedral chapter wishing to proceed to the election of a bishop had to receive prior permission from the King; and further, that the King had a right to approve of the bishop-elect before he was consecrated and received his ' Bull of promotion ' from the Pope. About this time, however, the Pope had begun to assume a right of ' providing ' a bishop to a vacant see – notably when there had been a disputed chapter-election[1]; and thereafter, and with increasing frequency during the fourteenth century (especially under John XXII, 1316-34), the Pope claimed that certain sees were reserved to him, and that to those sees he himself would provide a bishop whenever a vacancy arose. Admittedly *reservation and provision* eased the pressure on a cathedral chapter to elect this or that man as bishop; but reservation and provision were also financially profitable to the papal *curia* and gradually became the subject of abuse.

The reforming councils of Constance and Basle had attempted to curb papal provisions (and the papal taxes that went with them), but they had failed to do so; indeed Pope Martin V (1417-31) had succeeded in establishing a further claim that all bishoprics and abbacies (that is, the ' greater benefices ' which, in Scotland, were usually called the ' prelaces ') of an annual value of more than 200 gold florins[2] were reserved for papal provision. Reservation and provision carried to this extent not only deprived the cathedral chapters and abbeys of their rights to elect, it also deprived the King of any influence or control in the election of prelates who, by virtue of their office, were members of his parliament and his council. The man whom the King would prefer might not be the man provided by the Pope. Moreover, princes and kings were beginning to grudge the money that went to Rome in

---

[1] A wise move; for, when the members of a chapter had disagreed about their future bishop, concord within the chapter would be better secured by the promotion of someone who had not been one of the original candidates. It should be noted, moreover, that such a ' provision ' by the Pope was simply an extension of his admitted right to confirm, or quash, a chapter-election, and that sometimes the Pope quashed an election and then ' provided ' the man who had been elected.

[2] In 1431 the gold florin was worth 8s. sterling, or 18s. Scots.

payments made upon provision and in other ways. That is, ' authority ' and ' resources ' were both involved – the two major problems that had confronted James I upon his return to Scotland in 1424.

In relation to resources, James saw much good money going to Rome in support of supplications, in the furtherance of suits, and as payments for provisions or for the right to draw a pension from the revenues of this or that benefice. Any provision to a see, for example, was now subject to a payment known as Common Services,[1] and Common Services might amount to 3,300 gold florins for promotion to St Andrews and 2,250 gold florins for promotion to Glasgow, with proportionate payments for other benefices according to their revenues. And a gold florin was at this time worth about one pound (Scots).

In relation to authority, James was anxious to ensure that the prelates of his realm would be men upon whose support he could rely: the Scottish Church, while identified with Rome, was not to be too strictly controlled from and by Rome.

James I took action immediately upon his return from captivity – though his moves were directed mainly against the drain of money to Rome and the individual negotiations of Scottish churchmen at Rome.[2] In his very first Parliament (1424) it was enacted that clerks (churchmen) or their procurators should not pass overseas without the special permission of the King; that no clerk was to purchase any pension to be drawn from a benefice, or to draw a pension previously granted; and that a duty of 3s. 4d. was to be paid on every £1 of gold or silver leaving the realm. In 1426 Parliament confirmed the preventive duty on the export of Money; and in 1427 and 1428 it was enacted that clerks

---

[1] At first paid voluntarily as an oblation to the Pope when consecrating a metropolitan, it soon became a compulsory payment exacted from all bishops upon their promotion; and no bishop could receive his Bull of promotion until full payment had been made. The payment was calculated as one-third of the annual revenues of the see, and was called ' Common Services ' because the monies so derived were divided *in common* between the Apostolic Camera (the papal exchequer) and the College of Cardinals. For smaller benefices half the net revenues of the first year (' first fruits ') were paid. Both payments were sometimes given the general term ' annates '.

As well as trying to curb the Pope's claims to reservation and provision, the ' reforming councils ' had also endeavoured to curb the payment of ' annates ', though again without success. In fact, if these various payments had not been made, the papal finances would have been crippled.

[2] It is worthy of note, however, that James I was also concerned with the decline in discipline within the Scottish monastic houses. In 1425 he addressed a strong letter to the abbots and priors of the Benedictine and Augustinian houses in Scotland urging them to shake off their sloth, to improve their discipline, and to counteract ' the decline of monastic religion, everywhere defamed and reduced to contempt within our realm '.

18

wishing to pass overseas were to obtain their foreign exchange in Scotland, were to inform the Chancellor of their reasons for wishing to go, and were to undertake that, when overseas, they would do no ' barratry ' – that is, they would not ' traffick ' in the purchase of benefices or pensions from benefices, or otherwise enter into individual negotiations with Rome.

Naturally these enactments aroused anger in Rome. Scottish clerics were to be denied access to the Roman Curia unless they had leave of the chancellor, and money that was Rome's due was to be withheld from her. James's chancellor, John Cameron, bishop of Glasgow, was adjudged to be responsible and, on the orders of Martin V, was cited to the apostolic see (1429). The citation was executed by William Croyser, archdeacon of Teviotdale, who came from Rome as a special nuncio for that purpose, but, on the petition of James to the Pope, the citation was withdrawn (1430). In 1433, however, the new Pope, Eugenius IV (who had succeeded Martin V in 1431), cited Cameron anew, and on the old charge of promoting legislation against the Holy See. Again Croyser executed the citation, and, this time, Croyser was himself summoned to the next Parliament to answer the King's charges of barratry and treason. In his absence he was found guilty and condemned to be stripped of his benefices, while intercourse with him at Rome was strictly forbidden. In letters to the Scottish Estates, in 1435, Eugenius asked them to intercede with James for the rehabilitation of Croyser and his restoration to his benefices; and in further letters of 1436, in which he denounced the Scottish bishops as ' Pilates rather than prelates ', the Pope threatened to exercise the full censures of the Church. A few months later, however, both the Pope and James I apparently thought it prudent to seek a compromise: possibly, if an impartial nuncio were to be sent to Scotland, some agreement might be reached in personal negotiations. A nuncio (the Bishop of Urbino) was accordingly appointed and sent to Scotland where he arrived about Christmas 1436; but, soon after he had been formally received, and before he could open his negotiations, the King was assassinated.

Undoubtedly James I had been influenced by the efforts of the Council of Basle to check both papal provisions and papal claims to annates, and was using the Council in his struggle against papal centralisation. Undoubtedly, too, James was endeavouring to protect the resources and the authority of the Scottish crown. It should be noted, moreover, that other rulers were striving towards the same end.

In 1438 (the year following James's murder) Charles VII of France, by the Pragmatic Sanction of Bourges, was able to secure some abatement of the papal claims to provisions, to annates, and to ecclesiastical jurisdiction; and in 1439 Germany was likewise able to limit papal claims. In effect, while the Pope had successfully withstood the reforming councils, and had succeeded in retaining, and even in extending, his rights of provision (with the accompanying payment of annates), he was now finding himself unable to resist the pressure, or action, of individual kings and, accordingly, was compelled to compromise.

Already in England a compromise had been reached whereby the King suggested the man whom he would like the Pope to provide, and the Pope provided accordingly. And soon, in Scotland, papal provisions to bishoprics of men certain to be acceptable to the King became almost so regular that some compromise was probably also at work. For example, in 1454, George de Schoriswod, provided to Brechin, was James II's confessor and became the Chancellor; and in 1457 Ninian Spot, provided to Galloway, was the Comptroller, and Thomas Spens, provided to Aberdeen, was the Keeper of the Privy Seal. It is especially noteworthy that these three bishops were, or became, important officers of state.

These provisions were made in the reign of James II, and were possibly made as the result of some understanding between the Pope and the King. In the reign of James III, however, in 1469 and 1471, Parliament, supporting royal policy, enacted that abbeys which had not previously been 'provided' from Rome should not be 'purchased' there; and in 1482 and 1484 the acts against 'barratry' – against 'the purchasing of pensions' and against the sending of money to Rome 'for promotions and pleas' – were renewed. Finally, in 1485, parliament sent a petition to the Pope that he would delay promotions to benefices for a period of six months so that the King might have an opportunity of supplicating the Holy See for the promotion of 'sic personis as is thankfull to his hienes' [that is, such persons as were acceptable to the king], for, the petition concluded, the prelates of the realm have the first vote in the King's Parliament and secret council.

James III, it should be remembered, was deep in trouble with certain sections of the nobility[1]; it was more than ever essential that

---

[1] Already in 1483 Pope Sixtus IV had issued Bulls commanding the Scottish nobles and prelates to obey the King.

he should be able to rely upon the support of the clerical estate; and that could be best ansured if the prelates were men of his own choosing. It is thus not altogether surprising that the request of 1485 was favourably received. In 1487 Pope Innocent VIII granted an indult[1] to James III in which he conceded that promotions to vacant prelacies would be delayed for at least eight months so that, during that period, the King could put forward his supplications (in other words, his suggestions) to the Pope.[2]

If, in the past, it had been common practice for the King to make suggestions to the Pope, now the King had gained a recognised right to have his suggestions awaited and considered. Moreover, for at least eight months[3] the King could promote to any vacant benefices to which the bishop would have made the promotion,[4] and for at least eight months the King could draw the temporal revenues of the see – mainly the revenues from its endowments of land. The Pope, on the other hand, still retained his right of provision; and, more important, ' common services ' were still paid.

The indult was not necessarily a perpetual privilege – though its wording spoke of James III ' and your successors, Kings of Scotland ' – but, despite some evidence of attempts by individual churchmen to evade both the indult and the acts against barratry, the system of ' recommendation by the King ' and ' provision by the Pope ' was now generally observed.[5] In 1526, moreover, Parliament went a stage further and boldly stated that it was the *rule* that ' when prelacies, such as bishoprics or abbacies, fell vacant the nomination [and ' nomination ' is far stronger than ' recommendation '] thereof pertained to the King

[1] A special privilege granted by the Pope authorising something to be done outside the normal law and practice of the church.

[2] And, in the preceding year, a legate sent by Innocent VIII had presented the Golden Rose to James as a mark of papal favour (see *supra*, p. 139, n. 2) and, by using the censures of the Church, had striven to support the crown.

[3] And the period would usually be even longer than that, for a newly promoted bishop could not exercise authority within his see until he held his Bull of promotion which was not until he had paid his ' common services ' and the raising of so large a sum was not always easy.

[4] In 1450 the bishops had agreed that during a vacancy in any see the King had the undoubted right of filling any lesser benefices normally filled by the bishop of the see; this royal right had been confirmed by Provincial Councils of the Scottish Church in 1457 and 1459; and it had been further confirmed by parliament in 1462 when it was stated to be an ' old and undoubted custom '.

[5] After the battle of Flodden, where James IV died excommunicate (*infra*, p. 285, n. 2), Pope Leo X tried to argue that the indult had ceased to be effective and that Scottish prelacies were now at his disposal; but in 1519 he confirmed the indult by Bull.

and the provision to the Pope '; and in 1535 the Pope not only admitted the King's right to *nominate*, but also extended the official period of delay from eight months to twelve months.

In these further concessions granted in 1535, the Pope was undoubtedly influenced by Henry VIII's contumacy and the English King's breach with Rome. Scotland, at all costs, had to be kept faithful to the Holy See. But, because of that, the Scottish King, knowing the strength of his position, began to nominate, and the Pope, fearful lest Scotland should follow the example of England, began to provide, men who were unworthy of holy office. Steadily in the King's nominations and the Pope's provisions there was less and less regard for the spiritual welfare of the church. No longer was it necessary for the King to make a grant of lands as a reward for service, or as a gift to a favourite; all that was necessary was to name his man to the Pope so that the Pope could provide him to some rich benefice. The officers of state could be paid in a like way.[1] So, in nomination and provision, promotions to benefices became more and more scandalous. James IV had secured the promotion of his illegitimate son, Alexander, as archbishop of St Andrews at the age of eleven[2]; but even that paled before James V's supplication to the Pope and the Pope's provision of three of the King's illegitimate sons, while still infants, to the Abbeys of Kelso and Melrose, to the Priories of St Andrews and Pittenweem, and to the Abbey of Holyrood respectively.[3] Moreover, following the death of James V, the Scottish Parliament calmly decreed that, when these sons of the King had drawn from the revenues of their abbeys funds sufficient to maintain them according to their estate, the remaining revenues were to be regarded as available for the general needs of the crown. In effect those important monasteries became, for the time being at least, part of the patrimony of the crown.

One after another, the great abbeys and priories had now fallen into the hands of illegitimate sons of the royal house or into the hands of the nobility; their revenues were used solely to support this or that noble lord in a life of luxury and idleness, or, at best, in the pursuit of

[1] We have already noted this in the reign of James II, and in the reign of James IV the Secretary (Patrick Paniter) had been promoted to the abbey of Cambuskenneth and the Treasurer (James Beaton) had been promoted to the bishopric of Whithorn and later to the archbishopric of Glasgow.

[2] But he was sent abroad to study, at one time reading under Erasmus at Padua and Siena; he did much for the straitened university of St Andrews; and he fell with his father at Flodden.

[3] A fourth illegitimate son was provided to the Priory of Coldingham, and a fifth to the Charterhouse at Perth.

secular ambitions; and the lord held his office *in commendam*,[1] delegating to others the spiritual work of his benefice. Almost every important monastic house was held by a ' commendator '; high offices in the church were filled by men who had little regard for the care of souls but craved the revenues they could enjoy; and corruption grew apace. Moreover, once a member of this or that noble family had secured an important office in the church, others of the same family were apt to be given offices beneath him; and even the episcopate showed a like family connection.[2]

At first, the Popes, by exercising their right of provision, had safe-guarded the church from royal or baronial pressure which might work to its detriment. They had favoured men of ability and upright life. But a practice that began in defence of the church became so debased that, in the end, it was to be one of the causes of the church's downfall – indeed, the Roman Catholic historian, Lesley, writing in the second half of the sixteenth century, saw in the indult of 1487 the main cause of the corruption in the Scottish Church that led to the Reformation.[3]

James I had viewed the payment of money to Rome as a drain upon his realm that could be ill afforded; to those who preached reform in the sixteenth century Rome appeared to be more concerned with money than with the care of souls. Certainly money paid to Rome could secure ' dispensation ' from many irregularities. A priest could purchase a right to hold two or more livings – whereby the spiritual needs of some of the people were neglected; priests and laymen alike could purchase the legitimation of their illegitimate children; Rome, upon payment, would grant a release from this or that vow. And now, by the nefarious connivance of the Pope and the King, prelates could be promoted whose lives were often as scandalous as their appointments.

As early as the second half of the fourteenth century Wycliffe had

---

[1] Literally, *in trust*. Originally, an office, such as that of abbot or prior, would be ' commended ', often to a bishop, to hold, with all its revenues, until an abbot or prior was provided. But abuse had crept in, and now abuse had become greater still when lay-lords were provided to such offices, with their large revenues, for life.

[2] Three successive Chisholms were Bishops of Dunblane from 1487 – a brother succeeding his brother, and a nephew succeeding his uncle; and we find Chisholms holding the offices of arch-deacon, dean, and subdean. In Dunkeld, Robert Crichton strove to succeed his uncle, George Crichton, and eventually did so; and in St Andrews, David Beaton succeeded his uncle James Beaton. So also, in the first half of the sixteenth century, we find three Stewarts successively Bishops of Caithness, two Gordons Bishops of Aberdeen, and two Hepburns Bishops of Moray.

[3] Though James I's letter (referred to, *supra*, p. 265, n. 2) shows that, a full fifty years before the indult, the monastic houses were becoming corrupt through luxury and ease of living.

denounced the growing corruption in the church and the lax lives led by many of the clergy. To Wycliffe, no man whose manner of living was against the law of God could be a priest. In 1406 or 1407, as we have seen, James Resby had been burned at Perth for preaching Wycliffe's doctrine that holiness alone gave spiritual authority. In 1425 Parliament had passed an act against heretics and lollards; and in 1433 there had been a second martyrdom – that of Paul Crawar at St Andrews. But reforming opinions were not stifled. In 1494, we hear of the Lollards of Kyle whose ' articles ' not only denounced pardons and indulgences but also attacked the papacy and held that ' every faithful man or woman is a priest '. In 1525 and 1535 there were further acts against heresy and, also, against the importation, holding and using of any of the writings of Luther. In 1528, Patrick Hamilton, a grandson of James, first Lord Hamilton, and of royal descent, was burned at St Andrews for maintaining ' divers heresies of Martin Luther and his followers ' – and ' the reek of Master Patrick Hamilton infected as many as it blew upon '.

In the early mediaeval period the Church had undoubtedly ' sought religion and its increase ' and had influenced the lives and thoughts of men. Scholars and thinkers had pursued their studies within its precincts, it had advanced knowledge and all the arts, and it had contributed largely to the growth of a body of law whereby men could know and enjoy justice. Lovely illuminated manuscripts – of the gospels, or of service books – and majestic cathedrals and beautiful abbeys were witness to man's desire to praise and honour God with man's noblest handiwork. Yet even then the seeds of decay had already been sown in the appropriation of parish churches notably to bishoprics and monasteries.[1] With continuing appropriations – and at the time of the Reformation nearly nine-tenths of the parish churches in Scotland had been appropriated – and with all their endowments of piety, the bishoprics and monasteries had become too wealthy, so that high office in the church had become attractive to unworthy men and, in the end, the ' shepherds' only care ' had been ' to find pasture for themselves '. Popes and princes alike had contributed to the decay.

When first referring to the appropriation of parish churches we noted, briefly, that the great wealth concentrated in the higher offices within the church had led to a neglect of the parishes and of parish work. The larger part of the revenues of the appropriated parish churches was now being taken by cathedrals, monasteries, and collegiate

---

[1] *Supra*, pp. 125-7.

churches; the 'living' was impoverished; and, as a result, many a parish became ill-served by an illiterate and underpaid priest who, needy and greedy, pressed for offerings which his poor parishioners could ill afford. The exaction of mortuary dues (the cow and the 'upmaist cloth') was denounced by James V and scathingly satirised by Lyndsay in the *Thrie Estaitis*; the feeling of the common people was aptly expressed in their saying, 'Nae penny, nae paternoster'; and, through this, there had grown up an anti-clericalism which was both widespread and deep.

This drawing away of the revenues of the parish churches had two other ill-effects. Little or nothing was available for the poor of the parish, and little or nothing for the repair of the parish church. A statute of the Provincial Council of 1549 enjoined that, where churches had been appropriated, alms were still to be distributed as of old, and the churches were to be kept in repair; but that was merely reiterating a law which in many parts had long been flouted. In 1556, when Archbishop Hamilton wrote to the Dean of Christianity of the Merse calling his attention to the ruinous state of a number of parish churches within his deanery, he complained that, in a great many, 'choirs as well as their naves were wholly thrown down and as it were levelled to the ground; others were partly ruinous or threatening collapse in respect of their walls and roof; they were without glazed windows and without a baptismal font, and had no vestments for the high altars and no missals or manuals, so that their parishioners could not hear the divine services or masses therein as befits good Christians, neither could masses be celebrated nor the church's sacraments administered'. And the murmurings of the poor were to culminate, on the eve of the Reformation, in the 'Beggars' Summonds'.[1]

It is small wonder that the church, corrupt and unable to minister to the needs of the people, was losing its hold over the people's lives and thoughts. Nevertheless, although the movement for reform was spreading fast, men were not yet ready to break away from Rome.

NOTE

The Archbishoprics of St Andrews and Glasgow

The tradition of parity among the bishops of Scotland remained unbroken until 1472; and when, in that year, Pope Sixtus IV issued a Bull erecting St Andrews into a metropolitan and archiepiscopal see in favour

[1] *Source Book of Scottish History*, VOL. II (2nd edn.), pp. 151-52, 168-69. See also *infra*, p. 315.

of Patrick Graham and his successors, the Pope's action was ill received by the King and the other bishops alike. Patrick Graham, the bishop of St Andrews, had opposed the royal policy with regard to ' barratry '; in 1466 he had been provided by the Pope to the rich abbey of Paisley *in commendam*; and in 1471 he had gone to Rome, obviously to seek papal support. The Bull of 1472, undoubtedly granted at Graham's request, not only showed a breach of the acts against barratry, but also, by its very wording, indicated the disfavour with which those acts were viewed in Rome. The King treated Graham as a traitor and ordered the temporalities of the see to be seized into his own hands; an appeal was made to Rome; and Graham was eventually deposed (1478), to die some three or four years later, virtually a prisoner and almost certainly insane.

The erection of St Andrews into a metropolitan see was, in itself, a desirable step, but it had been too long delayed, and came too late. The other bishops disliked their new status as suffragans of St Andrews,[1] and succeeding archbishops were not men of the stature required to reform the Scottish church.

Following the final rebellion against James III, and the murder of the king, Robert Blackadder, bishop of Glasgow, was much in favour with the new government, whereas William Scheves, archbishop of St Andrews, had been a supporter of the opposing faction. That, together with Glasgow's old jealousy of St Andrews, and her claim to be a ' special daughter ' of the apostolic see,[2] may account for a decision of Parliament in 1489 that the see of Glasgow should be erected into an archbishopric. The decision was forwarded to Rome; it was followed by direct supplications from James IV himself; and finally, in 1492. Pope Innocent VIII erected Glasgow into an archiepiscopal see, with the sees of Dunkeld, Dunblane, Galloway (Whithorn) and Argyll (Lismore) as its suffragans. The remaining sees remained within the province of St Andrews.[3]

---

[1] The Bishop of Aberdeen received exemption from the jurisdiction of St Andrews from 1474 to 1480, the Bishop of Glasgow received exemption in 1488, and the Bishop of Moray was exempt from about 1509 to 1514.

[2] *Supra*, p. 137, n. 2.

[3] At a later date the see of the Isles was also brought within the province of Glasgow, but Dunkeld and Dunblane were restored to the province of St Andrews (Cf. *supra* p. 122, n. 4).

CHAPTER XXVIII

The Reign of James IV

THE PERIOD covered by the reign of James IV was one of transition – a change which had already begun in the luckless reign of James III gathered pace. Old concepts were being questioned; new ideas were being mooted; new movements were astir; and in that time, when the whole of Europe felt an upsurge of the spirit, Scotland suddenly seemed to come into her own. She was ruled by a popular king who was brave and energetic and ready to give a welcome to all that was new; trade increased, and the east-coast ports grew in importance; there was a firmer rule of law; the new learning reached Scotland, and there was a flowering of all the arts. Scotland suddenly began to prosper. Her friendship and alliance were sought in the courts of Europe; her ships were feared and respected on the seas; her poets found music in words.

For this period, we are fortunate in possessing a contemporary account of Scotland written in 1498 by a Spanish ambassador, Pedro de Ayala, who had come to Scotland in 1496 in an attempt to persuade James to abandon the old alliance with France. There is fulsome praise of the King. James IV is ' of noble stature . . . and as handsome in complexion and figure as a man can be '. He speaks six languages in addition to English and Gaelic; he says his prayers; he is active and moves throughout his kingdom to administer justice and to collect his rents; and the Scots do not now ' dare to quarrel so much with one another ' as they formerly did, for the King executes the law without respect to rich or poor. The King, however, is rash in warfare; he does not take care of himself; and he is not a good captain because he begins to fight before he has given his orders. Then follows an estimate of the royal revenues – very much an overestimate. Immense quantities of fish are caught and exported, and there are large flocks of sheep; but although the corn is good the Scots ' do not cultivate the land '.[1]

---

[1] Agricultural implements were, of course, still very primitive. But although the old cumbersome wooden plough, that required some eight oxen or scraggy horses to draw it, and that often stuck, was still in use and was used until the invention of the iron swing-plough in the eighteenth century, Ayala himself gave the main reason for the failure of Scottish agriculture when he added that arable and pasture were let

and on the whole the people are poor. The women are courteous, graceful and handsome, and are ' absolute mistresses of their houses '; and, though again we must discount the exaggeration, ' the towns and villages are populous; the houses are good, all built of hewn stone, and provided with excellent doors, glass windows, and a great number of chimneys '.[1]

Ayala's rosy picture was intended to influence the Spanish Court in the hope of arranging a marriage between James IV and a Spanish bride; and yet, despite his exaggerations, there is evidence of the advances that had been made during the latter half of the fifteenth century. Aeneas Sylvius Piccolomini (later Pope Pius II), who had visited Scotland in 1435, had had a far different story to tell – though his picture also was coloured, this time adversely, for, after a tempestuous voyage, and in fulfilment of a vow to God for his safety, he had performed a painful winter pilgrimage with great bodily suffering. According to Aeneas Sylvius, Scotland, because of its cold climate, produced few crops; the houses for the most part were built without lime, with roofs of turf, and with ox-hides for the doors of the humbler dwellings; the poor begged almost in a state of nakedness; there was little refinement and there were few luxuries, so much so that even bread was a ' dainty '.

Whatever may be Ayala's other exaggerations, however, there is independent and ample evidence that James was a strong and energetic King who endeavoured to hold the law to his people. In moving throughout his kingdom to maintain the law and his authority, more-

' by leases of three years '. These short leases, or ' tacks ', of three or five years were the curse of Scottish agriculture, and short leases for small farmers were the common rule until the ' improvements ' and the ' improving landlords ' of the eighteenth century. No tenant with a short lease would develop his land or improve his buildings since, if he did so, the land, at the close of the lease, might be let to another tenant or his own rent might be raised. John Major, a Scottish historian writing soon after Ayala's comment, saw that this was the problem and in his *History of Greater Britain* offered the solution: ' If the landlords would let their lands in perpetuity, they might have double and treble of the profit that now comes to them – and for this reason: the country folk would then cultivate their land better beyond all comparison, would grow richer, and would build fair dwellings '. To some extent, as we shall see later, the problem was met by the development of feu-ferme tenure (see *infra*, pp. 295-6), but, save on the crown lands, it was a long time before feu-ferme tenures were enjoyed by the smaller tenants.

[1] Ayala must have noticed that even in Edinburgh most of the houses were still built of wood and roofed with heather or thatch. Not until 1677 was there an official attempt to ensure that new buildings, and repairs or alterations to old buildings, were of stone and ' sclaitt or tyll '.

over, James IV at once tackled the problem of the Highlands and Islands. We can trace his movements in the official records of the time, and there we find that he was north of the ' Mounth ' in 1490, twice in 1493 he was in the Highland west, while in 1494 and 1495 he was three times in the Isles.

These early expeditions to the west and to the Isles were necessitated by the turbulence of the MacDonalds who, in the Western Isles, had long been beyond the reach of the King's law. In 1491, Alexander of Lochalsh, the nephew of John, lord of the Isles, and his confederates had suddenly marched from Lochaber and, after seizing the royal castle of Inverness, had despoiled the lands of the sheriffdom of Cromarty.[1] Then, turning to ravage the lands of the Mackenzies of Kintail, with whom they were at feud, the MacDonalds were surprised and defeated on the river Conon and driven out of Ross. In turn, the Mackenzies began to harry and to spoil. The end of this story of rapine was the final forfeiture of the lord of the Isles in May 1493 and the annexation of his lands – though James allowed him to remain at the royal court with an ' honourable maintenance ' – and thereafter, proceeding to the Isles in person, James received one after the other the submission of the chiefs.[2]

Later, there was again trouble in the west. James marched from the south and Huntly from the north, while Sir Andrew Wood and Robert Barton led a naval expedition to the Isles. MacDonalds, Macleans, Macleods and Camerons, fighting under Donald Dubh, grandson of the Lord of the Isles, were only crushed after much fighting; and in 1504, Ross and Caithness were erected into sheriffdoms, and justices-depute and sheriffs-depute were appointed for the Isles both north and south.[3] But, having broken up the confederacy that had been held together by the Lord of the Isles, James IV strove hard

[1] Some Highland historians say that James, persuaded by interested and partial counsellors, had granted to the Campbells lands which had formerly belonged to the MacDonalds. More likely, however, the MacDonalds were making a new claim, by force, to the earldom of Ross. John, earl of Ross, had been forfeited in 1475 (when his sentence for treason took account of the earlier treasonable negotiations in the treaty of Westminster-Ardtornish), and, when he was restored in 1476 and given the title of Lord of the Isles, certain of his lands, including the earldom of Ross, were still withheld by the crown.

[2] Yet in the summer of 1494, immediately after another royal expedition *apud insulares,* John of Isla seized Dunaverty and hanged the king's governor; but, with four of his sons, he was taken prisoner by MacIan of Ardnamurchan and all five were hanged.

[3] Though not until much later did these measures become really effective.

to secure the friendship of Highland chiefs; and it is probably significant that at Flodden even some of those Highlanders who had earlier fought against the King fought and died by his side. On the other hand, like his predecessors, James, at times, did not hesitate to ' play off ' clan against clan, and Huntly and Argyll, as Lieutenants of the King, in the north and in the south-west, respectively, were gradually given powers that were too great, and which they used to advance their own interests – as a result of which there was to be yet further trouble in the north and west.

At this time, too, the central government became associated more and more with Edinburgh as a capital. We have seen that in the reign of James III Edinburgh had come to be regarded as the ' principal burgh ' of the kingdom. In the reign of James IV the supreme courts of justice were becoming centralised there; when James strove to improve the work of Council and Session the causes of poor litigants were to be heard in Edinburgh; and in 1501, in preparation for his marriage to Margaret Tudor, the King began to build a new royal residence there – the Palace of Holyroodhouse.

James, moreover, dominated in his realm. He held nine Parliaments between 1488 and 1496, but thereafter Parliament met only in 1504 and 1509. The Council, however, was increasingly active both in hearing legal causes and in the administration of the realm, sitting separately, or splitting into two parts, for these two important functions – and in its sittings for administrative and political business we have the genesis of the Privy Council. Yet in all this James probably played an important personal part, interesting himself in all things. He interested himself in civil justice and its improvement; he rode on the justice-ayres, ' driving the ayres ' as they had never been driven before, putting down lawlessness – notably on the Borders – and increasing his revenues through fines and forfeitures. It was the King himself who encouraged and developed the royal navy, and who was in close touch with his sea-captains, Sir Andrew Wood and the Bartons; it was the King who was interested in the development of artillery.

But the King also encouraged the new learning. A third university, King's College, Aberdeen, was founded in 1495; an Education Act was passed by Parliament in 1496; and in 1507 Chepman and Myllar received a licence to set up ' ane prent ' (a printing-house) in the Southgate (now the Cowgate) of Edinburgh.

The Education Act of 1496, which is popularly attributed to Bishop Elphinstone of Aberdeen – who was also the prime mover in the founding of the university there[1] – endeavoured to ensure that those who administered the law should be trained in a knowledge of the law, though we have no evidence that its provisions were ever effective. The act prescribed that the eldest sons of all substantial barons and freeholders were to be put to school as soon as they had reached the age of eight or nine; they were to remain at school until they were well grounded in Latin; thereafter they were to study ' art and law ' for a further three years so that they could acquire ' knowledge and understanding of the laws '. This was to be done under a penalty of twenty pounds; and the whole purpose of the act is revealed in its hopeful statements that thereby ' justice may reign universally through all the realm ', that the heritable judges in baronies and sheriffdoms ' may have knowledge to do justice ', and that henceforward the poor people would have no need to seek the king's own court for remedy in their own small causes. That is, the intention was twofold: an endeavour to secure a better administration of the law in the localities, and, through that, to relieve the central courts of causes brought by litigants who feared that their own local courts would be unable or unwilling to give them justice.

Again, when Chepman and Myllar received their licence to bring into Scotland the necessary ' stuff ' to set up ' ane prent '[2] they were to print the books of the law and the acts of Parliament (which are named first in their licence) together with chronicles, mass-books and breviaries, and to sell their works ' for competent prices '. Once more there appears to be the same stress upon a knowledge of the law, and once more Bishop Elphinstone – who stands out in this period as a man apart – appears to have been a prime mover in this new development. But Chepman and Myllar possibly found the law too complex; there is no evidence that they printed either books of the law or acts of Parliament.[3] The works that have survived from their press are

[1] When other prelates were importing luxuries from the Continent, Elphinstone was importing wheel-barrows and gunpowder (for quarry-blasting) to further the building of his university.

[2] Andrew Myllar, a Scotsman, had learned the art of printing in France. Two books printed by him at Rouen in 1505 and 1506 are still preserved. Walter Chepman was an Edinburgh merchant who, presumably, provided the necessary finance. Scotland, however, was late in the field. Movable type and a press had been used by Gutenberg at Mainz about 1454; there was a printing press in Paris as early as 1470; and Caxton had set up his press at Westminster in 1476.

[3] It is perhaps unnecessary to stress that we have no knowledge of books that may have been printed but of which no copies have survived. Nevertheless the first printed acts of Parliament were probably those of the Parliaments of 1535 and 1540,

mainly ballads and poetry, including some poems of Henryson and Dunbar, though by June 1510 they had completed their magnificent printing of the Aberdeen Breviary in two noble volumes – again with the encouragement of Elphinstone.[1]

Robert Henryson (?1430 -?1506), who had already written some of his best work in the reign of James III, has been called ' the Scottish Chaucer '. His *Testament of Cresseid* is a continuation of Chaucer's *Troilus*, and much of it, it has been said, ' Chaucer would have been proud to call his own '. But his most characteristic poems are his *Moral Fabillis of Esope* which, set in a Scottish background, are not only delightful to read but also reveal both intimacy with nature and a wide humanity. ' He looks out on the animal world and finds that it is an exact counterpart to the world of men '; his creatures are often ' the poor commons ', and his ' morals ' denounce oppression and stress the joys of a simple life –

> Blissit be sempill lyfe withouttin dreid;
> Blissit be sober feist in quietie:
> Quha hes aneuch, of na mair hes he neid; [*enough*
> Thocht it be litill in to quantitie. [*though*

William Dunbar (?1460 -?1520) was of harder fibre. He can still feel intensely, but in him there is little of Henryson's warm humanity. He is a veritable master of verse, and writes and rhymes for the sheer joy of music in words. ' No other Scottish poet is so sensitive to the magic of words; no other Scottish poet is master of such a range of subtle musical effects '.[2] But his only compassion tends to be for himself, and he has nothing of Henryson's feeling for his fellow-men.

Possibly Dunbar accompanied the ambassadors who went to London in 1501 to negotiate the marriage of James IV and Margaret Tudor, and there wrote the poem in praise of London, each stanza ending

London thow art the floure of Cities all

printed by Davidson in 1541. There was then a gap until 1565 when Lekprevik printed the acts of the Parliament of 1563, which were quickly followed, however, in 1566, by a volume of the acts of the Parliaments from 1424 to 1564.

[1] The licence granted to them had referred to ' mass-books, manuals, matin-books and portuus books [portable breviaries], after our own Scots use [i.e. as opposed to the Sarum use], and with legends of Scots saints, as are now gathered and eked by the reverend father in God, and our trusty councillor, William [Elphinstone], bishop of Aberdeen '.
[2] R. L. Mackie, *King James IV of Scotland*, pp. 172, 174, 181.

but the careful Henry VII limited his appreciation to a gift of twenty merks. *The Thistle and the Rose*, and a shorter poem beginning

> Now fayre, fayrest off every fayre,
> Princess most pleasant and preclare,
> The lustyest one alyve that bene,
> Welcum of Scotland to be Queene!

were written to welcome Margaret Tudor to Scotland. *Blyth Aberdein*, written to commemorate Queen Margaret's visit there, when she was on a pilgrimage to Tain (1511), is in striking contrast to his *Satire on Edinburgh* in which, with a refrain

> Think ye nocht schame

he condemns the narrow streets, the crowded buildings, the smells, the scolding women, and the many beggars in the midst of a rich town.

From the poems of Dunbar we gain a far better picture of Scotland in the days of James IV than we do from the report made by Ayala. Dunbar criticises the delays of justice and the need for a stricter rule of law – in spite of James's attempts to improve the courts and to hold the law to his people; he writes of the low state of morals; above all, his poems contain many lines that give us a picture of the King himself – his early licentiousness, his instability, his liberality, his love of amusement, his dabblings in science,[1] and his desire for military glory and renown. Through this last aspect of James IV's character the sudden flowering of Scotland was to droop on the field of Flodden.

In the international relations of Scotland, James came into conflict with England when he supported the Yorkist pretender, Perkin Warbeck, against Henry VII. Warbeck had arrived in Scotland in November 1495, almost certainly at the invitation of James. James had not hesitated to accept him as Richard, duke of York, and had found a bride for him in Lady Catherine Gordon, daughter of the Earl of Huntly; and, in return for Scottish aid, Warbeck had promised the surrender of Berwick. But, when James raided the northern counties of England in the autumn of 1496, there was no rising in support of the

---

[1] Dunbar's *Ballat of the Fenyeit Freir of Tungland* is a lampoon on an Italian, Damien (well described in Lesley's *History*), who gained the ear of the King by pretending to be able to multiply gold and to have the secret of the elixir of life. James fell an easy prey to his impostures, made him Abbot of Tongland, and, as the *Accounts of the Lord High Treasurer* reveal, spent much money in furthering Damien's experiments.

Yorkist pretender (as the Scots had been led to expect); in the first two days Warbeck quarrelled with the King over the slaughter of ' my own people ' and the seizure of their cattle; he left the Scottish army in dudgeon; and the raid achieved nothing. Thereafter Scottish enthusiasm for the Warbeck cause waned and vanished. Warbeck, accompanied by his wife, left Scotland, sailing from Ayr, in July 1497, in a ship, not inappropriately called the *Cuckoo*, which had been provisioned and equipped by the King – who was now doubtless glad to see him go.[1] After the great raid against Norham at the end of the same month (a raid which was abandoned upon the approach of an English army under the Earl of Surrey), a truce was made and, in 1499, was extended to endure until one year after the death of the survivor of the two sovereigns. In 1502 the truce became a treaty of ' perpetual peace ', sealed by James IV's marriage, in 1503, to Henry VII's elder daughter, Margaret.[2] That peace, although sorely tested after the accession of Henry VIII in 1509, endured until the eve of Flodden.

In other international relations we find James corresponding with the Emperor Maximilian (who was also a supporter of Perkin Warbeck) and suggesting, at the time of the Warbeck adventure, an alliance between them. In 1502 James sent a small Scottish force to the help of his uncle, Hans, king of Denmark, who was struggling against the rebellious Swedes supported by the Hanseatic town of Lübeck[3]; but thereafter, although continually urged by Hans to send further support, James confined himself to diplomatic pressure, though in 1510 he allowed the Bartons to engage in some very profitable privateering at the expense of Lübeck. In another field, in 1506 and 1507, he entered

[1] After his further inglorious adventures in Cornwall and Devon, and his capture and later execution (1499), his wife was courteously entertained by Henry VII, who placed her in the household of his queen, Elizabeth.

[2] We are told that, when the marriage was being discussed in the English Council, some of Henry VII's councillors objected that if the King's two sons [Arthur and Henry] were to die without issue then the kingdom of England would fall to the King of Scotland; to which Henry replied that, if that should happen, Scotland would be but an accession to England, and not England to Scotland, for the greater would draw the lesser; and the King's answer silenced those who put the question, for it ' passed as an oracle '. There are those who would say that, when James VI succeeded Elizabeth, because of the failure of the English line, the ' oracle ' began to prove its truth. It is also to be noted that James IV's marriage to Margaret Tudor brought James IV, and, after his death, James V, close claimants to the English throne from the accession of Henry VIII in 1509 until the birth of Henry's daughter Mary, in 1516.

[3] Hans was the brother of James III's queen, Margaret of Denmark. Denmark, Norway and Sweden had been united under the treaty of Kalmar (1397), but the union was unpopular and unstable, and was particularly resented in Sweden.

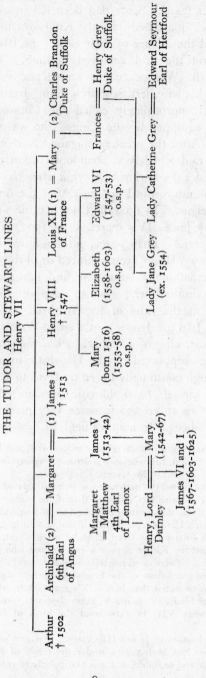

THE TUDOR AND STEWART LINES

Henry VII

Arthur † 1502

Margaret = (1) James IV † 1513 ‖ Archibald (2) 6th Earl of Angus

Henry VIII † 1547 ‖ Louis XII (1) = Mary = (2) Charles Brandon of France Duke of Suffolk

James V (1513-42) ‖ Margaret = Matthew 4th Earl of Lennox

Mary (born 1516) (1553-58) o.s.p. ‖ Elizabeth (1558-1603) o.s.p. ‖ Edward VI (1547-53) o.s.p.

Frances = Henry Grey Duke of Suffolk

Mary (1542-67) = Henry, Lord Darnley

Lady Jane Grey (ex. 1554) ‖ Lady Catherine Grey = Edward Seymour Earl of Hertford

James VI and I (1567-1603-1625)

282

into negotiations to try to prevent the dismemberment of the Duchy of Gueldres.[1]

But all international relationships were now influenced by the power of France. The Spanish missions to Scotland in 1495 and 1496, and all the English missions sent by Henry VII and Henry VIII had the one aim of detaching Scotland from her old alliance with France. France had become too powerful for the peace of Europe. The great French fiefs of Burgundy, Anjou and Brittany had fallen to the crown one by one. France had become compact under a strong central monarchy with a developed military organisation; and, under Charles VIII and Louis XII, this new France was looking for expansion in Europe, particularly in Italy where she saw many small states with much wealth and with much corruption. But Spain, too, had changed with the marriage of Ferdinand and Isabella and the union of Aragon and Castile; and Spain also had claims in Italy. As a result, for over fifty years France and Spain fought each other in Italy. England, because of her traditional foreign policy and her strategic interests, could not allow France to become too powerful. And, in Scotland, James IV, bound to England by his marriage to Margaret Tudor, and by a new treaty of ' perpetual peace ', but still influenced by the old alliance, found his position gradually becoming more and more difficult. For long he hoped to secure and maintain peace in western Europe by organising a new Crusade against the infidel Turk, in which England, France and Spain should all participate – under his leadership. But the Crusade never materialised. And international politics finally compelled James to decide between the new friendship with England and the old friendship with France. He chose the old friendship and died at Flodden.

The road to Flodden began in Italy, where Julius II, ' the warrior Pope ' who was seeking to unite Italy under his own rule, formed a league with Louis XII and the Emperor Maximilian – the League of Cambrai (1508) – to crush the strong power of Venice and to seize certain of its territories. Already, in 1507, Julius II had sent a hat and a sword to James IV[2] and had designated him ' Protector of the Christian Religion ' – the Pope hoping that, if England were to attack France, while France was helping the Pope against the Venetians, then James, as a faithful son of the Church, would attack England – though by the end of 1508 England also had joined the League of Cambrai. The

---

[1] James II's queen had been Mary of Gueldres.
[2] The sword sent to James by Julius is still preserved with the Scottish regalia.

result, however, was disconcerting. The Venetians were defeated by the French; but thereafter the French stayed on, and soon made themselves masters of Milan and northern Italy, which suited neither the Pope nor Spain. Moreover, Julius quickly realised that it would be impolitic to ruin Venice which, as a maritime power, was one of the main defences against the ruthless piracy in Mediterranean waters and against the steadily encroaching Turks.

Accordingly Julius began to look for ways and means to drive out the French; and Louis XII played into his hands by trying, through the French clergy, to summon a General Council of the Church to condemn the temporal warfare of the Pope. At once Julius seized his opportunity. Louis was denounced as schismatic; and the Pope was able to form a Holy League (1511) against France. The league was 'holy' in little save its name. France was to be crushed by those who feared her power. The league formed by Julius II was joined by Spain, looking for her own gains in Italy, by Venice, hoping to recover something of what she had recently lost, and, a little later, by the Emperor Maximilian, furthering the interests of Spain against those of France, and by England, fearful of French power and traditionally France's enemy.

Meantime, in England, Henry VIII had succeeded Henry VII in 1509 – and Henry VIII, no less than James IV, looked for renown. Moreover a number of incidents were now making for tension between Scotland and England. On the Borders, for example, Sir Robert Ker of Ferniehurst, a Scottish Warden of the Marches, had been killed at a 'day of trew' by 'the bastard Heron'; both Henry VII and Henry VIII had declined to take any action; and the affair still rankled in James's mind. Again, in the summer of 1511 when Andrew Barton, James's sea-captain, had been killed in a fight with the Howards and his two ships (the *Lion* and the *Jenny Pirwin*) taken as prizes, and when James had written to Henry demanding the return of the Scottish ships and the trial of the Howards in accordance with the treaty of peace, the English King had sent the arrogant reply that it was not customary to accuse a prince of breaking a treaty simply because he had done justice on a pirate.

In December of this same year James wrote to the Pope that Henry was deliberately making trouble between England and Scotland, attacking 'the Scots by land and sea, slaying, capturing and imprisoning', and that accordingly he presumed the treaty of 1502, renewed upon Henry VIII's accession in 1509, was no longer binding and that the breaking of it was no longer to be followed by the spiritual censures of the church[1] – but the Pope did not respond to the appeal.

Henry VIII's accession to the Holy League and his cavalier attitude towards James IV had brought the two countries to the brink of war. All the evidence reveals that James was reluctant to take up arms against England. But if a too powerful France was a danger to England, equally a weak France and a too powerful England would be a danger to Scotland.

In the summer of 1512 the old alliance was renewed between Scotland and France, in terms very similar to the treaty of Corbeil in 1326 and its confirmation in 1371. Henry, on his side, persuaded the Pope to warn James of the consequences to himself and to Scotland should he break the peace with England, and, almost on his deathbed, Julius II issued a bull executorial authorising the excommunication of James should he attack England.[2] The crisis was at hand. Henry, having joined the league against France, was anxious to show his prowess on the field of battle. James, in no mood to be friendly with England, was being moved by antipathies both old and new. Henry might send his ambassadors in an endeavour to secure peace between the two realms; but Henry had treated James with calculated contempt, and had even re-stated the old English claim to suzerainty over Scotland.

In May 1513 the Earl of Shrewsbury landed with a small force at Calais, and, on the last day of June, Henry himself landed there with further forces under his own command. On 16 August he defeated the French in the Battle of the Spurs. A week later (22 August) James led the Scottish host over the Border – to the fatal field of Flodden – not solely in the interests of France.

The decision to invade England was taken by James himself, against the advice of his elder statesmen, including Bishop Elphinstone and the Earl of Angus. In Henry's absence in France, the English army that marched to meet James was led by the Earl of Surrey who proved to be a better general than the Scottish King. Furthermore, Henry, upon embarking at Dover, had charged Surrey to watch the Scots, and

---

[1] It is important to note that when the treaty of perpetual peace was made in 1502 it was confirmed by the Pope (Alexander VI), and the papal confirmation placed the breaker of the treaty under the spiritual censures of the church. This accounts for James's letter to the Pope.

[2] Because of this, and because of the sanctions laid down in Pope Alexander VI's confirmation of the treaty of 1502, James died at Flodden an excommunicated king.

Surrey had spent the early weeks of August in making preparations for a speedy mobilisation of the northern levies (should that prove to be necessary) and in moving his artillery to Newcastle.

Having crossed the Border on 22 August 1513,[1] James spent a fortnight in taking the castles of Norham, Wark, Etal and Ford – profitless work that wasted men and time, though no good general would leave hostile fortresses in his rear; and by then sickness and desertion had already begun to take their toll. That wasted fortnight, moreover, proved the worth of Surrey's earlier preparations. The opening days of September saw his forces from Lancashire and York-shire, Cheshire, Durham, Northumberland and the Borders assemble to the number of nearly 20,000 men. All were well armed (mainly with bills – eight-foot long axes with curved blades) and well led. At Alnwick, on 4 September, they were joined by Lord Howard with 1,000 men from the fleet. James's host was probably about the same size as Surrey's.

Fearing that James, upon hearing of his approach, might retreat to the Border, and determined to bring the Scots to battle, Surrey now sent a challenge to James, offering to do battle with him on Friday, 9 September, at the latest. It was a move taken in full knowledge of the character of the King: a move well calculated to keep James in the field. James accepted the challenge: he would wait for Surrey until noon on the 9th.

But when Surrey came into touch with the Scottish army he found it on the west side of the valley of the Till[2] in a well-nigh impregnable position on Flodden Edge, facing east-south-east, and with its guns covering the only approach. Surrey had issued his challenge, but to attack such a position would be to invite almost certain defeat. It was then that the English commander made his risky but brilliant move. Marching past the Scottish position, he crossed to the east side of the Till – unmolested by James, who stayed in his ' fortress ' when he might have made a dangerous attack on Surrey's flank or on his crossing of the Till – and, further north, recrossed to the west again by Twizel Bridge and a near-by ford. He had placed himself between James and the Scottish line of retreat. Then, moving south, he made for Branxton Hill, lying to the north-west of Flodden Edge. He, too,

---

[1] In an earlier raid, at the beginning of August, the Scots, under Lord Home, had been badly mauled upon their return from burning and plundering in Northumber-land.

[2] The Till flows into the Tweed about three miles south of Norham.

would take up a strong position and thereby compel the Scots to fight at a disadvantage when they strove to make their way back to Scotland.

Seeing the peril in which Surrey seemed likely to place him, James left his position on Flodden Edge and, with some difficulty turning his whole army round, moved in haste to Branxton Hill. He was there first, for the English had the more difficult ground to cross, and the encounter began late that same afternoon.

The Scottish guns, possibly not yet in proper positions, or possibly placed too high on the hill to be sufficiently depressed to reach the advancing English below, had the worst of an opening artillery duel. The English gunners, firing better than their adversaries, soon began to inflict heavy losses in the Scottish ranks. An advance down the northern slope of the hill, and away from that galling gun-fire, became imperative. The issue should be settled by ' hand-strokes '. But it was not in solid phalanxes of spearmen, not in the close ' schiltrons ' that had won the day at Bannockburn, that the Scots moved down the hill to engage the enemy. With their ranks already broken by the English gunfire, and worried by the rough and slippery ground,[1] they moved down the hill in disorder and, without a close formation, had none of the advantages of the old schiltron of spears. More than that, in the ' hand-strokes ' that now ensued the Scottish spears, eighteen feet long, proved no match for the English eight-foot bills. The Bishop of Durham, writing to Wolsey after the battle, says, ' our bills quit them very well . . . for they shortly disappointed the Scots of their long spears wherein was their greatest trust '. Apparently the English bills, with sweeping strokes, broke the Scottish spears; the Scots had then to rely upon their swords; and, in such encounters, the longer bills could beat down upon the Scots before they could reach their enemies with the sword. So, again, the Bishop of Durham wrote of ' large, strong and great men that would not fall when four or five bills struck on one of them at once '.

The battle became little less than a massacre. Scotland lost her King, nine earls, thirteen lords, one or more members of almost every important family in the land, and, with them, the thousands of ' mere uncounted folk '. The English reckoned that more than 10,000 Scots were killed, and their reckoning was probably not far wrong; their own losses were probably not more than 1,500, and few of those were

---

[1] Many of them had even thrown away their shoes in order to have a better grip on the ground.

men of rank. The 'Flowers of the Forest' had been cut down; and many a family mourned its dead.

Scottish bravery had been proved; and later it was to be enshrined in the words of Scott –

> The stubborn spear-men still made good
> Their dark impenetrable wood,
> Each stepping where his comrade stood,
> The instant that he fell.

But more than bravery is required in battle. Scotland suffered defeat partly through the greater efficiency of the English bill, partly through the better handling of the English guns, partly through the better training of the English levies, and partly also through the folly of her King. Not only had James failed to make an attack on Surrey as the English column wound its way up the valley, or even an attack during Surrey's risky crossing of the Till, but also, in the fight itself, he had rushed upon the enemy and given no further word of command. The contemporary English chronicler, Edward Hall, might write, 'O what a noble and triumphant courage was this, for a king to fight in a battle as a mean soldier', but the King should have directed the battle instead of throwing away his life in the thick of the fight.[1] Ayala's comment, made fifteen years before, had been tragically shown to be true. Had James retained the command, even defeat might not have been disaster. Surrey's men were weary; they had advanced through difficult ground in evil weather; they were short of victuals, and, worse than that, had had no beer or ale for a full three days. To them the victory seemed to be a miracle.

For long in Scotland, the battle was seldom mentioned by name. The official records and registers, when referring to those who died there,[2] say only that they died 'in campo bellico', or 'in the field'. In that field the prime of the land lay, 'cauld in the clay'.

---

[1] The story of the dwindling circle around the King is almost certainly legendary. James, brave and impetuous, was probably killed fighting with the foremost.

[2] By an act made at Twizelhauch on 24 August 1513, the heirs of those killed in action against the enemy were to succeed without payment of relief and without the King enjoying the casualties of wardship and marriage. A similar concession had been granted to the heirs of those who were slain at Harlaw, was later to be granted for the battle of Pinkie, and apparently thereafter became customary.

CHAPTER XXIX

The Finances of the Crown

FROM TIME to time, as we have seen, attempts had been made to strengthen the finances of the crown – for the king's revenue had to meet all the expenses incurred in the government of the realm as well as the needs of the royal household.

Under David II Parliament had twice endeavoured to check the alienation of crown lands so that the King could ' live of his own ' – that is, so that the revenue from the royal lands and the king's burghs together with the receipts from the customs, feudal casualties, the profits of justice and so forth would be sufficient for all crown purposes.[1] James I had tried to improve the administration of the crown finances by dividing the work of the Chamberlain between two new officers – a Comptroller, responsible for crown ' property ', and a Treasurer, responsible for ' casualty '; he had striven to prevent the drain of money to Rome; and he had added, by forfeiture, a number of large estates to the crown.[2] Under James II, the forfeiture of the Black Douglases had brought further estates to the crown; and, by a new enactment, the customs and certain lands and castles were henceforth to be ' annexed ' to the crown – another attempt to prevent alienation. This new enactment, moreover, had opened with the words that, ' as the poverty of the crown is oft-times the cause of the poverty of the realm and many other inconveniences which are too long to express . . . '; and those ' inconveniences ' included taxation. Taxation was still regarded as an ' extraordinary ' source of revenue, to which recourse should be had only for extraordinary needs. The ' ordinary ' revenue of the crown should be sufficient for all ordinary needs. The King should be able to ' live of his own '.

But, with the development of the national economy, with increasing affairs of state, and, above all, with new methods of waging war, the ordinary revenue of the crown was proving hopelessly insufficient for crown needs.

In warfare the new and expensive weapon was artillery. Guns were expensive to make or to buy; they were expensive to move and expensive to fire; gunners, smiths, wrights, masons, quarrymen,

[1] *Supra*, p. 184.   [2] *Supra*, pp. 209-10, 265-7.

289

coopers and so forth had to be paid money wages. And none of this new expenditure could be met from the old feudal fighting services such as the render of one knight, or an archer, or a sheaf of arrows.

It is true that artillery gave the King a new power over his fractious nobility The King had his guns – weapons too expensive for the nobility to acquire and to maintain – and the king's guns could batter down the noble's castle. Thereafter a forfeiture would possibly meet the expense. But the capital expenditure incurred in building up a train of artillery, and the recurrent expenditure involved in maintaining it, threw a new and heavy strain on the royal finances.

A few small guns were probably imported into Scotland about the middle of the fourteenth century,[1] but the first official reference to royal artillery occurs in the Chamberlain's account rendered in 1385,[2] though further payments, in the same account, for saltpetre and sulphur ' ad municionem castrorum regis ' suggest that there were already guns in several royal castles. In 1430, according to Bower, James I imported a great brass bombard from Flanders, and at first most guns, and most of the gunners, came from there. James II used artillery to reduce the castles of Abercorn, Blackness and Threave – and died from the bursting of a gun at the siege of Roxburgh. Under James IV some early experiments were made in gun-casting at Stirling Castle, and later, and apparently more successful, experiments at Edinburgh Castle; and at Flodden the captured Scottish guns excited the envy of the English.

These early guns were of two kinds – *bombards*, or siege-guns,[3] of large calibre, firing ' gun-stones ',[4] and mounted on iron and wood carriages (' cradles ') which were usually drawn by oxen; and ' field guns ', called *curtals, serpentines, sakers, culverines,*[5] and a host of other names,[6] the smaller of which were usually carried in ' gun-carts '. The

[1] Barbour speaks of ' crakkis of wer ' (guns) as a novelty first seen by the Scots in their campaign in Weardale in 1327 (*The Bruce*, BOOK XIX, lines 394-400).

[2] *Exchequer Rolls*, VOL. III, p. 672. See also *supra*, p. 197.

[3] Hence the word, *bombardment*.

[4] The gun-stones were shaped by masons and quarry-men, and in the *Accounts of the Lord High Treasurer* there are many payments to quarry-men for ' correking gunstanis '.

[5] It is said that a curtal fired a shot of 60 lb; a demi-curtal a shot of 35 lb; a culverine a shot of 20 lb; a saker a shot of 10 lb, and a serpentine a shot of 4 or 5 lb; but there were many variations.

[6] In the *Complaynt of Scotland*, in a passage giving commands to gunners, we read of culverine moyens, culverine bastards, falcons, sakers, half-sakers, half-falcons slangs, half-slangs, quarter-slangs, head sticks, murderers, pasvolans, berses, double-berses and dogs.

larger field guns also fired gun-stones, but the smaller ones fired iron-shot. In addition there were ' hand-guns ' – hackbutts (which, when placed on a forked rest, were called ' hackbutts of croche ') and hacks, or demi-hacks, firing ' pellocks ' of iron or lead. In 1507 James IV had a ' hand-culverine '; the *Accounts of the Lord High Treasurer* contain references to shooting-matches at Holyrood and to target-practice at Newhaven; once, in May 1508, the King paid fourteen shillings (probably ' danger-money ') to a keeper at Falkland to accompany him in stalking deer with his culverine; and gradually, over the next five years, he acquired no less than five hand-guns.

When the large bombards were moved from one place to another, squads of men had to be sent on ahead to ' smooth the way ', the sheriffs of the shires through which the guns would pass had to be warned to have relays of oxen in readiness, and labourers with picks and shovels, together with smiths and wrights, had to accompany the guns to attend to the various breakdowns that might occur. So, when the guns were moved, we find references in the records to the bell-man being sent through the streets of Edinburgh ' for workmen to take wages '. And the ' wages ' were a further heavy burden on crown finance.

The arrangements made to move the king's artillery for the ' great raid ' against Norham in 1497[1] are entered in full in the *Accounts of the Treasurer*. In addition to the oxen that would be provided or requisitioned on the way, 179 horses and 110 drivers were also hired ' to draw the artailyerie ', at a cost of £114 a week; to smooth the way, 221 men, with shovels, spades, picks and mattocks, were hired at 6s. a week each (making a weekly total of £66 6s.); to fashion and ' correct ' the gun-stones, 61 quarrymen and masons were hired at 9s. 4d. a week each (making a weekly total of £28 10s.); and the wages of twelve wrights, four smiths, and a cooper (for the powder-barrels) came to £8 a week. In addition, the great bombard *Mons*[2] had her own team of 100 workmen, and five wrights and smiths, costing £32 a week; and yet, despite a payment of 14s. to the minstrels that ' playit before Mons doune the gait ' [the High Street of Edinburgh], she broke down on the outskirts of the town when seven wrights took nearly three days to make a new ' cradle ' for her at a cost of £2 10s.[3]

It might be argued that all this was special expenditure for a raid on England; but, with the steady development of these new weapons of war, the provision and maintenance of the royal artillery in the later

[1] *Supra*, p. 281.   [2] ' Mons Meg ' is still to be seen at Edinburgh castle.
[3] *Accounts of the Lord High Treasurer*, VOL. I, pp. 346-50.

years of the reign of James IV was costing well over £5,000 a year.

The heavy financial burden of the new weapon had already been realised in the reign of James II, when there was apparently a half-hearted attempt to secure co-operation from the nobility. In 1456 Parliament thought it ' speedful that the King make request to certain of the great barons of the land that are of any might to make carts of war, and in each cart two guns, and each of them to have two chambers, with the rest of the gear that pertains thereto, and a cunning man to shoot them '. But there is no evidence that the act was put to execution. Indeed, the King probably saw the danger of allowing the nobility to have guns with ' cunning men to shoot them ', and deemed it advisable that the new deterrent should remain a royal monopoly; and later enactments refer only to the provision and supply of ' carts of war ', without any reference to guns.

But now the costs were rising at an alarming rate.

Warfare by sea was also becoming more and more expensive, and ships too were armed with guns. In the reign of James III ships like the *Yellow Carvel* were simply armed merchantman; and ' skeely skippers ', though helped to some extent by the King, hoped to recover their outlays by taking the merchantmen of other nations under ' letters of marque ', which were virtually authorisations to commit acts of piracy. James IV, however, spent vast sums on a royal navy and royal men-of-war.

James's first big ship, the *Margaret*, took two and a half years to build and was armed with twenty-one guns. The cost of her building and equipment was about £6,000. But that was a trifle compared with the outlay on the ' great ' *Michael*, which took over four years to build[1] and which cost over £30,000. Pitscottie, who may have derived his figures direct from Sir Andrew Wood, the King's admiral, tells us that the *Michael* was 240 feet long, with walls 10 feet thick, and inside her walls she was 35 feet in beam. His further description (which sounds exaggerated) tells us that her armament consisted of six cannons on every side, with three great basilisks – two at her stern and one at her prow[2] – and three hundred smaller guns, ' moyen and batterit falcons and quarter falcons, slangs, pestilent serpentines, and double dogs,

---

[1] In the *Accounts of the Lord High Treasurer* we can trace her under construction in 1507 and she was launched, but not completed, in 1511.

[2] The *Accounts of the Treasurer* show that some of her great guns required six carts each to carry them.

with hackbutts and culverines '; her complement, over and above her captains, skippers and quarter-masters, was ' three hundred mariners to sail her, six score gunners to use her artillery, and one thousand men of war '.[1] And he concludes his account with a story characteristic of the King – when the ' great ' *Michael* had been launched and was lying off-shore, James tested her by firing a cannon-ball at her, but it ' shook her not, and did her little scathe '.

When James finally broke with Henry VIII, and assembled his host for the ill-fated campaign that ended with Flodden, the *Michael*, the *Margaret*, and at least three other royal ships were victualled[2] and made ready and sailed for France to join the ships of Louis XII; but they sailed under the Earl of Arran, and not under one of James's skilled sea-captains, and James's navy, built at great cost, did nothing apart from raiding the English stronghold of Carrickfergus.[3]

But ships, in addition to the wages of carpenters, wrights and other craftsmen (many of whom came from France), and the cost of their materials and equipment, required docks, repair-shops, ware-houses and other services. Some harbour accommodation for the smaller vessels was already available in the eastern ports; but James IV established new naval dockyards at the Pool of Airth[4] and at Newhaven, where the ' great ' *Michael* was built. And when the ships were manned wages had to be paid to both sailors and soldiers. The wages of a sailor appear to have averaged thirty-five shillings a month; a skipper received £7 or £8 a month.

All-in-all, towards the end of his reign James IV was spending well over £15,000 a year on the royal navy.

Further expenditure on the armed forces also arose through the need for extended military service in the field. The old feudal service was limited to forty days,[5] and all the king's lieges between sixteen and sixty were expected to obey the summons to the host,[6] unless they

---

[1] In one official reference the names of 295 ' mariners of the great ship ' are listed but the gunners number only fourteen.

[2] The victualling of the *Michael* included 3,000 gallons of ale, 240 marts, 5,300 ' stock ' fish, 13,000 loaves of bread, and 200 stones of cheese.

[3] The *Michael* never returned to Scotland. In 1514 she was sold to Louis XII for forty thousand francs, and, according to Buchanan, this noble ship rotted away in the harbour at Brest.

[4] On the Forth, about eight miles east of Stirling.

[5] In 1496 there is a clear reference to the lieges giving forty days' service in time of war, and serving at their own expense, as had been customary in the past; but service for twenty days appears to have been more common.

[6] Such a complete mobilisation probably took place only in the immediate neigh-bourhood of the king's own person. There was no effective machinery for ' shire

had received royal licences to 'bide at hame.'[1] From time to time Parliament had laid down the arms and armour which the lieges were expected to bear when serving with the host, and sheriffs and barons were ordered to hold regular 'wappinschaws' (weapon-showings) to ensure that those within their jurisdictions possessed the weapons that accorded with their status. Much of this however, was merely paper legislation. When the King called out the host the organisation was primitive, the response varied, and those who joined his banner, although undoubtedly brave, and many of them at home in the saddle, had had little or no training as fighting-units.

But such a cumbersome, ill-organised and temporary army, unwilling to leave the demands of steading and farm, was useless for any regular or continuing military duty such as that of garrisoning the Border strongholds. Thus, as early as the reign of James III (and possibly earlier), the government had begun to employ 'wageouris' – regular soldiers receiving wages for their service: usually two shillings or two shillings and sixpence a day, or, sometimes, ten shillings a week.

Over and above this new expenditure arising out of new methods of warfare, there were also increasing costs in the government of the realm. Not only was there a growing civil service but also, as Scotland became more and more involved in European politics, there were increasing expenses in diplomatic negotiations.[2] Ambassadors were expensive to send and expensive to receive. For example, within the course of a few months in 1512 departing English ambassadors received a present of plate costing £120, a departing French ambassador received plate costing £115, and a departing Spanish ambassador received a purse containing approximately £100.

Finally, while James III may have amassed treasure and kept it secretly, James IV was openly prodigal. For his marriage to Margaret Tudor his two gowns of cloth of gold, lined with fur, cost over £650 each, and the hangings and canopies of the royal chambers in the new palace of Holyroodhouse cost approximately £1,000.

On rare occasions a small tax or 'contribution' would be imposed by Parliament; but the Scots never suffered taxations gladly, and the

levies ', and much depended upon the action and authority of the local sheriff or lord.

[1] Burgh communities frequently paid large sums ' to bide at hame ' or, alternatively, furnished a quota of mercenaries (' wageouris '). Individuals purchased licences often on the ground of ' heavy corpulence ' or ' extreme sickness '.

[2] The index to the *Acts of the Parliaments of Scotland* under the heading ' Embassy ' is eloquent of the sudden increase in diplomatic activity in the reigns of James III and IV.

collection of a tax was always a slow, difficult, and never-completed task. An occasional forfeiture might help matters for a brief while, and James IV, as we have seen, ' drove ' the justice-ayres and derived a fair revenue from their amercements and compositions. Ayres at Jedburgh in 1498 and 1499, for example, yielded £2,455 and £2,015 respectively; an ayre at Lanark in 1500 yielded £1,750. But many of these amercements were paid in cattle or kind – and we have references to the payment of drovers ' pro agitando ' the cattle to the royal larders. The main sources of revenue were still the great customs, the royal lands, the king's burghs, the profits of justice and feudal casualties. And the royal revenue was now far too small for the many calls that were made upon it. In an average year, at this time, the total revenue from all regular sources was probably not more than £30,000 (Scots), or, roughly, £7,500 sterling. It was clear that more money had to be found for the many needs of the crown.

More money was found in two ways – by increasing the revenue drawn from the crown lands, and by exploiting the wealth of the Church.

As we have seen, the old feudal fighting services contributed nothing to the new *money* needs of the crown – though the income from the feudal casualties of relief, wardship and marriage (or their profitable sale to others) should not be underestimated. But obviously the economic position would be vastly improved if the King could draw money-rents from the crown lands. Money rents were already being paid by many tenants under short tacks (or leases) of three or five years; money rents were paid by the burghs; and by now most of the important burghs had been granted feu-ferme charters. The Church, which required money for many purposes (including the payment of annates or common services, and payments for various negotiations with the Holy See), had long been granting tenures in feu-ferme for its own lands.[1] The crown, too, needed money for many purposes. Why should not the crown likewise develop tenures in feu-ferme for the crown lands ? And lands held in feu were not only held on a perpetual heritable tenure in return for a fixed annual money-rent, but also, in return for the many advantages of such a perpetual tenure,[2] the tenant could be called upon to pay a goodly sum for the granting of a feu-ferme charter.

[1] Although the grant of a feu-ferme charter was virtually a permanent alienation and, if not ' to the evident utility of the church ', was contrary to canon law.

[2] The advantages are sometimes stated in the feu-ferme charter: ' That, from the assured hope to them and their heirs of enjoying and holding a tenure in perpetuity, some reasonable advantages in the increase of " improvement " would accrue – in

In 1458 the King had been urged to ratify sub-infeudations in feu-ferme (provided the ferme was of a reasonable amount and not prejudicial to the crown), and thereby 'give example' to others. In 1504, Parliament gave authority to the King to set in feu-ferme the crown lands, both 'annexed' and 'unannexed'. In 1540, a similar act spoke of feuing as being 'to the great profit of the crown'. And in 1584, Parliament, considering 'the daily increase of the charges and expenses' of the royal household, ordained that henceforth all lands falling to the crown by escheat, forfeiture, or otherwise were to be annexed to the crown and were to be held of the crown 'only in feu-ferme' for the payment of feu-duties and not otherwise.

The records reveal that James IV soon saw the advantage of the act of 1504, and that from 1508 onwards much feuing of the crown lands took place. The accounts also show that, where lands had previously been held on a short tack (or lease), and were now feued, the feu-duty was much larger than the old rent; and naturally so, because of the benefits enjoyed by the tenant under a perpetual heritable tenure. Also, because of those benefits, substantial sums in hard cash were paid by tenants for a grant of tenure in feu-ferme. Nevertheless it should be noted that, because of the continuing fall in the value of money, the feu-duties received by the crown, which could never be raised, became gradually of less and less worth. It should also be noted that although, in the second half of the reign of James IV, those crown lands which were held for money-rents had their rents increased (or 'highted'), the increases were quickly offset in a like way.

Thus from the reign of James IV onwards, the crown revenues benefited by the receipt of a greater number of feu-duties, with occasional capital payments for the granting of feu-charters, and by increased rents. And we find that certain of the Lords of Council were appointed to be 'Commissioners of the Crown Lands', to be responsible for the administration of the crown lands, for the fixing of rents, for setting lands in feu-ferme and for the collection of rents and feu-duties.[1]

suitable buildings, lands put under new cultivation, the recovery of "waste", the planting of trees, the raising of fish in fresh water and by means of stanks, the construction of dove-cots, orchards, pleasaunces and warrens, together with the enrichment in movable goods of the tenants holding the same lands thus set in feu-ferme' (Cf. *Source Book of Scottish History*, VOL. II (2nd edn.), p. 241).

[1] In miniature all this can be traced in the later administration of the Forest of Ettrick which had fallen to the Crown with the forfeiture of the Black Douglases in 1455.

Turning to the Church, and slightly anticipating what must be said later, we have ample evidence that the Church was wealthy while the crown was poor. The Church at this time possessed almost half the wealth of the kingdom: its revenues, as we know from the records, were in excess of £300,000 a year, while the royal revenues, as we have seen, were still only some £45,000 a year. The crown, however, was already tapping the great wealth of the Church in various ways. By abusing the indult of 1487, it could grant a vacant benefice as a reward to some civil servant or as a favour to this or that lord, and thereby avoid a drain upon its own resources; it could also enjoy the temporalities of vacant benefices for the better part of a year or more.[1] We have noted too, that, with Henry VIII's defiance of Rome and papal endeavours to keep Scotland faithful to the Holy See, abuse of the indult had become more and more scandalous. More than that, papal fears lest James V should follow Henry's advice and example, and break with Rome, were soon exploited to wring papal sanction for the diversion of certain church revenues to state purposes – as, for example, in the founding and endowment of the College of Justice, when there was also further abuse in the disposal of the church revenues assigned for that purpose.[2]

But the wealth of the church could be attracted to the state in other ways. When a ' Protestant ' party began to emerge in Scotland, with a leaning towards an alliance with England, the prelates of the Roman Church showed themselves willing to give money to the crown in the hope of preserving both the old alliance and the old faith. Indeed, they were quick to see that the survival of the old faith (and therewith their retention of the Church's wealth) had become largely dependent upon the survival of the old alliance. So, in the end, we find the Scottish Church of its own accord making ' contributions ' or ' a tax of the clergy ' to crush heresy in Scotland and, above all, to oppose any alliance with heretical England. In May 1543, for example, just before the treaties of Greenwich were negotiated by the Regent Arran (who was then leaning towards an Anglophil and Protestant policy), a meeting of the clergy at St Andrews (called by Cardinal Beaton) resolved to raise £10,000, by a tax upon prelacies and benefices, ' to maintain the liberty of the Church and to preserve the State ' – in other words, to save the Church by maintaining the old alliance with France. In succeeding years such ' contributions ' multiplied. Moreover, since 1522, if not earlier, the Church had been contributing

[1] *Supra*, pp. 268 ff. [2] *Infra*, pp. 306-7.

one-half of all national taxations, and the apportionment of the payment of any tax had now become one-half from the church, one-third from the barons, and one-sixth from the burghs – whereas, previously, the apportionment had generally been two-fifths from the church, two-fifths from the barons and one-fifth from the burghs.[1]

Much of this was vastly similar to the payment of insurance premiums. The ' contributions ' made by the Church and the taxations of the Church were small in relation to its wealth. But if Scotland were to follow the example of England the Church might well lose all.

At the same time it must again be stressed that, although the Scottish Kings still professed obedience to Rome, they themselves, by taking advantage of Rome's difficulties and by diverting church revenues to secular purposes, helped to contribute to that decay in the Church which was one of the causes leading to the Reformation.

[1] In 1468, if not earlier, Parliament had adopted the method of fixing the sum to be brought in by a tax and leaving each estate responsible for its own share, at first in equal proportions but, in 1472, and generally thereafter, in the proportions of two-fifths of the total amount from the clergy, two-fifths from the barons, and one-fifth from the burghs. Sometime between 1501 and 1522, however, the clergy had been burdened with one-half of the total of a tax, leaving one-third to be raised by the barons and one-sixth by the burghs.

CHAPTER XXX

The Reign of James V

SCOTLAND WAS in no immediate danger after the disaster of Flodden. The Earl of Surrey was short of supplies; the weather was appalling; and, above all, Henry VIII, whose chief interest lay in his campaign in France, realised that the Scots, with their heavy casualties, and with an infant King, could be of no further trouble for some time to come.

Yet, if Scotland had been drawn into the tangle of European politics in the reign of James IV, now, more than ever, Scottish politics were to be influenced by events in Europe – notably the rivalry between the French King, Francis I, and the Emperor Charles V, the preaching of Luther and the German Reformation, and, finally, Henry VIII's breach with Rome.

Charles V, who became Emperor in 1519 (against the strong candidature of Francis I), was the grandson of Maximilian. When he succeeded to the Hapsburg lands, however, he was already ruling Spain, Naples and Sicily, and drawing upon the wealth of the New World overseas (as the grandson of Ferdinand and Isabella), while from his father, Philip of Burgundy, he had inherited the Netherlands. The ramifications of his wide empire extended further still through marriages: two of his sisters married the kings of Denmark and of Portugal; his son, Philip of Spain, married Mary Tudor; and Catherine of Aragon, Henry VIII's first wife, was his aunt.

But, if the once-powerful France was now encircled, Charles V's empire was widely scattered and not easily held. For example, the Emperor needed the friendship of England if he was to use the English Channel for easy communication between Spain and the Low Countries. Moreover, although France was England's traditional enemy, a new concept of a ' balance of power ' was emerging. It was not clear that Henry VIII would necessarily ally with the Emperor against France, and Henry's divorce from Catherine of Aragon tended to throw Henry and the Emperor into opposite camps.

All this affected Scotland; and, at a later stage, European politics were reflected in the various negotiations for the marriage of Scotland's King. France still wanted the ' auld alliance '; England still wanted

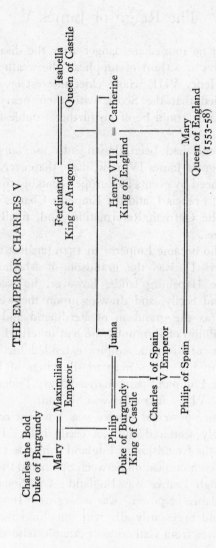

THE EMPEROR CHARLES V

Charles the Bold Duke of Burgundy

Mary = Maximilian Emperor

Ferdinand King of Aragon = Isabella Queen of Castile

Philip Duke of Burgundy King of Castile = Juana

Henry VIII King of England = Catherine

Charles I of Spain V Emperor

Philip of Spain = Mary Queen of England (1553-58)

to be safe from an attack from the north; and England, France and the Emperor all negotiated for Scotland's friendship and support.

James IV had named his Queen as regent in the event of his death; and, within a fortnight of Flodden, she was duly appointed as guardian of the infant King and Regent of the kingdom. The King was crowned at Stirling, and the Earls of Angus, Arran and Huntly, and James Beaton, archbishop of Glasgow, were associated with Margaret as her councillors. Yet it would appear that, almost at once, certain of the nobility sent secret letters to France, to John, duke of Albany,[1] inviting him to come to Scotland to take over the regency; and when, in August 1514, the Queen Mother (who was still only twenty-four years old) married Archibald Douglas, sixth earl of Angus (who was about the same age), the invitation to Albany was urgently renewed. The Red Douglases were powerful enough already without the young King being in Douglas hands. And at last, in May 1515, Albany arrived in Scotland to assume the regency of the realm. He was confirmed in his regency, he was made guardian of the King, and the two offices were to be held by him until James V reached his eighteenth year.

The new regent was virtually a Frenchman, speaking only French[2] – a severe handicap for that tactful handling of jealous and headstrong nobles which had always been necessary in the Scottish council and court – but, with the death of the King's young brother, Alexander, towards the end of 1515 or early in 1516, he was next in succession to the throne. Naturally Henry VIII, anxious to wean Scotland from the auld alliance, disliked the idea of a Scottish regent who was a Frenchman and also next in succession to the Scottish throne. He had made a temporary peace with France in the preceding August, and thereafter had done all he could to prevent Albany leaving France – and, when Albany sailed for Scotland, Henry had even tried to intercept him on his way.

At first Albany showed both energy and ability. The young King was taken from his mother and entrusted to the keeping of a small group of nobles who supported the regent; the Queen Mother fled to England[3]; and an abortive resistance-movement headed by Arran and

[1] Son of Alexander, duke of Albany, the second son of James II (see the Table on p. 262).
[2] The Scottish chronicles were translated into French for him so that he could know something of the history of the country of which he was now regent.
[3] She was at Harbottle, Northumberland, in October 1515 when she gave birth to a daughter, Margaret Douglas, who was to marry Matthew Stewart, fourth earl of Lennox, and to become the mother of Darnley.

Lennox was easily crushed. Henry VIII, striving to oust Albany from the regency, now informed the Scottish Estates that if they wished to have peace with England they must send Albany back to France; but the English King's imperious message merely strengthened the Regent's position and party and, in November 1516, Parliament formally declared Albany to be the ' second person of the realm ' – that is, heir presumptive to the crown.

In the following summer Albany returned to France, for a ' brief visit ' (which, however, lasted for four years), and, while there, strengthened the auld alliance by the treaty of Rouen (1517). The new treaty re-affirmed the old arrangements for mutual help against English aggression, but, in addition, it was agreed that James V should marry a daughter of Francis I – a clause in the treaty which was not fulfilled until twenty years later when James married Madeleine de Valois.

Prior to his departure, Albany had appointed a council of regency, to govern the country during his absence, which, in an endeavour to secure some order of tranquillity, he had made a council of all parties (including Huntly, Argyll, Angus and Arran), while, as a gesture to Henry VIII, the Queen Mother had been allowed to return to Scotland. But all these endeavours were useless. Almost at once one of Albany's lieutenants, the Sieur de la Bastie, whom he had made Warden of the East March in succession to Lord Home,[1] was ruthlessly murdered by the Homes of Wedderburn; the Queen Mother began proceedings of divorce against Angus; and a long-standing feud between Angus and Arran came to a head in a street fight in Edinburgh (1520), when the Hamiltons, striving to oust the Douglases from the capital, were themselves driven out – a fight which became known as ' Cleanse the Causeway ' or, in other words, ' cleanse the streets of Edinburgh of all the Hamiltons '.[2]

But Albany still stayed in France. It may be that, with the election of Charles V as Emperor in 1519, Francis I, seeing himself threatened on all sides, now became doubly anxious to be on friendly terms with

[1] Lord Home had been executed by Albany, in 1516, for treasonable intrigue with England.

[2] Pitscottie's account of this affair contains one of his best stories. He relates that Gavin Douglas, bishop of Dunkeld, and uncle of Archibald, sixth earl of Angus, striving to bring the Hamiltons and Douglases together in peace, called on James Beaton, archbishop of Glasgow, a supporter of the Hamiltons, and asked for his help as mediator. But when the Archbishop, striking his breast, declared on his conscience that he knew nothing of the intentions of the Hamiltons, his own armour rattled beneath his vestments. Whereupon Gavin Douglas replied, ' Faith, my lord, but yours is a poor conscience, for I heard it clatter '.

Henry; and thus Francis, probably seeking to gratify Henry, definitely strove to keep Albany in France. Nor can Albany have been over-desirous to return to the hard task of trying to govern the Scottish nobility. With the outbreak of war between France and the Emperor in the autumn of 1521, however, and with France becoming apprised of a treaty that had been concluded between Henry VIII and Charles V, the auld alliance once more appealed to the French King. After all, in any war between Charles V and Francis I, England was almost bound to be on the side of the Emperor, partly because of her long-standing tradition of war with France, and partly because of her cloth-trade with the Netherlands. It is not surprising that Albany now returned to Scotland (November 1521).

In July and August 1522, English forces raided and harried the northern coast of France, and in September, in fulfilment of the treaty of Rouen, Albany led the Scottish host to the western march for an invasion of England. But, at the Border, the Scottish nobles refused to invade England. Partly this was a ' Flodden complex ', which was long to persist; but, more than that, Albany in one of his letters to France, complained that the Scots lords were saying their wars with England were merely in the interests of France and they were weary of fighting for others.

The refusal of the Scottish lords to march into England was a clear indication of a changing attitude towards the old alliance; and Albany, whose position had been rendered difficult, and who saw that he could do little in Scotland to help France, returned thither in the following month (October 1522). Again Henry tried to have Albany removed from the regency. In January 1523 he offered, in return for the removal of Albany, a long truce and the marriage of his daughter Mary to James V. His offers, however, were mistrusted and rejected. Turning again to force, Henry sent the Duke of Norfolk (the son of ' old Surrey ' of Flodden) over the Scottish border to ravage and to waste. Kelso was burned in June and Jedburgh in September, and ' the scourge of the Scots ' left ' neither house, fortress, village, tree, cattle, corn nor other succour for man ' in his wake. On the day of the burning of Jedburgh, however, Albany once more landed in Scotland, bringing with him men and guns. Again the Scottish host was led to the Border – this time on the east – and again the Scottish nobles refused to cross into England. This second refusal convinced Albany of the hopelessness of his task. In May 1524 he once more returned to France – this time on the understanding that if he did not return to Scotland before September 1524 his regency would be at an end. He did not return, and his regency was over.

The broken periods of the regency of Albany reveal a continuance of the old alliance with France and an attempt, by France, to strengthen that alliance by the treaty of Rouen. But, as we have seen, there is also a change of attitude in Scotland: Scotland is not to be used as a pawn of France. And, amid the old Scottish factions and feuds, it is possible to see two parties emerging – one favouring an alliance with England, the other an alliance with France; though personal ambitions and personal hatreds are still apt to be deciding factors.

With Albany's return to France, and with the Earl of Angus still in France (whither he had gone after ' Cleanse the Causeway '), the Earl of Arran now came to the fore; and Arran and Margaret, the Queen Mother, represented a party favourable to an alliance with England rather than with France. In July 1524 they arranged for the ' Erection ' of the King – James, then twelve years old, was brought from Stirling to Edinburgh, placed on a throne, and publicly invested with crown, sword and sceptre. A guard of 200 men was sent by Henry to act as a bodyguard for his nephew; in August the officers of state who had been appointed by Albany were discharged; a Parliament held in November confirmed the appointments made by the Queen Mother and Arran; and James Beaton, now archbishop of St Andrews, and always a supporter of the old alliance, was placed in confinement. The ' English faction ' was, for the time being, supreme. In June of the same year, moreover, the Earl of Angus had arrived in London from France, and in October he returned to Scotland – also in favour of an alliance with England. In February 1525 he was confirmed by Parliament in all his former dignities, offices and lands and in March he was made Warden of the East and Middle Marches.

All seemed to be going well for the English faction; but Angus and Arran were still at feud, and Angus and Margaret, despite a temporary reconciliation, were wholly unable to work together. The English faction was divided within itself – Arran, next in succession to the crown after Albany, must not have too much power; the headstrong Margaret was always in opposition to Angus. Moreover, when Francis I was defeated and captured at Pavia (1525), there was again the fear that a weak France might mean a too-powerful England, even though Wolsey, pursuing a tortuous and opportunist diplomacy, now made an alliance with France against the Emperor. Indeed, at this stage, both parties in Scotland were at a complete loss in their diplomacy; if, indeed, it can be said that the nobles of either party had a policy that was dictated by considerations other than personal ones.

Because of the many divisions among the nobility, and because almost every noble house was distrusted by the others, Parliament, in July 1525, agreed that the King should remain ' in company ' with certain lords and prelates, ' quarterly ', according to a system of rotation. Those for the first ' quarter ' were the Earl of Angus and Gavin Dunbar, archbishop of Glasgow; and Angus, having secured the person of the King, ' would in no wise part with him '. Thus, in June 1526, when the Estates declared that since James had now reached the age of fourteen his royal authority should henceforth be in his own hands, that meant, simply, that royal authority was in the hands of Angus. And likewise, when the same Parliament declared that the King should appoint royal officers as he thought expedient, that meant as Angus thought expedient. As had happened in November 1524 the Scottish Parliament had merely acted as the tool of the faction then in power; but the Red Douglas, emulating Lord Livingston and Lord Boyd, keeping the King in his own hands[1] and filling the offices of state with his kin and friends, virtually ruled Scotland until the King's escape in the spring of 1528. Then, when the King's supporters gained control, the Angus Douglases were forfeited. For a while Angus successfully defied the King at Tantallon; but he was compelled to take refuge in England, and he did not return to Scotland until after Solway Moss and the death of James V.

Once more, however, Scotland became involved in the tangle of European politics. The Emperor's forces after heavily defeating the French in Italy, had made the Pope their prisoner. But Catherine of Aragon, from whom Henry was now contemplating a divorce, was the Emperor's aunt. A divorce from Catherine would antagonise the Emperor, and was little likely to be granted by his prisoner. Yet although Wolsey's diplomacy might try to draw England and France closer together, England had an important trade with the Low Countries, which formed part of the Emperor's possessions. The Emperor, too, began to see the value of Scotland as a possible ally. Scotland also had considerable trade with the Low Countries. Perhaps the Emperor might even be able to find a bride for James V and so seal the alliance. But the Emperor's suggested match – his sister Marie, the

---

[1] An attempt by Scott of Buccleuch to free the King was defeated; and in a further attempt Lennox was slain.

widowed Queen of Hungary[1] – was attractive to neither party, and, as soon as Francis I heard of the Emperor's approach, he again suggested a French marriage, though this alliance with England against the Emperor (if it could be relied upon) was more valuable to him than alliance with Scotland, and the treaty of Rouen had faded into the background.

It will be seen that brides had now been suggested for James V by France, England, and the Emperor. James, it may be said, was being courted in high quarters. But James was short of money[2]; he was determined that when he did marry he would marry a well-endowed bride; and, while the rich bride who would not upset European diplomacy was difficult to find, James's financial difficulties were becoming more and more pressing. There was only one other source of money – the Church. In 1531 James approached the Pope for a permanent subsidy of £10,000 a year from the revenues of the Church in Scotland ' for the protection and defence of the realm '.

The European situation was favourable to James's request. The Pope was still virtually in the Emperor's power, and the Emperor, trying to wean Scotland away from the old alliance with France, had just concluded a treaty with Scotland furthering her commercial relations with the Netherlands. Above all, Henry VIII, demanding a divorce from Catherine of Aragon (the Emperor's aunt), was putting the Pope to defiance, and in Europe heresy was spreading apace. It was essential that Scotland should remain true to Rome. Yet £10,000 a year was a startling demand.

At first the Pope temporised. Then he granted the imposition of a tithe for three years. Finally, when it was urged that the £10,000 a year could be used to establish a College of Justice[3] (half of whose members could be churchmen), and that the Roman Church in Scotland could survive the assaults of heresy only if law and order were maintained, he agreed. In September 1531 Clement VII issued a Bull authorising an ecclesiastical subsidy of £10,000[4] a year for the maintenance of a College of Justice in Scotland as long as James and his

---

[1] Her husband had been killed on the bloody field of Mohacs (1526), vainly fighting against Suleyman the Magnificent.

[2] As we have seen, James IV had spent recklessly on the army and navy, and the period 1513-28 had not been conducive to recovery.

[3] In effect a supreme central civil court. A ' college ' is a society instituted for certain common purposes and possessing special rights and privileges; and the name is still used in that sense in, for example, the College of Surgeons.

[4] Strictly, 10,000 ducats *auri de camera*, equivalent, roughly, to £10,000 (Scots).

successors remained true to Rome. And in the following year (1532) James undertook in Parliament to establish the College and also to maintain the authority of Rome and the freedom of the Church.

In other words, James had bargained to remain true to Rome provided he was allowed to use part of the church's revenues for state purposes. The precedent was dangerous. More than that, however, the prelates, viewing a standing contribution of £10,000 a year with alarm, and well aware of James's pressing needs, now entered into an agreement with the king that, instead of this heavy annual subsidy, they would pay to him £72,000 in eight half-yearly instalments over the next four years, which the King could use as he wished, and thereafter would provide, for the endowment of the College of Justice, £1,400 a year, in perpetuity, which should be met from certain benefices assigned for that purpose.

In 1535, the succeeding Pope, Paul III, issued a Bull confirming the erection of the College (and also confirming the agreement with the prelates whereby £1,400 a year was to be provided from benefices within their patronage); and in 1541 Parliament ratified the institution of a College of Justice to consist of fourteen judges (seven churchmen and seven laymen), to sit under a President (who was to be a churchman), and with power to the King to add ' extraordinary lords '.

The limited finance of £1,400 a year was, from the very first, inadequate; it meant less than £100 (Scots) a year for each of the judges; and further provision had eventually to be made. But, for the first time, Scotland had a central civil court with a paid judicial bench.[1]

The erection of the College of Justice was partly a financial expedient, partly an attempt to secure a more efficient administration of civil justice. And, in relation to law and order, James did not neglect the difficult parts – the Highlands and the Borders. An attempt by the Earl of Argyll, the King's Lieutenant in the west, and James Stewart, earl of Moray, the King's Lieutenant in the north, to advance their own interests at the expense of the MacDonalds, had led to a gathering in arms of the MacDonalds of Islay and the Macleans of Duart, and there had been much mutual ravaging and wasting of Campbell and MacDonald lands.[2] In the spring of 1531 the King determined to lead

[1] For later changes in the constitution of the College of Justice (the Court of Session), see *Source Book of Scottish History*, VOL. II (2nd edn.), p. 52.

[2] In the case of the Macleans there was also a background of feud. Lauchlan Maclean of Duart had married Catherine, daughter of Archibald, second earl of Argyll, and, tiring of her, is said to have had her placed on a rock (still called the ' Lady's Rock '), which was exposed only at low tide, intending to drown her (1523). She

his army northwards in person; but, when the chiefs had laid their cause before him and had voluntarily come into his will, it appeared that Argyll and Moray had determined upon a ' danting of the Isles ' largely for their own ends. With justice, Argyll was deprived of his office and temporarily imprisoned, and, for the rest of his reign (and largely through the loyal efforts of the Macdonalds of Islay), James had no further trouble in the southern isles.[1] Further north, however, in 1539, Donald Gorme of Sleat, chief of the MacDonalds of Skye, in alliance with the Macleods of Lewis, once more strove to regain the lost earldom of Ross, but when, at the outset of his campaign, he died of a wound received in the siege of Ellandonan, the attempt collapsed.

James now determined upon a display of force. In May 1540, with a large and well-armed fleet, he sailed from the Forth to Orkney and thence to Lewis, Skye, Mull and Islay, and by Kintyre back to Dumbarton. From every disaffected part he brought back with him the local chiefs: some were released upon promise of obedience and the giving of hostages; others were still in confinement at the time of his death. So, we are told, there was as ' greit quietnes and obedience ' in the Isles as in any other part of the realm, and ' gude compt and payment ' was made of the King's rentals there.

On the Borders, always a difficult part of the land, the Armstrongs of Liddesdale had long defied the wardens of Scotland and England alike, and had boasted that they would be ordered by neither King. Nor were some of the Border lords and lairds – Bothwell and Home, Maxwells, Johnstons, Scotts and others – any better. Some were certainly intriguing with England; and, quite apart from the mainten- ance of law and order, and the pacification of the Border lands, there was the danger that Border incidents might give Henry VIII an excuse for Border devastation. In 1530 James placed a number of these March lords and lairds in close ward and, leading a veritable army to the Border, hanged ' Johnnie Armstrong ' of Gilnockie and some forty of his followers. Johnnie Armstrong may have been ' nane the waur o' a hanging ', but he was probably more of a nuisance to England than to the Scottish King. The ballad makes him a hero; popular tradition accused a ' graceless ' King of treachery; and it was said that

was luckily rescued by a passing boat; but, in revenge, her brother, Sir John Campbell of Cawdor, later murdered Duart in Edinburgh.

[1] For a detailed account of these troubles, see Gregory, *History of the Western Highlands and Isles* (1836), pp. 132-43.

the trees upon which he and his followers were hanged[1] withered away in manifestation of the injustice that had been done.

Yet it should also be noted that, seeking to hold the law in the ' broken parts ' of his land, James was strengthening the government. Argyll and Moray and the Border lords were reminded of the power of the King; and when, in 1536, James left Scotland to bring back a bride from France, the government, in his absence, stood firm.

As we have seen, James, in 1532, declared his determination to maintain the Roman Church. Henry, on the other hand, had already broken with Rome, and the breach quickly widened with his marriage to Anne Boleyn, the Act of Supremacy, and the suppression of the monasteries. Henry strove hard to persuade his nephew to follow his example; but James refused and, in addition to remaining true to Rome, remained true also to the old alliance.

James was still unmarried, and was still being courted in high quarters. In 1532 the Emperor sent him the Golden Fleece; in 1534 Henry VIII sent him the Garter; and in 1536 Francis I admitted him to the Order of St Michael. There was a possibility, as late as 1534, that he might marry Mary Tudor; a little later, the Emperor suggested marriage into the royal house of Denmark, and then into that of Portugal; and although, in 1536, James contracted to marry Mary of Bourbon, daughter of Charles, duke of Vendôme – at the same time stipulating the ' wealth ' she was to bring with her – he was so bitterly disappointed when he saw the lady that he at once broke off the match. At last, however, James married. On 1 January 1537 he married Madeleine, the eldest surviving daughter of Francis I. After twenty years the marriage clause in the treaty of Rouen had finally been fulfilled.

A marriage with Madeleine had been discussed at intervals since 1530, but the poor health of the princess had made Francis reluctant to agree. And only eight weeks after she had bent down to kiss the soil of her husband's kingdom, the young Queen, ' of pleasand bewtie, guidlie favour, luffing countenance and cumly manners ', died (7 July 1537). Again James sought a bride in France; and in June 1538 he married Mary of Guise-Lorraine, the eldest daughter of the Duke of Guise.

James's declared intention to maintain the Roman Church, his adherence to the old alliance, and his successive French marriages roused Henry's anger and fear.[2] Henry, denounced as a heretic, an

---

[1] At Caerlanrig, about ten miles south-west of Hawick on the road to Langholm.
[2] It is also interesting to note that Henry had thought of Mary of Guise, a lady of ' majestic stature and graceful proportions ', as a possible fourth bride for himself.

adulterer, and a despoiler of the Church, saw facing him the possibility of attack from a league of the Roman Catholic powers; and in the north lay Scotland, true to Rome, and united by marriage with one of the greatest houses in France. Striving to come to some agreement with James, Henry secured a promise from him that he would meet him at York (September 1541); but, although Henry made the long journey, he journeyed in vain. Neither Scottish King nor Scottish embassy came to meet him. James's privy council, and notably the churchmen, had feared the possibilities of such a meeting and had dissuaded the King. Further angered, and determined to teach James a lesson, Henry now loosed the northern levies on Scotland. In August 1542 Sir Robert Bowes crossed the Border to raid Teviotdale, but was heavily mauled by the Earl of Huntly at Haddon Rig. The Duke of Norfolk was more successful – and Roxburgh, Kelso, and a number of smaller places were burned.

In reply, James assembled the Scottish host; but, at Fala Muir, the nobles refused to march further – they would not march to the Border, much less cross it into England. There was the old argument that the war was a war for France; there was a new argument that, if James were to be killed, he had no child to succeed him.[1] But the refusal at Fala Muir was made only some three weeks before the attack on England which met with disaster at Solway Moss: and the reason for those two different events lay in other factors that were now at work.

In England, the 'Reformation', although achieved by agreement between the bishops and the king, had neverthelsss resulted in a complete break from Rome and in the seizure of some of the wealth of the Church. And there were those in Scotland who viewed Henry's actions with approval. Some looked upon the wealth of the Church and compared it with the poverty of the land; some looked to the endowments that pious ancestors had fondly made; others were inclining towards a new faith that had come from Germany, that condemned ' pilgrimages, pardons, and other such baggage ', and that made the Word of God an open book. To all these, an alliance with England was preferable to an alliance with France. A party favourable to a new faith and a new alliance was growing stronger.

Yet there were also others who, while remaining faithful to the

---

Catherine of Aragon had been divorced; Anne Boleyn had been beheaded; and Jane Seymour had died a few days after giving birth to Edward (VI).

[1] Two sons, James and Arthur, born of Mary of Guise, had both died in infancy; Mary had not yet been born.

Church of Rome, realised the corruption of too many of its servants. Among these was the King himself who, after seeing a performance of Lindsay's *Satyre of the Thrie Estaitis* in January 1540, is reported to have charged the Archbishop of Glasgow (Gavin Dunbar), and several bishops who were present with him, to reform their ways and manner of living, otherwise he would send six of the proudest of them to his uncle of England (Henry VIII) and, as they were treated, so would he treat all others who did not amend. But although James urged and desired reform,[1] he did not desire a ' reformation '. Nor did he wish to break the old alliance with France.

It may be that David Beaton (who had succeeded his uncle, James Beaton, as archbishop of St Andrews), a staunch upholder of the old faith and the old alliance, urged James to further action after the fiasco at Fala Muir. Was not the maintenance of the old alliance essential for the maintenance of the Roman Church ? If the old hatred of England could be revived, all might yet be well. Certainly James collected another army – apparently with help from the Church – but that army, caught in marshy ground between the Esk and the Sark, suffered an ignominious and overwhelming defeat. It is said that some of the nobles took umbrage at the assumption of the command by Oliver Sinclair, the King's favourite (who was captured ' fleeing full manfully '), and that some of those who were inclined to the new faith suspected they had been put in the forefront of the battle to be smitten there. But the Scottish staff work was incredibly bad, and the Scottish host had little heart for the fight to which it had been led.

Solway Moss was fought on 24 November 1542. On 7 or 8 December 1542 Mary of Guise gave birth of a daughter, Mary. On 14 December 1542 James V died.

Mary, now Queen of Scots, was one week old.

[2] Cf. *Supra*, p. 272.

CHAPTER XXXI

The Reformation - I

THAT THE Roman Church in Scotland stood in need of reform is amply evident from the statutes of its own Provincial Councils which, in 1549, 1552 and 1559, strove too late to correct abuses which had for too long undermined the Church's influence and brought contempt upon its prelates and priests.

In 1549 the Scottish Churchmen, assembled in their own Provincial Council, declared that there appeared to be two main causes of ' heresy ', namely, ' the corruption of morals and profane lewdness of life in churchmen of almost all ranks, together with crass ignorance of literature and of all the liberal arts.' Therefore, in their Council, they set themselves to remedy those abuses within their Church. The statutes then passed are eloquent of the crying need for reform. We find statutes against the incontinence of the clergy, and against their intemperance and negligence; statutes forbidding them from using the revenues of the church to endow their illegitimate children; statutes commanding the examination of priests in their ability to read and to expound the Scriptures, and ordering parsons and bishops to preach in person at least four times a year; together with other, more general, statutes for the amendment of life and morals so that ' those who correct others be not themselves guilty '. That such statutes were long overdue is evident from contemporary writings. That unfortunately they remained paper-statutes, and were not observed, is clear from a report made to Pope Paul IV by Cardinal Sermoneta in 1556 in which a number of these abuses, together with others, were once more denounced, and the Pope was urged to take measures to secure correction and reform; while in 1559 many of these statutes were passed again, in even stronger terms, in what was to be the last Provincial Council of the Scottish Church.

This decay in the Roman Church in Scotland, evident in its own statutes, is also referred to in the histories written by contemporary churchmen. John Major, scholar and divine, whose *History of Greater Britain* was published in Paris in 1521, traced the growth and persistence of corruption to the Church's wealth. Because of its wealth, offices in the Church had become attractive to men who sought, not a spiritual life, but a life of ease and luxury. In the words of Major, the wealth that had been bestowed upon the Church was ' the offspring of a truly pious sentiment, but piety, the mother, was smothered by luxury, the wanton daughter '. On the other hand, John Lesley, bishop of Ross, whose *History of Scotland* was published in Rome in 1578, attributed the corruption in the Church to the abuse of the indult of 1487 so that, as we have already seen, promotion to high office in the Church had become a valuable part of the royal patronage, often being made simply to suit the needs of royal policy or the royal purse.

Whatever the cause, most of the bishops and abbots, with few and notable exceptions, now led secular and often disreputable lives to the neglect of their spiritual office. These prelates of a wealthy church, moreover, had shown little care or thought for the humbler clergy within the parishes, where the priests were often ignorant and under-paid, and led lives that were little different from those of the members of their flock. All this was realised by the Church itself; but the attempted reforms came too late and were ineffective. Already, in 1541, an enactment of Parliament had spoken of the ' unhonesty and misrule of kirkmen both in wit knowledge and manners ' as being the reason why the kirk and kirkmen were despised and contemned.

This contempt for a corrupt Church, moreover, was quickened with the public performance of morality plays and with the circulation of books and broadsheets now made possible by the growth of printing. In 1543, 1549 and 1552 we read of slanderous bills, writings, ballads and books which were circulating to the defame of the Church and churchmen. None of these early broadsheets has survived, but some indication of their contents may perhaps be gathered from Sir David Lyndsay's play, *Ane Pleasant Satyre of the Thrie Estaitis*,[1] and from the collection of *Gude and Godlie Ballates*, made by the brothers Wedderburn of Dundee,[2] in which, in addition to metrical vernacular versions of a catechism, the Creed, the Commandments, and certain psalms, there are also lampoons on the Church and its priests.

But, while Provincial and General Councils alike had recognised

[1] We do not know when the *Satyre* was first printed, but we know that it was performed before James V, his queen, and the lords of council at Linlithgow on Epiphany 1540. In his works Sir David Lyndsay (*c.* 1490-*c.* 1555) attacked corruption in both church and state: in the church, in his *Satyre*; in the state, in his *Testament of the Papyngo*. In his *Supplicatioun anent Syde Taillis* he even attacked absurd female fashions. His *Historie of Squyer Meldrum*, on the other hand, is a long epic of its hero's many adventures, military and amatory.

[2] Again we do not know the date of the first printing. The earliest surviving edition is that of 1578, though there is reference to an earlier edition of about 1570.

abuse and had agreed upon the necessity for reform, already men had appeared who preached reform and who spoke to the people. Much earlier, Wycliffe had held that no one could hold holy office unless he led a holy life. More recently Luther had denounced 'indulgences', and in 1517 had nailed his thesis to the doors of a church in Wittenberg. Patrick Hamilton had been burned before the College gate in St Andrews in 1528 for a belief in faith that 'made man and God friends'; and at St Andrews George Wishart was burned in 1546. 'Heresy' had become more than an attack upon the corruption in the Church: now it was held that the Church could be reformed only by reforming its doctrines.

The preaching of the early martyrs, Resby and Crawar, had shown the influence of Wycliffe and Hus. Patrick Hamilton had been influenced by Luther; and in 1525 and 1535 acts of parliament had condemned the 'damnable opinions of the heretic Luther' and had striven to prevent the entry into the realm of Lutheran books and writings. With Luther had come a new belief in faith: 'If a Christian has faith he has everything. . . . Faith unites Man to God'; and Patrick Hamilton had re-affirmed that faith brought 'Man and God together'. Wishart, however, had been influenced by the preaching and work of the Swiss reformers at Zürich, and laid stress upon the rejection of all beliefs and practices for which no warrant could be found in the Word of God. That reliance upon scriptural warrant was henceforth to be a cardinal point in the preaching of the Scottish reformers and was to be central in their Confession of Faith.

So came the desire for a new Church to preach the faith, a Church pure and undefiled and free from all man-made ceremony and invention. Where in the Word of God was there warrant for the ceremonies of the Church of Rome, the authority of the Pope, and the invocation of saints? Above all, the Mass of the Roman Church, said in a tongue unknown to most of those who attended, was held to be far different from Christ's words and actions in the Last Supper as they were recorded in the Gospels. The Mass, too, was celebrated as a propitiatory sacrifice for the sins of the living and the dead, and, in the Mass, the priest was interposed between God and his people; but a true 'communion' meant the full participation of the people in the 'Lord's Table', there to break bread and to take the cup in remembrance of Christ and therein to renew their faith and find union with God. Only thus could Christ's command be obeyed by men.

Yet how were the people to know the story revealed in the Gospels if the Word of God was denied to them ? In the Roman Church the Scriptures were held to be a holy mystery, to be read and interpreted to the people by priests alone. By 1530, however, copies of Tyndale's translation of the New Testament were reaching Scotland through the east-coast burghs; and, with the reading of the Gospel, arose a great yearning for 'the unsearchable riches of Christ'. A new belief and a new faith stirred in men; and the Reformers could justify their preaching by the printed Word.

Added to all this, the time was one of change. Old values were being questioned; new thoughts and beliefs were abounding. A new world had been discovered across the seas; trade and commerce were growing apace; towns were assuming a greater importance; news and ideas travelled between countries, and within countries, and were discussed as never before. There was an upsurge in the minds of men.

Finally, to the poor, and they were many, the Church was no longer the supporter of those in distress. It retained its wealth largely for its own ease. On 1 January 1559 the 'Beggars' Summonds' mysteriously appeared on the doors of friaries and hospitals. It ordered the Friars to quit their houses, which had been endowed for the maintenance of the poor, so that the poor could enter into possession of foundations which were theirs by right. And, in the first riot at Perth, it was the houses of the Grey Friars and the Black Friars, together with the Charterhouse, that were looted and despoiled.

All this lies in the background of the complex movement called the Reformation. And now, too, we must take account of the political situation which, in the end, turned a movement for the reformation of religion into a rebellion against the state.

James V had died in December 1542, three weeks after the rout at Solway Moss. Mary, Queen of Scots, was exactly one week old. For a brief period there was a struggle for the regency between Cardinal Beaton, archbishop of St Andrews, the advocate of the old faith and the old alliance, and the Earl of Arran, heir presumptive to the throne, who had leanings towards Protestantism and who favoured a new alliance with England and with an English king who had broken away from Rome. Thus the struggle for the regency had both a political and a religious aspect. Henry VIII, moreover, quick to seize his chance, had promptly sent back to Scotland a number of the Scottish lords who had been captured at Solway Moss and who, moved by bribes and promises, had entered into assurances with him to further the cause of the English alliance and to secure the marriage of the infant Mary to Henry's son, Edward, later Edward VI.[1] And with these ' assured lords ' came also the forfeited Douglas, earl of Angus, a strong supporter of an alliance with England.

Arran soon won the struggle for the regency. Beaton was seized and imprisoned by the Douglases, and, in the middle of March 1543, a Parliament formally declared Arran to be the governor of the realm. The same Parliament also passed an act permitting the lieges to have and to read the Bible in English translation (though it forbade ' disputes ' or the ' holding of opinions '), and ambassadors were sent to England to discuss the English marriage.

For those who favoured the old alliance and the old faith the position was critical. The imprisoned Beaton contrived to send messengers to France representing the danger to the Church and the peril to French interests; and, regaining his liberty, by bribery or connivance, towards the end of March, at once conspired with John Hamilton, abbot of Paisley, half-brother to Arran, a man of far stronger character than the governor and a devoted member of the Roman Church. A little later, and possibly as a result of Beaton's urgent communications, Matthew, fourth earl of Lennox, returned to Scotland from France – and Lennox could claim to be next in succession to the crown if the divorce of the first Earl of Arran were to be proved invalid.[2] Moreover, that both France and the Papacy realised the danger of the events then taking place in Scotland is clear from the appearance in Scotland, a few months later, of two French envoys, La Brosse and Ménage, and a papal legate, Grimani.

Meanwhile the negotiations with England still went on. On 1 July 1543 two treaties (the treaties of Greenwich) were agreed – a treaty of marriage: on the conclusion of her tenth year Mary was to marry Edward; and a treaty of peace: there was to be peace between Scotland and England until a year after the death of either Mary or Edward. These treaties with England, the ' old enemy ', were nevertheless far from popular. Arran was accused of having ' sold the young Queen to

---

[1] They had agreed to do all they could to break the alliance between France and Scotland; to hand over Mary into Henry's hands, to be brought up by him until she could be married to Edward; and to help Henry to become the ' director and protector ' of the realm of Scotland. Some of them had even signed secret articles that, in the event of Mary's death, they would help Henry to take over the government of Scotland. But although they had taken English gold, Henry was soon to complain that they did little in return.

[2] *Supra*, pp. 260-3.

316

the English '; the ' assured lords ', who had taken Henry's money, did little in return to help the English cause; Beaton and Hamilton actively urged the old alliance and the old faith; and finally Arran himself wavered and then changed. Little more than a week after the treaties had been solemnly ratified at Holyrood (25 August 1543), Arran suddenly re-embraced the Roman faith, did penance for his apostasy, and made Beaton and Mary of Guise, the Queen Mother, members with him in a new council of government.

It is possible that Beaton and Hamilton had reminded Arran in no uncertain terms that his legitimacy, and thereby his position as heir presumptive to the throne, depended upon the validity of his father's divorce; that a divorce granted by the Church could be rescinded by the Church; and that, if the divorce were to be rescinded, Matthew, fourth earl of Lennox, would become heir presumptive to the throne. Certainly in December 1543 a new Parliament annulled the treaties of Greenwich, renewed the alliance with France, and re-affirmed the laws against heresy. Beaton was re-instated as Chancellor. The Cardinal had not laboured in vain; but, while the Scottish Parliament had again shown itself to be little more than the tool of the faction then in power, it is also clear that the English ambassador was right when he wrote that the people ' hated England and stood by France '. Moreover, Henry VIII had alienated the Scots by his overbearing attitude. He had assumed the air of an overlord, demanding the custody of Mary and the succession in the event of her death, and he had seized, in breach of the treaty, a number of Scottish merchantmen.

This complete reversal of policy, however, meant that Henry VIII, denounced by the Pope, soon to be again at war with France, and devoid of friends and allies, had once again to reckon with a hostile Scotland in the north. Cheated of the prize which he thought was in his grasp, angry and disillusioned, Henry determined to teach the Scots a lesson. And the lesson took the form of the destructive invasions by the Earl of Hertford in 1544 and 1545. Possibly these invasions could be called ' actions for breach of promise ' – for the marriage of Mary to Edward had been broken off; certainly the ' English Wooing ' was a brutal attempt to bully the Scots into marrying their Queen to a suitor of England's choosing.

In 1544 Hertford burned Edinburgh, Holyrood and Leith; and in 1545 he boasted of the burning of seven monasteries (including Dryburgh, Melrose and Kelso) and over 240 villages and towns. Lennox, in opposition to Arran, and active in Henry's interests, also harried in the West Marches and Annandale; and the MacDonalds entered into treaty with Henry, swearing allegiance to him and binding themselves to do all they could to the annoyance of the regent.

When they saw their burning houses the women of Edinburgh might well cry out, 'Woe worth the Cardinal',[1] and lament a policy that had brought such ruin in its train; but Hertford's devastations were hardly likely to commend an English alliance. Instead they revived old hatred of the English aggressor and identified the old alliance (and the old faith) with national independence.

But if Henry's 'rough wooing' ruined his plans for the marriage of Mary and Edward (and whatever other plans he may have had in mind), on the other hand a steadily increasing attempt to crush all heresy, which Beaton now encouraged, tended to unite those who had embraced the new faith. As a result, religious persecution, culminating in the martyrdom of George Wishart (1 March 1546) had a political as well as a religious aftermath. If the new faith were to be embraced by many, and if a united Protestant party were to arise, that party could look only to England for support. And 'the sword of the Lord and of Gideon' had already been seen: at the seizure of Wishart, the 'servant of the Lord' had caused a two-handed sword to be taken from one of his followers, called John Knox.

The martyrdom of Wishart, together with a 'deadly feud' against Beaton, led to the assassination of the Cardinal in his castle at St Andrews less than three months later (29 May 1546). Knox insists in his *History*[2] that Beaton was slain in vengeance for 'the shedding of the blood of that notable instrument of God, Master George Wishart', and because Beaton had been, and remained, 'an obstinate enemy against Christ Jesus' (which, to Knox, meant an enemy to the new faith); but, significantly, the Leslies played a leading part in the murder, and there was old feud between the Leslies and the Cardinal. Knox also tells us that Beaton's dying words were, 'Fye, fye; all is gone' – and those words could be deemed prophetic.

With the help of Mary of Guise, Beaton had successfully opposed the scheming of Henry VIII and had maintained the old policies and the old faith. His murderers, on the other hand, proclaimed themselves to be the upholders of the 'true faith' and, fortifying themselves

[1] 'Woe be to the Cardinal'.
[2] A vivid account of the Reformation by one who played a leading part in the struggle. Although its bias is obvious, it is, nevertheless, remarkably trustworthy in detail.

in the murdered Cardinal's castle, looked to England for aid. Opposing parties in Scotland were taking shape; and the ' Protestants ', or ' Reformers ', holding a strong castle in arms, were there steadily joined by others of the Protestant faith – and also, perhaps, by some of little or no faith at all. Thither, to St Andrews, in the Easter of 1547, came John Knox, looking for security; there Knox received a call to become the castle's minister. But the looked-for English aid failed to come; instead, in July 1547, the ' Reformers ' in the castle were compelled to surrender to a French attack. Some were placed in French prisons; others, including John Knox, were put to row in the French galleys.[1]

Meantime, in January 1547 Henry VIII had died; and in France, in March 1547, Francis I had died. With the death of Francis I and the accession of Henry II, French court intrigue brought the house of Guise into a position of power. Francis, second duke of Guise, and his brothers became influential in French policy; and, in Scotland, their sister, Mary of Guise, was the Queen Mother. With the death of Henry VIII, Hertford, now the Protector Somerset, continued the policy of ' rough wooing '; and, although at one time he suggested safeguards for Scottish independence if only the Scots would agree to the marriage of Mary and Edward, his campaign of 1547, which included the rout and massacre of the Scottish army at Pinkie, merely stiffened the opposition to England and increased Scotland's reliance upon France.

After their success at Pinkie, the English seized and fortified Haddington, only eighteen miles from Edinburgh and a strategic centre which commanded Lothian. After their defeat at Pinkie, the Scots appealed to France for the protection of their kingdom.

Scotland's appeal was answered – but there were conditions. France would defend the liberties of Scotland, but Mary was to be sent to France so that, in due course, she could be married to the Dauphin. This was formally agreed in the treaty of Haddington (July 1548), concluded with the French plenipotentiaries in the camp of the Scottish army then besieging the town; and, a few weeks later, Mary set sail for France. Meantime Arran still remained regent. In 1549 he was granted the French duchy of Châtelherault. In the same year his half-brother, John Hamilton, succeeded the murdered Beaton as archbishop of St Andrews.

[1] Released early in 1549, Knox became a preacher in England under the Protestant Edward VI. With the accession of the Roman Catholic Mary Tudor he fled to the Continent and became a preacher to Protestant congregations – first at Frankfurt-am-Main, and then at Geneva. At Geneva he was attracted by Calvin's religious and political doctrines which were henceforth to influence all his work.

With the treaty of Haddington the five-year-old Mary had been committed to the ' faith and credit ' of the French king, and France, for the defence of Scotland, soon established there a force of some 6,000 to 8,000 well-trained soldiers led by officers who had gained experience in the wars in Italy. The treaty of Haddington, in effect, had given France a double hold over Scotland. We are told that when Henry II heard of it he ' leaped for blitheness, and was so blithe that it seemed incredible '; yet naturally so, for, as the Queen Mother wrote, the decision to send Mary to France ' put all things into the hands of the French king '.

Henry II certainly hoped that if an English army could be committed to Lothian he would be able the more easily to recover Boulogne.[1] That, indeed, happened. England lost on both fronts. There was a first, unsuccessful assault on the English garrison holding Haddington – unsuccessful, if we are to believe Knox, mainly because of two miraculous shots from the English ordnance[2] – but that was only a check; Haddington soon fell, and the English were ' clean dung out of Scotland '. On the other front, France regained Boulogne. In 1550 Scotland was included in the treaty of peace (the treaty of Boulogne) between England and France.

But, if France had saved Scotland from English designs, who was to save Scotland from the designs of France ? Henry II undoubtedly had hopes far beyond the recovery of Boulogne. We are told that when he heard of the arrival of Mary in France he declared ' France and Scotland are now one country '; and in 1550, with the conclusion of the treaty of Boulogne, he was speaking of ' maintaining the kingdom of Scotland in the obedience of our son the Dauphin '. With the treaty of Boulogne, Scotland was freed from the English, but the French forces, steadily reinforced, still stayed on; and when, in 1558, Mary Queen of Scots married the Dauphin Francis, the auld alliance seemed to be more firmly sealed than ever before.

But already there were those in Scotland who had begun to question the trend of affairs. What would be the position of Scotland when Francis became King of France ? Would not Mary remain in France

---

[1] By a treaty of 1546 England was holding Boulogne as guarantee for the payment of a French indemnity.

[2] ' Which God so conducted that . . . the bullets rebounded from the wall of the Friar Kirk to the wall of Saint Katherine's Chapel, which stood direct foiranent it, and from the wall of the said Chapel to the said Kirk wall again, so oft, that there fell more than an hundred of the French at those two shots only ' (*History of the Reformation in Scotland*, ed. Dickinson, VOL. I, p. 106).

as Queen of France ? Would she not govern her kingdom of Scotland from France ? Was that perhaps the reason for the continued maintenance of French soldiers on Scottish soil ? Would not Scotland then become little more than a French possession ?[1] And for those who had embraced the reformed religion there was a further question – would not France, true to the Church of Rome, at once determine their destruction ?

Thus, when the Reformers, calling themselves the 'Army of the Congregation of Christ Jesus', finally took up arms to defend their cause, they were able to make Protestantism a national movement against French imperialism; whereas, only a few years previously, the maintenance of the old alliance and, with it, the Roman Church had been a national movement against English aggression. In a declaration of their cause the Reformers were able to proclaim that they took 'the sword of just defence' not only for the reformation of religion, but also that 'the liberty of this our native country may remain free from the bondage and tyranny of strangers'. And those 'strangers' were the French.

[1] The danger was greater than that. Mary, before her marriage, and Mary and Francis after their marriage, entered into solemn agreements to observe and keep the laws, liberties and privileges of Scotland; and, later, both Henry II and Francis (as King of Scots) bound themselves to maintain the immunities and ancient liberties of the Scottish realm. We now know, however, that, three weeks before her marriage, Mary had signed secret documents of a vastly different purport, whereby, in the event of her decease without issue, she made over to the King of France her kingdom of Scotland and such rights as she had or might have to the kingdom of England. (See *Source Book of Scottish History*, VOL. II (2nd edn.), pp. 158-60. For Mary's rights to the English crown, see *infra*, p. 325.)

CHAPTER XXXII

The Reformation - II

IT IS possible that, in the period immediately following the treaty of Boulogne, Arran (now Duke of Châtelherault, and still Regent) and his half-brother, John Hamilton (now Archbishop of St Andrews in succession to the murdered Beaton), were quick to see that the sending of Mary to France and the continued presence of French troops on Scottish soil might result in an alliance between the Protestants and those who, for various reasons, feared or disliked the increasing influence of the French. Thus the issue of what is known as ' Hamilton's Catechism ' may have been part of an endeavour to meet the danger by trying to satisfy some of the demands for reform within the Church.

In January 1552 a Provincial Council of the Scottish Church had openly admitted that neither the prelates nor the inferior clergy had, as a rule, ' such proficiency in the knowledge of the holy Scriptures as to be able, by their own efforts, rightly to instruct the people in the Catholic faith and other things necessary to their salvation '; and accordingly, to combat such clerical ignorance, the Council had decreed that a Catechism in the Scots tongue, which had already been prepared and approved, should be printed and put in use. ' Hamilton's Catechism ' was published and distributed to the churches in the following August. Its publication was significant. Described on its title-page as ' ane commone and catholik instructioun of the christin people in materis of our Catholik faith and religioun ', and written in simple and moving language, it reveals, in places, a spirit of compromise, an attempt to meet some of the points raised by the reformers. Indeed, one notable passage on justification by faith was little different from the declarations of Martin Luther and from the views for which Patrick Hamilton had been burned.[1]

But, admirable as it was, this attempt at instruction and reform came too late. The Catechism itself helped to call attention to the ignorance of the clergy which had prompted it; and the corruption in

---

[1] See *Source Book of Scottish History*, VOL. II (2nd edn.), pp. 145-50. Archbishop Hamilton was certainly not opposed to some measure of reform, but it should be noted that tradition ascribed the authorship of the ' Catechism ' to John Winram, sub-prior of St Andrews, who later joined the Reformers and took part in drafting the ' Confession of Faith ' and the ' Book of Discipline '.

the Church was not solely due to ignorance. Moreover those who had feared the growing French influence in Scottish affairs were now finding that their fears were justified.

In December 1553 Mary became eleven years old and so entered her twelfth year. The French court soon found lawyers to maintain that, being in her twelfth year, the Queen of Scots was virtually twelve years old and was therefore legally of age to govern in her own name. That, in effect, meant that, while Mary would continue to reside in France, Scotland would be governed in her name by her own delegates. And who could be more suitable to govern Scotland in the Queen's name than the Queen's own mother, Mary of Guise ? In a Parliament of April 1554 the regency was formally transferred from Arran to the Queen Mother. Technically Arran resigned; but he was certainly not anxious to demit office, and pressure (or bribery) was brought to bear upon him – in particular, he was freed from accounting for all his intromissions with crown property (including the crown jewels and furnishings) during the period of his regency.

With Mary of Guise as regent, there was an immediate increase of French control. Frenchmen were appointed to offices of state, Scottish fortresses were garrisoned by French soldiers, and the French ' began to think themselves more than masters in Scotland '. As early as 1555, amid murmurings of lords and commons alike, it was necessary to pass an act against speaking evil of the Queen Regent and the French; and undoubtedly there was a steadily growing antipathy to both the French officers and the French soldiers, some of whom were guilty of outrage and excess. Nevertheless those who had embraced the new faith enjoyed toleration – for a while. English Protestants were allowed to find refuge in Scotland from Roman Catholic persecution under Mary Tudor, who had succeeded to the English throne in 1553; and in the autumn of 1555 John Knox was allowed to visit Scotland from Geneva and to stay, preaching and exhorting, for well-nigh a year. Possibly, in the political interests of France, and to combat any claim by the Earl of Arran to the Scottish throne, the Queen Regent was endeavouring to avoid serious trouble in Scotland. But again, John Hamilton, archbishop of St Andrews, was the half-brother of Arran, and Arran would succeed to the throne if Mary were to die without issue. Since the young Queen's health was reported to be far from good, the Hamiltons, in the opposite camp, may also have wished at this juncture to be ' well thought of '.

But with toleration the numbers of the Reformers steadily increased.

Already they were strong in the east-coast burghs and in the south-west; many lairds and barons were embracing the new faith; and now even some of the nobility were supporting the Protestant preachers.

Early in 1557 there was apparently some hope of a rising, both political and religious. In March a number of Scots lords wrote to John Knox at Geneva inviting him to return to Scotland where he would find the faithful ' ready to jeopard lives and goods in the forward setting of the glory of God '; then they decided that the time was ' not yet ripe ', and Knox, having reached Dieppe in October, received there further letters advising him to stay awhile. In the following December (1557), however, some of the leading Protestant nobles, calling themselves the ' Congregation of Christ ', subscribed a Common Band (which, being a religious band, was later called a ' Covenant '), binding themselves to ' apply our whole power, substance, and our very lives, to maintain, set forward, and establish the most blessed word of God ' and to ' labour at our possibility to have faithful Ministers purely and truly to minister Christ's Evangel and Sacraments to his people '. And thereafter, as Knox admits in his *History*, ' the Lords and Barons professing Christ Jesus ', that is, the Protestants, frequently convened in council, and their discussions in council covered both religion and ' policy '.

The ' face ' of a reformed church was revealing itself. Some of the Protestant lords openly associated themselves with the preachers; some maintained preachers in their own households; and the leading preachers found that more and more they could rely upon temporal support.

Sometime in the following year a number of the ' temporal lords and barons ' who were desirous of reform presented certain ' articles ' to the Queen Regent. They spoke of the ungodly and dissolute lives led by spiritual men, and the failure of Provincial Councils to secure reform; they asked for the sincere preaching of God's word in parish churches on Sundays (or at least on every third or fourth Sunday), for more qualified curates and vicars, for the Sacraments to be adminis-tered in the English tongue, and for the common prayers and litanies also to be said in English. They also asked for some mitigation of clerical exactions at Easter-time and at the time of burials, and some reform in the ' long process ' and ' exorbitant expenses ' of the con-sistorial courts. The Queen Regent passed these articles to Archbishop Hamilton and, at his instance, they were considered at a Provincial Council held early in 1559 – again an indication of the Queen Regent's desire for an understanding and of Hamilton's interest in reform. Some reforms were attempted – clerical exactions were to be mitigated,[1] and there was to be more efficient supervision of the parishes and of the lives and qualifications of parish priests; but the request for services and the administration of the Sacraments in the English tongue was refused.[2]

Meantime in France, in April 1558, Mary had married the Dauphin, Francis, and in England, in November 1558, Mary Tudor had died and had been succeeded by Elizabeth. And, with the accession of Elizabeth, most of the anti-papal legislation of Henry VIII's reign was renewed and the prayer-book of Edward VI brought back into use. Once more the Reformers in Scotland could look to England for aid.

But Elizabeth, Henry VIII's last surviving child, was the daughter of Anne Boleyn; she knew that the Roman Church had never recognised the divorce from Catherine of Aragon; and, with that, she knew also that, in the eyes of Rome, she was neither a legitimate daughter of Henry VIII nor legitimate Queen of England. In the eyes of Rome, and of the great continental Roman Catholic powers, France and Spain, the rightful Queen of England was Mary, Queen of Scots, the direct and lawful descendant of the marriage of James IV and Margaret Tudor, even though Henry VIII had endeavoured to cut out the descendants of his elder sister Margaret in favour of the descendants of his younger sister Mary.[3] Within two months of Elizabeth's accession, Francis and Mary, King and Queen of Scotland, and the future King and Queen of France, had assumed the title of King and Queen of England and Ireland. The policy of France was abundantly clear, and for Elizabeth, as for the Protestants in Scotland, politics and religion were inseparably intertwined.

And, at this very juncture, Mary of Guise, the Queen Regent, appears to have decided that the days of toleration and compromise were over. How far she was influenced by an increasing contempt of her authority, how far she was influenced by instructions reaching her from France, it is impossible to say. It may be that, with the agreement

[1] Notably those at burials – the 'corpse present', the 'kirk cow', and 'the grey cloak that haps the bed'; exactions which James V had tried in vain to end or to reduce.
[2] Though it may have been partly to meet that request that the 'Twopenny Faith' – a moving statement, in the vernacular, of the nature and meaning of the 'Sacrament of the Altar' which was to be read to the people at the time of the Sacrament – was now published (1559).
[3] See the Table on p. 282, and infra, p. 333, n. 2.

of the first draft of the treaty of Câteau-Cambrésis (which not only brought the war between France and Spain to an end but also marked a drawing together of France and Spain for the extirpation of ' heresy '), she received instructions from France to crush the growing Scottish movement for reform. According to Knox, in his hatred of the Regent, and of all her actions, she now began ' to spew forth and disclose the latent venom of her double heart '. Certainly there was a change in her attitude when an ' intercession ' on behalf of the Protestant preachers was received with the forthright answer that they would be ' banished out of Scotland, albeit they preached as truly as ever did St Paul '.

The preachers continuing to preach, the more important of them were summoned to Stirling ' to underlie the law ' (10 May 1559); whereupon the ' brethren ', the Protestant lords and lairds, assembled at Perth, though without armour, to support their preachers. And ' in this meantime that the preachers were summoned ', John Knox again returned to Scotland (2 May 1559). At Perth, on 11 May, he preached a sermon ' vehement against idolatry '. A boy threw a stone; an image was broken; a riot broke loose; and the houses of the Black Friars and the Grey Friars, together with the Charterhouse, were looted and despoiled.

No government could allow such lawlessness to pass unchecked. The Regent assembled her forces and marched towards Perth. The Army of the Congregation gathered in arms. The reformation-rebellion had begun.

There was some marching and counter-marching, but little fighting. The Queen Regent was largely dependent upon her small force of trained French troops, for many of the nobility, with their followings (the basis of any Scottish army), were either favourable to the Re-formers, or resentful of the Regent's reliance upon the French, or, perhaps, hopeful of gaining something of the wealth of a Church that was now in peril. The Reformers, on the other hand, had no forces comparable with the trained French levies. Nevertheless, by the end of June the Army of the Congregation had succeeded in occupying Edin-burgh, while the Regent and her French troops fortified themselves in Leith – a useful strategic base for the recapture of Edinburgh as well as a port to which French supplies and reinforcements could be sent.

A series of useless challenges and answers between Edinburgh and Leith now ensued. Wearying of these, the Lords of the Congregation ' deposed ' the Queen Regent, in the names of Francis and Mary (thereby assuming a delegated authority which they did not possess), transferred the government of the realm to a new ' Great Council ', and prepared for an assault on Leith (October 1559). But the long period of ' challenges and answers ' had enabled the French to fortify Leith to some purpose. The assault was repulsed; more than that, the French issued out of Leith and so harassed the Reformers that ' many fled away secretly, and those that did abide (a very few excepted) appeared destitute of counsel and manhood '. The Army of the Congregation retreated in disorder from Edinburgh to Stirling – part going thence to Glasgow and part to Fife.

Now, more than ever, English aid was essential to save the Reformers from disaster and utter defeat. And now, at last, Elizabeth, who had hitherto confined her help to smuggling small sums of money across the Border – some of which had been intercepted and had never reached the Reformers – actively intervened. In January 1560 an English fleet under Admiral Winter anchored in the Forth, and so cut the French sea-communications. No further supplies and reinforcements could reach either the Regent in Leith or the French troops who had set out to engage the forces of the Reformers in Fife. At the beginning of April an English army, under Lord Grey, crossed the Border, and combined English and Scottish Protestant forces began a second siege of Leith held mainly by the troops of Roman Catholic France.

Hitherto, for many reasons, Elizabeth had been reluctant to intervene openly in the Scottish struggle. By the Anglo-French clauses in the treaty of Câteau-Cambrésis England was pledged not to make war on France. That might not mean much – in those times[1] – but intervention in Scotland might lead to a war with France for which England was wholly unprepared. Elizabeth, too, was not as yet secure on the English throne; if she helped rebellious subjects in another realm might not rebellious subjects in her own realm seek outside help in a like way ? – and there were still many Roman Catholics in England who might rise against her Protestant policy. Moreover, one of the leading Scottish reformers was a certain John Knox, who had written a book against women rulers; and although Knox's book – *The First Blast of the Trumpet against the Monstrous Regiment of Women* – had been directed against the rule of Mary of Guise and Mary Tudor (both Roman Catholics), and although he later wrote to Elizabeth grudgingly conceding that if she humbled her heart she could yet prove herself to be exceptional – like the blessed Deborah in Israel –

[1] Nevertheless both Winter and Grey were instructed that they were acting on their own authority; thus, if necessary, Elizabeth could officially disown their actions.

many of the statements in his work had aroused her natural resentment.[1]

Elizabeth had intervened solely in her own interests. Her belated decision to send the much-needed help to the Army of the Congregation – a step that had been constantly urged by Cecil – was dictated by the danger of French support for Mary's claim to the English throne, which has already been noted. Immediately after the death of Mary Tudor, Henry II of France had had Mary publicly proclaimed in Paris as 'Queen of England, Scotland and Ireland'; Francis and Mary had assumed the English royal arms; and, in July 1559, Francis and Mary had become King and Queen of France. To fail to intervene might well give France a control over Scotland that would imperil Elizabeth's throne. Was it not evident that French imperialism might include England as well as Scotland? The old danger, feared by Henry VIII, that France might use Scotland as a northern base, was too great not to be met.

Thus Elizabeth's intervention could be regarded as a purely defensive move; and the treaty of Berwick (February 1560), whereby English aid became a reality,[2] was little more than a treaty of mutual defence. It declared that because the French intended to conquer Scotland and to unite it to the crown of France, therefore Elizabeth, at the request of the Scots, took Scotland under her protection and maintenance, but only for the preservation of its freedoms and liberties and to save it from conquest, and only during the time of the marriage of Francis and Mary and for one year thereafter. English forces were to be sent with all speed into Scotland; and the Scots, in turn, promised to send support to England should England be invaded by France. Finally, and because Elizabeth did not relish the thought of aiding subjects who were in rebellion against their lawful rulers, the Scots testified and declared their due obedience to their Queen provided she

[1] Three brief passages will suffice to explain that resentment –

'To promote a Woman to bear rule, superiority, dominion or empire above any realm, nation or city is repugnant to Nature; is contumely to God, a thing most contrarious to his revealed will and approved ordinance; and, finally, it is the subversion of good order and of all equity and justice.'

'Where Women reign or be in authority, vanity must needs be preferred to virtue; ambition and pride to temperance and modesty; and, finally, avarice must needs devour equity and justice.'

'As for Woman, it is no more possible that she, being set aloft in authority above man, shall resist the motions of pride, than it is able to the weak reed or to the turning weathercock not to bow or turn at the vehemency of the unconstant wind.'

[2] Winter's fleet had entered the Forth *before* the conclusion of the treaty of Berwick; but the English army, under Lord Grey, entered Scotland only after the treaty had been signed.

and her husband, the King of France did nothing that tended to the subversion and oppression of the just and ancient liberties of their kingdom. In the whole treaty there was not a word about religion. To Elizabeth the crisis was a political one; and Knox was later to speak of her as ' neither good Protestant nor yet resolute Papist '. It has been well said that English forces took part in the final battle of the Scottish reformation-rebellion purely because Elizabeth was not sure of the validity of her mother's marriage-certificate.

Leith, although stoutly defended by the French troops of the Queen Regent against a new assault and siege by combined English and Scottish forces, was at last starved into surrender. Mary of Guise, moreover, ill and dying, had entered the castle of Edinburgh on 1 April for greater security and medical attention, and had died there on the night of 10-11 June. With the arrival of commissioners from France authorised to negotiate a peace, the Scottish reformation-rebellion came to an end with the treaty of Edinburgh (July 1560).

The treaty of Edinburgh was made between England and France – for the French commissioners held that their King and Queen could not conclude a treaty with Scottish subjects who had been in rebellion against them. By the treaty, France recognised Elizabeth's right and title to the English throne; Francis and Mary were to abstain from using and bearing the title and arms of the sovereign of England and Ireland; the French and the English forces were to be withdrawn from Scotland; and there were to be no future warlike preparations in England against France, or in France against England. Again not a word was said about religion. The treaty was the natural corollary to Elizabeth's defensive intervention; by it she secured the withdrawal of the French forces from Scotland and her recognition, by France, as the lawful Queen of England.

In addition to the treaty, however, certain ' Concessions ' were granted to the Scots to settle essentially Scottish questions. By the Concessions the fortifications of Leith were to be destroyed; the French troops there were to be sent home[1] and no French forces were again to be brought into Scotland; no stranger (in effect, no Frenchman) was henceforth to hold office under the Crown; there was to be a general act of oblivion, and Francis and Mary were to take no action against any who had joined the Congregation; the Estates of Scotland

---

[1] A letter from Cecil to the English Council tersely comments that the French were glad to be gone; the English were glad to carry them (in English ships); and the Scots were glad to curse them on their way.

22

were to meet in August 1560; and finally, on the question of religion, it was granted that, ' Whereas on the part of the nobles and people of Scotland there have been presented certain articles concerning religion and certain other points in which the lords deputies [the French commissioners] would by no means meddle, as being of such importance that they judged them proper to be remitted to the King and Queen; therefore the said nobles of Scotland have engaged that in the ensuing Convention of Estates some persons of quality shall be chosen to repair to their Majesties and remonstrate[1] to them the state of their affairs . . . and to understand their intention and pleasure. . . . '

Thus, while Elizabeth had gained the security and recognition for which her English contingents had fought, the whole question of religion, for which alone many of those in the Army of the Congregation had fought, was left undecided – to be submitted to Francis and Mary for their consideration. But, for Knox and his fellow-preachers, and for many of the lords, lairds and burgesses who had joined the Army of the Congregation, the whole struggle had been one to secure the ' true religion '. To them, this happy victory, this glorious end, had shown ' how wondrously the light of Christ Jesus had prevailed '. Hence, although religion had been passed by in the treaty of Edinburgh, and virtually passed by in the Concessions, the Reformers were quick to turn a political victory into a religious victory also. To them it was essential to establish the true religion forthwith. There were too many risks inherent in delay: notably, there could be little doubt about the answer that would come from Francis and Mary – if, indeed, they deigned to send any answer at all.

The Estates met in August 1560, in accordance with the Concessions, and forthwith, despite the wording of the Concessions, the authority and jurisdiction of the Pope were abolished, the celebration of the Mass was forbidden, a Confession of Faith (a full statement of Protestant doctrine, drawn up by the ministers and engrossed in the register of Parliament) was approved, and all doctrine and practice contrary to the Confession were condemned.

This meeting of the Estates (called the ' Reformation Parliament ') was attended by over a hundred small barons and lairds – all fervent Protestants – who claimed a right to sit as freeholders of the King, although, as we have seen, neither the act of 1426 nor that of 1428 had ever been fully operative.[2] But the actual wording of the Concessions had been, ' the Estates shall be summoned to the Parliament

[1] Represent. [2] Supra, pp. 213-15.

according to custom: and it shall be lawful for all those to be present at that meeting who are in use to be present . . . .' Were these small barons and lairds ' in use to be present ' ? Was the Parliament of August 1560 a lawful Parliament ? More than that, in the Concessions the whole question of religion was to be remitted to Francis and Mary for *their* decision. But Parliament itself had legislated in matters of religion. Were these Protestant enactments of the Reformation Parliament lawful and valid ?

Mary never ratified either the treaty of Edinburgh or the enactments of the Reformation Parliament.[1] Thus, throughout the whole of her personal rule from 1561 to 1567 the religious question remained unsettled. Shortly after her abdication (or deposition) in 1567, however, another meeting of the Estates re-enacted the anti-papal legislation of 1560 and again engrossed the Confession of Faith in the register of Parliament; and this time the royal assent was given by the Regent Moray in the name of the one-year-old King James VI. More than that, when the infant King was crowned, the Earl of Morton, in the name of the King, took a new coronation oath which included a clause that the sovereign would maintain the true religion and would preserve it to the utmost of his power.

A Protestant Church had supplanted the Church of Rome; the old alliance with France had been broken; and a new alliance with England had been born. Two Protestant countries, Scotland and England, were drawing together, and the way was being prepared for James VI to succeed Elizabeth and to rule over both realms as a Protestant king.

Nevertheless the Reformation had fallen far short of all that Knox and his fellow ministers had hoped and prayed for. While the Confession of Faith had been engrossed in the register of Parliament, the Book of Discipline – a plan, drawn up by Knox and others of the ministers, for the establishment of the reformed church, and its endowment out of the wealth that had been bestowed upon the Church of Rome[2] – had been passed by. The old church still retained the larger part of its revenues; its prelates and priests remained undisturbed in their benefices; its structure was still intact. A new faith had been accepted; but the new church had been given neither establishment nor endowment for the furtherance of the faith.

[1] To have ratified the treaty of Edinburgh would have meant abandoning her claim to the English throne; to have ratified the enactments of the Reformation Parliament would have meant abandoning her religion.

[2] See *infra*, pp. 348-51.

CHAPTER XXXIII

Mary Queen of Scots

FOR A whole year – from August 1560 to August 1561 – Scotland had no established government. Mary was still in France; her mother, the Queen Regent, had died, and no new regent had been appointed to take her place. For some twelve months the government appears to have been largely in the hands of the Lord James Stewart, Mary's half-brother, and the Duke of Châtelherault, both important leaders of the victorious Congregation, together with William Maitland of Lethington acting as their Secretary.

Probably neither the Lord James Stewart nor Châtelherault desired or expected the return of Mary. The Lord James could not forget that only the accident of birth had debarred him from the crown.[1] Châtelherault certainly remembered that he was next in succession to the throne; and, if Queen Elizabeth could be persuaded to a Protestant marriage with his son, a Hamilton might yet rule Scotland, and England too. Indeed, following the meeting of the ' Reformation Parliament ', an embassy was sent to England to propose that marriage, and stress was laid on the fact that the Hamiltons were heirs presumptive to the Scottish crown; but Elizabeth replied that she was ' not at present disposed ' to marry.

Whatever may have been the hopes of the Lord James Stewart and the Hamiltons, however, they were rudely shattered by the unexpected death of Mary's husband, Francis II, in December 1560, and by Mary's resolve to return to her own country. No longer Queen of France, she was still Queen of Scots. And what would be the outcome when Mary, brought up in the Roman church, returned to govern a nominally Protestant realm ?

Lesley states that a number of the Roman Catholic bishops and lords knowing of Mary's intention to return to govern her own kingdom, sent messengers to her urging her to land in the north where she would find faithful and true service from all. Certainly from the Protestant party, the Lord James Stewart went to France to give counsel to the Queen, and his counsel was that she should ' press no matters of

[1] He was a natural son of James V by Margaret Erskine, daughter of John, fourth Lord Erskine.

332

religion '. Perhaps, too, he promised that she could have her own Mass privately in her own chapel.[1] The Queen determined to follow the advice of the Lord James. On 19 August 1561, Mary, not yet nineteen years old, landed in Scotland to take over the government of her native realm; and she landed, not in the north, but at Leith.

According to Knox, ' the very face of heaven, the time of her arrival, did manifestly speak what comfort was brought unto this country with her, to wit, sorrow, dolour, darkness and all impiety. For, in the memory of man, that day of the year was never seen a more dolorous face of the heaven than was at her arrival. . . . The sun was not seen to shine two days before, nor two days after. That forewarning gave God unto us '. To Knox, Mary was a Papist, and so to be distrusted and feared. But, although Mary did little that touched the reformed church, the six years of her personal rule were to close tempestuously, with ' sorrow and dolour ' for the Queen herself.

By the treaty of Edinburgh, Elizabeth had secured France's recognition of her right and title to the English throne. Mary, however, had refused, and continued to refuse, to ratify that treaty, thereby maintaining her claim to be the rightful Queen of England – or at the very least to be recognised as Elizabeth's rightful successor. Elizabeth, on her part, equally consistently refused to acknowledge Mary's right to the succession.[2] The attitudes of both queens were natural. Mary regarded herself as the rightful Queen of England; if she was willing to accept Elizabeth as the *de facto* Queen, surely she could be given recognition of her right, *de jure*, to be Elizabeth's successor. Elizabeth, on the other hand, feared that to acknowledge Mary as her successor would be to strengthen Roman Catholic opposition to her own rule; it might even encourage some zealot to cut short her life and thereby hasten the accession of the legitimist Roman Catholic Queen. Slightly

---

[1] See the account of the instructions given to the Lord James (Knox's *History*, ed. Dickinson, VOL. I, pp. 354-5); though that account may have been coloured by the light of subsequent events.

[2] By Henry VIII's will, and by act of Parliament, the succession went to the issue of Henry's younger sister Mary, and not to the issue of his elder sister Margaret. If Elizabeth were to die without issue, then the crown of England was due to pass to a Seymour (see the Table on p. 282). Or was Henry VIII's will, with its accompanying confirmation by Parliament, irrevocable ? Could not the throne of England pass to Mary, Queen of Scots, the descendant of his elder sister Margaret ? The situation was complex and dangerous; and, had Elizabeth not recovered from an attack of small-pox in 1562, England might have been torn by a civil war between those who favoured the Seymours and a Protestant succession and those who favoured Mary Stewart and a return to the Roman faith.

to vary her own words, an acknowledgment of Mary's right might be tantamount to wrapping herself in her own winding-sheet.

Thus it is easy to understand why Maitland of Lethington, who was now Mary's Secretary, and who, with the Lord James Stewart, largely influenced Mary's policy in the early years of her reign, was unable to secure any form of reciprocal recognition between the two queens. Moreover the difficulties of Lethington and the Lord James lay not only in trying to curb Mary's ambitious claims by some form of compromise agreement, but also in trying to restrain a strong Protestant faction which demanded that Mary should be compelled to embrace the new faith and rule a Protestant country as a Protestant Queen.

On the very first Sunday after Mary's landing a riotous demonstration broke out at Holyrood against the Mass that was celebrated in the chapel royal for the Queen and her household[1]: and then it was the Lord James Stewart, seeking to compromise, or merely fulfilling a promise he had made to the Queen, who held the door against the angry mob. On the following day Mary – probably on the advice of the Lord James – issued a proclamation in which she ordered the state of religion which she found 'publicly and universally standing' at the time of her arrival to be maintained, but in which she also forbade all tumults and interference with her servants and household for any cause whatsoever.

There were murmurings among 'the godly'; but Lethington argued that, with time, Mary might yet be brought round to 'sweet reasonableness'; and a calmer atmosphere soon prevailed. As one ardent reformer declared, 'At the first I heard every man say, " Let us hang the priest "; but after that they had been twice or thrice in the Abbey [of Holyrood, at the Queen's Court], all that fervency was past. I think there be some enchantment whereby men are bewitched '. And the enchantment was undoubtedly the Queen.

A few months later there was further compromise when the Privy Council agreed to some financial provision for the urgent needs of the reformed Church. Hitherto, with the rejection of the Book of Discipline, the Roman clergy, still in legal possession of their benefices, had continued to enjoy their revenues, while the ministers of the reformed church had had no assured incomes and were living as 'poor amid the poor', dependent upon the 'benevolence' of others. Now,

---

[1] Possibly a Protestant service had been or was being held in the adjoining Abbey Church which was then in use as a parish church for Canongate.

by an act of the Privy Council, one-third of the revenues of all benefices was to be collected annually and used partly to provide stipends for the ministers and partly for the ' support of the Queen's Majesty '. To Knox, this was to give the reformed church only part of one-third of all that which it should enjoy of right. His comment was, ' I see two parts freely given to the Devil [the two-thirds still retained by the holders of Roman benefices – though some had embraced the reformed faith], and the third must be divided between God and the Devil [the one-third to be divided between the ministers and the Queen]. Well . . . ere it be long the Devil shall have three parts of the Third[1]; and judge you then what God's portion shall be.' Certainly as the years passed by, the Queen took more and more of the one-third and less and less was available for the stipends of the ministers.[2]

Nor, despite certain hesitancies, did Mary show any singular favour to those of her own faith. When, in 1562, during a ' progress ' in the North, the Queen met with ' manifest tokens of disobedience ' from the Gordons, she allowed the Lord James Stewart to crush the most powerful Roman Catholic family in Scotland. The Lord James, to whom Mary had recently granted the earldom of Moray (though the grant was then kept secret), defeated Huntly (who probably still held the earldom of Moray *de jure*) in a pitched battle at Corrichie. Huntly died on the field, possibly from apoplexy; the Gordons were forfeited; and shortly thereafter the Lord James received a further charter of the earldom of Moray, the grant being now made public.[3] In the following year (1563), moreover, Archbishop Hamilton and a number of the Roman clergy were warded for celebrating Mass in violation of the proclamation of August 1561. Not unnaturally there were many who began to ask what was to be feared from a queen who crushed Huntly and who allowed the priests of her own church to suffer for their faith.

But Mary had not embraced the reformed faith, and the more fervent Protestants, including John Knox, were not blind to the dangers

---

[1] That is, none of the one-third would be available for the ministers.

[2] The total of the one-third varied from year to year, owing to deductions, remissions and exceptions; roughly, it amounted to about £72,000, of which at first about £26,000 was allowed to the ministers. The latter sum steadily decreased, and, moreover, the diminishing sum had to be allocated to an increasing number of ministers, exhorters and readers.

[3] It would appear, indeed, that Mary elevated the Protestant Lord James Stewart at the expense of the Roman Catholic Earl of Huntly, and Knox, in his *History*, speaks of ' malice ' between Huntly and the Lord James – which would be understandable.

that still threatened. Preaching at the time of the Parliament in 1563, Knox did not spare his words –

The Queen, say ye, will not agree with us. Ask ye of her that which by God's word ye may justly require, and if she will not agree with you in God, ye are not bound to agree with her in the Devil. Let her plainly understand so far of your minds; and steal not from your former stoutness in God, and he shall prosper you in your enterprises.

That outspoken passage was evoked by the current rumours of a marriage for the Queen. For if Mary were to marry into one of the great Roman Catholic houses – if she were to marry Don Carlos of Spain, as was then bruited, or any of ' the children of France, Spain or Austria ' – then the Protestant faith in Scotland (and in England also) might well be gravely imperilled. So, in the same sermon, Knox sounded the warning,

This, my Lords, will I say, . . . whensoever the Nobility of Scotland professing the Lord Jesus, consents than an infidel (and all Papists are infidels) shall be head to your Sovereign, ye do so far as in ye lieth to banish Christ Jesus from this Realm; ye bring God's vengeance upon the country, a plague upon yourself, and perchance ye shall do small comfort to your Sovereign.

For this sermon Knox was summoned before the Queen[1]; and when, angrily, she demanded, ' What have ye to do with my marriage ? Or what are ye within this Commonwealth ? ' there came the quick reply, ' A subject born within the same, Madam. And albeit I neither

[1] This was Knox's fourth and final interview with Mary. Although the accounts all come from Knox's own pen (in his *History*) certain notable passages in the earlier interviews deserve quotation. In the first interview (4 September 1561), after Knox, in the pulpit of St Giles, had thundered against the Mass, he had argued that subjects might resist their Princes in matters of religion; to which Mary, ' amazed ', had answered, ' Well, then, I perceive that my subjects shall obey you [Knox], and not me; and shall do what they list, and not what I command: and so must I be subject to them, and not they to me.' To which came Knox's reply that he sought only ' that both princes and subjects obey God ', which, to him, meant ' embrace the Protestant faith '. The second interview (15 December 1562) came after Knox had preached against the vanity of Princes and the danger that they were more exercised in their delights (including the Queen's dancing) than in reading and hearing God's word; and when, at his dismissal from the interview, some had muttered, ' He is not afraid ', he had answered ' Why should the pleasing face of a gentlewoman effray me ? I have looked in the faces of many angry men, and yet have not been afraid above measure.' At the third interview (in April 1563), when the Queen had asked Knox to use his influence to prevent the Roman Catholics in the West from being punished for observing their own rites, Knox had reminded her that princes and subjects alike were bound to observe the laws, that the ' Sword of Justice is God's ', and that if the ruler failed to do justice, then the servants of God [the Protestants] could do so.

be Earl, Lord, nor Baron within it, yet has God made me (how abject that ever I be in your eyes), a profitable member within the same.'

Knox's fears were certainly not without foundation. In western Europe the Wars of Religion had begun. The Netherlands were held down by Spain, and a Spanish army was in occupation. In France the Huguenots were fighting to avoid suppression. At Trent a General Council of the Roman Church, while calling for reform in the Church and a higher zeal for the Roman faith, had also rejected all Protestant doctrine and had called for the extirpation of heresy.

Elizabeth, too, was not blind to the dangers that threatened. She left Mary in no doubt that any marriage with France, Spain or Austria would inevitably mean hostility between England and Scotland. And yet the only alternative that Elizabeth proposed was marriage to her own favourite, Lord Robert Dudley, earl of Leicester – whom she was probably reluctant to lose, and to whom, as merely a newly elevated subject, Mary was not in the least attracted.

For a whole year the marriage of the Queen of Scots was the subject of diplomatic activity, rumour and counter-rumour. Then, in the autumn of 1564, Elizabeth persuaded Mary to allow the forfeited Matthew, fourth earl of Lennox, to return to Scotland[1]; and his son, Darnley, followed early in 1565. What Elizabeth's motives were, we shall never know. The Lennox Stewarts were suspected of trafficking with Papists, and, for a time, the Earl and his wife had been imprisoned on that suspicion. If Mary (now twenty-two) were to fall in love with ' the long lad ' Darnley (aged twenty), a marriage between Mary and Darnley would unite the two nearest claimants to Elizabeth's throne[2]: and both were Roman Catholics. It may be that Elizabeth, anxious to keep Leicester at her court, allowed her personal feelings to overcome her statecraft. Sir James Melville, Mary's ambassador at the English court, says that Elizabeth hoped that Mary would be attracted to Darnley and so would forget Leicester.[3] Or again, it may be that Elizabeth secretly hoped that Mary would fall in love with Darnley – better a marriage with Darnley then a marriage into one of the great continental Roman Catholic Houses.

[1] Lennox had gone to England in 1544 where, later that year, he married Margaret daughter of Archibald, sixth earl of Angus, and Margaret Tudor (see the Table on p. 262). He had remained in England, had entered Henry VIII's service, and had been given English estates. As a result, he was declared guilty of treason and forfeited.

[2] See the Table on p. 282.

[3] It is to be remembered, however, that Melville wrote his *Memoirs* late in life, when memory may have given way to imagination.

All this is conjecture; the facts are that Darnley arrived in Scotland in February 1565 and that the question of Mary's marriage was quickly settled. By the middle of April 1565 she had so fallen in love with Darnley that ' she could forsake all others and be content with her own choice '.

On 29 July 1565 Mary married Darnley according to Roman Catholic rites.[1] The day before the marriage Mary had issued a proclamation, by heralds, that Henry, Lord Darnley, should be ' named and styled ' King; and, on the day after the marriage, the proclamation was made again when, of all those who were present, not one so much as said ' Amen ', save only Darnley's father, Lennox, who cried out, ' God save his Grace '. That prayer was to be unanswered.

These details are significant. It was not simply, as Buchanan avers, that heralds had been given the functions of council and parliament. Nor was it simply the old jealousy of a noble house raised to kingship. There was something more. The sudden marriage with Darnley, taking place within six months of his arrival in Scotland, affected too many interests, and too many persons and parties. The Queen had married a Lennox Stewart, and the Hamiltons saw an end to their long held hopes of kingship. For the Lord James Stewart earl of Moray, and for Lethington, the marriage spelled the end of compromise, the end of their wishful-thinking that Mary could be ' allured into sweet reasonableness ', the end, too, of their ' guidance ' of the Queen. For Knox and all those who were fervent for the Protestant faith, the marriage was a union of Papists, and was to be feared for all that might follow. But, for Mary herself, her marriage meant a new chance – a chance to take everything into her own hands, to be free from the old restraints of Moray and Lethington, and from the unwelcome advice of Knox.

A fortnight before her marriage, and doubtless to allay alarm and to disarm all opposition, Mary had issued two proclamations stating that she had no intention of molesting her good subjects in the freedom of their consciences and religion. Nevertheless, a number of the

[1] Mary and Darnley were both grandchildren of Margaret Tudor (see the Table on p. 282), and, since they were so closely related to one another, a papal dispensation was necessary to enable them to marry. Mary, however, was so anxious for the marriage of her choice that she could not wait for the dispensation and, when it was granted, it had to be antedated. It is also to be noted that the dispensation was granted on a promise by Mary and Darnley that they would defend the Roman faith to the utmost of their power, but, as it happens, their marriage and its aftermath actually freed Scotland from the danger of a counter-reformation supported by France or Spain.

Protestant lords had convened at Stirling, in arms, determined to demand complete assurances for the maintenance of the reformed faith before they would give their consent to the Queen's marriage. Mary, however, had no intention of asking for their consent: and by the haste of her marriage forestalled their demand. Moreover, when the Protestant lords still remained together in arms, the Queen, in answer, assembled her own supporters to oppose them.

But no longer were the Protestant lords united as of old. Moray and Lethington, by their previous policy of appeasement and compromise, had split the ranks of the Army of the Congregation of Christ Jesus. Some had supported them; others had opposed them, foretelling that no good would come from shaking hands with the Devil. Long, long ago, Moray had guarded the chapel door of the Queen's Mass; long, long ago, Knox had urged that the Queen should be compelled to embrace the new faith. Knox had claimed the right of subjects to resist the idolatry of their rulers; Moray had opposed him. Knox and Moray had become strangers to one another.

And now two armed forces were in the field – one led by Moray, the other by the Queen. On 26 August 1565 those Protestant lords and lairds still willing to fight under Moray and Châtelherault (though not solely for the old cause of the ' true Evangel ') rode into Edinburgh. They were only some 1,200 strong. Hearing that the Queen with her supporters was riding to meet them, they beat a hasty retreat. Then followed the ' Chase-about-Raid ' when, however much her followers might weary, ' the Queen's courage increased man-like, so much, that she was ever with the foremost '. And the end of the Queen's chase was that Moray and his associates were compelled to flee into England, where, later, Elizabeth, still fearful of subjects in rebellion against the lawful authority, and yet probably angry because in this instance they had failed, gave them a scolding reception and refused their request for aid.

Mary was now supreme, with all power in her own hands. And now, tragically, she discovered that Darnley was not fit to be a king. Devoid of manly qualities, inconstant, unstable and weak, he was also headstrong, intolerant and proud. Bitterly disappointed, Mary refused to give him any royal authority (though the royal writ ran in the names of Henry and Mary, or *rex et regina*) or to grant his reiterated requests for the ' crown matrimonial '.[1] And, in discovering the mistake of her

[1] A grant of the crown matrimonial would have meant that, if Mary pre-deceased Darnley and left no issue, Darnley would continue to reign as king.

marriage, and determined to rule all things in her own way, she made a further mistake in continuing to seek advice from the members of her household to the exclusion of Darnley and the nobility alike.

A proclamation issued at Dumfries by Moray and his associates during the Chase-about-Raid had declared that they were moved to take action because of the evident danger to the Protestant faith and also because of Mary's neglect of the advice and counsel of her nobility and her reliance upon 'strangers . . . men of base degree'. Those strangers of base degree included her musician-secretary, David Riccio ('her trusty servant Davy', or 'that poltroon and vile knave Davie', as Knox called him); and Riccio was now viewed with a suspicion probably greater than he deserved. To the Protestants he was a papal agent; to the nobility he was an upstart whom they found 'always speaking with her Majesty'; to Darnley he was a rival, the man to whom the Queen gave confidences which she denied to her husband.

Darnley had even baser thoughts. Jealous, jaundiced and unstable, he entered into a plot with the Protestant lords who had been driven out in the Chase-about-Raid and who were due to be forfeited in life, lands and goods in a Parliament that was to be held on 12 March 1566. A 'band' was made: the Protestant lords were to be pardoned and allowed to return to Scotland; 'the religion' (that is, the Protestant faith) was to be maintained; Darnley was to be given the crown matrimonial and, if Mary were to die without issue, Darnley was to succeed to the throne; if necessary, the Queen was to be coerced into agreement; and, as a first step, Riccio was to be murdered.

How far the Protestant lords were sincere in their promise of the crown matrimonial is doubtful; but the first step was duly taken on the evening of Saturday, 9 March 1566. James Douglas, fourth earl of Morton, secured the approaches to Holyrood; and Darnley, Lord Lindsay of the Byres, Lord Ruthven and his son, and others associated with them gathered within the palace itself. Then, when Mary was at supper in her private chamber, they burst into the room, dragged the doomed Riccio from behind the very skirts of the Queen and, to the accompaniment of angry recriminations between Mary and Darnley, stabbed him to death in an adjoining chamber, the king's own dagger (said to have been used by Ruthven) being left sticking in the dead man's breast. On the following day, Sunday, 10 March, Darnley, by proclamation, discharged the Parliament which was due to meet on the Tuesday to pass doom of forfeiture on Moray and those who had been with him in the Chase-about-Raid; and, on the evening of the same Sunday, Moray and his friends rode into Edinburgh.

So far all seemed to have gone according to plan. On Monday, 11 March, Mary, virtually a prisoner in her own palace, received Moray and his adherents. Openly she promised forgiveness; secretly she vowed revenge. She planned escape. She easily persuaded the cowardly and unstable Darnley to desert his fellow-conspirators and to take her part. In the early hours of Tuesday, 12 March, Mary and Darnley slipped out of Holyrood and rode to Dunbar – a castle belonging to James Hepburn, fourth earl of Bothwell. From there the Queen quickly rallied her supporters. On Sunday, 17 March, in face of the forces she had gathered, Moray and his friends retreated from Edinburgh; the murderers of Riccio – Morton, Lindsay and the Ruthvens – fled to England; Knox fled to the West country; and on Monday, 18 March, Mary made a triumphant re-entry into the capital.

For a second time two armed forces had opposed each other; and for a second time Mary had prevailed. But there was a difference; and it was not merely that a new group of nobles, including Morton, Lindsay and Ruthven, were now proclaimed traitors while Moray and the other lords of the Chase-about-Raid were received back into favour.

To the Queen, Darnley had denied all knowledge of the plot that had led to the murder of Riccio, and had confessed only to being ' art and part ' in the home-bringing of Moray without Mary's knowledge and consent. But Darnley had deserted his fellow-conspirators and had connived at the Queen's escape; nay more, he had fled with her. His fellow-conspirators retaliated by revealing to Mary his full complicity in the plot. Mary, who had previously guessed all, now knew all. And that meant that she knew not only of Darnley's complicity in the death of Riccio but also of his endeavour to gain the crown matrimonial by murder and coercion. Perhaps, too, she wondered how far her brutal husband had hoped to go. At the time of Riccio's murder, and that terrifying scene when armed men with drawn daggers had broken into her private room, she was six months pregnant with child.[1] Had Darnley, the desirer of the crown matrimonial, basely hoped for a miscarriage that might result in a still-born child, her own death, and kingship for himself ? Hitherto she had simply despised Darnley. Now she hated him.

It is not difficult to sympathise with the unhappy Queen. Young – she was not yet twenty-four years old – proud and gifted, she found herself in an environment that had taxed the strongest kings. Force,

[1] Her son, James VI, was born on 19 June 1566.

341

faction and feud still dominated Scotland as of old; and to old contentions was now added that of 'the religion'. Mary had need of a
consort who was strong, trustworthy and wise: a consort who could
give her sound advice in difficulty, and comfort and strength in time of
need; but also a consort who would temper any headstrong ambition
and youthful pride. Instead, she had married Darnley, who was
cowardly and callous, brutal and base.

Henceforward in the tangled skein of evidence that has come down
to us there is one continuous thread – Mary's loathing and hatred of
Darnley: increased, perhaps, by the knowledge that his body was now
diseased through licentious indulgence. But a divorce might affect
the legitimacy of her infant son; and she is said to have bewailed that
she saw 'no outgait'. Nor was the Queen alone in her hatred. Darnley
was hated by well-nigh everyone else. By Moray, Lethington, Bothwell
and many another lord he was hated for his insolence and arrogance;
by the fugitive murderers of Riccio he was hated for betrayal. Certainly
another plot was hatched; and, although we may never know the
truth of all its ramifications, there was now a suspicious sequence of
events.

On 20 December 1566, the Queen, by act of Council, showed a new
tenderness towards the ministers of the reformed church, assigning
towards their stipends a definite portion of the 'Thirds' and giving
to the reformed church the right of collection. On 23 December, by
a grant under the privy seal, she restored to John Hamilton, archbishop
of St Andrews, his old consistorial jurisdiction – a jurisdiction which
included marriage cases. Furthermore, although in 1564 Commissary
Courts had been established to exercise the jurisdiction formerly
enjoyed by the consistorial courts of the Roman Church, Mary's grant
discharged the commissaries from exercising their jurisdiction within
the diocese of St Andrews. The next day, 24 December, Mary
pardoned Morton and a large number of those who had been associated
in the murder of Riccio, allowing them to return to Scotland.

Little more than six weeks later, during the night of 9-10 February
1567, Kirk o' Field, where Darnley was lodging, was 'blown up wi'
pouder' and the king was found, strangled to death, in the adjoining
gardens. On 3 May 1567, in the Commissary Court of Edinburgh, the
Lady Jean Gordon secured a divorce from her husband, Bothwell,[1] on
the grounds of adultery. And on 7 May 1567, at the instance of
Bothwell, the newly re-established consistorial court of the Archbishop

---

[1] They had been married as recently as February 1566.

of St Andrews nullified his marriage to the Lady Jean Gordon on the ground that they were within the forbidden degrees.[1]

Meantime, on 24 April, when Mary was on her way back to Edinburgh from Stirling (where she had been to see her infant son) she was intercepted by Bothwell and taken to his castle at Dunbar. Whether or not she was taken willingly, we shall never know. Her friends, equally with her later accusers, had noted an undue familiarity towards Bothwell in recent months, and the evidence relating to her ' abduction ', although contradictory, suggests willingness rather than the reverse. Nor shall we ever know what happened at Dunbar, and what was the relationship between Mary and Bothwell there. All that can be said with reasonable certainty is that Mary, in her reaction against Darnley, had been attracted to Bothwell.

On 6 May Bothwell rode back into Edinburgh with the Queen, ' leading the Queen's Majesty by the bridle as captive '. John Craig, Knox's colleague in Edinburgh, was asked to proclaim the banns of marriage between Mary and Bothwell, but refused to do so without written warrant from the Queen. When Mary's warrant was brought to him, charging him to make the proclamation, he did so but, at the same time, publicly denounced the marriage he proclaimed.[2] On 15 May 1567 Mary and Bothwell were married at Holyrood by the Bishop of Orkney according to the rites of the Protestant church.

This hasty marriage, three months after Darnley's murder, shocked public opinion. Whether or not Mary knew of the plot that had culminated in Darnley's murder, and whatever that plot was, and whether or not Bothwell had seduced her and placed her under constraint, she had married the man whom popular opinion had branded as the murderer of the King, and the man whom within the last fortnight, had

---

[1] But a dispensation to marry had been sought and granted, and apparently was now conveniently suppressed. It should be added that the judge-delegate in the consistorial court later complained that he had given sentence of nullity under threats and pressure.

It is also to be noted that in this tangled drama of events the Lady Jean Gordon, a devout Roman Catholic, obtained her divorce in the civil (Protestant) commissary court, while Bothwell, a Protestant, obtained his decree of nullity in the Roman Catholic consistorial court.

[2] The fearless Craig also denounced Bothwell before the Privy Council, referring to the laws relating to adultery and ravishing, the suspicion of collusion between Bothwell and his wife (the Lady Jean Gordon), the sudden divorce, the new proclamation of marriage to the Queen, and lastly the suspicions that had been raised in connection with Darnley's death which Mary's marriage to Bothwell would confirm. His account can be read in the record of the General Assembly for 30 December 1567 (*Booke of the Universall Kirk*, VOL. I, p. 115).

been divorced in an Edinburgh court for adultery. Even the Pope, in the following month, gave his decision to have no further communication with the Queen of Scots ' unless, indeed, in times to come he shall see some better sign of her life and religion '.

For the third time in Mary's brief personal reign two armed forces opposed each other. The ' Confederate Lords ' declared that they were in arms to deliver Mary from Bothwell and her enemies, to secure the person of the young Prince, and to prosecute the murderers of the King. Exactly one month after her marriage to Bothwell, Mary surrendered to the Confederate Lords at Carberry, without risking battle (15 June 1567), and after urging Bothwell to make good his escape.[1]

The Queen was imprisoned by the Lords in Lochleven Castle, and there, on 24 July 1567, she was compelled to demit the crown to her infant son James, to appoint her half-brother, the Earl of Moray, as regent, and to appoint certain lords to act until Moray could be recalled from France.[2] Five days later (29 July 1567) the one-year-old James VI was crowned, and in December 1567 a Parliament, held by the regent Moray, ratified the action taken by the Lords at Lochleven.

Less than a year later, on 2 May 1568, the Queen escaped from Lochleven and made her way westwards to the Hamilton country, where she hoped for Hamilton support against the Lennox Stewarts now represented by the infant king.[3] Defeated at Langside (13 May 1568), she fled over the Border into England.

Naturally Elizabeth found Mary's presence in England disconcerting. Mary was a sister-sovereign who sought asylum; but Mary was also a claimant to Elizabeth's throne while, on the other hand, the Regent

---

[1] Bothwell fled north and was sheltered for a while in Spynie Castle by his kinsman, the Bishop of Moray. Thence he made his way to Orkney and to Shetland and from there to Norway. Having no papers, his ship was taken and he was placed in custody as a privateer. Taken to Bergen, he was confronted by the Lady Anne Throndssön, whom he had married in Denmark in 1560, and who now accused him of desertion. The authorities, not knowing what action to take, kept him in confinement. He died in prison, in 1578, after a long illness and with his mind deranged.

[2] He had left Edinburgh for St Andrews the day before Darnley's murder – possibly knowing that the King was to be killed, but possibly not knowing the manner of the killing. Although he later returned to Edinburgh, he left Scotland for France about the middle of April.

It is impossible not to be suspicious of Moray. Had he been disinterested in his earlier ' guidance ' of the Queen, or had he subtly led her into difficulty ? Had he ' looked through his fingers ', anticipating what the end would be ? Why was he so conveniently absent at every crisis ?

[3] It should be remembered that, if Mary were not restored, and if James VI died, as lawful king of Scotland, without an heir, the crown would pass to Darnley's brother, Charles, to the exclusion of the Hamiltons.

Moray, who now governed in Scotland, was a firm believer in friendship with England. Above all, perhaps, Mary was a Roman Catholic who had been forced to flee from rebellious Protestant subjects. If an attempt were to be made to restore this Scottish queen to her rightful throne, it might bring together all those who adhered to the Roman faith in both Scotland and England; it might even bring in the great continental powers of France and Spain; and the restoration of Mary to her rightful throne might mean the throne of England as well as the throne of Scotland. In any such attempt Mary could be a magnet drawing to her side all the scattered elements of political and religious discontent in Elizabeth's own realm.

Possibly all these considerations were in Elizabeth's mind when, at Mary's request, she agreed to an enquiry into the actions of the ' rebellious ' Scots. At York, and later at Westminster and Hampton Court, Commissioners appointed by Elizabeth heard at wearisome length the charge of ' rebellion ' brought by Mary against her subjects, and the counter-charge by Moray and his adherents that Mary was unfit to rule her kingdom. Now, suddenly, the Casket-letters were produced[1]; but, since the originals ' disappeared ' a few years later, leaving us with translations only, and since it is impossible to check their statements against evidence that we know to be trustworthy, the question as to whether or not they were genuine must still be held ' not proven '.[2] The production of the Letters, however, so besmirched Mary's character that it was virtually impossible for her ever to regain her former honour and estate – an inevitable outcome of which Moray cannot have been unaware. Finally, on 10 January 1569, Cecil made a non-committal statement on behalf of Elizabeth which gave leave to Moray and his adherents to return to Scotland ' in the same estate ' as that in which they were when they came to England – that is, Moray was to return as Regent for the infant James VI: and that meant that Mary was to remain in England, to all intents and purposes a prisoner.

Throughout the whole of the enquiry the scales had been heavily loaded against the unfortunate Queen, and the accepted rules of law had been little observed. Elizabeth undoubtedly felt more secure with Scotland under Moray's control, and her fear that Mary might be a danger to her own throne was soon shown to be real. In October

[1] They were said to have been found in a silver casket taken from one of Bothwell's servants, Dalgleish.

[2] Probably the best analysis of the evidence is still that contained in Andrew Lang's *The Mystery of Mary Stuart*.

1569, the rising of the 'Northern Earls' included among its aims the release of the Scottish Queen. The rising was crushed, and the disaffected north was despoiled and overawed; but in January 1570, in a letter to Cecil, Knox did not hesitate to write, 'If ye strike not at the root, the branches that appear to be broken will bud again'. His meaning was obvious, and it was reinforced when, two years later, the Ridolfi plot, though only a plot on paper, came to light.

Meantime, in Scotland, Moray had been active and resolute; but in January 1570 he was assassinated by a Hamilton in Linlithgow; a small English force, in retaliation for a Border raid, seized the opportunity to harry the Hamilton lands; and Archbishop Hamilton, taken prisoner at the capture of Dumbarton Castle (held by Lord Fleming in the name of the Queen), was hanged, without respect to his office or his age, for art and part in the murder of Moray (April 1571). Now open civil war was raging between the 'King's-men' and the 'Queen's-men'. In an attempt by the Queen's-men to break up a convention of the King's men, at Stirling, in September 1571, the new Regent, the Earl of Lennox (Darnley's father), was killed. His successor as regent, the Earl of Mar, died just over a year after his appointment, and was succeeded by the Earl of Morton (1572). There was little quarter on either side, though gradually the King's-men prevailed until at last Edinburgh Castle, held by Kirkcaldy of Grange, was the only important stronghold still in the hands of Mary's supporters.

Then, once more, as in 1560, Elizabeth actively intervened. For a second time an English army crossed the Border to help in the siege of a Scottish stronghold. In May 1573 English artillery helped to batter down Edinburgh Castle; and Kirkcaldy of Grange, a brave soldier, an old companion with Knox in the French galleys, but now too loyal to a doubtful cause, was hanged.

Elizabeth's decision to intervene, and her subsequent support of Morton in the regency, up to the very time of his execution in 1581,[1] were clear pointers that she had determined to keep Mary in England. A friendly north was essential. On the Continent, the 'Wars of Religion' were being fought with bitterness and no mercy. Already the Pope had declared Elizabeth excommunicate and deposed, thereby encouraging rebellion against her authority and an attack upon her realm, and in 1580 another Pope gave a ruling that the assassination of the English Queen would be no sin. Thus, when William of Orange, the Dutch Protestant leader, was assassinated in 1584, excitement in

[1] See *infra*, p. 354.

England and fear for the life of Elizabeth led to the Bond and Act of Association for the safety of the Queen. If there were to be an attempt on Elizabeth's life, then the person in whose interest the attempt was made, or who was privy to the attempt, was to be pursued to death.

Mary was now more strictly guarded, but still hoped for release. After sixteen years of imprisonment it is little wonder that she clutched at any scheme that offered her a chance of freedom again. In 1585, Anthony Babington held out that prospect of release. His plot was incredibly stupid, and he himself the most stupid of conspirators. Walsingham played with him as a cat plays with a mouse; but, in the intercepted correspondence, Mary had approved of the assassination of Elizabeth. Her fate was sealed. Elizabeth might say she would have been glad of ' some other way ' of dealing with the unhappy Mary Stewart; but parliament, council and people demanded justice, and Elizabeth finally signed the death warrant. On 4 February 1587 (unknown to the still wavering Elizabeth), the English Council sent the warrant to Fotheringay, and on 8 February Mary died on the scaffold there. It was the only solution. Mary was too dangerous to be alive. Roman Catholic might was gathering for its greatest trial of strength with Elizabeth and England. Whether or not justice was served at Fotheringay, expedience demanded the death of Mary Stewart.

James VI, approaching the manly age of twenty-one, played an ignoble part. He was determined to succeed Elizabeth on the English throne, and he had her vague promise that she would not prejudge his title. Although in turns he both prayed and threatened, in the end he silently acquiesced in his mother's death. James could not forget that Mary's claim to the English throne came before his own; more than that, the success of a Roman Catholic invasion (for which the Spanish shipyards were known to be already at work) might even restore Mary to the throne on which he sat. With James VI also, expedience prevailed.

CHAPTER XXXIV

The Crown and the Kirk

IT MAY be said that Mary's brief personal reign was little more than an interlude which has acquired unwarranted attention from the fast-moving drama of its closing months. An interlude: for, with the deposition of Mary in 1567, the reformation settlement of 1560 was at once confirmed, and the Confession of Faith was re-engrossed in the register of Parliament.[1]

Yet although, in 1567, as in 1560, the Confession of Faith was approved, the Book of Discipline, which had been drafted by Knox and his fellow ministers in 1560,[2] was passed by in both 1560 and 1567. The Book of Discipline, which would have devoted the wealth of the Roman church to the work of the church reformed – in stipends for the ministers, in the furtherance of education, and for the relief of the poor – did not commend itself to the greater part of the Lords. We may say that ' Faith ' was not followed by ' Works '; we may agree with Knox that ' avariciousness would not suffer this corrupt generation to approve . . . the Policy . . . of the godly ministers '; and yet, looking back, we can now see that the schemes advocated in the Book of Discipline were so far-reaching as to be little short of ' devout imaginations '.

Like the Confession of Faith, the Book of Discipline claimed to be firmly based on the Word of God.[3] In it, Knox visualised church and state working hand-in-hand. With the people ' all professing Christ Jesus ' and all subject to a ruler who would rule ' according to the law of God ', church and state would be the twin pillars of God's house on earth. Yet the very rejection of the Book showed that Scotland was far different from the ' perfect city ' of Geneva, and that in Scotland church and state were not to be one.

According to the Book of Discipline the church and the people were to be closely bound together. Each minister was to be elected

[1] *Supra*, p. 331.

[2] The Book of Discipline, or certainly a first draft of what is now known as the Book of Discipline, had been drawn up between 29 April and 20 May 1560. That is, it was a ' blueprint ' of the policy to be adopted when victory had been won.

[3] ' Protesting, that if any man will note in this our Confession any article or sentence repugning to God's holy word . . . ' (The Confession of Faith). ' For as we will not bind your Wisdoms to our judgments further than we be able to prove the same by God's plain Scriptures . . . ' (The Book of Discipline).

by the congregation of the church he was to serve, and was to be examined in ' life and manners, doctrine and knowledge '. To assist each minister (and principally in maintaining religious discipline) elders, chosen from the congregation of the church, were to be elected annually. For collecting and administering the revenues of the church a deacon was to be appointed. And the elders and the deacon were to report on the life, manners, study and diligence of the minister, once a year, to the Superintendent. The Superintendents, who, in their administrative and supervisory functions, were much like bishops, were to be appointed to dioceses (a term that was retained), and the first appointments were to be made by the ' godly ' state. In his diocese the superintendent was to plant and erect churches; he was to be a preacher, preaching in the different churches within his diocese; and, as he passed from place to place in his diocese, he was to examine ' the life, diligence and behaviour of the ministers, the order of their churches, and the manners of the people ', and to consider the provision for the poor and the instruction provided for the youth.[1]

In its sections dealing with education, the Book stressed the necessity for the education of youth under the supervision of the church. Every church (that is, every parish) was to have a schoolmaster able to teach at least grammar and the Latin tongue. In rural parishes, where this might not be possible, the minister or reader was to give elementary education and to act as schoolmaster. In ' notable towns ', and especially in the head burghs of dioceses, there were to be ' colleges ', with paid teachers, providing courses in Latin, Greek, Logic and Rhetoric. The three existing universities – St Andrews, Glasgow and Aberdeen – were to be maintained and endowed; and the existing degree courses were to be revised so that students, having gained a background in Arts, could specialise in divinity, medicine or law. In the home there was to be systematic reading of the Bible, while every head of a household was to ensure that his children, family and servants were instructed in the principles of the Christian religion. And the whole object of education was clearly defined: that men might be the better able to serve the church and the commonwealth.

The proposals relating to the poor were left somewhat vague and ill-defined, but the relief of poverty was clearly laid upon the church. The poor were to return to their native parishes and there the parish churches were to make arrangements for their support.

---

[1] All much like the ' visitations ' which the bishops of the Roman church were supposed to conduct but which they had for long neglected.

In addition there was some anticipation of the modern Welfare State. There were to be variable stipends for the ministers – for, while all of them would require money for books, some would be bachelors while others would have wives and families, and some would need to travel more than others; there were to be ' educational allowances ' for the children of ministers, and pensions for ministers' widows and orphans; there were to be variable university fees, according to the rank of the parent and his capacity to pay; and there were to be university bursaries for the poor.

All this, however, could be done only through the transfer of the vast wealth of the Roman Church. The stipends of the superintendents and the revenues of the universities were to come from the rents and feu-duties derived from the land-holdings of the bishoprics. The ministers, the schools and the poor were to be supported by the teinds (or tithes), which were still to be paid, but which were now to be ' reasonably taken ' and paid direct. The rents and feu-duties of the monastic houses were not included in the scheme – possibly because it was realised that, as they had already largely fallen into the hands of the nobility, they were now largely irrecoverable.

But these essential financial proposals were undoubtedly the main reason for the rejection of the ' godly policy '. In many instances a bishopric or monastery had arranged with a ' tacksman ' that, in return for paying a lump sum, he could collect both its tithes and its land-rents in this or that district. Moreover, hundreds of parish churches (each with its teinds and often with land-endowments as well) had been assigned to cathedral chapters or monastic houses. Thus the problem of separating the teinds (for the payment of ministerial stipends and the maintenance of the schools and the poor) from the land-rents (for the support of the superintendents and the universities), and the further problem of ensuring that local teinds were paid direct to the local parish minister, were probably beyond the administrative capacities of the time. Even some seventy years later, in the opening years of the reign of Charles I, a statesmanlike scheme to evolve some order in the payment of teinds brought upon the king the odium of ministers and laymen alike.

Apart from the difficulties inherent in the scheme, moreover, there was naturally opposition from those lords who had already ' greedily gripped ' church possessions, or who had kith and kin in the enjoyment of benefices. And what of the position of the Crown itself? In national taxations, as we have seen, one-half of any tax had been paid by the church. If all the revenues of the church were to be devoted to the superintendents, the ministers, the universities, the schools and the poor, how could the Crown raise further taxes without doubling the proportions to be paid by the barons and by the burghs?

Perhaps it is not surprising that the Book of Discipline was passed by. On the other hand it may be thought surprising that the whole structure of the Roman church was still left intact. That is to say, while, in 1560, the jurisdiction of the Pope was abolished, the Mass proscribed and a Protestant Confession of Faith accepted, bishops and priests were still left undisturbed in their benefices and the monastic houses were not ' dissolved '. Again too many of the lords were commendators of monastic houses, or had other interests at stake. Thus, while the bishops, abbots, priors and priests of the Roman church performed no spiritual office but still drew the revenues of the benefices,[1] the ministers of the reformed church preached the new faith but lived largely on the ' benevolence of others '. In effect, two churches existed side by side – one, silenced and well-endowed; the other, active and miserably poor. And the active reformed church was steadily organising itself in kirk sessions and with a General Assembly.[2]

As we have seen, when, in 1567, Mary was deposed, and the Lord James Stewart, earl of Moray, became regent, there was still no attempt to give effect to the provisions of the Book of Discipline. Nor were any of the Roman clergy ejected from their livings.[3] Too many interests were still affected. Nevertheless, steps were taken to ensure that as the benefices of the old church fell vacant they would be filled by ministers of the church reformed. Accordingly it was enacted that as parish churches fell vacant their patrons were to present ' qualified persons ' – that is, ministers of the reformed faith – for examination and admission by the superintendents; and, four years later, in January 1572, by what has been called the ' Concordat of Leith ', it was agreed that henceforth as episcopal sees fell vacant they were to be filled by bishops nominated by the crown but examined and admitted by a

[1] Less the one-third collected for the Queen and the ministers under the arrangement made in 1562 (supra, p. 335).

[2] The first General Assembly of the Church met in December 1560 and thereafter, for a time, met twice a year. Much like a ' parliament ' for the church, it was at first attended by barons, commissioners of burghs, and certain of the ministers.

[3] Not until 1573 was it enacted that all those who held benefices, or who enjoyed any church revenues, and who refused to accept the Confession of Faith, were to be deprived of their benefices or holdings; and under this act certain ejections at last took place.

' Chapter ' composed of ministers, and the new bishops were to be subject to the General Assembly in all things spiritual.

The Concordat of Leith received the approval of Knox, and yet, even before he died that same year (November 1572), he had seen that the appointments of these new reformed bishops could be subject to abuse. And, under the regent Morton (who assumed office on the day of Knox's death), the appointments of the new bishops were blatantly accompanied by agreements under which part of the episcopal revenues were diverted to secular purposes or secular pockets, while the ministers were still living as ' poor amid the poor '. There may have been little new in this, but it was the setting which Andrew Melville found in Scotland upon his return from Geneva in 1574, and which led him to draw up a second Book of Discipline in which, for the first time, we find a condemnation of episcopacy and, with it, the doctrine of the parity of ministers – the groundstone of Scottish presbyterianism.

This second Book of Discipline again stressed that all its claims were based on the Word of God. Like the first Book of Discipline it demanded that the whole ' patrimony ' of the church should be devoted to the ministers, the schools, the poor, and ' other affairs ' of the kirk, so that those who served God could be ' provided for without care or solicitude '. But in addition, however, it also declared that bishops with authority over their brethren, ' pastors of pastors ', were unlawful before God, for all God's ministers were equal, one with another. Authority and discipline were to be maintained, not by dignitaries, but by a hierarchy of church courts, including elders as well as ministers, and later defined as the kirk-session, the presbytery, the synod and the general assembly. The examination and admission of ministers was to be by presbyteries. The general assembly was to be essentially a gathering of ministers and elders, representing the lower courts in the hierarchy, and it was to have authority over all men, lay as well as spiritual, in ' ecclesiastical causes '. This authority of the assembly, moreover, derived from the authority of the church which was ' different and distinct ' from the authority of the state. For, as the Book laid down at the very beginning, the kirk ' has a certain power granted by God ' and flowing direct from God; the kirk has no head on earth – its only head is Christ, the spiritual king and governor. So, if the civil magistrate transgressed ' in matters of conscience and religion ', he had to submit to the discipline of the kirk; and it was the duty of the kirk to ' teach ' the civil magistrate how to exercise his civil authority ' according to the Word '.

Here was far more than a renewed claim to the wealth of the Roman church for the work of the church reformed. Here too, there was far more than a condemnation of bishops and a claim that all God's servants were equal. Here, in effect, was a threatened theocracy: a kirk that would ' teach ' (which might well mean dictate) a policy to the state. With the kirk claiming a right to instruct the civil authority in those matters that were of ' conscience and religion ', and with the kirk claiming to be the judge of what those matters were, the authority of the king could be heavily invaded. Indeed, to drive the argument to its logical conclusion, where lay the need for a king's council when the ministers claimed that they were in counsel with God ?

James VI was quick to perceive that the kirk and its ministers could soon be claiming to control almost every aspect of royal policy; on the other side, Andrew Melville was fearless in asserting an authority for the kirk that was separate from, and above, the authority of the state. In 1584 he did not hesitate to tell the king's Privy Council that they ' presumed over boldly ' to ' control the ambassadors and messengers of a king and council greater than themselves and far above them '; and in 1596 he told James VI, not that church and state were the twin pillars of a Christian commonwealth, but that there were two kings and two kingdoms in Scotland, and one was ' Christ Jesus the King, and his Kingdom the Kirk, whose subject King James the Sixth is, and of whose kingdom [he is] not a king, nor a lord, nor a head, but a member '. It is not surprising that James was later to declare that Scottish presbytery agreed ' as well with monarchy as God and the Devil ', or that he roundly asserted ' No bishop, no king '. And that axiom, ' No bishop, no king ', provides the key to James's policy in his ensuing struggle with Melville and the kirk.

Taking his cue from England, James saw that in episcopacy, with bishops chosen and appointed by the crown, lay his only hope of royal control over the church, perhaps even his only hope of some royal control over the state. So, in the contest between the crown and the kirk, James strove for the supremacy of the crown, supported by an episcopal church; Melville strove for a church which contained no bishops, who might be tools of the king, and a church which, under its General Assembly, was independent and free from any control by the state.

This struggle between the king and the kirk first came into the open in the events that followed the arrival in Scotland (in 1579) of Esmé

Stewart, Lord d'Aubigny.[1] D'Aubigny, ingratiating and handsome, had at once become a close favourite of the thirteen-year-old James. He was created Earl of Lennox in 1580, and Duke of Lennox in 1581; he was given command of the king's bodyguard; and the uncompromising regent, the Earl of Morton – who had brought stability to the realm – was accused by Captain James Stewart[2] for art and part in the murder of Darnley, was imprisoned and later executed (June 1581). And Captain James Stewart had by now been created Earl of Arran.

But the ministers strongly suspected Esmé Stewart of being a papal agent; rumours of Roman Catholic plots and conspiracies were rife; and even Elizabeth had thought it wise to send warning letters to the young King. To lull these alarms and suspicions, James, Lennox, and the members of the royal household had subscribed, in January 1581, a Confession of Faith (known as the ' King's Confession ', or the ' Negative Confession ' – because of its denial of all religion and doctrine that was not in accord with the Confession of 1560), and in March 1581 had given orders for this Confession to be subscribed throughout the whole realm.[3] The ministers, however, remained far from reassured, and increasing evidence of Roman Catholic intrigues and plots deepened their suspicions of Lennox. Nor were the ministers without the support of a number of the nobility who disliked the sudden ascendancy of Lennox and Arran and their influence over the King, and who were perturbed by the undoubted plots that were afoot, including plots for the restoration of Mary to the Scottish throne.

In August 1582 the Earls of Mar and Gowrie, with Lord Lindsay and Lord Boyd, seized James, *more Scottico*, at Perth and compelled him to accompany them to Ruthven Castle. Arran was seized soon afterwards; Lennox was compelled to obey an order to leave Scotland (December 1582)[4]; and the ' Ruthven Raiders ' held the young king in their power for some ten months until his escape in June 1583. Meantime, in October 1582, the General Assembly of the kirk had

---

[1] Esmé Stewart was the son of John Stewart, Lord d'Aubigny, and grandson of John, third earl of Lennox. He was thus a cousin of James VI. Moreover, with the forfeiture of the Hamiltons, and with the death in 1576 of Darnley's brother Charles, sixth Earl of Lennox, who left only a daughter, Arabella Stewart, Esmé Stewart was a near heir to the Scottish throne.

[2] This adventurer, hand-in-glove with Lennox, was the second son of Andrew, Lord Ochiltree, and, strange as it may appear, John Knox had been his brother-in-law.

[3] This ' Negative Confession ' was later made the basis of the National Covenant of 1638.

[4] He retired to France and died there shortly afterwards (May 1583).

given its approval to the ' Raid of Ruthven ' (an approval which James never forgot or forgave), regarding it as an ' act of reformation ' that had delivered ' the true religion . . . from evident and certain dangers ' and had preserved the person of the King from ' no less peril '.

With James's escape in June 1583, however, Arran was at once restored to favour, and Andrew Melville, accused of treason, took refuge in England. A second plot, in which the Earls of Mar, Gowrie and Angus played the leading parts, and which was directed against Arran, failed. Gowrie was executed; Mar and his associates fled to England; and to England also fled a number of the leading ministers who had supported both the Ruthven Raiders and this second plot.

Arran was now in complete ascendancy, though hated more than ever by nobility and ministers alike; and James, taking his revenge for the approval given by the General Assembly to the Raid of Ruthven, now struck at the roots of all that Melville had claimed for the kirk. In May 1584 the so-called ' Black Acts ' declared the King to be head of both church and state; affirmed to the King and his council jurisdiction over all persons both spiritual and temporal; discharged all judgments of the church that were not approved by King and Parliament; forbade any assembly of the church to be held without the King's permission; forbade the preaching of any sermon in contempt of the King or of the proceedings of the King's council; and laid down that the government of the church was to be by bishops responsible to the King.

Little more than a year later, however, the killing of Lord Russell, son of the Earl of Bedford, at a Border ' day of trew ', enabled Elizabeth to demand the surrender of Arran as the instigator of Russell's death. Elizabeth, who was anxious for a Protestant league with Scotland,[1] not only distrusted Arran but also wished to effect a reconciliation between James and the ' Protestant Lords ' who had taken refuge in England. In October 1585, after ineffective diplomatic exchanges, she ' let slip ' these ' Banished Lords '; they recrossed the Border and were at once joined by their friends. For a time it looked as though armed conflict was inevitable, but Arran's courage failed him and his ascendancy was at an end.[2]

Andrew Melville and the other presbyterian ministers now returned

[1] *Infra*, p. 362.
[2] In 1595 he was killed by James Douglas of Parkhead, a nephew of the Regent Morton, in revenge for his denunciation of Morton which had led to Morton's imprisonment and execution.

to Scotland, and in February 1586, at a conference of councillors and ministers at Holyrood, agreement was reached on a compromise intended to reconcile the rival claims of the Crown and the Kirk. Henceforth bishops were to be presented by the King to the General Assembly for election and admission; each bishop was to be appointed to a particular kirk which he would serve as a minister; he was to be subject to a presbytery or ' senate ', chosen from the ministers within his bounds, through whose advice he would appoint to vacant parish churches; and in ' life and doctrine ' he was to be answerable to the General Assembly. This compromise was accepted by the next General Assembly – though not without much discussion – and a scheme of presbyteries, twenty-two in number, was drawn up, each of which was to have a ' moderator ' who would be either a bishop or a commissioner.[1] But the compromise, mainly owing to the Act of Annexation in the following year, never became effective.

By his Act of Annexation (1587), which he later bitterly regretted, James, possibly trusting too much to the advice of his chancellor, John Maitland,[2] unwittingly struck a severe blow at the episcopal system which he was striving to erect. As was to be constantly the case, the King was spendthrift and short of money; accordingly, on the argument that former royal endowments of the church had seriously impoverished the crown, and to avoid placing unbearable taxations upon the people, the crown now resumed, by annexation, all the temporalities still pertaining to any ' archbishop, bishop, abbot, prior, prioress ' and ' whatsomever other prelate '. The manses and glebes of the parish churches were left untouched; but, for the rest, the ' possessors of great benefices ' were stripped of everything save their principal dwelling-places. Who now would want to be a bishop ? There was a ' temporary eclipse of episcopacy '; and the ministers shrewdly forgot the compromise of 1586.

Then, once again, extraneous events played a part – this time greatly to the advantage of the kirk.

In February 1592 the Earl of Huntly, who had received a commission

---

[1] Originally a ' commissioner ' was a minister commissioned to carry out the functions of a superintendent; here the commissioner in a like way was to be a minister commissioned to carry out the functions of a bishop.

[2] Younger brother of William Maitland of Lethington. Their father, Sir Richard Maitland (1496-1586), was a competent poet (his best work is probably his *Solace in Age*) who, however, also collected specimens of early Scots poetry. In the Maitland MSS., and in the equally valuable Bannatyne MS. (the collection of George Bannatyne, 1545-1608), much early Scottish vernacular poetry has been preserved.

from James to ' bring in ' the Earl of Moray (on a charge of aiding and abetting the lawless activities of Francis Stewart, earl of Bothwell[1]), exceeded his commission and barbarously slew the ' Bonnie Earl ' at Donibristle. In view of the fact that there was feud between Huntly and Moray, James's commission to Huntly was singularly ill-advised. More than that, however, Huntly was a Roman Catholic, while the ' Bonnie Earl ' was the son-in-law of the ' Good Regent ' Moray. Worse still, although Huntly was warded for a brief period in Edinburgh castle he was soon released and not brought to trial.

Amid a general outcry, notably in the sermons of the ministers, that James's royal authority was ' contemptible ', that he allowed the Earl of Bothwell to put him to defiance and Huntly to commit murder with impunity, and that he even favoured Huntly as a Roman Catholic, James, again on the advice of Maitland, now Lord Thirlestane, agreed to an Act of Parliament which has been called the ' Golden Act ' or the ' Magna Carta of the Church of Scotland '. By this act, James ratified all the liberties and privileges previously granted to the reformed church, gave to the kirk the right of calling General Assemblies (though at each General Assembly the king or the royal commissioner was to name the date and place of the next meeting[2]), granted the right of synods and presbyteries to meet, declared that the acts of 1584 (the ' Black Acts ') were not to take away ' the privilege that God has given to the spiritual office bearers in the kirk ' in matters of religion and discipline, and finally declared that henceforth presentations to benefices were to be directed to presbyteries.

Yet James was still a hater of presbyterianism and of the independence asserted by the ministers. To James, parity of ministers was ' the mother of confusion '; and the independence asserted by the ministers was little short of an attempt to govern the government. Then, for a third time, unforeseen circumstances affected the course of

[1] The son of John Stewart, a natural son of James V, and Jean Hepburn, the sister of Mary's Bothwell. He had been created Earl of Bothwell by James VI in 1587. In 1591 Bothwell had repeatedly put the King to defiance and revealed the weakness of the royal authority. He had broken into the tolbooth of Edinburgh and carried off a prisoner; he had escaped from his ward in the castle of Edinburgh; had been outlawed and twice thereafter had appeared in Edinburgh and insolently challenged the authorities; and finally he had made his way into Holyrood and into the King's own chamber, greatly to the terror of James.

[2] But no provision was made whereby a General Assembly could be called if the king or royal commissioner, being present, did *not* name the date and place of the next meeting – a loophole of which James took advantage in his continued struggle with the kirk after his accession to the English throne.

the conflict between the claims of the ministers and the king's insistence upon some royal authority over the church.

In March 1596 the King's continuing leniency towards the Roman Catholic earls, Huntly and Erroll,[1] had been criticised in the General Assembly, and the ministers had not spared their words; in September of the same year Melville had taken the King by the sleeve and called him ' God's sillie[2] vassall '; and in November, David Black, minister in St Andrews, had refused to acknowledge the jurisdiction of the Privy Council when charged with uttering ' unreverent, reproachful and infamous ' words in a recent sermon. Then, in December, came a sudden and unexpected tumult in Edinburgh, the cause of which is not known with certainty, but which gave James his chance. Denouncing both the burgesses and the ministers, James left Edinburgh and by act of Council proclaimed it to be no longer the capital of the kingdom.

Edinburgh, it is true, was soon able to recover its status and privileges by payment of a fine of 20,000 merks, but, touched in their pockets, its burgesses were henceforth more wary in their support of the ministers. Moreover, by making generous grants from the temporalities of the bishoprics and abbacies which he had annexed to the crown, James was able to secure the support of many of the nobility – support from those who received as well as from those who hoped they might receive.

The ministers were now fighting their battle almost alone. And James was quick to see that not all the ministers were as unyielding and resolute as Andrew Melville. By taking advantage of the clause in the act of 1592 which enabled the King or his commissioner to name the date and place of the next meeting of the General Assembly, James now began to summon Assemblies to meet in places like Dundee, Perth and Montrose, where opinion was less radical than in the south, and where the atmosphere was likely to be less perfervid.

And now, by a combination of astuteness, subtlety and plain common-sense, as well as by bribes, flattery, threats and some chicanery – all of which is sometimes called his ' kingcraft ' – James was able gradually to graft an episcopal form of government upon a presbyterian church.

His first step was to persuade a General Assembly, held at Dundee in May 1597, to appoint commissioners ' to give advice to his majesty

[1] *Infra*, pp. 364-7.
[2] *Sillie*: not in its modern sense of *foolish*, but in its earlier sense of *feeble* and *frail*.

in all affairs concerning the welfare of the kirk '. Andrew Melville had given the King advice enough; but, as Calderwood records,[1] the commissioners ' being exalted so high as to have access to the king when they pleased ' soon became the ' king's led horse ' and concurred with the king by giving him the advice he wanted. In December 1597, when they had recommended that the ministers should have representation in Parliament, James at once agreed and, in the same month, secured an act whereby ministers whom the King pleased ' to provide to the office, place, title and dignity of a bishop, abbot or other prelate ' should have seat and vote in Parliament, and that accordingly vacant bishoprics, now and to come, should be filled by ministers of the kirk.

The King astutely professed that his sole desire was to give the kirk a voice in the government of the realm; he denied any intention to introduce ' papistical or Anglican bishopping '; but the supporters of Melville's true presbyterianism saw here the thin end of the wedge.[2] Moreover the King had not disguised his views in *Basilikon Doron*[3]; his opponents had secured a copy of the book; and they had noted that in it the king had written that there were some among the ministers who were learned and modest and who, if preferred to bishoprics, would not only re-establish the old spiritual estate in parliament, but would also defeat the demand for parity, ' which I can not agree with a monarchy '.

A cautious General Assembly, meeting at Montrose in March 1600, resolved that the representatives of the kirk in parliament should be chosen by the King out of a list drawn up by the kirk, and could be deposed by the kirk; that they were to be responsible to the General Assembly; that they were to discharge no episcopal functions, and were to be called ' commissioners ' and not ' bishops '; and that they were to be continued in office from year to year. James's answer (October 1600) was to appoint ministers of his own choice to the vacant sees of Ross, Aberdeen and Caithness, paying no regard to the safeguards laid down by the General Assembly; and these three bishops, together with a fourth bishop appointed to the see of Moray, sat and voted in a Parliament held in November 1600. The King had firmly inserted

[1] *History of the Kirk of Scotland*, VOL. v, p. 644. Calderwood (1575-1650) wrote as a perfervid presbyterian.

[2] One minister even compared the act to the wooden horse of Troy.

[3] A book of advice for his son, Prince Henry, which James had just written and which was printed for private circulation probably towards the end of 1598 or early in 1599.

the thin end of the wedge. Here was the beginning of an episcopal church.

Admittedly these bishops had as yet no place in the government of the kirk; but by further ' kingcraft ' James was eventually able to secure a church controlled by bishops who presided over synods, who admitted ministers, and who enjoyed a consistorial jurisdiction.[1] All that, however, came only after his accession to the English throne.

[1] See *Source Book of Scottish History*, VOL. III, pp. 54-61.

CHAPTER XXXV

James VI and the Accession to the English Throne

IN AUGUST 1560 over 100 small barons and freeholders (all fervent Protestants) had thronged the ' Reformation Parliament ', vaguely relying upon the act of 1428 but also claiming that, as there was no better place than Parliament in which they could serve the commonwealth, they ought to be present there to ' be heard, to reason, and to vote '. Their attendance had been accepted, but it had conflicted with the terms of the Concessions, and the validity of the Parliament had been called in question.[1]

Again, in December 1567, when Mary had been deposed, and when affairs once more were critical, a number of small barons had presented themselves at the Parliament held by the regent Moray in the name of the one-year-old James VI – doubtless to demonstrate their support of the new government. And now, in 1567, an attempt was made to regularise the position. By one of the articles put forward ' for the common weal of the realm ', and said to have been ' approved ', it was declared that since by ' law and reason the barons of this realm ought to have vote in Parliament as a part of the nobility ' henceforth, whenever a Parliament was summoned, the sheriff of each shire was to call together the barons of the shire so that they could choose one or two commissioners to represent the shire; and the expenses of the elected commissioners were to be met by the rest of the barons whom they represented. Significantly this system of representation was recommended ' for safety of numbers at each Parliament ': the small barons were mainly Protestants, and the regular attendance of shire commissioners (rather than the haphazard presence of those who decided themselves to come) would give the Protestant party steady support for its political programme. It could rely upon a safe majority. On the other hand, there is no mention of freeholders; and it looks as though the freeholders were now to be disfranchised.

Owing to the defective nature of the Parliamentary records, it is impossible to say whether or not this ' approved article ' became statute

---

[1] *Supra*, pp. 330-1. It is to be noted, moreover, that the act upon which they relied was one which had relieved the small barons and freeholders from the burden of personal attendance and had endeavoured, instead, to establish a system of shire commissioners.

law. Certainly there is no record of the election of shire commissioners, or of the attendance of shire commissioners at Parliaments and Conventions of Estates. Certainly, too, at times of crisis – as, for example, at the election of the regent Mar (September 1571) and the election of the regent Morton (November 1572) – the small barons still turned up in 'goodly numbers' to support the government: but they turned up as individuals and not as representatives of the shires.

Yet clearly it was essential that the composition of Parliament should be known and definite. More than that, uncertainty in its composition might mean uncertainty in the furtherance of a Protestant policy. And the need for a strong Protestant government, with certainty in its retention of power, was one of the factors leading to the county franchise act of 1587.

In March 1585 Philip II of Spain and the Duke of Guise proclaimed their 'Catholic League' for the extirpation of all heresy. Most of the Netherlands, 'a pistol pointed at the heart of England', had already fallen into the hands of Spain; the fate of Protestant Europe appeared to hang in the balance; and Elizabeth sent hastily to James asking him to conclude with England a Protestant League, offensive and defensive, to combat the threat from Roman Catholic might.

A league with England was accepted by a Convention of Estates in July 1585, although it was not finally concluded until July 1586[1] when Arran had been overthrown.[2] Meantime, in a Parliament held in December 1585, a petition had been presented to the king and the Estates representing the need for both king and Parliament to be 'well and truly informed of the needs and causes pertaining to his loving subjects in all estates, especially the commons of the realm', and asking for the revival of the 'good and lovable' act of 1428. And out of this petition came the franchise act of 1587 which, with only a few later modifications, determined the county franchise until the Reform Act of 1832.

The act of 1587, which recited James I's act of 1428 in full, was little more than a straightforward re-enactment of that measure.[3] Commissioners (two from each shire – but only one from each of the small shires of Clackmannan and Kinross) were to be elected by the small barons and freeholders, and the expenses of the commissioners were to be met by those whom they represented. The commissioners were to have votes in both Parliaments and Conventions of Estates,

[1] For its details, see *Source Book of Scottish History*, VOL. III, pp. 441-3.
[2] *Supra*, p. 355.   [3] *Supra*, p. 214.

and their representatives on the Committee of the Articles[1] were to be equal in number to the representatives of the burghs. Finally, because the petition of 1585 had suggested that the right to take part in the election of county commissioners should be limited to those small barons and freeholders who held land, direct of the King, of the annual value of at least forty shillings, and because the petition was recited in full in the preamble to the act, that voting qualification was now regarded as part of the act itself.[2]

The small barons and freeholders undoubtedly represented a strong Protestant group, at a time when a strong Protestant government was essential, but the background to this county franchise act is also interesting in other ways. James VI was faced with a problem similar to that which had faced James I – Parliament was largely an assembly of the great feudal lords. The burghs, as we have seen, tended to be more interested in the deliberations of their own Convention of Royal Burghs than in the deliberations of Parliament.[3] The theory of a clerical estate was still maintained, but the clerical estate was virtually non-existent. While four or five bishops still sat, James had not yet established his episcopal system; and the abbots and priors were nearly all commendators who, although forming part of the spiritual estate, were ' of the nobility ' and thought and acted like the nobility.[4] In effect Parliament contained too many great lords, only a few burgesses, and no real clerical estate. To bring in the small men would help to offset the power of the great lords.

In another aspect, the King, always short of money and always spendthrift, could the more easily secure the ingathering of a taxation (and taxations were already multiplying) if the small men, as well as the great lords, had agreed to its imposition. Equally, if the small men were present in Parliaments and Conventions they could strive to protect their fellows by opposing any exaggerated demands from the King.

Finally, it is significant that the small men, eager and anxious to have voice and vote in Parliament, now regarded representation as a privilege whereas, in 1428, it had probably been rejected as a burden. This was part of a new political consciousness which had been stimu-

[1] *Supra*, pp. 215-7.
[2] So arose the ' forty shilling freeholder '. So, too, those holding land, direct of the king, of a lesser value were now definitely disfranchised.
[3] *Supra*, chap. xx.
[4] When, after the act of annexation, James began to erect the lands of the monasteries and priories into ' temporal lordships ', the ' lords of erection ' sat as lords temporal.

lated by the Reformation movement; and its strength is to be seen in the fact that, in order to further their petition of 1585, the small men were willing to make a 'handsome contribution' of £40,000 to the King. Because of some delay in the forthcoming of this 'contribution', the act of 1587 did not become effective until 1594; and, even then, not all the shires elected commissioners. Gradually, however, in steadily increasing numbers, shire commissioners took their places in Parliaments and Conventions of Estates.

Nevertheless James VI, in another aspect of his 'kingcraft', was soon able to use the method of electing the Committee of the Articles to gain control of that Committee and, therewith, control of the legislation put before the House. After his accession to the English throne, moreover, he secured a close relationship between the Lords of the Articles, the Privy Council and the Court of Session, and, with the 'king's men' dominating those three bodies, James could ensure that the legislature, the executive and the judiciary did all things according to the king's own pleasure.[1]

In the background to the act of 1587, as we have seen, lay the Roman Catholic League between Philip II and the Duke of Guise, and the Protestant League between Elizabeth and James. The act was passed in July 1587; and, a year later, in August 1588, most of the surviving galleons of Philip's 'Invincible Armada', striving desperately to round the northern capes, were broken to pieces on Scottish and Irish coasts. But there were still a number of Scottish lords – notably the Earls of Huntly and Erroll in the north, and John, Lord Maxwell, in the south-west – who, remaining true to the Roman faith, continued to intrigue for its restoration. Moreover, according to a contemporary estimate the majority of the people in the northern counties, as well as in Dumfriesshire and Wigtownshire, were favourable to Rome. And James himself, while willing to enter into a Protestant League with Elizabeth (and to receive for his 'support' a pension of £4,000 a year), was nevertheless reluctant to appear as an uncompromising Protestant prince. Already intent upon the succession to the English throne, he could not forget that there were still many Roman Catholics in England, especially among the nobility. Who could tell what the future religion of England would be?

In February 1589 Elizabeth's agents intercepted a packet of letters from Huntly, Morton (that is, John, Lord Maxwell), and Lord Claud Hamilton, which, written to Philip in the name of the Roman Catholics in Scotland, expressed regret at the failure of the Armada and suggested

[1] See *Source Book of Scottish History*, VOL. III, pp. 234-8.

that in any future enterprise a Spanish force should be landed in Scotland whence it could easily make trouble in England. ' Good Lord, methink I do but dream ', wrote the English Queen, when forwarding the letters to James, ' no king a week would bear this '; the traitors must be forthwith ' clapped up '. Faced by Elizabeth's angry letter, and by the clamour of the ministers, James had perforce to take some action. Huntly was warded in Edinburgh Castle, and yet, on the day following his ward, the King, who had a ' tenderness ' for him, dined with him, ' kissed him often, and protested he knew he was innocent '; and within a few days the Earl was free again. But, almost at once, and possibly in an attempt to seize the King's person (as had been done before) and also to dispose of John Maitland, his close adviser, Huntly and Erroll entered into a band with Crawford, Bothwell and Montrose. There was to be a move on Edinburgh from both the North and the Borders. James, learning that the earls were marching against him, summoned his lieges. The move from the south petered out. Bothwell, Huntly and Erroll retired northwards, and James came up with them and their followers (who are said to have numbered 3,000) at the Brig o' Dee. There the Earls, losing the courage to do battle against their sovereign, surrendered. Yet James still avoided resolute measures. Although the earls had plotted against the person of their King, and had risen in arms against the royal authority, thereby incurring the penalties of treason – namely, forfeiture of life, lands and goods – again they were merely warded, and again, within a few months, they were released.

In this same year (1589), however, James committed himself to a Protestant marriage with Anne, daughter of Frederick II of Denmark, and, in romantic fashion, sailed from Scotland to bring home his bride from across the sea (May 1590). On the other hand, still compromising, he did not bring Huntly to book for the murder of the ' Bonnie Earl of Moray ' (February 1592),[1] and, within a few months thereafter, a further Roman Catholic intrigue was exposed.

In December 1592 a number of letters and certain blank documents (the ' Spanish Blanks ') subscribed by Huntly, Erroll and Angus, were seized in the possession of George Ker (younger brother of Lord Newbattle) just as he was about to sail from the Firth of Clyde. According to a royal proclamation, issued on 5 January 1593, the letters revealed a treasonable conspiracy to bring strangers and Spaniards into the realm of Scotland to overthrow the monarchy and the true religion;

---

[1] *Supra*, pp. 356-7.

but thereafter James strove to parry the loud demands of the ministers and the people of Edinburgh for action rather than proclamation. There was a strong suspicion that the King himself was not averse to the use of Scotland for a Spanish invasion of England – provided Philip II did not take the English crown for himself – and that among the intercepted letters there had been one ' which tuiched the king with knowledge and approbatioun of the traffiquing '.[1] It is possible, but hardly likely, that James may have toyed with the idea that, if England were to be conquered by Spain, and a heretic Elizabeth overthrown, he could then be ' converted ' to the Roman faith and rule both Scotland and England as a Catholic prince. Certainly in a document drawn up about June 1592 James had weighed up the pros and cons of the conquest of England by a Spanish force with Scottish help, and the wording of his ' reasons ' suggests that the Crown of England meant more to him than the religion of its ruler and its people.[2] On the other hand the character of the argument indicates that this was an ' academic exercise ' and little more.

For their treasonable conspiracy in the affair of the ' Spanish Blanks ' Huntly and Erroll finally appeared before the King in October 1593 and offered to submit themselves to trial, but, a few weeks later, James came to an agreement with them that if they renounced the errors of popery or, alternatively, left Scotland, no action would be taken against them. Neither earl took advantage of this agreement and both were forfeited. Yet they paid little heed to that; and when, in July 1594, the good burgesses of Aberdeen arrested a known papal agent and, with him, three strangers also ' suspect to be papists ' on a ship that had arrived from Calais, they were compelled to deliver their prisoners to Angus, Huntly and Erroll under the threat that otherwise the ' gryt forcis of the saidis erlis . . . lyand about the toun ' would ' invaid and persew the samen with fyre and sword '. Word soon reached James of the arrest and the release, and, in the face of this affront to the royal authority, the king once more summoned the lieges to accompany him to the north. Before he could march, the young Earl of Argyll had rashly opposed Huntly and Erroll at Glenlivet, and had been heavily defeated (October 1594); but when James, with his stronger forces, and accompanied by Andrew Melville and others of the ministers (whom he took with him to give them proof of his zeal against papists),

---

[1] Calderwood, *History of the Kirk of Scotland*, VOL. V, p. 251.

[2] See ' The Spanish Blanks and the Catholic Earls ' in *Collected Essays and Reviews of Thomas Graves Law* (ed. P. Hume Brown), pp. 244-76, and particularly pp. 268-71.

arrived in the north-east, Huntly and Erroll, for the second time, shrank from battle against their King. Their houses of Strathbogie and Slains were destroyed, and the Earls were compelled to observe the earlier agreement and to retire abroad. They were back again in Scotland in 1596, when they were favourably received by James and their forfeitures soon reduced (1597); but thereafter the northern earls took no further part in Catholic intrigues. In the south-west, moreover, John, Lord Maxwell (and titular Earl of Morton), who had apparently ceased to be an active 'trafficker' in the cause of Rome, had been killed in a 'clan battle' with the Johnstones, near Lockerbie (December 1593).[1]

With the death of Lord Maxwell, and the quiescence of Huntly and Erroll, the ministers breathed more freely – though certain of the 'Octavians' (eight commissioners of Exchequer whom James, always short of money, had appointed in January 1596 to restore the royal finances) were accused of Roman Catholic leanings and were suspected of securing the return of Huntly and Erroll. A number of the King's officers of state were also reputed to be Roman Catholics. Certainly the Queen herself embraced the Roman faith about 1600.

The year 1600, however, was more notable for the strange episode known as the 'Gowrie Conspiracy'. In August 1600, when James was hunting near Falkland, he was persuaded by Alexander, Master of Ruthven, and brother of the Earl of Gowrie, to ride to Gowrie House in Perth to interview a man who, according to Ruthven, had been seized with a pot full of coined gold. At Gowrie House the King was led through various chambers, each carefully locked behind him, until he was brought to a small turret room where he found himself confronted by an armed man. In a struggle that then ensued, James managed to reach the window and to give the cry of 'Treason'. Those who had ridden with him to Gowrie House rushed to his rescue and both the Earl of Gowrie and his brother were slain. The story of the armed man in the turret room, and what happened there, rested solely upon James's own account; there were many who did not believe his story; and whether there was a Gowrie conspiracy against the King, or an attempt by the King to ruin the House of Ruthven, will never be known. As was openly said at the time, Gowrie and his brother had been killed and so could never give their own account of what had happened.[2]

---

[1] The large number of face slashes received in this fight gave rise to the phrase 'a Lockerbie lick'.

[2] The most recent analysis of the 'Gowrie Conspiracy', by W. F. Arbuckle.

And now James began to devote all his attention to the ' great prize ' – the succession to the English throne. Elizabeth had told him she would not prejudge whatever ' right, title or interest' he might have or claim to have; but beyond that she would not go. She would not name him as her successor. Moreover, although James was the obvious Protestant successor, the line of Henry VII's daughter Margaret was still excluded by Henry VIII's will which had been confirmed by the English Parliament[1]; nor was it clear whether the Bond and Act of Association precluded James from the succession as a result of his mother's complicity in the Babington plot.[2]

The King's renewed endeavours to secure an episcopal form of government in the Scottish Church may well have had a purpose additional to that of controlling the fractious ministers; for James was fully aware that Presbyterianism was anathema to Elizabeth and to the English churchmen. Uniformity in the Churches would be a royal advantage. Yet it was still not certain that Protestantism would prevail: and James did not hesitate to make careful diplomatic approaches to the Pope. How far he was prepared to go, however, is another matter; he may merely have been calculating that Roman Catholic help (or perhaps an absence of Roman Catholic opposition) might be his if he held out a vague prospect of emulating Henry IV who became King of France as a Protestant in 1589, but in 1593 became a Roman Catholic in order to unite his realm. In politics, the ' auld amitie ' with France was renewed, and James's agents were busy in the minor courts of Europe. Above all, James entered into an important secret correspondence with Cecil. He was convinced that Cecil could secure his accession; and Cecil's letters were certainly encouraging and full of wise advice.

Although in 1598, 1599 and 1600, James had taken measures indicative of a determination to use force of arms in support of his claim, everything moved steadily in his favour. During the years from 1601 to 1603 Cecil was definitely on his side, even indicating, in his letters, an acceptance of James as Elizabeth's successor; the English armed forces were controlled by Cecil's supporters; and there was no real rival to James's claim. In Scotland, Roman Catholics and Protestants alike wanted James, a Scot, to succeed to the English throne;

(*Scottish Historical Review*, VOL. XXXVI), suggests that there *may* have been a conspiracy against the king, but the verdict must be one of ' Not Proven '.

[1] Cf. *supra*, p. 333 n., and the Table on p. 282.

[2] See *supra*, pp. 346-7.

in England, Protestants looked for the maintenance of the ' true religion ', and Roman Catholics could expect toleration. In the closing months the English Council was ready to proclaim James as King.

On 24 March 1603, Elizabeth, the last and greatest of the Tudor line, died; and less than three days later, on the Saturday night, Sir Robert Carey, travel-stained and weary, brought the news to Holyrood. James VI of Scotland had become also James I of England.

In a message to his people the delighted King told them that ' where I thought to have employed you with some armour, now, I employ only your hearts, to the good prospering of me in my success and journey '. London and Edinburgh were not far apart: ' I shall visit you every three years at the least, or oftener, as I shall have occasion '.

James lost no time in assuming his inheritance. He left Edinburgh on 5 April 1603 and reached London on 7 May. He was to reign until 1625; but the year 1617 was to be the one solitary ' occasion ' when he visited his native realm.

CHAPTER XXXVI

Scotland in the Time of James VI

THE ACCOUNT of an English traveller, Fynes Moryson, who visited Lothian and Fife in 1598, confirms the impression gained from other sources that in many respects Scotland was still a poor country, with a still primitive economy. Its main exports from the east-coast burghs to France and the Low Countries were wool, skins, smoked or dried fish, and coarse cloth ' both linnen and woollen, which be narrow and shrinkle in the wetting '[1]; its main imports were iron, timber ('eastland burdis'), pitch, tar, wine, fine cloths, and a few luxuries. This trade, moreover, was never in large quantities – only in 'small fardels', or 'sma' sums'.

Both the government and the merchants were aware of the disadvantages inherent in the continuing export of raw materials, but since the export of wool had to meet the import of necessities like iron and timber, a Scottish cloth industry could be developed only by disrupting the whole pattern of exchange. From time to time, indeed, attempts were made to restrict the export of wool and the import of cloth; foreign weavers, mainly Flemings, were encouraged to settle in Scotland and to work there; and in 1597, for the first time, an import duty (of a shilling in the pound) was laid upon all foreign merchandise coming into the realm. But, in general, the old pattern of trade was to continue for a further half-century and more.

Usually there was a sufficiency of plain food – salt meat, wild fowl and game, fish, oats and barley, kale, peas and beans; but a backward agriculture meant that periods of dearth (and even starvation) were not unknown, and there was ' no Art of Cookery '. Nor was there much ' furniture of Household stuffe '.[2] Even the King's palace of Holyroodhouse was sparsely furnished, and strenuous efforts were made to improve both the building and its furnishings in readiness for Anne of Denmark. At that time, too, the begging letters sent out by

[1] There was also a fairly considerable export of barrelled fish (mainly herring and salmon), and a smaller export of salt (from salt pans) and a little knitted hose.

[2] Here Fynes Moryson adds that the bedsteads were ' like Cubbards in the wall, with doores to be opened and shut at pleasure '; and early in the seventeenth century we are told that Gordon of Abergeldie had ' ane clos kaisset bed, lokkit and bandit ' in which, presumably, he felt secure from draughts and enemies alike.

James VI to meet the expenses attendant upon the Queen's arrival reveal the poverty of the Scottish court. Not only does the King beg for money, which is ' scarce in these parts ', but also from the Laird of Barnbarroch he begs for ' such quantity of fat beef and mutton on foot, wild-fowls and venison, or other stuff meet for this purpose, as possibly ye may provide and furnish ', from the Laird of Caldwell he demands ' a hackney for transporting of the ladies accompanying the queen '... and from the Earl of Mar he solicits the loan of a pair of silken hose for his own person.

In the countryside the baron would have his ' ha' house ', built of well-dressed stone, and the laird and tenant-farmer might have a ' fair dwelling '. A royal rental of 1541 had stipulated that the king's tenant in feu-ferme had to have an ' honest mansion ', containing hall, chamber, pantry and kitchen, with barn, byre and doocot, and with a garden well hedged in – though it may be questioned how often the stipulation was observed. But the houses of the common folk were roughly built of stone and turf, or of turf alone, low and squat, with a ridged or crutched roof thatched with heather or turves. There would be a hole in the roof to act as a chimney for the central hearth, one window at the most, and a doorway probably hung with a hide. Even in the middle of the seventeenth century an English traveller in Scotland, Richard Franck, was amazed to see sheep grazing on the roofs of these low houses; and, a little later, another traveller, Thomas Kirke, spoke of the houses of the common people as ' very mean, mud-wall and thatch ', and added that ' in some parts, where turf is plentiful, they build up little cabins thereof, with arched roofs of turf .'[1] These primitive dwellings had usually only one room, or two rooms at the most, with a floor of beaten earth. Their plenishings were practically non-existent: a stool perhaps, an iron pot, and a few wooden platters and spoons. In winter, the cattle shared the limited accommodation with the human occupants. Filth predominated, as also did disease – notably the ' itch '.

Communications were still difficult: the roads were little more than beaten tracks, leading from burgh to burgh, or from bridge to bridge. These ' roads ' were almost impassable for wheeled vehicles and difficult to traverse, but there were apparently many wooden bridges and the stone bridges were often graceful and well-built.

---

[1] Houses built of turf could still be seen in some parts of the Highlands in the second half of the nineteenth century. It should be noted, however, that turf roofs are still sometimes used on modern houses in the Faeroes and Norway where they have proved to be well adapted to climatic conditions.

The methods of working the land had hardly changed from early times. Oats or bere (an inferior barley) would be grown on the 'infield' for three or four years with steadily diminishing yields; the land would then lie fallow for three or four years or more (and, in that time, become choked with weeds) and a patch of almost equally poor 'outfield' would be brought into cultivation. The old heavy ox-plough still ploughed the rigs that were separately owned and were divided by ditches or baulks; while 'community working' made it difficult, if not impossible, for any one member of the community to introduce improvements in method. There were practically no hedges enclosing 'fields'. Much of the land was wet and sour – mainly because it was ill-drained – and accordingly the hill-sides, where there was natural drainage, were brought into cultivation to such an extent as to surprise English travellers. Thomas Morer, visiting Scotland in 1689, found it 'incredible' how much of the hill-sides were ploughed when, 'to our thinking, it puts 'em to greater difficulty and charge to carry on their work than they need be at in draining the valleys'. Feuing, with its benefit of perpetual heritable tenure, had encouraged some improvement, but more than a hundred years were still to elapse before there were outstanding changes in Scottish farming.

In the burghs, on the other hand, signs of progress could be seen. Stone houses were now steadily replacing houses built of wood, though the many burgh 'acts' made in 'feir and dreddour' of fire – notably that heather, broom, whins and 'other fewall' must not be stacked in closes, and that naked lights must be shielded in a 'bowet' – indicate that wooden houses still predominated.[1] Within his house, however, the wealthier merchant[2] might have better furniture and more comforts and luxuries than many a baron or laird. Most barons had lands but little pence, for their rents were largely paid in victual; but the merchant had money through trade and, with trading connections overseas, could import continental luxuries for his own use. His house, usually reached by a 'forestair' running up from the street, might consist of only two or three rooms above his booth, but those rooms were often well furnished: a settle perhaps, one or two carved oak chairs, one or more oak aumries (or cabinets), oak chests, a bed fitted with curtains,

---

[1] Fires in the burghs were of frequent occurrence and were often disastrous. As late as 1624, 1652, and 1688 there were destructive fires in Dunfermline, Glasgow and Kilmarnock respectively.

[2] Some merchants now became very wealthy. George Heriot (' Jingling Geordie ') founded Heriot's Hospital in Edinburgh, and in 1601 James VI was said to owe £180,000 (Scots) or £15,000 (sterling) to Thomas Foulis and two other merchants.

and perhaps a small table. The solar (or principal room) and the bed-chamber would probably be hung with arras, or have carved panelling, and the ceiling might be painted with a repeating pattern. There would be comfortable cushions; a good supply of napery; probably some of the spoons and table-ware would be of silver and others of pewter; and the kitchen would be well supplied with pots, cooking utensils, and dishes. But in all burghs sanitary arrangements were still non-existent. Even in Edinburgh, ' the cheif and principall burgh of the kingdome ', the Privy Council in vain ordered the magistrates to take action to prevent the streets, vennels, wynds and closes from being ' overlaid and coverit with middingis and with the filthe and excrementis of man and beast '.

The burghs, however, were still small. The six leading burghs in point of size and wealth were Edinburgh, Dundee, Aberdeen, Perth, Glasgow and St Andrews, and it is doubtful if any others had more than 2,000 inhabitants[1]; most burghs, it is clear, had far less, and many had only a few hundreds. The total population of the country was probably about 850,000.

In burghs and landward areas alike, breaches of the peace were of constant occurrence. The local lord was still largely a law unto himself; nobles and their followers were the cause of many a fracas in the burgh's streets[2]; the royal authority was frequently put to defiance; and more often than not the royal officers were partial and venal. Central and local records are full of references to ' murder, burning, ravishing of women, violent reif, slaughter, common theft and reset of theft ', or, more frequent still, ' wrangous, violent and masterful spoliation '. ' Deadly feuds ' were still the order of the day. They were denounced by James VI in his *Basilikon Doron*, and upon at least two occasions the King took extraordinary measures to try to end them. On Sunday, 14 May 1587, he invited all the nobles who were then attending a Convention of Estates in Edinburgh to a banquet at Holyrood, where, after drinking to them thrice, he solemnly exhorted them to maintain friendship with one another, and threatened to be an enemy to the one who first broke the peace. Not content with that, on the next day, in the evening, he led a procession of his nobility through Canongate to the market cross of Edinburgh, two abreast, each holding the other by the

[1] Stirling and Ayr, the next most important burghs, may each have had about 2,000 inhabitants.
[2] Edinburgh, indeed, where rival houses frequently met at councils or at court, was said to have been ' the ordinary place of butchery, revenge, and daily fights '.

hand, and each a mortal enemy to his companion. At the market cross a table was laid with wine and sweetmeats, and there, once more, the young King made his nobles drink to each other and to peace and happiness. Again, in December 1595, grieving that deadly feuds had 'altogether disordered and shaken loose' the realm, and that slaughter had become a daily occurrence, James summoned over thirty of the nobles and barons who were at feud with one another to wait upon him at certain days and places so that, with the advice of their friends, their quarrels might be reconciled. But the records prove that neither of these royal efforts was effective. Nor had any success attended an attempt in 1587 to re-establish the justice-ayres and to supplement them by appointing in every shire certain 'honorable and worthie personis being knawin of honest fame' to be 'kingis commissioners and justices in the furtherance of justice peax and quietness', similar to the English Justices of the Peace.

In the Highlands and on the Borders where, owing to the difficulties of communication and access, the royal authority was less effective still, James also tried to find new methods of securing some measure of control. In 1587 Parliament enacted that, under a 'General Band', all chiefs of clans and all 'landlords and bailies of the lands on the Borders and in the Highlands where broken men have dwelt or presently dwell' were to find sureties (landed men in the Lowlands) for the peaceful conduct of those on their lands. Anyone thereafter suffering injury from 'broken men' could pursue the surety who had been found, and the 'chief' or 'landlord' in addition to being bound to satisfy his surety was to be mulcted in a heavy fine. The 'Band', however, was no more successful than similar earlier expedients.

Ten years later, in 1597, all 'landlords, chieftains and leaders of clans, principal householders, heritors and other possessing, or pretending right to possess, any lands in the Highlands and Isles' were ordered to produce their titles before the Lords of Exchequer before 15 May 1598. They were then to find sureties for regular payment of their rents and services to the Crown, and for the observance of law and order within their lands, with the penalty that those who failed to produce their titles and to find sureties would forfeit their holdings. Since it was well known that few Highland chiefs would be able to produce titles for their lands, this act gave the King an opportunity to forfeit and to regrant in those cases where he thought such action desirable. And, when certain of the MacLeods failed to produce their titles, the Isles of Lewis and Harris and the lands of Dunvegan and

Glenelg were declared to be forfeit and at the King's disposal. These lands were now granted by James to an association of Lowland lairds which, since its members came mainly from Fife, became known as 'The Gentlemen Adventurers of Fife'. The 'Adventurers' were to hold the lands free of crown rents for a period of seven years, so that they might develop and improve them; but thereafter they were to pay rental in money and victuals to the crown.

There is evidence that James had exaggerated ideas of the 'incredible fertility' of these outlying parts of the realm, and that, through the 'Adventurers', he hoped to secure not only law and order but also a considerable increase in crown revenue. The 'Adventurers' (accompanied by artificers and labourers) first endeavoured to 'colonise' Lewis (October 1599); but disease, insufficient supplies, and the natural hostility of the Lewismen forced them, after three attempts, to abandon the project.[1]

In the case of the MacGregors who, largely through the high handed actions of Campbell of Glenorchy, had become a 'landless clan' and 'broken men', James did not shrink from a policy of attempted extirpation. In 1590, certain of 'the wicked clan Gregor', continuing in 'blood, slaughters, herschips, reifs and stouths', had murdered the King's forester in Glenartney, and then, according to the accepted account, had cut off the dead man's head and had carried it to their young chief in Balquhidder. There, the whole clan being assembled, each man had laid his hands upon the bloody head, had avowed his approval of the deed, and had sworn to defend those who had done it. The Privy Council granted 'letters of fire and sword' to the Earl of Huntly to be used against the MacGregors, but, through the influence of Campbell of Cawdor, the chief and his clan escaped destruction. Early in 1603, however, and again through Campbell cunning, the MacGregors took part in a raid upon the Lennox when the Colquhouns of Luss were defeated with great slaughter at Glenfruin and much spoil was carried away. This time there was to be no escape: the MacGregors were to be extirpated; and the task was entrusted to Argyll who had persuaded them to attack the Colquhouns. All who had fought at Glenfruin were outlawed; the name of MacGregor was proscribed; their chief, Alasdair, was hanged; and Argyll, for his services in hunting down the clan, was rewarded with a grant of Kintyre. Later, the Privy Council decreed that no former member of the clan might carry any weapon save only a pointless knife for his

[1] In 1607 they finally sold their 'rights' to Mackenzie of Kintail.

meat, and that not more than four of them might meet together at any time for any purpose.[1]

In an entirely different field, however, Scotland showed, and continued to show, considerable progress. Although the [First] Book of Discipline, with its comprehensive proposals for education in school, college and university, had been rejected, the Reformed Church still strove to ' plant ' schools as wells as kirks. In the landward areas many ministers acted as schoolmasters in their parishes; in the burghs the kirk-sessions co-operated with town councils in the furthering of burgh schools; and the Church never abandoned Knox's concept of a school for every parish. The University of Glasgow was given new life under Andrew Melville who introduced there a new curriculum and new methods of teaching which constituted so radical an improvement as to be known as the *nova erectio* (1577); the University of St Andrews was reorganised and reformed, likewise with a ' new foundation and erection ' (1579), and Andrew Melville's acceptance of the office of Principal of St Mary's College meant that the reforms were given full effect; and at Aberdeen, where King's College apparently resisted reform, George, fifth earl Marischal, founded a new university (Marischal College), in 1593, in which the ' order ' was to be similar to that established by Andrew Melville in Glasgow.[2] In Edinburgh, James VI granted a charter to the town council in 1582 giving it leave to erect a college and making available the lands and buildings of the collegiate church of St Mary in the Fields[3]; and the ' Town's College ', a University of Edinburgh under the control of the town council, opened its doors in 1583.

In the realm of learning, George Buchanan, who had been James's tutor, was acounted the finest Latin scholar of his time, and his

[1] The enactments against the MacGregors were not repealed until the reign of George III, when the name was restored to the ' nameless clan '. That members of the clan survived was due to the widespread re-setting (or receiving and sheltering) of individuals by other clans, although heavy fines, payable to Argyll, were imposed upon those found guilty of re-setting MacGregors.

[2] A year earlier, in 1592, a charter had been granted to Sir Alexander Fraser enabling him to erect a university in his burgh of Fraserburgh (Faithlie), and a small college eventually took shape there. But the competition from Marischal College was too strong; Fraserburgh was small and remote and was strongly presbyterian; and, with James VI's establishment of episcopacy, the college of Fraserburgh lapsed after a tenuous life of some eight or nine years.

It should also be noted that in 1581 we have reference to an article before Parliament ' for erection of ane college in Orkney '; but nothing more is known of this project.

[3] The ' Kirk o' Field ' of Darnley's murder.

Rerum Scoticarum Historia, despite its early legends and its later denigration of Mary, was a remarkable work for its time, going through many editions and remaining the best history of Scotland until the works of Thomas Innes, William Robertson, Lord Hailes and John Pinkerton appeared in the eighteenth century. Sir John Skene of Curriehill had prepared his editions of *The Lawes and Actes of Parliament*, 1424-1597, and of *Regiam Majestatem*, and had published his valuable law dictionary, *De Verborum Significatione*. John Napier of Merchiston was already at work on many inventions including his ' artificial numbers ' which we now know as logarithms. While the King himself, pedant and poet, furthered a proposal, made in a General Assembly at Burntisland in 1601, for a new translation of the Bible – a proposal that eventually led to the ' Authorised Version '.

A statement made in 1572 by an English agent in Scotland has often been quoted: ' Methinks ', wrote Sir Henry Killigrew to Lord Burghley, ' I see the noblemen's great credit decay . . . and the barons, borough and such-like take more upon them '. And Killigrew was right. Under the guidance of the ministers of the church reformed, and in alliance with the ministers, the burgesses and the small barons and lairds gained a new political consciousness and therewith assumed a new importance. A ' middle class ' began to make itself heard more and more in the affairs of the realm. As for the nobility, the Act of Annexation of 1587[1] had brought in to the crown the lands and revenues of the bishoprics, abbeys and priories, and, when James began to grant away some of these lands and revenues as temporal lordships, the nobility tended to become courtiers and supporters of the King in all his doings. The old struggle between the King and the nobility waned when the King had lands and wealth to bestow. And, after James's accession to the English throne, there was a vast increase in the royal patronage at his disposal, with a corresponding increase in the attachment of his Scottish nobles.

Already, too, the King had shown that he could secure faithful servants and officers of state who could be instruments of the royal will. Nor did they necessarily come direct from the nobility. The most distinguished of them, Thomas Hamilton (' Tam o' the Cowgate '), later earl of Haddington, James's Secretary of State from 1612, and Lord President of the Court of Session from 1616, came from a family of Edinburgh burgesses.

The old order was changing; a new order was slowly taking shape.

---

[1] *Supra*, pp. 356, 358.

Select Bibliography

A. RECORD PUBLICATIONS

Livingstone, M., *A Guide to the Public Records of Scotland.* 1905.

Accounts of the Lord High Treasurer of Scotland, 1473-1566. Edited by Thomas Dickson and Sir James Balfour Paul. 11 vols. 1877-1916.

Accounts of the Masters of Works, 1529-1615. Edited by Henry M. Paton. 1957.

Acts of the Lords Auditors of Causes and Complaints, 1466-1494. Edited by Thomas Thomson. 1839.

Acts of the Lords of Council in Civil Causes, 1478-1495. Edited by Thomas Thomson. 1839.

Acts of the Lords of Council in Civil Causes, 1496-1501, with some *Acta Auditorum et Dominorum Concilii*, 1469-1483. Edited by George Neilson and Henry Paton. 1918.

Acts of the Lords of Council in Public Affairs, 1501-1554. Edited by Robert Kerr Hannay. 1932.

Acts of the Parliaments of Scotland, 1124-1707. Edited by Thomas Thomson and Cosmo Innes. 12 vols. in 13. 1814-1875.

Border Papers. [1560-1603]. Edited by Joseph Bain. 2 vols. 1894, 1896.

Calendar of Documents relating to Scotland, 1108-1509. Edited by Joseph Bain. 4 vols. 1881-1888.

Calendar of State Papers relating to Scotland, 1547-1603. Various editors. 12 vols. 1898- . In progress.

Chronicles of the Picts, Chronicles of the Scots, and other Early Memorials of Scottish History. Edited by William F. Skene. 1867.

Documents and Records illustrating the History of Scotland. [1237-1307]. Edited by Sir Francis Palgrave. 1837.

Documents Illustrative of the History of Scotland, 1286-1306. Edited by Joseph Stevenson. 2 vols. 1870.

Exchequer Rolls of Scotland, 1264-1600. Various editors. 23 vols. 1878-1908.

Foedera. Edited by T. Rymer. 4 vols. 1816-1819, 1869.

Hamilton Papers. [1532-1590]. Edited by Joseph Bain. 2 vols. 1890, 1892.

Ledger of Andrew Halyburton, Conservator of the Privileges of the Scotch Nation in the Netherlands, 1492-1503. [Edited by Cosmo Innes.] 1867.

Letters of James V. Edited by Denys Hay. 1954.

National Manuscripts of Scotland. Facsimiles. [1094-1649.] 3 vols. 1867-1871.

Register of the Great Seal of Scotland, 1306-1668. Various editors. 11 vols. 1882-1914.

Register of the Privy Council of Scotland. First Series. 1545-1625. Edited by John Hill Burton and David Masson. 14 vols. 1877-1898.

Register of the Privy Seal of Scotland, 1488- . Various editors. 5 vols. 1908- . In progress.

Rotuli Scotiae. [1291-1516]. Edited by D. Macpherson and others. 2 vols. 1814, 1819.

B. Narrative and Literary Sources

Adomnan, *Life of Columba*. Edited by Alan Orr Anderson and Marjorie Ogilvie Anderson. Edinburgh, 1961.

Barbour, John, *The Bruce*. Edited by William Mackay Mackenzie. London, 1909.

Bower, Walter, *Scotichronicon*. Edited by Walter Goodall. 2 vols. Edinburgh, 1775. [See also *Liber Pluscardensis*.]

Calderwood, David, *History of the Kirk of Scotland*. [1524-1625]. Edited by Thomas Thomson and David Laing. 8 vols. Wodrow Society, 1842-1849.

Chronicle of Melrose. Edited by Alan Orr Anderson, Marjorie Ogilvie Anderson and William Croft Dickinson. Facsimile edition. London, 1936. [*The Chronicle of Melrose*, translated by Joseph Stevenson. London, 1856.]

Chronicon de Lanercost. [1201-1346]. Edited by Joseph Stevenson. Bannatyne and Maitland Clubs, 1839. [*The Chronicle of Lanercost*, 1272-1346, translated by Sir Herbert Maxwell. Glasgow, 1913.]

Complaynt of Scotland. Edited by James A. H. Murray. Early English Text Society, 1872.

Diurnal of Remarkable Occurrents. [1513-1575]. Edited by Thomas Thomson. Bannatyne and Maitland Clubs, 1833.

Dunbar, William, *Poems*. Edited by John Small and Æ. J. G. Mackay. 3 vols. Scottish Text Society, 1893.

Fordun, John, *Chronica Gentis Scotorum*. Edited and translated by William F. Skene. 2 vols. Edinburgh, 1871, 1872.

Fragments of Scottish History [edited by Sir John Graham Dalyell]. Edinburgh, 1798. [Contains the ' Diary of Robert Birrel ' (1532-1605), ' The Late Expedition in Scotland under the Earl of Hertford, 1544 ', and Patten's 'Account of the Expedition into Scotland under the Duke of Somerset, 1547 '.]

Gray, Thomas, *Scalacronica*. [1066-1362]. Edited by Joseph Stevenson. Maitland Club, 1836. [*Scalacronica*, translated by Sir Herbert Maxwell. Glasgow, 1907.]

The *Gude and Godlie Ballates*. Edited by David Laing. Edinburgh, 1868.

Henryson, Robert, *Poems*. Edited by G. Gregory Smith. 3 vols. Scottish Text Society, 1906-1914.

Knox, John, *History of the Reformation in Scotland*. Edited by William Croft Dickinson. 2 vols. Edinburgh, 1949.

——, *Works*. Edited by David Laing. 6 vols. Edinburgh, 1895 [Reprint].

Lesley, John, *History of Scotland*. [1437-1561]. Edited by Thomas Thomson. Bannatyne Club, 1830.

Liber Pluscardensis. Edited and translated by Felix J. H. Skene. 2 vols. Edinburgh, 1877, 1880. [The *Liber Pluscardensis* is largely founded upon Bower's *Scotichronicon* (q.v.), which is still untranslated.]

Lindsay, Robert, of Pitscottie, *Historie and Cronicles of Scotland*. [1437-1575]. Edited by Aeneas J. G. Mackay. 3 vols. Scottish Text Society, 1899-1911.

380

Lyndsay, Sir David, of the Mount, *Poetical Works*. Edited by David Laing. 3 vols. Edinburgh, 1879.

Major, John, *History of Greater Britain*. Edited and translated by Archibald Constable. Scottish History Society, 1892.

Melville, James, *Autobiography and Diary*. [1556-1601]. With a ' Continuation ' called *A True Narratioune of the Declyneing Aige of the Kirk of Scotland*. Edited by Robert Pitcairn. Wodrow Society, 1842.

Melville, James, of Halhill, *Memoirs of his own Life*. [1549-1593]. Edited by Thomas Thomson. Bannatyne and Maitland Clubs, 1827.

Moysie, David, *Memoirs of the Affairs of Scotland*. [1577-1603]. Edited by James Dennistoun. Bannatyne and Maitland Clubs, 1830.

Orkneyinga Saga. Translated and edited by A. B. Taylor. Edinburgh, 1938.

Pitscottie, see Lindsay, Robert.

Spottiswoode, John, *History of the Church of Scotland*. [To 1625]. Edited by M. Russell and Mark Napier. 3 vols. Bannatyne Club and Spottiswoode Society, 1847-1851.

Vita Edwardi Secundi. Edited by N. Denholm-Young. Edinburgh, 1957.

Wyntoun, Andrew, *Orygynale Cronykil of Scotland*. Edited by David Laing. 3 vols. Edinburgh, 1872-1879.

C. GENERAL HISTORIES AND WORKS OF REFERENCE

Anderson, Alan Orr, *Early Sources of Scottish History*, 500-1286. 2 vols. Edinburgh, 1922.

——, *Scottish Annals from English Chroniclers*, 500-1286. London, 1908.

Black, George F., *The Surnames of Scotland*. New York, 1946.

Brown, Peter Hume, *History of Scotland*. Library edition. 3 vols. Cambridge, 1911.

Burton, John Hill, *History of Scotland*. Second edition. 8 vols. and Index. Edinburgh, 1873.

Chalmers, George, *Caledonia*. New edition. 7 vols. and Index. Paisley, 1887-1902.

Craigie, Sir William (editor), *A Dictionary of the Older Scottish Tongue from the Twelfth Century to the end of the Seventeenth*. Chicago and Oxford, 1931- . In progress.

Dalrymple, David, Lord Hailes, *Annals of Scotland*. [1057-1371]. Third edition. 3 vols. Edinburgh, 1819.

Dickinson, William Croft, Donaldson, Gordon, and Milne, Isabel Arnot, *A Source Book of Scottish History*. Second edition. 3 vols. Edinburgh, 1954, 1961.

Donaldson, Gordon, *Scotland, Church and Nation through Sixteen Centuries*. London, 1960.

Dowden, John, *The Bishops of Scotland*. Glasgow, 1912.

Dunbar, Sir Archibald H., *Scottish Kings*. Second edition. Edinburgh, 1906.

Easson, David Edward, *Medieval Religious Houses: Scotland*. London, 1957.

Hailes, Lord, see Dalrymple, David.

Keith, Robert, *An Historical Catalogue of the Scottish Bishops down to the Year 1688*. Edited by M. Russell. Edinburgh, 1824.

Lang, Andrew, *History of Scotland*. Third edition (vols. I and II). 4 vols. Edinburgh, 1903-1907.

Paul, Sir James Balfour (editor), *The Scots Peerage*. 9 vols. Edinburgh, 1904-1914.
Scott, Hew (editor), *Fasti Ecclesiae Scoticanae*. Revised edition. 8 vols. Edinburgh, 1915-1950.
Scottish Historical Review, Vol. 1 (1904)- . In progress.
Thomson, J. Maitland, *The Public Records of Scotland*. Glasgow, 1922.
Tytler, Patrick Fraser, *History of Scotland*. [1249-1603]. Second edition. 9 vols. Edinburgh, 1841-1843.

D. PARTICULAR PERIODS

Prehistoric Times

Childe, Vere Gordon, *Prehistoric Communities of the British Isles*. Edinburgh, 1940.
——, *Prehistory of Scotland*. London, 1935.
——, *Scotland before the Scots*. London, 1946.
Fox, Sir Cyril, *Personality of Britain*. Fourth edition. Cardiff, 1952.
Piggott, Stuart, *British Prehistory*. Oxford, 1949.
——, *Scotland before History*. Edinburgh, 1958.

Roman Times

Burn, A. R., *Agricola and Roman Britain*. London, 1953.
Collingwood, R. G., *Roman Britain*. Second edition. Oxford, 1937.
Crawford, O. G. S., *Topography of Roman Scotland*. Cambridge, 1949.
Haverfield, F. J., *Roman Occupation of Britain*. Edited by Sir George Macdonald. Oxford, 1924.
Macdonald, Sir George, *The Roman Wall in Scotland*. Second edition. Oxford, 1934.
Miller, S. N. (editor), *The Roman Occupation of South-Western Scotland*. Glasgow Archaeological Society, 1952.
Richmond, I. A., *Roman Britain*. Harmondsworth: Penguin Books, 1955.
——, (editor), *Roman and Native in North Britain*. Edinburgh, 1958.

Celtic Scotland

Anderson, Joseph, *Scotland in Early Christian Times*. Edinburgh, 1881.
Chadwick, H. M., *Early Scotland*. Cambridge, 1949.
Duke, John A., *The Columban Church*. Edinburgh, 1957 [Reprint].
Dumfriesshire and Galloway Natural History and Antiquarian Society, *Transactions*, Third Series, vol. xxvii (1948-49). ' Whithorn Volume '.
Jackson, Kenneth, *Language and History in Early Britain*. Edinburgh, 1956.
Skene, William F., *Celtic Scotland*. Second edition. 3 vols. Edinburgh, 1886-1890.
Stenton, Sir Frank, *Anglo-Saxon England*. Oxford, 1943.
Wainwright, F. T. (editor), *The Problem of the Picts*. Edinburgh, 1955.
Watson, William J., *History of the Celtic Place-Names of Scotland*. Edinburgh, 1926.

Mediaeval Scotland

Balfour-Melville, E. W. M., *James I, King of Scots.* London, 1936.
Barron, Evan Macleod, *The Scottish War of Independence.* Second edition. Inverness, 1934.
Barrow, G. W. S., *Feudal Britain.* London, 1956.
Cooper, Thomas MacKay (Lord Cooper), *Supra Crepidam.* Edinburgh, 1951.
Coulton, G. G., *Scottish Abbeys and Social Life.* Cambridge, 1933.
Dunlop, Annie I., *The Life and Times of James Kennedy, Bishop of St Andrews.* Edinburgh, 1950.
Fergusson, Sir James, *William Wallace.* New edition. Stirling, 1948.
Lawrie, Sir Archibald Campbell (editor), *Annals of the Reigns of Malcolm and William, Kings of Scotland.* Glasgow, 1910.
——, *Early Scottish Charters, prior to 1153.* Glasgow, 1905.
Origines Parochiales Scotiae. Edited by Cosmo Innes and others. 2 vols. (in three). Bannatyne Club, 1851-1855.
Powicke, Sir Maurice, *The Thirteenth Century.* Oxford, 1953.
Ramsay, Sir James H., *The Genesis of Lancaster, 1307-1399.* 2 vols. Oxford, 1913.
Ritchie, R. L. Graeme, *The Normans in Scotland.* Edinburgh, 1954.
Stenton, Sir Frank (editor), *The Bayeux Tapestry.* London, 1957.

From 1488 to 1603

Black, J. B., *The Reign of Elizabeth.* Second edition. Oxford, 1959.
——, *Andrew Lang and the Casket Letter Controversy.* Pamphlet. Edinburgh, 1950.
Brown, P. Hume, *George Buchanan.* Edinburgh, 1890.
——, *John Knox.* 2 vols. London, 1895.
Bruce, John (editor), *Correspondence of King James VI with Sir Robert Cecil and Others.* Camden Society, 1861.
——, *Letters of Queen Elizabeth and King James VI of Scotland.* Camden Society, 1849.
Buchanan, George, *Rerum Scoticarum Historia.* See Gatherer, W. A.
Clifford, Arthur (editor), *The State Papers and Letters of Sir Ralph Sadler.* 2 vols. Edinburgh, 1809.
Dickinson, Gladys (editor), *Two Missions of Jacques de la Brosse, 1543, 1560.* Scottish History Society, 1942.
Donaldson, Gordon, *The Reformation in Scotland.* Cambridge, 1960.
—— (editor), *Accounts of the Collectors of Thirds of Benefices, 1561-1572.* Scottish History Society, 1949.
Fleming, David Hay, *Mary Queen of Scots.* Second edition. London, 1898.
——, *The Reformation in Scotland.* London, 1910.
—— (editor), *Register of the Minister, Elders and Deacons of the Christian Congregation of St Andrews, 1559-1600.* 2 vols. Scottish History Society, 1889, 1890.
Gatherer, W. A., *The Tyrannous Reign of Mary Stewart.* [A translation, with editorial notes, of George Buchanan, *Rerum Scoticarum Historia*, Books XVII-XIX.] Edinburgh, 1958.
Henderson, T. F., *Life of Mary Queen of Scots.* 2 vols. London, 1905.

Keith, Robert, *History of the Affairs of Church and State in Scotland*, 1527-1568. 3 vols. Spottiswoode Society, 1844-1850.
Lang, Andrew, *James VI and the Gowrie Mystery*. London, 1902.
——, *John Knox and the Reformation*. London, 1905.
——, *The Mystery of Mary Stuart*. New edition. London, 1901.
Lee, Maurice, *James Stewart, Earl of Moray*. New York, 1953.
——, *John Maitland of Thirlestane*. Princeton, 1959.
McCrie, Thomas, *Life of Andrew Melville*. New edition. 2 vols. Edinburgh, 1899.
Mackenzie, William Mackay, *The Secret of Flodden*. Edinburgh, 1931.
Mackie, J. D., *The Earlier Tudors*. Oxford, 1952.
Mackie, R. L., *King James IV of Scotland*. Edinburgh, 1958.
—— (editor), *Letters of James IV*, 1505-1513. Scottish History Society, 1953.
Mathieson, William Law, *Politics and Religion*. 2 vols. Glasgow, 1902.
Percy, Lord Eustace, *John Knox*. London, 1937.
Pollen, John Hungerford (editor), *Mary Queen of Scots and the Babington Plot*. Scottish History Society, 1922.
——, *Papal Negotiations with Mary Queen of Scots*. Scottish History Society, 1901.
Robertson, Joseph (editor), *Inuentaires de la Royne d'Escosse*. Bannatyne Club, 1863.
Smith, G. Gregory, *The Days of James IV*. London, 1900.
Teulet, A. (editor), *Papiers d'État . . . relatifs à l'histoire de l'Écosse au XVIᵉ siècle*. 3 vols. Bannatyne Club, 1852-1860.,
——, *Relation Politiques de la France et de l'Espagne avec l'Écosse au XVIᵉ siècle*. 5 vols. Paris, 1862.
Thomson, Thomas (editor), *Acts and Proceedings of the General Assemblies of the Kirk of Scotland*, 1560-1618 (*Booke of the Universall Kirk of Scotland*). 3 vols. Bannatyne and Maitland Clubs, 1839-1845.
Tough, D. L. W., *The Last Years of a Frontier*. Oxford, 1928.
Willson, D. Harris, *James VI and I*. London, 1956.
Winzet, Ninian, *Certain Tractates*. Edited by James King Hewison. 2 vols. Scottish Text Society, 1888, 1890.

E. LEGAL AND CONSTITUTIONAL STUDIES

Cooper, Thomas Mackay (Lord Cooper), *Select Scottish Cases of the Thirteenth Century*. Edinburgh, 1944.
——, *The Scottish Legal Tradition*. Pamphlet. Edinburgh, 1949.
Dickinson, William Croft (editor), *Court Book of the Barony of Carnwath*, 1523-1542. Scottish History Society, 1937.
——, *Early Records of the Burgh of Aberdeen*, 1317, 1398-1407. Scottish History Society, 1957.
——, *Sheriff Court Book of Fife*, 1513-1522. Scottish History Society, 1928.
Hannay, Robert Kerr, *The College of Justice*. Edinburgh, 1933.
Innes, Cosmo, *Lectures on Scotch Legal Antiquities*. Edinburgh, 1872.
Mackenzie, William Mackay, *The Scottish Burghs*. Edinburgh, 1949.
Mackie, J. D., and Pryde, G.S., *The Estate of Burgesses in the Scots Parliament and its relation to the Convention of Royal Burghs*. St Andrews, 1923.

Murray, David, *Legal Practice in Ayr and the West of Scotland in the Fifteenth and Sixteenth Centuries.* Glasgow, 1910.

Neilson, George, *Trial by Combat.* Glasgow, 1890.

Pagan, Theodora, *The Convention of Royal Burghs of Scotland.* Glasgow, 1926.

Pitcairn, Robert (editor), *Ancient Criminal Trials in Scotland.* 3 vols. in 4 (11 parts). Bannatyne and Maitland Clubs, 1829-1833.

Pryde, George S. (editor), *Ayr Burgh Accounts*, 1534-1624. Scottish History Society, 1937.

Rait, Robert S., *The Parliaments of Scotland.* Glasgow, 1924.

Stair Society. *An Introductory Survey of the Sources and Literature of Scots Law.* Various contributors. Edinburgh, 1936.

——, *An Introduction to Scottish Legal History.* Various contributors. Edinburgh, 1958.

Thomson, J. Maitland, *The Public Records of Scotland.* Glasgow, 1922.

[*Note*: Scottish feudalism, early land tenures and the organisation of society in the twelfth and thirteenth centuries must be studied in the charters. Most of the surviving monastic and episcopal cartularies have been printed by historical clubs and societies; and there are many charters in the family histories edited by Sir William Fraser. A list (complete up to 1935) of manuscript charter collections, of printed cartularies, and of family histories and other works containing printed charters is given by William Angus in *Sources and Literature of Scots Law* (ut supra), pp. 259-264.]

F. Ecclesiastical History (General Works)

Bellesheim, A., *History of the Catholic Church in Scotland.* Translated by D. O. Hunter Blair. 4 vols. Edinburgh, 1887-1890.

Cunningham, John, *The Church History of Scotland.* Second edition. 2 vols. Edinburgh, 1882.

Dowden, John, *The Bishops of Scotland.* Glasgow, 1912.

——, *The Mediaeval Church in Scotland.* Glasgow, 1910.

Easson, David Edward, *Medieval Religious Houses: Scotland.* London, 1957.

Grub, George, *An Ecclesiastical History of Scotland.* 4 vols. Edinburgh, 1861.

Hannay, Robert Kerr, *The Scottish Crown and the Papacy.* Historical Association: Pamphlet, 1931.

Henderson, G. D., *The Claims of the Church of Scotland.* London, 1951.

Herkless, John, and Hannay, Robert Kerr, *The Archbishops of St Andrews.* 5 vols. Edinburgh, 1907-1915.

MacEwen, Alexander R., *A History of the Church in Scotland* [to 1560]. 2 vols. London, 1913, 1918.

Patrick, David (editor), *Statutes of the Scottish Church*, 1225-1559. Scottish History Society, 1907. [See also Robertson's *Concilia*.]

Robertson, Joseph (editor), *Concilia Scotiae: Ecclesiae Scoticanae Statuta*, 1225-1559. 2 vols. Bannatyne Club, 1866. [See also Patrick's *Statutes*.]

G. Social and Economic Conditions

Brown, Peter Hume (editor), *Early Travellers in Scotland.* Edinburgh, 1891.

——, *Scotland before 1700 from Contemporary Documents.* Edinburgh, 1893.

——, *Scotland in the Time of Queen Mary.* London, 1904.

SELECT BIBLIOGRAPHY

Chambers, Robert, *Domestic Annals of Scotland.* Third edition. 3 vols. Edinburgh, 1874.
Franklin, T. Bedford, *A History of Scottish Farming.* Edinburgh, 1952.
Grant, I. F., *The Social and Economic Development of Scotland before 1603.* Edinburgh, 1930.
Innes, Cosmo, *Scotland in the Middle Ages.* Edinburgh, 1860.
——, *Sketches of Early Scotch History.* Edinburgh, 1861.
Lythe, S. G. E., *The Economy of Scotland, 1550-1625, in its European Setting.* Edinburgh, 1960.
Symon, J. A., *Scottish Farming, Past and Present.* Edinburgh, 1959.
Warrack, John, *Domestic Life in Scotland, 1488-1688.* London, 1920.

H. The Highlands and Islands; Orkney and Shetland

Adam, Frank, *The Clans, Septs and Regiments of the Scottish Highlands.* 4th edition, revised by Sir Thomas Innes of Learney. Edinburgh, 1952.
Clouston, J. Storer (editor), *Records of the Earldom of Orkney.* Scottish History Society, 1914.
Darling, F. Fraser, *Natural History in the Highlands and Islands.* Glasgow, 1948.
Donaldson, Gordon (editor), *The Court Book of Shetland,* 1602-1604. Scottish Record Society, 1954.
——, *Shetland Life under Earl Patrick.* Edinburgh, 1958.
Goudie, Gilbert, *The Celtic and Scandinavian Antiquities of Shetland.* Edinburgh, 1904.
Gregory, Donald, *History of the Western Highlands and Isles.* Second edition. London, 1881.
Innes, Sir Thomas, of Learney, *The Tartans of the Clans and Families of Scotland.* Revised edition. Edinburgh, 1950.
Kermack, W. R., *The Scottish Highlands: A Short History.* Edinburgh, 1957.
MacDonald, Colin M., *The History of Argyll.* Glasgow, 1950.
Mackenzie, W. C., *The Highlands and Isles of Scotland: A Historical Survey.* Revised edition. Edinburgh, 1949.
Simpson, W. Douglas (editor), *The Viking Congress,* 1950. Edinburgh, 1954.
Skene, William F., *The Highlanders of Scotland.* Edited by Alexander MacBain. Stirling, 1902.

I. Education, Literature, Art and Architecture

Cant, R. G., *The University of St Andrews: A Short History.* Edinburgh, 1946.
——, *The College of St Salvator.* Edinburgh, 1950.
Cruden, Stewart, *The Scottish Castle.* Edinburgh, 1960.
Finlay, Ian, *Art in Scotland.* Oxford, 1948.
——, *Scottish Crafts.* London, 1948.
Grant, Sir Alexander, *The Story of the University of Edinburgh.* 2 vols. London, 1884.
Grant, James, *History of the Burgh Schools of Scotland.* Glasgow, 1876.
Hannah, Ian C., *Story of Scotland in Stone.* Edinburgh, 1934.
Hannay, Robert Kerr, 'The Universities of Scotland' in H. Rashdall, *The Universities of Europe in the Middle Ages.* New edition, edited by F. M. Powicke and A. B. Emden. Oxford, 1936.

386

Henderson, G. D., *The Founding of Marischal College, Aberdeen*. Aberdeen, 1947.
Henderson, T. F., *Scottish Vernacular Literature*. Edinburgh, 1910.
Herkless, John, and Hannay, Robert Kerr, *The College of St Leonard*. Edinburgh, 1905.
MacGibbon, David, and Ross, Thomas, *The Castellated and Domestic Architecture of Scotland*. 5 vols. Edinburgh, 1887-1892.
——, *The Ecclesiastical Architecture of Scotland*. 3 vols. Edinburgh, 1896-1897.
Mackenzie, Agnes Mure, *An Historical Survey of Scottish Literature to 1714*. London, 1933.
Mackenzie, William Mackay, *The Mediaeval Castle in Scotland*. London, 1927.
Mackie, J. D., *The University of Glasgow, 1451-1951*. Glasgow, 1954.
Millar, J. H., *A Literary History of Scotland*. London, 1903.
Rait, Robert S., *The Universities of Aberdeen*. Aberdeen, 1895.
Scott, Sir Walter (editor), *Minstrelsy of the Scottish Border*. Revised and edited by T. F. Henderson. 4 vols. Edinburgh, 1932.
Scott-Moncrieff, George (editor), *The Stones of Scotland*. London, 1938.
Wittig, Kurt, *The Scottish Tradition in Literature*. Edinburgh, 1958.
[*Note:* The county inventories published by the Royal Commission on the Ancient and Historical Monuments of Scotland are invaluable for the study of ancient and historical monuments – prehistoric, Roman, mediaeval and early modern up to (and where there are special reasons later than) 1707.]

J. ATLASES, MAPS AND GAZETTEERS

Bartholomew, John (editor), *Survey Atlas of Scotland*.
——, *Survey Gazetteer of the British Isles*.
Groome, F. H. (editor), *Ordnance Gazetteer of Scotland*. 6 (or 6 in 3) vols.
Johnston, W. and A. K., *Gazetteer of Scotland*.
Ordnance Survey. Map of Britain in the Dark Ages – North Sheet.
   Map of Monastic Britain – North Sheet.
   Map of Roman Britain.
Royal Scottish Geographical Society, *Early Maps of Scotland*. Edinburgh, 1936.

K. BIBLIOGRAPHIES

Black, George F., *List of Works* [in the New York Public Library] *Relating to Scotland*. New York, 1916.
Ferguson, Joan P. S., *Scottish Family Histories held in Scottish Libraries*. Edinburgh, 1960.
Hancock, P. D., *A Bibliography of Works Relating to Scotland* [published in the years] *1915-1950*. 2 vols. Edinburgh, 1960. [See also Mitchell and Cash.]
Mackie, J. D., *Scottish History*. Cambridge (for the National Book League), 1956.
Matheson, Cyril, *A Catalogue of the Publications of Scottish Historical and Kindred Clubs and Societies, 1908-1927*. Aberdeen, 1928. [See also Terry.]

Meikle, Henry W., *Scotland*. Cambridge (for the National Book League), 1950.

Mitchell, Sir Arthur, and Cash, C. G., *A Contribution to the Bibliography of Scottish Topography*. 2 vols. Scottish History Society, 1917. [See also Hancock.]

Stair Society. *An Introductory Survey of the Sources and Literature of Scots Law*. Various contributors. Edinburgh, 1936.

Stuart, Margaret, *Scottish Family History: A Guide to Works of Reference on the History and Genealogy of Scottish Families*. Edinburgh, 1930.

Terry, Charles Sanford, *A Catalogue of the Publications of Scottish Historical and Kindred Clubs and Societies*, 1780-1908. Glasgow, 1909. [See also Matheson.]

Index

Northumbria, Tostig, earl of 71
— Waltheof, earl of 75, 77n
Norway 37 and n, 40-1, 146-7, 163n, 281n
Nunneries 133n

'Octavians', the 367
Orkney, early settlements in 12n, 15, 19, 34n; Romans in 25; Norse in 5, 38-40, 120; acquired by crown 24 and n, 225; death of Hakon in 41; death of 'Maid of Norway' in 146; James V in 308; proposed college in 376n
— bishop of. See Bothwell, Adam
— bishopric of 122n
— Sigurd, earl of 53, 70
— Thorfinn, earl of 53, 55 and n, 70
— William St Clair (Sinclair), earl of 42
— Patrick Stewart, second earl of 250
Ormond, Hugh Douglas, earl of 253, 255-6
Oswald, king of Northumbria 46 and n, 47, 48n
Oswiu, king of Northumbria 46n, 47-8 and n
Otterburn, battle of 199, 252-3, 261
Owen, king of Strathclyde 38-9

Paisley, abbey of 123, 125
— burgh of 157, 247
Parishes, erection of 124-5; appropriation of parish churches 125-7, 271-2, 350
Parliament, origins of 106-7; its functions 106-7, 192; summons to 107, 187, 189; representation in 7, 185ff., 213-4 and n, 215, 330-1, 359-64; lords of 213, 215, 363; speaker (of commons) to be elected 214-5; requests to 266, 302; notification and publication of acts of 212, 278 and n; ecclesiastical enactments of 206, 265-8 and n, 269, 271, 273, 313-4, 316-7, 330-1, 348, 355, 357; economic enactments of 183, 208-9, 230, 235-6, 256-7, 289, 294-5; education act 277-8; judicial enactments of 153, 208, 211-3 and n, 225-6 and n; military enactments of 10, 292, 294; political enactments of 182-4 and n, 208-9 and n, 211-2, 224, 233 and n, 234, 237, 256-7, 302, 304-5, 317, 323, 344, 374; committees and commissions of 192-3, 212, 215-6 and n. See also Articles, Committee of the; General Council
Parliament, 'Reformation', 330-1; 361 and n
Paschal II, pope 136
Paul III, pope 307
— IV, pope 312

Peebles, burgh of 160, 239, 242-3, 247-9
Pembroke, Aymer, earl of 163
— Gilbert, earl of 80
Penda, king of Mercia 46n, 48n
Percy, Henry 157, 173, 178
Perth, burgh of 6, 116, 125, 139, 147, 157, 162-3, 176, 179, 186, 204, 207-8, 220-1, 243-4, 271, 326, 354, 358, 367, 373
— castle of 6, 166-7, 180
— church of 228-9
— Inch of 201
— religious houses of 217, 269n, 315, 326
— treaty of 41-2
Philip II, king of Spain 299-300, 362, 364-6
— IV, king of France 159, 161 and n, 174; letter from Scots parliament to 166
Piccolomini, Aeneas Sylvius (Pius II), his description of Scotland 274 and n, 275 and n
Picts, origins of 21, 32-4 and n; invasions by 5, 22, 28-9; kingdom of 33-4, 37, 39, 70; conversion of 44, 46; culture of, and Pictish sculptured stones 35; their law of succession 34-5 and n; and the Scots 35, 37, 46
Pinkie, battle of 2n, 288n, 319
Piperden, clash at 217n
Pitscottie, Lindsay of. See Lindsay
Pius II, pope. See Piccolomini
Plague, outbreaks of 245-6
Pleas of the Crown 93 and n, 104
Poets and poetry 8 and n, 110, 272, 279-80, 313n, 356n. See also Dunbar, William; Henryson, Robert; Lyndsay, Sir David
Population, estimates of 22, 119n, 251, 373
Premonstratensians 122n, 129
Presbyteries 352, 356-7
Prestonpans, 228; battle of 2n,
Primogeniture, law of 55-7
Privy Council, composition of 364; enactments of 334-5, 373, 375-6 and n; rebuked by the ministers 353, 358; Bothwell denounced before 343n
Protestantism, its rise 271, 314-5, 323-4
Provincial Councils, holding of 141-2 and n; enactments of 268n, 272, 312-4, 322, 324-5 and n
Provision to benefices, system of 264 and n, 267, 270

'Raid of Ruthven' 354-5
Randolph, earl of Moray. See Moray
Reformation 4, 126-7, 207, 241n, 248, 260, 272, 298, 312ff.

INDEX

— — son of James V 357*n*
— Margaret, dau. of Robert III, countess of Douglas. *See* Douglas
— — dau. of James I 217
— Mary, countess of Angus. *See* Angus
— — dau. of James II 225 and *n*, 260
— Robert, son of Murdac, duke of Albany 196
— Sir Robert, assassin of James I 196, 218
— Walter, son of Murdac, duke of Albany 196, 210
— *duke of Albany. See* Albany
— *earl of Arran. See* Arran
— *earl of Bothwell. See* Bothwell
— *earl of Buchan. See* Buchan
— *earl of Lennox. See* Lennox
— *earl of Moray. See* Moray
— *earl of Orkney. See* Orkney
Stirling Bridge, battle of 158 and *n*
— burgh of 6, 14, 111, 113*n*, 116, 119, 125, 158, 167, 179, 186, 228, 237, 247-8, 256, 258, 304, 326-7, 339, 343, 346, 373*n*
— castle of 6. 69, 78, 97-8, 102, 109, 158, 161, 166-8, 179, 203, 222, 255, 257, 290; keeper of, *see* Livingston, Sir Alexander
Strathbogie, David of, earl of Atholl. *See* Atholl
Strathclyde, kingdom of 33, 35-6, 39, 70
Strathearn, Malise Graham, earl of, deprived of earldom and created earl of Menteith 210, 254. *See* Menteith
Succession, acts of 169-70, 176, 182, 194-5
— collateral 54; yields to primogeniture 55-7
Superintendent, office of 349 and *n*
Surrey, Thomas Howard, earl of, repulses Scots 281; at Flodden 285-8, 299
— John de Warenne, earl of 156, 158, 178
Sutherland 8*n*; early settlements in 15; Norse in 5, 38 and *n*, 120; inbringing of 40; troubles in 226
Sweyns, of Knapdale 174*n*
Sybilla, queen of Scots 74
Sylvius, Aeneas. *See* Piccolomini
Symeon of Durham, cited or quoted 72, 134

Tacitus, cited or quoted 23 and *n*, 24 and *n*, 25 and *n*, 31-2
Tain, sanctuary at 163; Margaret Tudor at 241, 280
Talbot, Richard, lord of Mar. *See* Mar
Tantallon castle 210*n*, 305
Taxation 119*n*, 294-5, 297-8
Teinds, payment of 124-5

Teviotdale 199, 310
— archdeacon of. *See* Croyser
Thanages 67
Thirds of Benefices 335 and *n*
Thirlestane, John Maitland, first lord (1590-5), his background 356*n*; policy of 356-7; opposition to 365
Thorfinn, earl of Orkney 55 and *n*, 70
Threave Castle 252
Thurstan, archbishop of York 76, 135*n*, 136
Toisech, office of 60-1
Townships, early 61-2, 66
Trade 7, 111ff., 185, 191, 230*n*, 370 and *n*
Trades, Incorporated 235-6 and *n*
Traprain Law 20, 31*n*
Treasurer, duties of 209-10, 243, 289
Trinitarians 132, 133
Trinity College, Edinburgh 229 and *n*
Tudor, Arthur, son of Henry VII 281*n*, 282
— Margaret, queen of Scots 261-2; her marriage to James IV 277, 279, 281 and *n*, 282-3, 294, 325; visits Aberdeen 241, 280; visits Tain 241, 280; her marriage to sixth earl of Angus 259, 282, 301-2, 304; appointed guardian 301; flees to England 301 and *n*; returns to Scotland 302; favours English alliance 304; and the succession to throne of England 325, 333*n*, 368
— Mary, dau. of Henry VII, and the succession to the throne 282, 325, 333*n*
Turgot, bishop of St Andrews, election and consecration of 134-5, 138; returns to Durham 135; his *Life* of St Margaret 121
Turnberry, bond of 144
Turnbull, William, bishop of Glasgow, founds Glasgow university 229
Tweed, river 6, 39 and *n*, 63, 70, 73, 76, 79, 81, 153-4, 159, 286*n*; valley of 5, 7, 16
Twizelhauch, act at 288*n*
'Twopenny Faith' 325*n*
Tyndrum, defeat of Bruce at 163
Tyne, river 25-6, 36, 72-3, 76-7

Umfraville, Ingram de, guardian of Scotland 160
Union of the Crowns 2, 11, 217, 231, 369

Valois, Madeleine de, queen of Scots, her marriage to James V 302, 309; death of 309
Veere, staple at 230*n*
Verneuil, battle of 196, 199, 209, 253
Vienne, John de, commands French force in Scotland 198-199

407

INDEX

Vikings, the. *See* Norse
Vitrified forts 20
Votadini 20, 31 and *n*

Wake, Thomas, lord of Liddesdale 173, 178
Wallace, Sir Malcolm, of Elderslie 157
— Sir William, his initial resistance 157-8; his victory at Stirling 158; letter from, to Lübeck and Hamburg 158; governs Scotland 158-9; his defeat and subsequent career 159; example of 160; capture and execution of 161
Walter, sixth High Steward (1309-26), his marriage 169-70, 196, 197*n*, 251
Warbeck, Perkin, receives support from Maximilian 281; supported by James IV 244, 280-1; his subsequent career 281*n*
Wardlaw, Henry, bishop of St Andrews 206
Warenne, John de, earl of Surrey. *See* Surrey
Wark Castle 286; burning of 221
Wars of Independence 2, 6, 105, 110, 156ff., 165ff.
Weardale, campaign in 290*n*
Wedderburns, of Dundee, their book of *Gude and Godlie Ballates* 313
Western Isles, machair of 8*n*; communications in 9; Norse in 5, 37-40, 120; inbringing of 40; cession of 41-2; royal authority in 3, 40, 42, 109, 223-4, 275-6
Westminster-Ardtornish, treaty of 223-4, 257, 276*n*
Westmorland 74, 77, 80, 167
Whitby, 'Synod' of 47-8 and *n*, 49-50, 120
Whithorn, bishopric of 50, 120, 122*n*, 145, 269*n*, 273
— cathedral of 122 and *n*, 129
— early missionaries at 43-4
Wigtown, Archibald Douglas, earl of, and third earl of Douglas. *See* Douglas
— Thomas Fleming, second earl of 252
— earldom of 252, 255
Wigtownshire, Christianity in 43
William I, king of England (1066-87), his claim to the throne 70*n*, 155; landing of 71, 94 and *n*; invades

Scotland 72; his agreement with Malcolm III 56*n*, 72, 73, 148; and Domesday survey 1; death of 72*n*
— II, 'Rufus', king of England (1087-1100), his claim to throne 155; his relations with Scotland 56, 73-4, 148
— I, 'the Lion', king of Scots (1165-1214) 53, 144, 150-1; accession of 57; invades England 77; his capture 77, 137; does homage 78; and the quitclaim of Canterbury 78; his marriage 78*n*; his relations with John 78-81; quarrels with the papacy 138-9; founds Arbroath abbey 125; defeats Guthred 58, 90*n*; secures North 40; death of 57; feudalism under 67, 83*n*, 86-8, 90-1, 108; burghs in reign of 112-3, 116, 118, 238, 244
— fitz Duncan. 53, 56 and *n*
— the 'Boy of Egremont' 53, 58*n*
— de Lamberton, bishop of St Andrews 160, 162, 163, 170
— of Newburgh, cited 76-7, 113
Windsor, church council at 134
Winram, John, sub-prior of St Andrews 322*n*
Winter, Sir William, admiral, commands English fleet 327 and *n*, 328*n*
Wishart, George, his teachings 314; martyrdom of 314, 318
— Robert, bishop of Glasgow, guardian of Scotland 143, 145; resists English 157, 162-3, 170
Wolsey, Thomas, Cardinal, receives report on Flodden 287; his policy 304-5
Wood, Sir Andrew 276-7, 292
Wycliffe, John, influence of 207, 270-1
Wyntoun, Andrew of. *See* Andrew of Wyntoun

Yolande, queen of Scots, marries Alexander III 143
York 23, 25, 28, 80-1, 134, 159, 161, 171*n*, 223, 310, 345
— archbishops of, claim to be metropolitan in Scotland 50, 134ff.; their claim rejected 140-1; province of 50, 120, 122*n*, 134. *See also* Thurstan
— treaty of 1, 80-1, 148, 153